'This book is as necessary to read and absorb as the two that preceded it, not for a better understanding of the milieu in which Clark was writing, but for a better understanding of the human condition … the last pages are incredibly moving and compound the sheer, Technicolor humanity of what we have read before' Simon Heffer, *Literary Review*

'The skill in the diaries and memoirs of most politicians lies in the delicate airbrushing out of their faults and weaknesses. Alan Clark's self-portrait, on the other hand, is defiantly warts-and-all … His three volumes of diaries will ensure his immortality'
Craig Brown, *Mail on Sunday*

'Ever present in this volume is his preoccupation with the illness that finally claimed him. It is more sombre, infinitely more foreboding than his other work … The last entries, by Jane recording Alan's final days, are hugely moving … This is simply the best book I have read since – well, since the last Clark oeuvre' Steven Norris, *The Times*

'A rare record of what it is like to be dying by a master of the English language' Bevis Hillier, *Spectator* (Books of the Year)

'This volume of Clark is better on small details of an indulged life, of Eccles cakes and stilton, the vanity of his timed runs up flights of stairs, his befriending of jackdaws whose pellets he takes abroad for good luck' Quentin Letts, *Daily Mail*

'The last diaries are a muted version of the others, full of stengun judgments, scorn, candour and opinion – also ambition recollected in imperfect tranquillity'
Edward Pearce, *Tribune Magazine*

'Alan Clark's relationship with God in these diaries is both funny and moving … These diaries do not stalk the corridors of power. There is very little high-level gossip, but some of our favourite characters from the early diaries make appearances … As his hypochondria gives way to real sickness, his moral gambling to terror, his selfish and equivocal attitude towards his wife to absolute love and gratitude, the diaries assume an immense sadness and profundity ... Alan Clark was not a good man, but he was a dazzling diarist. He writes, self-pityingly: "I suppose I will be remembered for the Diaries." He will, and for this one most of all. A grand love story eclipses a political career'

Sarah Sands, *Daily Telegraph*

'A long way from the acerbic knockabout looked for by Clark's admirers ... The latter part of the book is darkened by the diarist's recognition that [those] frissons of demise are no illusion: he has brain cancer ... the journal of a disappointed man becomes that of a mind at the end of its tether. At the same time the heartless, even caddish, candour gives way to impassioned avowals of devotion to a sorely tried wife. When he finally abandons his pen, Jane Clark adds her own brief log, in which reciprocated devotion sits uneasily with sick-room grue. "I love God," she writes, "but this is such a cruel way to demolish such a brilliant brain"'   E.S. Turner, *TLS*

'Pure pleasure ... there ought to be a constant supply of Alan Clarks'   Sue Townsend, *Mail on Sunday* (Books of the Year)

Alan Clark, educated at Eton and Oxford, read for the Bar but did not practise. He was Tory MP for Plymouth Sutton 1974–1992 and for Kensington and Chelsea, 1997–99. He had various junior ministerial appointments in the Margaret Thatcher and John Major governments of the 1980s. He was best-known for his Diaries (three vols) which *The Times* placed in the Samuel Pepys class. They were filmed by the BBC with John Hurt as Clark and Jenny Agutter as Jane Clark.

Alan Clark died in 1999.

Ion Trewin is a London publisher. Originally a journalist, he was Literary Editor of *The Times* 1972–79. He was Alan Clark's editor and publisher for the original 'Diaries' and following his death edited two further volumes of the celebrated diaries. In 2008 he edited and introduced THE HUGO YOUNG PAPERS: Thirty Years of British Politics Off the Record (Allen Lane) which won the Channel 4 Political Book of the Year Award 2009. Married with a son who is a literary agent and a daughter who is a teacher, he has since 2006 been literary director of the Man Booker prizes. He was chairman of the Cheltenham Literature Festival 1996–2007.

THE LAST DIARIES

DIARIES

In and Out of the Wilderness

ALAN CLARK

Transcribed and Edited,
with Introduction and Notes,
by Ion Trewin

PHOENIX

A PHOENIX PAPERBACK

First published in Great Britain in 2002
by Weidenfeld & Nicolson
This paperback edition first published in 2003
by Phoenix,
an imprint of Orion Books Ltd,
Orion House, 5 Upper St Martin's Lane,
London WC2H 9EA

An Hachette UK company

5 7 9 10 8 6 4

A CIP catalogue record for this book
is available from the British Library

ISBN 978-0-7538-1695-0

Typeset by Selwood Systems, Midsomer Norton
Printed and bound in Great Britain by
Clays Ltd, St Ives plc

The Orion Publishing Group's policy is to use papers that
are natural, renewable and recyclable products and
made from wood grown in sustainable forests. The logging
and manufacturing processes are expected to conform to
the environmental regulations of the country of origin.

www.orionbooks.co.uk

'Diaries are so intensely personal – to publish them is a baring, if not a flaunting, of the ego … These are not "Memoirs". They are not written to throw light on events in the past, or retrospectively to justify the actions of the author. They are *exactly* as they were recorded on the day; sometimes even the hour, or the minute, of a particular episode or sensation.'

Introduction, *Diaries*, 1993

'God this is a filthy pen, I'm going to change it.'

Qatar, 12 May, 1991

'How delicious is "the quiet hour". There are few more agreeable (intellectual) conditions than a pot of Indian tea, a nice pen (earlier I was fussed because I could only find a biro) and a blank page.' 11 February, 1995

CONTENTS

ILLUSTRATIONS

The photographs in *The Last Diaries* are a
selection from the Clark family albums.

GLOSSARY

AC – Alan Clark
Jane – sometimes Janey, BLJ
James – AC's elder son (aka 'Boy', 'Jamie')
Julie – married to James
Angus – James and Julie's son
Andrew – AC's younger son (aka 'Tip', 'Tip-book', 'Tup', 'Cin', 'Lilian')
Sarah – married to Andrew (together aka 'The Amazings')
Albert, Archie – Andrew and Sarah's children
Colette – AC's sister (aka 'Celly')
Colin – AC's brother (aka 'Col', 'Pin')
Lord Clark – AC's father, Kenneth Clark (aka 'Bonny papa')
B'Mama – AC's mother, Jane Clark (aka 'Bonny mama')
Pam – Jane's mother, living in Benalmadena in Spain (aka 'Ma')
Nick – Nick Beuttler, Jane's brother, living in France

STAFF AND ESTATE

Lynn Webb – housekeeper, and her husband Ken
Edwin ('Eddie') Wilson – retired groundsman, and his wife Peggy
Brian Harper – head gardener

ANIMALIA

Tom ('T.O.') – Jack Russell terrier, 'head of the house'

Eva ('E') – Rottweiler
Hannah and Lëhni – Rottweiler sisters
KK – James's labrador
Bok – Bokassa, labrador, successor to KK
Max, George, 2Boy, Bromley, TC – jackdaws

WESTMINSTER

Sue Line – secretary at the House of Commons
Alison Young – secretary at the House of Commons
Pat – driver at the Ministry of Defence
Patricia (Trish) Sill Johnston – secretary at the House of Commons

CONSTITUENCIES

Barbara Lord – Conservative agent, Kensington and Chelsea
1a – Chelsea Manor Street, SW3, the Kensington and Chelsea
    Conservative Association headquarters

HOUSES AND LOCATIONS
SALTWOOD

The Mains – another name for Saltwood Castle
The Castle: various rooms including the Great Library; the
    Tower offices (winter and summer); the Red Library; the
    badge room (glory hole of mainly car parts); the archive
    room; Peggy's pantry; the Green Room (the Clarks' informal
    sitting room in the old staff wing); the asthma rail (by the back
    door); Rabies Room; the Knights Hall
Pavillon – summerhouse by the swimming pool, which the
    Clarks gave themselves as an anniversary present
Lady Conway's Bridge – across the moat and linking Garden
    House to the Castle; widened during Lady Conway's
    ownership of Saltwood
MFS GH and MFS GL/Gt Hall – 'My Father's Study'. There are
    two, one in the Garden House, the other in the Great Hall,

behind the Great Library.

Garden House (GH) – a large bungalow, designed by John King in the old kitchen garden in the grounds of Saltwood, for Lord and Lady Clark, when they moved out of the castle in 1971

Sandling – the railway station for Saltwood

Gossie Bank – a steep climb at the far end of Grange Farm, Saltwood; AC often refers to the time he takes to ascend it

The Seeds – a large arable field at Grange Farm, Saltwood

The Bailey (inner and outer) – the two courtyards (see also lawns)

Courtneys (aka 'the Secret Garden')

ALBANY

B5 Lower/Upper – Piccadilly chambers which AC inherited from his mother. The Upper, more an attic, had once been servants' quarters

ERIBOLL

The Lodge – principal house on the estate

Shore Cottage – Jane's croft at Eriboll, where Jane and AC always stay

The Creaggan Road – connects Loch Eriboll to Loch Hope by way of the Creaggan Ridge, some seven miles in length and climbing from sea level to 600 feet at the ridge

Foulain – a shepherd's cottage at the foot of the loch

Strathbeg (sometimes Stra'beg) – a remote croft at the head of the Polla Valley

Arnaboll and Cashel Dhu – crofts on the Loch Hope side of the estate

Ardneackie – the peninsula that juts out into Loch Eriboll

Birkett Foster – rocks that reminded AC of a seascape by the Victorian painter, Myles Birkett Foster

ZERMATT

Châlet Caroline – the Clarks' house in the village, which they built in the early 1960s
The Kiosk – built by the Clarks in 1985, adjoining the châlet
Trift – an inn at an early stage in the ascent to the Rothornhutte
Othmars – an inn on the Blauherd

BRATTON-CLOVELLY

Town Farm – an early home; in west Devon, near Okehampton and about three-quarters of an hour's drive north of Plymouth

SEEND MANOR

Broomhayes – near Devizes in Wiltshire; retained by the Clarks when they moved to Saltwood. Latterly the home of Andrew and Sarah Clark

RYE

Watchbell Street – including No 11, where the Clarks lived after they married

HOUSE OF COMMONS

House Library – House of Commons, a favourite spot for writing
Dean's Yard – an office, mainly for secretaries, by Westminster Abbey
1 Parliament Street – where AC had an office after his return to the Commons in 1997
White Office – ministerial office in the Commons during AC's time at the Ministry of Defence

SOME CARS AND RELATED MATTERS

(where cars mentioned in this volume are transitory purchases, they are sometimes identified within the text)

The Mews – composite name for various vintage car dealers' establishments in Queen's Gate, London

Coys – dealers in classic cars

Macrae & Dick (Derek Presley) – Land Rover dealers at Inverness

P. & A. Wood (Andy Wood) – specialists in Rolls-Royce and Bentley

Scott Moncrieff – purveyors and restorers of classic cars

The Discovery – Land Rover

Big Red – S-type Bentley Continental, number plate AC1800

Hen 3-litre – Bentley

New Bing – Bentley Continental S1 manual

KGV – Rolls-Royce Silver Ghost

R Cont – Green Bentley manual

Toyota – Truck used for wooding

Bustard – Bentley 4¼-litre

Bang Bang – R Cont manual with Bradley Brothers body

Barnato – Bentley 4¼ made for Wolf Barnato

C-Type – Jaguar XC13

XK 120 – owned by AC since his undergraduate days

Little Silver – Porsche 911 Carrera Cabriolet

Chapron – the Citroën, the decapotable, the very last of the DS cabriolets, built in 1978 to special order; belonging to Jane

THEBUS – 'the bus' – Transit van, at Eriboll

VDP – Vanden Plas

Winter Car – 1967 Chevrolet

Summer Car – 1967 Chevrolet

Buick – Straight 8

Old Ministerial – Jaguar bought by AC when at MoD

Citroën Mehari – a little plastic truck with an air-cooled engine and a very light footprint used for clearing grass. A kind of mobile wheelbarrow

Argocat – at Eriboll, performs the same function as the Mehari, but will also go through peat bogs, and swim

Hymac – mechanical digger at Eriboll

Countax – successor to the Westwood ride-on mower

Atco – cylinder mower for inner Bailey

SLANG

ACHAB – (lit.) 'anything can happen at backgammon', a saying originally from 'the Room' at Brooks's where games can swing at a late stage on an unpredictable run of the dice, used often as a consolation in times of depression. Adaptable in other circumstances, substituting 'politics' for 'backgammon'

AF – what AC called aortic fibrillations, not literally, but circumstances that set the heart racing

Dave-at-eight – getting up in time for the arrival of the official car, driven by Dave (or whoever the driver was)

Greywater – diarrhoea

Grunge – country clothes

Cutting peat – sometimes literally at Eriboll, but also getting away from it all

Lenin Stadium – anxiety so extreme it induces physical symptoms

Longies – long johns

Norwegian Embassy – weak at the knees

Piccolo – minor, but telling, as in 'piccolo triumph'

Sadismoid – as sadistically, though less *transitive* in meaning; the suffix -moid, or moidly, is often attached to adjectives

Satisly – arousing satisfaction, inducing complacency

Softies – recreational clothes

Thompson/plopson – defecation

too-hot-Henry – a phrase used by an actor during filming on location at Saltwood

Venice train – completely asleep on a journey

'w' – walk, as in going for a walk

white screen – computer

ABBREVIATIONS

NAMES

AC	– Alan Clark
AH	– Archie Hamilton MP
'ASPERS'	– John Aspinall
BLJ	– Beloved little Jane
CH	– Charles, Charles Howard
CS	– Christopher (aka 'Daisy') Selmes
DD	– David Davis MP
EG/EDG	– Euan Graham
'FRANCO'	– Frank Johnson
JM	– John Major MP
GJ	– Tristan Garel-Jones MP
LPF	– L.P. Fassbender, accountant
MH	– Michael Howard MP
MRDH	– Michael Heseltine MP
TK	– Tom King MP
'WOLF'	– Adolf Hitler

ACRONYMS

BB	– Big Book, otherwise *The Tories: Conservatives and the Nation State 1922–1997* (published 1998)
CGT	– Capital Gains Tax
CCO	– Conservative Central Office
CUCA	– Cambridge University Conservative Association
DE	– Department of Employment

EDM	– early day motion
EMT	– early morning tea
FP	– famous person
K&C	– Kensington and Chelsea constituency; Kent and Canterbury Hospital
KTH	– Kensington Town Hall
LCA	– love, care and attention
LLG	– loch like glass
MOS	– *Mail on Sunday*
MFT	– Minister for Trade
MOD	– Ministry of Defence
NOW	– *News of the World*
O/D	– overdraft
OECD	– Organisation for European Co-operation and Development
OUCA	– Oxford University Conservative Association
PC	– Privy Counsellor
PFD	– Peters, Fraser & Dunlop, literary agents
PQ	– Parliamentary Question
RREC	– Rolls-Royce Enthusiasts' Club
RUSI	– Royal United Services Institute
SE	– Stock Exchange
SEDOC	– out-of-hours doctor service in Kent
SOS	– Secretary of State
UBS	– Union Bank Suisse
UCH	– University College Hospital, London
VGL	– very good looking
WD	– 'wet' dream

INTRODUCTION

Alan Clark started keeping a regular diary in 1955 when he was still in his twenties. On quitting the House of Commons in 1992 he edited and published a selection from his decade as a junior minister in the Thatcher and Major governments and called quite simply *Diaries*. First published in 1993 to enormous success,[1] they were the start of his becoming, what he called, an FP, famous person. He did not demur; indeed subsequent entries often go on to rebound to the phrase, 'I was lionised ...', or at the very least, 'demi-lionised'.

In historical terms his account of Mrs Thatcher's downfall as Prime Minister is now seen as definitive. On a personal level his frankness caused little surprise to his friends, whether in how he came to make a ministerial statement in the Commons after indulging too liberally at a wine tasting or in recounting the attractions of a pretty face. Fool, Clark, fool! he would say. His diaries (sometimes he called them his journals, at others his memoirs) show a man who delights in writing, not least about pastoral events at his homes in Kent, Scotland, Switzerland and even in London (the Albany blackbird). Ask an admirer of the Clark diaries to name a favourite passage and it is odds on that the day he came to shoot a heron will figure high.

Before his death in 1999, and six years after the first publication of *Diaries*, Clark was persuaded (not least by financial considerations) that it was time, at last, to raid his past diaries for two further volumes: the 'prequel' to begin when he entered

---

[1] In paperback it is now titled *Diaries: In Power.*

politics in the early 1970s, and finally, to complete the trilogy, a sequel to the original, what happened in the 1990s after he first quit the House of Commons only to be elected again five years later for one of the Conservatives' most prized and copper-bottomed constituencies, the newly merged Kensington and Chelsea.

When he became ill in the late spring of 1999, with what turned out to be a brain tumour, he had done some preliminary work on the next volume.[2] The question of the third – and now final volume – was a matter for Clark's widow Jane. In deciding that it should go ahead she was mindful that it would not prove wholly pleasant reading for her, and that the 1999 entries would revive for her memories of her husband's final illness and death. However she also appreciated that her husband's standing would be incomplete without it. In fact Clark was writing until five weeks before he died. His script, rarely easy to read, became often shaky, increasingly minuscule. But despite the cancer his mental and intellectual powers were undimmed. Deciphering it, as ever with Clark's variable handwriting, was often laborious, but with Jane Clark's inestimable help I was defeated only rarely.

The original *Diaries* ended in February 1991. In his final entry he recounted being made a Privy Counsellor and walking back to Westminster, where he 'had a boring, overcooked lunch in the Members' dining room'. The new volume opens two days later with an intense affair, and ends in August 1999 with his love for Jane renewed and restated, but his own life coming to an end. Alan and Jane were married for 41 years. As Clark himself admits he was guilty at times of treating his wife appallingly, and even at one point in these diaries he thought of leaving her for someone else. But that thought never became a deed. These diaries, however, reveal an occasion when Jane's patience snapped, and she left him a note (see 14 December 1997). But of a more serious marital breach, in 1992, AC has left no comment, except evidence of pages torn from his diary.

---

[2] It was finally published a year after his death, as *Diaries: Into Politics*

Like his father Kenneth Clark, who in the early 1970s gave him Saltwood Castle in Kent, Alan was a hypochondriac. In this final volume the borderline between hypochondria and his own self-diagnosis of the ill health that is to come is tantalising for the reader. We know that Alan will die from brain cancer. He, however, does not, even though two years before his death he is writing increasingly of headaches, of an inability to defocus, of a weakness in one arm, of a spot on his lip, of changes in taste, appetite and sense of smell. He is capable of thinking the worst, but at this distance readers will share with his editor a surprise that despite test after test, no one in the medical profession identified the cause of his illness until it was far too late.

Politics remain a driving force. His decision to quit at the 1992 election was mostly to do with his exasperation at representing Plymouth Sutton. Clark and his Conservative association (as readers of *Diaries: Into Politics*, in particular, will recall) were often at daggers drawn. Clark found constituency surgeries particularly irksome. Even when he returned to Westminster five years later as MP for Kensington & Chelsea (could there have been a constituency more ideally matched to his talents and his personality?) there are rumblings about his lack of attention to detail. What he loved most about being a politician was Westminster itself, political gossip and debate. Shame about the constituents, he once joked in my hearing.

These last diaries are drawn in the main from eight A4 HMSO or 'Banner' hardback volumes of numbered lined pages (some pages are missing, as mentioned above, but there are no obvious gaps in the narrative). The paper quality is variable, and Clark's choice of pens often relies on whatever was available. He rarely writes in ballpoint; green ink is, as he says at one point, usually, but not exclusively reserved for holidays at Eriboll and Zermatt. These though were not the only diaries. At Shore Cottage, Eriboll, the far north of Scotland estate the Clarks acquired following the death of his father, he kept a diary to which photographs were added, and from this I have transcribed his account of the 'great walk' undertaken in 1991. The record

of the 1993 Alpine rally in which he drove his Rolls-Royce Silver
Ghost comes partly from an intermittent motoring diary. But
there are also entries on single sheets, often House of Commons
notepaper and not always slipped into the appropriate place. I do
wonder what other treasures may yet be found.

I am, though, surprised that he does not write more about
some of the key events in which he was involved during the
1990s, among them the Matrix Churchill trial (and the Scott
enquiry which followed), his legal action against the London
Evening Standard over their spoof 'Not the Alan Clark Diary',
the court case against one of the Clarks' Rottweilers after an
incident involving a BBC cameraman. He does not appear to
have written about either of his sons' weddings, although he
delights in recording the christening of grandchildren. But on
whether he was accepted into the Catholic Church shortly
before his death, as Father Michael Seed has claimed, the
evidence points firmly to the status quo. If Alan Clark had taken
this momentous decision while on his deathbed one can be
certain he would have written about it. God is never far from
his thoughts, or from his diary, and, nightly, he said his prayers.

With the best part of nine years of journals to draw from I
have had to be selective. As a writer, sometimes with crowded
days between entries, he is repetitious. He has a habit of
announcing what he will be doing the following week, and then
a week later giving an account of what happened. I have only
occasionally included both. With events described more recent
than in either of the two published volumes I have also disguised
three of the cast list.

Reliving his life through his diaries has been a rewarding
experience. He has an eye for what is important in politics. He
is good at spotting talent that will emerge later: both William
Hague and Iain Duncan Smith are mentioned well before their
leadership ambitions are tested. He is widely read: these diaries
contain references as varied as Chips Channon's diaries, Evelyn
Waugh's *Brideshead Revisited*, the *Faber Book of War Poetry* (edited
by his former parliamentary colleague, Kenneth Baker), A.W.

Kinglake's *Eothen*, Sapper's Bulldog Drummond novel *The Final Count* and, perhaps less surprising given its setting, John Buchan's *John Macnab*. But above all it is the richness of the life he leads and enjoys, despite frequent protestations of being depressed.

The question arose at a late stage as to how to end the volume. What I did not know when I began transcribing AC's journals was that Jane Clark had herself started a diary during the final weeks of her husband's life. It seemed appropriate therefore to describe what happened through her account. Jane at one point asked Al, who had by this time stopped writing, if he would like to continue by dictating entries to her. No, he said, it would be 'too melancholy'. Jane Clark's account, which I have edited, is by its very nature sad to read, and inevitably for someone bedridden at the end contains reports of bodily functions that some readers may feel are in excess, but that was a fact of Alan's last days. Yet it also has its moments of tenderness, of exasperation, even of humour. Jane Clark has showed herself to be a worthy fellow diarist as well as a devoted wife.

Ion Trewin
July 2002

EDITOR'S NOTE

Footnotes give the present and sometimes past – but rarely future – positions of individuals, usually at their first appearance. Nor is an MP's political allegiance shown except where this may be unclear from the text.

AC's occasional inconsistencies in style, dates, capitalisation and even English grammar, have sometimes been left as written. I have followed his own practice and, where appropriate, silently edited passages.

In the matter of financial dealings, AC often left out the final '000'. Thus the value of a picture given as, say, £300 is actually worth £300,000. I have not altered his way of expressing figures as the sums involved are usually obvious from the context.

In the case of a clearly intense affair, which was not revealed publicly at the time, I have felt it necessary to protect the name of the woman involved by referring to her throughout as 'x'.

IT

1991

Despite my resolve to keep 'x' out of this volume I find it practically impossible to concentrate effectively on anything else. She is in my thoughts the entire time, sometimes exclusively, some of the time in parallel, as it were, with whatever else one is meant to be doing.

The journey down to Reading University in the snow.[1] I was so dejected. She was quite perky. Very cold on arrival; no one to meet us. We sat at 'the bar', drank half a pint, G&T. I said 'all I really want to do is to kiss you …' She bridled. Enjoys it, but doesn't want to seem timid. After meeting up we were guided to the Common Room, then the Hall. They had totally balls'd it up, turned it into a *public* meeting packed with SWP [Socialist Worker Party] and anti-war groupies. I acquitted myself well and she was 'encouraged', and alone among the audience asked a helpful question. In the train back I felt immensely weary. When I leaned forward and put my elbows on the table she leaned back; but when I slumped back – and stayed back for the whole journey – she leant forward to counter this.

She looked incredible in her Russian hat, totally Zhivago. I hold this image in my mind at the moment; it gives me a nodule headache on the left side now, and a sort of despair really. How *is* this going to end? It's such agony. I haven't the nerve to cut it off.

It's preposterous. I'm actually *ill*, have been for a month, lovesick it's called. A long and nasty course of chemotherapy – but with periodic bouts of addiction therapy when I delude myself that I may be cured without 'damage'.

---

[1] AC, Minister for Defence Procurement, was speaking at a Reading University meeting in the midst of the Gulf War.

White Office   *Tuesday, 12 February*

Still regrettably obsessive. After Ministers TK[1] 'held me back';
he's nervous of me, still needs to pick my brain – in this case just
before going to Washington. But *won't* let me 'in on' anything,
TV, Radio (Archie [Hamilton][2] is on every day) or even
meetings with PUS and Mottram, CDS, Vincent,[3] etc etc,
because I will show him up in front of them.

   Lunched with Dilks[4] at Brooks's. His first words as we sat down
were 'How's the delightful "x"?' He was quite interesting about
Mrs T's 'Memoirs', said they could easily be ghosted – but it was
critically important that the 'ghost' should have access to all her
papers. It was something that ought to be spoken now with
Robin Butler, certainly ahead of the next General Election.[5]

Saltwood   *Sunday, 17 February*

On the way out to Bratton[6] yesterday (was it really only
yesterday?) we stopped at Brentor and I had a long, long prayer.[7]

---

[1] Tom King, MP for Bridgwater since March 1970; Defence Secretary since 1989.
[2] Archie Hamilton, MP for Epsom and Ewell since April 1978 and Armed Forces
Minister since 1988.
[3] Permanent Under-Secretary at Defence: Sir Michael Quinlan since 1988; Richard
Mottram, Deputy Under-Secretary since 1989; Chief of the Defence Staff,
Marshal of the RAF Sir David Craig since 1988; Field Marshal Sir Richard
Vincent, Vice CDS since 1987 and about to succeed as CDS.
[4] David Dilks, academic, newly appointed vice-chancellor, University of Hull; had
been research assistant, successively, to Anthony Eden, Lord Tedder and Harold
Macmillan; editor of *The Diaries of Alexander Cadogan* (1971).
[5] AC had discussed with Mrs Thatcher the writing of her biography (see *Diaries*, 4
January 1991). She was appalled at his estimate that it would take him a minimum
of three years. Sir Robin Butler had been Secretary of the Cabinet since 1988,
having been Mrs Thatcher's Principal Private Secretary, 1982–85.
[6] Town Farm, Bratton-Clovelly, Devon.
[7] Approached from the main Okehampton Road at Mary Tavy, this twelfth-century
Dartmoor church at the summit of Brentor stands all alone. Although it is a steep
walk, many thousands of visitors annually are attracted to it.

Should make me serene. And it does while I'm talking to God. But as soon as I stop doing so it comes seeping in. Because like all addicts I can vividly remember the incredible rush of vitality and well being that comes from a good 'fix'.

Then talk of an Election in May–June. Less than three months to go, it would seem or could be. And at that my life really will turn. A major crossroads – but I refuse to accept that thereafter it's all downhill to the grave. I just will not. ACHAB.[1]

I suppose it's better, perhaps, to put 'x' out of the way *now*. Honestly, I'm almost too weary to 'get involved'. The ache not quite as bad, lots of scar tissue there now. But, curiously, my principal concern is to find a way of starting with Jane. We had a horrible passage on Saturday night. Poor little darling – why should *she* be punished because I am being? [AC's question mark]

Last Friday I woke at 6-ish, took some EMT and 3 dry biscuits, boarded the 7.30 train at Charing Cross which didn't *leave* until it was 30 minutes late. BR now totally 3rd-world performer, no middle management in sight (too early) and periodic gabbled illiteration by a – plainly – platelayer drafted in to glottally 'try his hand at' the intercom. Got to Saltwood and loaded up Discovery. Set off at once in snow/fog/drizzle conditions and ground along M25, M3, A303 – many, many roadworks with piggy tailbacks – M4, got to Plymouth just after 4 p.m. feeling distinctly *dry* with exhaustion; just time to get a cup of tea and a scone and cream (I had no appetite – why?); then to surgery, people already making heads visible in a row through the looking glass of the outer office. A tall, strangely classy and distrait policeman who was my guard for the evening. A message from Alison[2] to ring her 'quite urgent', but naturally, she was engaged and NR [no reply] from the main switchboard so couldn't break in.

---

[1] AC was contemplating 'standing down' from the Plymouth Sutton constituency to which he was first elected in February 1974.
[2] Alison Young, AC's secretary since September 1988.

I started dealing with the mendicants, mainly complaining about their solicitors not being responsive enough. (What on earth am *I* meant to do about *that*?) Finally got through to Alison; she found me a number for Andrew Neil[1] who wished to speak 'before the deadline'. I had to spell WEDELN[2] for her. Then found I hadn't got a black tie − I was changing, as so often, into a dinner jacket in the upstairs lav. of the constituency office. Just got Jane at the hotel,[3] could she ask the manager? etc etc. Drove out to Crownhill; Nick Bennett, not a bad chap, some wives and relations at the Family Centre. Admiral Grose[4] turned up (without his wife). They are nice people − the families − though probably as wracked by trauma, infidelities or incest as any other grouping. I made a short speech − poll tax exemption − and then we moved on back into Plymouth.

The arrangements for Cecil[5] were characteristically gauche and irritating. The 'nobs', i.e. top table of about ten people had a room to themselves, with masses of drink ... untouched (but probably charged for) bottles. Then very late − doubtless blamed on me − we moved through increasingly resentful hoi polloi to the dining room. Cecil performed, just adequately, was good with questions − mainly hostile, and about interest rates. Most of the body of the room were characteristically Plymothian and 'rights'-type indignant. I escaped after dinner to our room − we had providentially booked into the Duke of Cornwall − but Jane valiantly remained downstairs chatting. At that same bar, indeed, and in that same dreary-decor room, where my adoption meeting had taken place in September 1972, nineteen years earlier.

---

[1] Andrew Neil, editor of the *Sunday Times* since 1983, executive chairman, Sky TV since 1988.

[2] 'Skiing. A technique using a swaying movement of the hips to make a series of short parallel turns.' (*The New Shorter Oxford English Dictionary*)

[3] The Clarks were staying at the Duke of Cornwall Hotel on Plymouth Hoe.

[4] Admiral Sir Alan Grose, Flag Officer Plymouth since 1990.

[5] Cecil Parkinson, MP for Hertsmere since 1983, a long-serving Minister under Mrs Thatcher, and former Conservative Party chairman; returned to the back benches in 1990.

MoD   *Thursday, 21 February*

Let's face it, I'm not really enjoying myself at all at the moment. I am distracted, more or less constantly, by the pain of my *maladie* and I can't concentrate on the really major points of strategic policy (I must write a 'Cosint Paper' on 'Geostrategic Policy 2000').

The Lady has now decided *against* my doing her biography – going for the big mechanistic technique of researchers and capable hacks. She's got no sense of art or scholarship at all, really. And has always been unreliable, loses her nerve and goes conventional.

Tuesday, 26 February

I have a tension headache. I'm eating very little (overnight down to 11.2 (+)[1]) not drinking at all. I do the [MoD] stairs to the 6th floor, one minute dead at a 'normal' swinging pace, 45 seconds *prancingly*.

There are so many things going to come to a head this year – but I can barely see things in perspective at all. Even quite calming things like sorting through my briefcase I can't 'face'. I suppose I'm in a pre-nervous breakdown condition.

MoD   *Thursday, 28 February*

The Gulf War is over. Too soon, I think. Bush[2] has ordered a ceasefire. Now a long and messy interlude with Saddam[3] stalling

---

[1] AC used imperial measures, thus weight was expressed in stones and pounds.
[2] George Bush, US president since 1989.
[3] Saddam Hussein, Iraqi president since 1979.

and dodging and quite likely to start shooting again. The
Foreign Office has no idea what it wants. Never seems to have
given any thought to the post-war pattern, the western military
presence, commitments – OBJECTIVES. I could write a
scintillating paper on this, but I'm exhausted and my morale is
at zero. Last night Mrs Thatcher (as she must now be called)[1]
chided me for being asleep on the bench when Tom was making
his statement.

An article in *The Times* by Oakley[2] – a man who always
ignores me – about the leaderless Right. No one mentions my
name. How quickly this can happen! There is now talk of a
General Election in June. Just time to claim, massively, some
allowances out of 91–92! Interviewed by Melanie Phillips[3] last
evening and she asked me about the adrenalin of power how it
keeps one going through this hellish existence; I said, 'But look
what happens when people retire or get flung out – they shrivel
up and get cancer immediately.'

MoD   *Monday, 4 March*

Darling Jane is looking a wee bit strained. She knows something
is up, and is quiet a lot of the time. But she doesn't question me
at all – just makes the occasional scathing reference. I do want
to make her happy – she's such a *good* person.[4]

And what of my medium-term plans? I must get rid now
of 'x'. What then? I *very* much wish an early Election. I

---

[1] Margaret Thatcher, usually referred to by AC as The Lady, although no longer
Prime Minister was still MP for Finchley; she was not created a life peer until 1992.
[2] Robin Oakley, political editor of *The Times* since 1986.
[3] Melanie Phillips, journalist with an influential column on the *Guardian* before
moving to the *Observer*.
[4] A few days later AC confesses: 'I fear I am as bad as I have ever been. No progress
at all. And darling Jane somehow knows. She was cross, just a little sad and puzzled
and listless. I would love to do something to really make her happy.'

popped over and spoke to Richard Ryder[1] this morning.
He was in agony from a recently (18 hours) ricked back –
playing tennis. But benign and delightful as always, said wait
until 20 April – but of course it doesn't matter giving late
notice to the constituency.[2] Registered my bid for a 'working
peerage' with a smile, but indicated approval. Also nodded
sagely when I said what a fool and how objectionable, was
TK.

Saltwood   *Sunday, 10 March*

God, is it already *10th* March? A quarter of the year gone by,
and I have done nothing, not answered a single letter, paid
a bill – still less 'played' with cars or other hobbies. I *must*
break out of the cycle, but I can only really effectively do
so by giving 'notice' in the next three weeks. The sheer
administrative complication that this entails compounds it.
This morning, woken up from a deep muck-sweat slumber by
Jane at 2.30 a.m. I lay awake for about 1½ hours, thought
among other things – I really would just as soon pack it in
now, just not go back to London *at all*. She rightly pointed out
I must see through Options,[3] the tank etc – leave my mark.
Then again, I suppose, the Cabinet changes at Easter – if there
is to be no General Election – but even Secretary of State
would almost have to ask – because of how it might have
been.

---

[1] Richard Ryder, MP for Mid-Norfolk since 1983 and government Chief Whip
since 1990.

[2] AC was subject to conflicting advice. Over lunch, three days before, Tony
Fanshawe (formerly Anthony Royle, MP for Richmond, 1959–83 and now a life
peer), told AC not to 'antagonise people' by leaving his 'standing down'
announcement until too late.

[3] The Ministry of Defence was, like other government departments, looking into
the future, in this case the role of the British armed forces into the twenty-first
century. AC concentrated on equipment.

Finances are now in a total mess – Coats at 160 +.[1] Vast new out-goings of Mains in prospect, lead roof, moat leaking. I fear it will have to be the Degas[2] because we will save the CGT by doing it through Andrew. Might yet scrape by as stock markets are recovering. But how do I see my future? Get the diary into shape as soon as you can, then really become a recluse, naturalist, pinpoint feats. Loch Shiel to Loch Eriboll.[3] A kind of upmarket Albert (if he was called Albert) Wainwright. With a hint, perhaps, of Poucher (and a touch of class, as Jane said, with Robin Fedden).[4]

But right at the moment, I am in really bad shape – shaking, inability to concentrate. The knowledge of this makes me *medically* apprehensive.

Winter office, a.m.   *Tuesday, 19 March*

In a state of abject depression – cross-streaked with apprehension so that my hands and forearms shake and feel watery. Poor old Archie H came into my office yesterday afternoon and stayed for ¾ hour whingeing on about end-of-an-era, all over, etc etc. The pretext was on being 'boxed-in' on Options, Treasury squeeze all that and I made some tangential slagging off of TK, his indecisiveness, inability to make any judgement

---

[1] Coats had amalgamated with the Clark cotton thread business, J. & J. Clark of Paisley, in 1896. AC's great-great grandfather had invented the wooden spool or bobbin. The decline (25½p in 1997) in the price of the Coats shares is never far from his mind.

[2] Edgar Degas's *Femme s'épongeant le dos*, left to AC by his father.

[3] AC's grandfather owned the whole of the Ardnamurchan peninsula, on the west coast of Scotland, to the south-west of Eriboll.

[4] *Alfred* Wainwright and W. A. Poucher, two indefatigable guides and proselytisers for the Lake District; today Poucher is the less well known. A chemist by training, who worked for thirty years with Yardley's, the cosmetics company, he climbed and photographed the uplands of Britain. He wrote more than thirty books and died in 1988. Robin Fedden, former deputy Director-General and Historic Buildings Secretary of the National Trust, author of *The National Trust Guide*.

save that of short-term political 'impact', 'how will it go in the house' etc. We are back to the old Conservative Government days, Eden at best. I said at least we broke the unions in the last decade, you won't hear much from *them* in the future. He agreed, but was still doleful. There's the general feeling that the baddies are getting away with it again – most apparent as Jane said at the weekend with all that fuss about the 'Birmingham Six',[1] yet one more excuse to slag off the police, wretched fellows. Jury wouldn't even convict an IRA gunrunner with their Kalashnikovs in the car and hands smelling of Semtex!

In the evening I went (with Alison) to Kensington Conservatives. *Very* clued up and intelligent and good company they were with many aspirant candidates. My address not *quite* up to standard, but questions sparkled. Dudley Fishburn[2] (whom I had warned Alison was a 'non-event') said nice things about me. His majority at a by-election I must admit is only 800.

Saltwood   *Saturday, 23 March*

Bruce Anderson rang,[3] and we gossiped around a bit. He is of the *agnostic* school concerning JM's private life.[4] But admitted that Norma had told him 'John's not nearly as much fun now; doesn't seem to have the energy … always into the boxes, etc'. Bruce said that Richard [Ryder] now 'pro' me, and there was some talk they might both come down for dinner and the night

---

[1] The 'Birmingham Six', six men who spent 16 years in prison after being wrongfully convicted of the 1974 Birmingham pub bombings.
[2] Dudley Fishburn, MP for Kensington since July 1988 when he succeeded the late Sir Brandon Rhys Williams. Kensington's merger as a constituency with Chelsea would not take place until 1997.
[3] Bruce Anderson, political journalist, currently with *Sunday Express*.
[4] The press had been full of concern at John Major's state of health. He had been PM for little more than 100 days, and was suffering from intermittent ear and throat infections. His wife Norma was quoted as saying, 'He's awfully tired and not getting enough sleep.'

at Easter. But he said my enemies were rampant, Douglas in particular.[1]

Charles P[2] had told him, 'Under no other Prime Minister would Alan have been either given office or promoted; and under any other Prime Minister he would long since have been sacked.' So I felt rather awful about already disowning the old Thatcherite rump the way I do. But actually, they're just a lot of old has-beens – all leaving public life. Who's going to lead them? Bruce said 'Michael Spicer'.[3] Well, *really*! Apparently John M made a long flat speech at Southport where the [Conservative] Central Council meeting (a fatiguing and probably somewhat disapproving body which I have never attended) is being held. TK, irritatingly, got a standing ovation – too easy after the Gulf – but MRDH [Heseltine][4] was greeted 'stonily'. I don't quite know what the Party is doing at the moment. It's a limbo year, which will, I suppose, suffer the planning blight for most of its course. For the first time ever, I believe, I watch the approaching springtime with gloom and apprehension. There is no way out of total agony on the w/e of 10 May[5] (cruelly and paradoxically the very solstice of physical delight and renewal).

Sunday's papers show the Party in considerable disarray – now likely to be aggravated by the six-point deficit shown in MORI. Although actually, it would be slightly more tolerable to be out under Labour than under a *new wave* Tory administration.

---

[1] Almost certainly a reference to Douglas Hurd, MP for Witney since 1983 (Mid-Oxon February 1974–83); Foreign Secretary since 1989. He and AC were on opposing sides of the Conservative Party.

[2] Sir Charles Powell, Private Secretary to the Prime Minister, 1984–91.

[3] Michael Spicer, MP for South Worcestershire and, like AC, elected in February 1974. Junior minister under Mrs Thatcher (Department of the Environment, 1990).

[4] Michael Heseltine, MP for Henley since 1974 (Tavistock, 1966–74), Cabinet minister in Thatcher governments, beaten in the 1990 Tory leadership election when John Major succeeded Mrs Thatcher; currently Environment Secretary, something of a poisoned chalice.

[5] An official visit, as Minister for Defence Procurement, to the Gulf States, following the end of the war.

I have no idea what the future holds this year. How, when, do I break it to Alison that I'm not standing, for example?

Saltwood   *31 March, Easter Sunday*

The special moisture in the spring air – if not the foggy inland – with the sun lightly obscured, but a luminous promise. We went to Communion this morning. I enjoy it now because of the opening prayer, whose significance (as with so much until now) I never before appreciated. '... to whom all hearts are open, all desires known, and from whom no secrets are hid ...'

Ashford Station (50 feet out!)   *Sunday, 14 April*

A great series in the *Sunday Telegraph* on 'the Mid-Life Crisis' today. It's going to be hard to come to terms with this – particularly in the knowledge that it's my 'fault'. Eleven years left, I suppose. If I'm lucky. I'm anxious about my nose (left side); my diabolic pressure must be sky-high; I tried to hold my breathing within the chest limits and got – at great cost – to 1¾ minutes (should be 2-2½) but on subsequent shots could only get it to 1.

This whole experience could take hold of as pre-cancerous.

Only good moment: I watched John Major[1] on *Walden*. He took it very well. I thought I'd ring Richard R and tell him; couldn't get through so switched to No 10. Yes he was there, could 'they' ring me back? Came through very quickly (though not as quickly as the Lady in crisis) and was *pathetically* glad to hear praise. 'Bless you, couldn't have come at a better moment'

---

[1] John Major was being criticised by, among others, Sir Alan Walters, former economic adviser to Margaret Thatcher, for his economic policies.

etc. I made reassuring crack about we all loved the Lady and her style 'none more than me ...' etc. But things more difficult now, people wanted it different. 'But have you seen today's papers?' *The Observer* – I couldn't remember anything *particularly* objectionable in *The Observer*, but looking at it afterwards, I suppose he must have meant Nick Wapshott's bitchy repetition of Mrs T's crack about 'the B-team'.[1] Fortunately I'd read the leader, which was broadly laudatory, in yesterday's *Times*, and quoted that. I think he was pleased. But where it's all going to end – like absolutely every other 'problem' which lies on us – God knows.

And talking of God – I went down to St Leonard's last evening to pray. Norman Woods[2] was there, pleasant and serious as always, counselling a handsome and classy couple about their Christening. I knelt and reflected on 'it' all. I almost asked Norman to hear my confession, but didn't/couldn't, though afterwards Jane said he would have. I was rather shocked to find how I prayed so selfishly. It was quite an effort to *focus* on the real purpose and to release darling Jane of her pain and sense of betrayal. She's going through exactly what I did in February – and I know what it's like – total hell (and in my own case all too likely to recur in slightly different form any minute). Only feebly did I give thanks for this wonderful life and all my blessings. Disgraceful.

White Office   *Thursday, 18 April*

Even allowing for the fact that it was mainly written in the train the standard of writing in the last entry is perfectly awful and indicates the level of mental disturbance from which I am presently suffering.

---

[1] Nicholas Wapshott, political editor of *The Observer* since 1988.
[2] The Rev. Canon Norman Woods, vicar of St Leonard's Church, Hythe.

Plymouth–Paddington train   *Saturday, 20 April*

I think, probably, I'm worse than at any previous point this year. The real problem is the *total* uncertainty hanging on prospects. I can't seem even to pray properly. Even last evening when I climbed to Brentor church. I could think things through, but make no real contact because, I suppose, what I really want to do is cruel and disreputable. My personal and political anxieties overlap inextricably. I had a rough meeting with the councillors (brilliantly thought up by Alison and organised by her). Some reasonable noises from Mount Gould and Efford, with some grumbling by (inevitably) Plympton St Mary and Erle, 'it's too late …' etc; then a whole list of what should be done tomorrow much of it impossible, a crash visit from Douglas Hurd (?!) etc. 'Well, if it's too late', I said, 'what's the point of doing these things?' Then (was it Campbell?) suggested that Michael Heseltine 'would go down very well' if he came here. 'Well, that's a good suggestion,' I said, 'because he's a bit short of places where he would go down well at the moment, and I expect he'd be glad of the invitation.'[1] More titters from loyalists.

All right, so I'm not standing again.

And 'x'? I've had so many breaks with her, but the day of the death sentence approaches. May, the magic month. At the end a solitary trip to Scotland. June and July the last months in public life. Will the obsession then be extinct – or at least diminishing?

Later – Tuesday
I just can't focus – the summer, the autumn, plans for the recess or 'leave'. Doesn't anyone go *abroad* at all? Will the Porsche or the ID decap [Jane's Citroën] be used? I sit at my desk in the

---

[1] As Environment Secretary Heseltine was unpopular, having to cope with the aftermath of the poll tax, one of the most hated measures of Mrs Thatcher's period as Prime Minister.

White Office getting impatient, watching the red phone light –
which has been on for 35 minutes.[1]

Albany   *Tuesday, 30 April*

An awful night, little more than three hours' fragmented sleep.
This morning Valerie[2] rang, claimed to be coming over in May
– so what?

Only good thing. Jane is better. Quite cured you could say. I
try and tell myself that this is what is really important. But (more
than) half of me says no it isn't – what counts is the incredible
joie de vivre, the physical and mental delight of being in love
and in the company of your adored. God alive! This confusion
has been going on for nearly five months. At least I do the stairs
in MoD, now weigh 11.6 and did Gossie last Sunday evening in
an incredible 2'28". All for what?

Later
In the White Office, with a batch of nasty questions (7 out of
top 13) all potentially awkward, and TK got me in to 'make sure'
that I was not going (presumably) to commit a 'gaffe'. First
impressions endure, and I suppose he is still conditioned by our
experience together when I was his junior minister in DE. And
all against a background of horrid (really horrid) personal
deprivation – which keeps recurring in a hundred different
ways, which affects my concentration.

[1] AC added his own footnote: 'turned out to be Keith Simpson'. Simpson, Special
Adviser to the Defence Secretary 1988–90, and a former lecturer in war studies
at Sandhurst, became Tory MP for Mid-Norfolk in 1997.
[2] Valerie Harkess, one of three women, a mother and two daughters, described by
AC as 'the coven' (see *Diaries: Into Politics* and *Diaries*).

Saltwood   *Bank Monday, 6 May*

Really vile weather. It's been like this for three weeks, blowing
so hard we can't even have a fire in the Green Room, rain, lawns
a mess, so cold that one naturally puts on longies. The Grahams[1]
came last night. EG looking incredible (though hair *very* white
in the centre and surprisingly old person soft and fluffy to the
touch). Funny and intelligent about medical matters, friends
who are dead. An excellent venison dinner, but the wine made
little difference to me. I am depressed, aimless. I see no future,
no objectives, no 'satisfaction' except possibly the traditional one
of 'getting things in order', a gift more to darling Jane than
anything else. Even when I went out in the Buick, this barely
registered, drove it badly, had forgotten how to change gear. I
never really want to see the Buick again, whereas I do sometimes pine for the Black Caddy. I am in bad shape, apprehensive
of my Gulf trip, ability to stay 'strong' this week and next. Max
[jackdaw] and his wife, appeared at the window this morning.
He *very* clearly and characteristically left me a pellet on the
windowsill, which I will take on my travels.

Saltwood   *Tuesday, 7 May*

Spent most of the day clearing the nettles of Lady Conway's
Bridge. Yet more capital expenditure threatening – to get
Barwick (presently doing the café wall) to make up the bridge
and then to get the roadman to 'dress' it when he does the drive.
But at tea I felt really gloomy. Recurrent pangs of 'x' all the time
I pulled, or *eradicated*, the nettles. But I know I shall have contact
with her this week. Once I acknowledge her loss, and it really is
'gone for good' how empty the whole thing will be? What will

---

[1] Euan Graham, long-standing friend. He had retired in 1984 as Principal Clerk of
Private Bills, House of Lords. He and his first wife, Pauline, were divorced in 1972.
By his second wife Caroline he had two daughters.

be my purpose in life? Just to stave off old age, I suppose, stay (outwardly) boyish for as long as I can watch people dying around me.

But not knowing where she is and what she is doing will be agony. Even worse than (as now) knowing what she *is* doing.

HE's residence, Qatar[1]   *Sunday, 12 May*

Out to Shaafa today and then to see Tip[2] who was magnificent, handsome, clear-headed and hugely popular with his brother officers. In great heat (43°) was shown round the 'sheds'. Impressive installations, promising recruits, grotty equipment (CVRT[3] and Chieftains and M60s). Our helicopter, a shabby Bell Huey, wouldn't start and we switched to another, even shabbier one. Our pilot – slightly James-like, young, blond. On the return journey he said we'd make a detour on the Jebel Akhdar. At the time I thought this sounded a bit dodgy, said nothing. Drank some camel's milk (quite delicious) in the mess, felt pretty good. But in fact he lined up a gorge with 3000 ft sides – less than 40-80 ft wide in places, climbed up to over 9000 ft looking at little villages, mud hut settlements etc. One of the most obviously dangerous things I have done for ages, and not enough lateral margin for side draughts or gusts ('whoops!' he said at one point). After it was over, and were all in the HS125, I, and the others, felt a real *high*. The beginning, it seemed, of 'feeling better'.

---

[1] For his official visit to the Gulf, AC flew on an HS 125 via RAF Akrotiri (Cyprus), and moved on to Oman before reaching Qatar.

[2] Andrew Clark was attached to the Sultan of Oman Armoured Brigade.

[3] Combat Vehicle Reconnaissance Track.

Saltwood (Long Garage)   *Sunday, 19 May*

I wouldn't have thought I could get lower, more depressed and unsettled. Partly, I suppose, because Jane is getting worse all the time, not eating anything (her weight is down to 8 stone, mine to 11.4 (*net*) I have lost 10½ lbs – nearly a stone). She has got a lot of confessions out of me, along the lines of what-do-you-do? when-did-you-do-it? type interrogation. I almost relish the admissions as of giving a dimension, a reminder of what occurred and has now ceased.

This continues to have a frightful effect on my routine, output, concentration. It's been running now for six months and *no sign whatever* of a diminishing of its intensity, quite the reverse in fact. Practically nothing gives me enjoyment any longer: cars, cleaning nickel with wire wool and Bluebell; the Heritage – that lovely May vision of the arboretum with its yellowy greens; politics – the 'comment' in the Sundays is total dross, I'm barely interested although vaguely *constater* that the Conservatives' fourth term is now in serious jeopardy in which case my title and even 'k' are now down the drain; Brooks's, the Mews, the company of 'friends' or journalists means very little. I said to Jane, the only things left that I like are seeing and talking to the boys (I had had a good conversation with James and Eriboll is ok, because Wimpey's[1] are going to step forward, also Tip was so fabulous in Oman with his lovely tidy quarters) and driving the Porsche. Yesterday we came back to Bratton in 3hr 24 minutes – Jane was very patient and good.

But she is *devastated* by what is happening. She knows, inevitably, that I still pine for 'x'. Yesterday she was so sweet to me on arrival, tried to seduce me on the lower end of the asthma rail. I would have loved to, but terrified over one more failure and disappointment. Sometimes she says, 'I love you so much, I really feel I ought to let you do whatever you want.' At other times she says I have destroyed so much there's no point,

---

[1] To extract gravel.

she won't even pray. What really hurts me is the knowledge of my own affliction. If I were younger I could hold both these women without trouble.

I'm not wholly wiped out, and I get little waves of hope that something might happen. God might dispense a favour. But he has given one so much. I've really had my quota already. I wonder how Scotland will be. Will that, too be a failure? Somehow, I think not, although the Whit weekend will be painful.

Eriboll: the great walk   *Saturday, 25 May*

Today I completed the great walk that has been on my mind almost since seeing it on the map some six or seven years ago.

Left the croft about 9 a.m. (later than I had hoped) and parked the Volvo at the end of the Stra'beg track at 9.18. I went via the bothy – unusually unoccupied although it is a holiday weekend – and made a short entry of my intention in their log, allowing a time of seven hours. Started the 'approach march' up the valley at 9.37.

Just within the hour, at 10.35, I crossed the fence into the Westminster [estate] territory having forded the Polla, and almost immediately began a very steep climb through birch and mossy peat gulleys, much riven by natural storm channels. Once above the tree line the gradient slackened, although great cliffs and cornices of peat showed the effect of flash flooding with water pouring off the Cranstackie ridge.

At twenty minutes past eleven I reached the stalkers track that runs up from Loch Dionard to the summit of Creag Staonsaid and on over to Glen Golly.

The cloud line was at about 1600 feet, and I had some difficulty in orienting myself on the descent to Dionard. My intention was to follow Alt an Essain Ghill up to the ford shown at the sortie from An Dubh Loch, then pick up the track that skirted the Creaggan Meall Horn. There are two burns – both quite difficult in spate – that run down here from the southern slopes of Creag Staonsaid, fordable today, but pretty foamy and dangerous I would judge in the autumn. As I worked my way down I saw very clearly the lines of the track (not shown on the O.S. 1:50 'Cape Wrath', but just delineated on the 1:25 Pathfinder of 'Arkle') that climbs up from Dionard on the w. side of the Alt an Essain Ghill. I searched for a ford (or 'leap') and just made it, losing my stalking stick, which I immediately pursued down stream. It got stuck between rocks a couple of times then freed as I approached and tumbled on. Finally I caught up with it and scrambled up the bank to the track. This is in reasonable repair, would carry an Argocat over this stretch though deteriorates to little more than a firm grassy spine higher up. Quite soon after, it seemed, at 12.30, I reached Coir an Dubh Loch, sinister and dark jade green, being fed by waters from Lolhan Ulbha above it. Cold drizzle, poor visibility. I ate my pack lunch and restarted at 12.32 getting on the steep early phase 'aortic fibrillation' – *passim* President Bush – but just thought sod it, and pressed on.

There is a burn (unmarked) that feeds Dubh Loch from Creaggan Meall Horn and the track plays with it sometimes skirting, sometimes deviating, but the actual turn to cross is very obvious and marked by good stepping stones. Within one hour, at 1.32, I reached the cairn where there is a junction with another track (not shown on the Pathfinder) and a gradual descent, increasingly grassy, follows the line of the Alt Horn, though well above it to the NW. The 'worst' of the traverse was now over and, exultant, I ran most of the way, feeling now that I had a 'record' time within my grasp. At half-past two I emerged from the Glen with Loch Stack visible on the right and a steep downward track – not unlike the first approach to the Trift ascent in Zermatt – leading into a Westminster pine plantation, now mature. Exited from this between two huge rocks, fifteen, sixteen feet high that framed the iron gateway. It took me nearly another hour's walking along the flat to follow the vehicle track around the eastern edge of the loch to the causeway, which joined the main road to Laxford Bridge. Here I slouched on the bank and ate the remains of my picnic, then walked westerly for another hour and a bit before sighting Jane and the 'Discovery' just past Stack Lodge. Whole time, well under seven hours, so that five, really, to the deserted croft at 'Lone' that marks the end of the walk. I saw no one, until the last point on the flat where I called to some 'serious' folk, well kitted out with nylon back packs and new climbing equipment. At first rebarbatif they may have thought that I was a scruffy laird questioning their rights. They became more amiable, but were, I judge, uneasy tyros. They didn't know where Eriboll was, even, and proclaimed their intention of climbing Foinaven and Arkle (different objectives surely?). Had the cloud line lifted the walk would have been even more fulfilling, and alarming. But there is no doubt that one is helped immeasurably by the tracks on the Westminster side. Natural judgement would have probably taken a different route skirting Creaggan Meall Horn earlier and following the burn in the Alt Horn much lower down.

A wonderful taste of the remote glens, and now whets the appetite for some of the crueller and steeper corries.[1]

Saltwood   *Sunday, 2 June*

Half-way through the year, and no let-up *whatsoever* in the misery factor. Quite the reverse in fact. Yesterday I had a raging temper tantrum after catching some 'pinks' with the Countax under the library windows. Bellowed and roared, threw my clothes around, cursed, cried etc. We were a tiny bit better at supper, but Jane had a bad night and this morning at breakfast staged a *duet* of wailing and recrimination in the course of which she threw and smashed a coffee cup, at the news that 'x' was in contact with the contractors about putting in a bathroom

---

[1] Elsewhere, AC summed up the great walk: 'as good as a "medical".'

at B5. After we'd calmed down went over to the Hardys at Sandling Park and strolled, for a little too long, among the rhodies and azaleas. When we got back I 'striped' the Bailey (first time this year). 'Tea' was at 6.45, and now I'm over in my father's study to record — what? That I still have no taste for anything — cars, heritage, politics, papers, paperwork, tidying, wine, company of friends — the endless variety of lovely May vistas is dross for me, all this for the very first time in my entire life. 'Nineteen ninety-one, the end of all the fun.'

I say, how is it all going to end? I don't know, I mean I suppose it *isn't* going to end, although the intensity of the pain, its obsessive and all-excluding nature may ease off. I'm in an impossible situation, impossible, that is, to conceive of any happy outcome. 'x' isn't really attracted to me any more; it's waning all the time. I *did* have one more chance, but I flunked it, and now I'm just the 'preferred escort'. But in any case, how *could* I run away from Jane? Thinking of her, and what *she* was doing and thinking will be just as painful and disturbing as, at present, is thinking (ditto) of 'x'. 'x' wants, half wants me to take her away for a little while. How the hell do I arrange this? And whose were those initials I saw in her diary for Friday lunch?

White Office												*Tuesday, 4 June*

Yesterday I went to see 'Dr' Page, Rowntree's successor.[1]

Young, absurdly so it seemed, but probably a contemporary of Tom Bates.[2] I told him my tale and he seemed concerned, asked a few faintly conventional questions about 'stress' and so on. Subjected me to an examination; blood pressure high ('it always is'), but he looked most piercingly into my eyes using a tiny, but powerful light and said that the blood vessels were normal. Took

---

[1] Dr Nick Page, who had taken over from the Clarks' long-time doctor, Dr Rowntree.
[2] Tom Bates, private consultant in Kent.

blood for 'tests', talked of giving hormones or whatever, asked about diabetes (urine sample), did nervous reactions (left side not so good). Said, disconcertingly, that testicles were 'atrophic', 'shrivelled' (in that case why do I still get WDs?). He seemed dismissive about my claim of good general health. I had climbed the MoD stairs in 42 seconds and the Eriboll/Stack walk, said that this was probably the way that stress was finding its impact on my good (i.e. normal) health pattern. Certainly it's true that it has been worse since I got to MoD. I can't bear to look at the records since then – so many lost opportunities.

My spirits were high when I left his surgery. But since then I have become depressed. My relationship with 'x' has altered – I fear irreparably, although we went through all this in February – and in any case it all poses such complexities.

Uncertainty, total uncertainty, and apprehension wreak their damage.

Sunday, 9 June

I am still miserable. I have been all year (with the exception of the long three weeks which I was recovering ground in end March early April). I just can't go on like this. I am being beastly to Jane; one had another awful night yesterday after I collapsed on hearing that Andrew had been sent a letter saying 'I am crying as I write this.' But really this incident, it's my way, I suppose, of venting my own despair. For once in my life I'm going to stick to the plan. *Nothing*, I'll try not even to see her until Thursday evening, and just see if she turns up from the train.

Yesterday I had a conversation with Richard R[yder] and he told me that the House would go on sitting into August. I can only get through August if I anaesthetise, a tourniquet, or whatever it is in July

A pretty awful day. We had planned to go into the arboretum

and clear wood. But for some reason the Toyota battery – perfectly all right when we put it away – had a dud cell and wouldn't start. There followed frequent battery changes; R Cont to Toyota, New Bing to R Cont, Mehari to Bang Bang in order to make place for hiding R Cont as peacocks were vandalising, I mean crazy scratching and leaping at their reflection in everything from the Shadow to S16.

Finally getting to the arboretum I made a balls of pruning the rowan tree,[1] didn't really get much done although Jane was incredible, staking and planting. I have a latent sore throat (yesterday also) and 'lost' my voice. It has no power, like an old person. So needed to shout for Tom[2] (and Jane). More impotence.

MoD   *Thursday, 13 June*

I'm really now quite thin and gaunt. I slept well – continuously indeed – but only for six-and-a-bit hours. Today I'm going *into the care of doctors* in that rather more indicative mode that one does, I suppose, in one's sixties; probably that most creepy of all specialities, the endocrinologist, glands etc. My hormone count was right down, and so will presumably want to take a lot more tests etc etc. Page, when he told me the reason, was slightly guarded. Similarly, I am clearly suffering from a resurgence of the nose place, slightly back and to one side.

Saltwood   *Saturday, 15 June*

A bad day. We had really been looking forward to a 'free' weekend, particularly the open Saturday. But James is here

---

[1] AC believed in the magical properties of the rowan.
[2] Tom, the Clarks' Jack Russell terrier, also known as T.O.

having run away from Sally.[1] *Désoeuvré* as always, standing around or going out to get cigarettes. So what the hell's going to happen here? I think they're irreconcilable – or is it irreconsilable? We drove over, having nothing better to do, to Mike Stallwood's[2] and I questioned him lightly about his arrangements and finances. The Eriboll account is o/d £20,000 and the same again next year I suppose as he's employing 2½ shepherds and the grant has been cut, the sheep sales don't cover the expenditure (the worst possible background for 'explaining' that we can't go ahead with Wimpey's; although my conversation with Colin Stroyan[3] disclosed that we *could* get out of it – at a cost of course. I still think we'll have to, because it will smash the estate, the endless sound of the crusher, breaking that special peace of the loch etc etc.) I will have nowhere to go on my retirement – hadn't I resolved to die on the Creaggan Road? Then again he's got all these 'military vehicles', quite unsaleable I suspect. He asked for a release (loan) of £20,000 from the Trust for 'investment' (i.e. speculation), which he wouldn't disclose as it always brought 'bad luck'. The idea is that he's going to Eriboll for a trial separation. But he can't live there alone indefinitely, and anyway half admits that he's drinking too much. And what does he do to occupy himself? So there we go – *worrying about James*, just as my parents, or mother particularly, worried about Col on and off all his life.

Then another setback. I don't think those bloody hormones are making the slightest difference. No night or morning erections – an initially, mildly heightened sexuality, I suppose. But this morning at breakfast Jane suddenly said – I think when I was trying to fluff her, on my knees – 'Having your skin-cancer tests?' (Having slyly seen, but not commented on, the bill for the path lab in the bathroom at Albany). I had to explain what it is for – unhappily cancer, but I needed, also, a path lab for my nose spot. Started whingeing, then went off to do the henhouses.

---

[1] Sally, James's second wife.
[2] Mike Stallwood, a dealer in militaria.
[3] Colin Stroyan, a friend of the Clarks, and a trustee of the Eriboll estate.

Jane and I finally had a short walk, snapping at each other. I said, 'this is going to be a very bad year, I know somehow that it is …'

'I wish you wouldn't keep on saying that, I really dislike it.'

So health, sex, money, politics (Labour now settled at 10 points ahead and *Mail on Sunday* openly plugging Heseltine again) all bad – and with a long run ahead.

Monday, 1 July

These entries are so few and far between. Testifying to the fact that 'x' and the anxiety she generates fill every waking hour that I'm not working. I don't concentrate on my work – particularly Saltwood paper work – although I can still garden manically, sit on mowers etc. I'm also terribly bad tempered and snappy.

Wednesday, 3 July

Yesterday in *The Times* I saw that they were 'looking for' a new chairman of English Heritage. I toyed with the idea. Could keep me in public life and, with House of Lords, and – fantasising now – would offer an attachment/platform for 'x' ('Oh she's mistress/lives with the Chairman of English Heritage').

As I write this, inevitably, I can get a heavy blood flow. It's too boring, the whole thing is controlled by the brain. (One minor plus is the virtual disappearance – after three scabbings each slighter than its predecessor – of the 'nose place'. Could this be the result of the hormone boost? More and more I think that the interaction of brain and blood is everything. Page wants me to go for another test on the 20th.)

Saltwood   *Sunday, 7 July*

A lovely fine day, really hot – so much so that I bathed (three
times) in *last year's* black water (at 72°!) and felt wonderful. As
we brought Saltwood to life, and looked at all the lovely vistas
and possibilities (in Garden House too) I thought there is so
much to do here. I must get a book, a couple of Saltwood
ledgers and write them up, so that the boys have something to
refer to – contents, vistas, possibilities. They or my grandchildren
would be interested.

King's Cross train   *Sunday, 14 July*

Last night we went to *The Magic Flute* at Glyndebourne. Frightful naff, pretentious audience, longueurs etc – but in fact it was
rather fun. David (Young)[1] had invited us, and he's always fun to
meet and talk to – though still with that slight hesitance,
deference almost, that was his undoing in the upper reaches of
the Party. He asked me (depressing) about my plans, implying I
would not be in the next Government. But as Jane and I agreed
this morning at EMT *at present* the Home Secretary[2] (also there)
went out of his way to chat; the Employment Secretary[3] made a
point of asking for a drink and a private meeting; 'Sir' Geoffrey
Leigh[4] was gravely courteous and I 'stung' him for an iced coffee

---

[1] Lord Young of Graffham (life peer 1984), brought into government (from the
Manpower Services Commission, where he was chairman) by Mrs Thatcher, and
successively Employment and Trade & Industry Secretary (1985–89); now
executive chairman, Cable & Wireless.

[2] Kenneth Baker had been Home Secretary since 1990. MP for Mole Valley since
1983 (Acton, March 1968–70; St Marylebone, October 1970–83).

[3] Michael Howard, Employment Secretary since 1990; MP for Folkestone and
Hythe since 1983, thus Saltwood was in his constituency. MH and AC also found
that they shared many political views.

[4] Sir Geoffrey Leigh, property magnate with strong arts interests; founded Margaret
Thatcher Centre, Somerville College, Oxford.

and a Dundee cake. All this will evaporate when we become penniless hermits.

The performance itself was 'jolly'. New wave director (Sellars) and librettist (some American poetess)[1] with huge photo back-drop of California, captions and text in flash red dot writing. Some, but fortunately very few obvious but pretentious 'in' jokes. The whole thing redolent of sex, from a slightly feminist style – which depressed me more. Is everyone now enjoying it? One good moment at supper when Lita [Young] squawked when Jane told her how old I was.

Bratton   *Saturday 20 July*

A nice free day here, until the 'frolic' (ugh) this evening. The place slowly coming round to shape up; the empathy and 'studio' giving it a new dimension and Campling's unfinished work[2] making the *link*. Tiny touches (some bare pelmets saved from being thrown out by the couple in the cottage) remind one of how untouched it has been since the days of our penury in the very early sixties – curtain rails in the dairy dining-room, e.g. This year we should get it really comfortable, and acceptably (though not by 'x's' standards) clean and tidy.

Then there is the restoring of the place. *Massive* expenditure (Jane has now very sensibly acceded to a total overhaul of Albany). The cars are unsaleable – except, possibly, the SS, my 'folly' (although I like it very much) and the R-type Continental. But if I'd kept the 8-litre money on deposit I could have bought the Napier for nothing (i.e. inclusive of profit of 225) we'd all be millionaires.

More uncertain is the career prospect. There could well be a

---

[1] Peter Sellars had revived his 1990 production with libretto by Alice Goodman.
[2] Robert Campling, painter of all things Bloomsbury, had partially painted a door at Bratton.

'standing start' reshuffle now, or in September. Albany just done up in time to entertain, but, as Jane said, 'no one will want to know us!'

MoD   *Tuesday, 23 July*

I parked the Porsche in the members' garage and walked along the cloisters and through the tunnel. A badge messenger acknowledged me deferentially. Not for the first time I reflected that all this will be over next year. This is my very last *chef des champs* summer. And I have *no* idea where or what I will be in July 1992. It is still less than a year ago that Ian[1] was murdered; his funeral and the start of the Gulf War with all its unhappy memories of Pavlovian alternatives. These twelve months have been sad for me. I've lost my love, seem to have become much poorer, and find my career becalmed (at lunch last week Bruce Anderson said, 'I don't quite know the Extel rating on Clark at present.' He meant – no dealings. It's over).

Are my relations with Jane set to improve? That would be some consolation.

MoD   *Wednesday, 24 July*

Incredibly tired. I drop off during meetings. It's muggy and humidly showery. Jane came up for the 'end-of-term lunch'. Soames was host, at the Cranbornes'.[2] I found it disparate and

---

[1] Ian Gow, MP Eastbourne, February 1974–30 July 1990, when murdered by an IRA car bomb. He became Mrs Thatcher's PPS in 1979. AC's chief friend in the Commons, he resigned from the government in November 1985 in protest at the Anglo-Irish Agreement.

[2] Nicholas Soames, MP for Crawley since 1983; Lord Cranborne, heir to the 6th Marquess of Salisbury, MP for Dorset South, 1979–87.

rather pointless. Too many guests – so a buffet. No butter (why?). I missed supper last night and breakfast this morning, but wasn't particularly hungry. Jane had had greywater yesterday and looked terribly thin, poor darling.

But the real point is … it is the end of the parliamentary summer – FOR EVER. This time next year I have *no* idea what I'll be doing or where. But I do know that I will no longer be a member of the House of Commons. No more chauffeur cars or solitary policemen. No more passes to flash. (But no more, I trust, wrecked Sunday evenings and Monday morning rushes.)

This, and my affliction, and the departure of my love, presently at her most blithe and feckless, make me very depressed, but with a 'nasty temper' lurking.

Saltwood   *Saturday, 10 August*

I don't really know what happened to last week. Not really very happy. This morning I said I was more unhappy than at any time since I could remember – Jane, too, she's terribly standoffish and cries at intervals. She is confronting me with things that I've done in the past which have been 'out' many times before and were 'kissed and made up' since, but still I'm basted. We had dreadful row coming back from Bratton. A journey which I drove continuously in the Discovery using m-way the whole way and with my foot absolutely flat down 95–100 in pretty thick traffic, under four hours, but small thanks I got etc etc. I've promised (a) not to whinge (b) not to swear (c) not to 'drive fast'. It's all part of the castrating syndrome.

There is a certain type of woman of which Jane is one and Valerie (to take an obvious and most emphatic example) is not who would rather have their man a eunuch than have him 'chasing around'.

Zermatt   *Monday, 19 August*

Arrived here after a long — but not disagreeable train journey from Zurich Flughaven. Dead tired and 'unwound' as one is in the train to Zermatt after a flight, we dozed intermittently and lolled in the heat. No picnic to stuff, Jane says she will never make me a picnic again, or clean my shoes. She looks 'a beauty', but very thin and washed out.

I am irreparably (short of a miracle) low, I simply do not see my way. How bitterly odious that I should have lost my sex drive at the very moment (sic) but all kinds of possibilities of liberation are, or were, open. Normally, indeed always in the past, it has revived in Zermatt.

On the way walking dreamily to the chalet from the station a group of young people approached. I felt a huge jealous rage. You can't pick up a paper without reading about how much everyone else is getting and how much they enjoy it. I used to think this was simply bluff and balls but now, after talking often with 'x', I know it isn't. There have been changes in attitudes and practices. I look at every couple, every man indeed with prurient curiosity and envy. And the effect it has on me is disastrous. My psyche totally blocks me.

I've been depressed before, of course, and recovered. We'll see …

Zermatt   *Saturday, 24 August*

Yet again the Zermatt magic has worked. Blissful in the chalet;[1] fine, dry, clear weather. Pleasant routine of late breakfast, picnic, expeditions. We're still too exhausted to read, or write or think. Sexual powers completely returned, back almost to the sixties

---

[1] Seven years later AC contemplated retiring to Châlet Caroline – 'a beach hut as Jane quite properly calls it'.

and later seventies. Jane 3 times in last four days, each one more pleasing than the last.

Saturday, 14 September

Arrived at Cromlix,[1] very sleepy, but relaxed and philosophic.

It took exactly 8 hours (including an hour stop south of Stoke at the Welcome Break) to do the 522 miles from Saltwood to Gleneagles, a total average of 65mph and cruising of 75mph. We left at 6 a.m. We ate a huge tea at Gleneagles, sent a few PCs ('horse-riding' for 'x'). Jane mentions 'x' periodically, but the atmosphere is much better – more flirty – even though she claims she will leave me if I do anything (*anything* as far as I can make out). Although I am quite open, joking, 'I want to fuck "x"...' I hope we will have a quiet, satisly week at Shore. It certainly should be better than in May. Then return at the weekend to face basic problems.

Shore   *Saturday, 21 September*

Very lethargic and depressed. The wind blows in squalls; Jane is silent and reproachful. (Why? Thinks I'm 'starting up again' with 'x' I suppose). Time seems to have foreshortened morning (sic) and Saltwood looms (we leave for Inverness this afternoon, and a particularly long sleeper journey that doesn't get in until 9.30 a.m.) with its mountains of uncleared paper and unordered 'statements'. Too soon – I am 'undecided', and fearful, about whether to go on the Brittany Rally – comes Party Conference and then ... a vacuum. Either a kind of limbo period in Parlt and the Dept in which nothing much happens and we wait for

---

[1] Cromlix House, a favourite hotel of the Clarks, near Stirling, Perthshire.

events that will cause the 'Polls' to fluctuate – or the dissolution and the End, in every sense, of an Era. Even so my preference would be for this last (sic) as I feel I would sort of lose ground, become obscure, in those last months. Or would I? Anything can happen at backgammon.

I have never been in a condition of such total uncertainty – not at least since I was trying to get a job in San Francisco in 1957. Yet at least we both have good *health*.

Blackpool train   *Wednesday, 9 October*

And so to the very last conference. One's written this before of course, but this time it's got to be the last one. I've got, at most, six months left in the House of Commons. I whinged a bit to Jane in the train on the way up, and she quite rightly said 'you could do *another* four years going down to Plymouth, stuck in the House of Commons, what, who, etc, are your …' True. But my chance of actually going to the Lords is 3–1 *at best*. Every diarist (except possibly Jim Lees-Milne[1]) toys reflectively with this idea. None of them made it. I've been sort of promised it by Chief Whip, Tristan, Tony R. etc. But doesn't really amount to anything.

I just don't see my way. I've lost so much ground – it's really only habit anyhow – with 'x'.

We had quite a nice room at the back of the hotel, changed, ran Alison through the ladies' cocktail party – providing her with some good 'contacts',[2] and then tagged on, just – Jane and I were on the point of going off to dinner on our own – to

---

[1] Whereas three of AC's favourite diarists, Sir Henry (better known as 'Chips') Channon, Leo Amery and Sir Harold Nicolson, were MPs, much of the career of James Lees-Milne centred around the National Trust (*Ancestral Voices* and *Prophesying Peace*).

[2] Alison was seriously considering going into politics, did in fact speak in the debate.

Bruce Anderson party which went on to the Victoria (including Tom Strathclyde, Sophy McEwan, Angie Bray, David Davis, the Needhams).[1] Drank too much. Randy in the night. Illish in the morning.

We listened to Heseltine's 'come-back'. Quite accomplished, though as always symbolic and vulgar. We steadfastly sat throughout the 'ovation'. Yet today (Friday) the camera showed him during John Major's speech looking spaced out, almost gaga. What was he thinking? This is the speech, the occasion, which I so narrowly missed, perhaps for ever? Or had he just had a little too much wine with journalists at lunch, before coming on the platform? John M is so lucid, and decent, and genuine. What a lucky escape we had.

As always I get depressed (*more* depressed I should say) watching the Cabinet move around congratulating each other on the platform. At dinner the weekend before, when I was telling how I had been twice proposed and twice blackballed for the Whips Office, David Davis said – 'if you'd been a whip I have no doubt that you'd have been in the Cabinet by now ...' I don't know, one mustn't be ungrateful for what has happened and all the good fortune that has come my way.

Plymouth train   *Thursday, 17 October*

I have got into a very good sexual relationship with Jane, so now have 'confidence'. She, incredibly, is insatiable. Would gladly do it 3 times every 24 hours! So this is a very great improvement on our relationship in the spring. It also changes a lot of parameters. I certainly don't want her to leave; it dulls the pining and the

---

[1] Lord Strathclyde, junior Minister in the Lords; Angie Bray, press secretary to the Conservative Party chairman (Chris Patten) since 1991; Sophy McEwan, a special adviser; David Davis, MP for Boothferry since 1987; Richard Needham, junior Minister in the N. Ireland Office, MP for Wilts North since 1983 (Chippenham, 1979–83) and his wife Sigrid.

dottiness of yearning for 'x'; it will ease the transition to 'civilian' life. I called for a miracle by the rowan tree, and the more I reflect on it the more I resolve it delivered.

I 'opened' on the second day of the Defence debate. I had been headache-light preparing the speech all morning. But by sylphless cutting (of Civil Service balls, on-the-record stuff) and adlibbing on Julian Amery,[1] regiments and Labour problems, a put down of 'Captain Browne'[2] much acclaim – whips, Godfrey Barker the next day.[3] This may well be the last speech I ever make in the House of Commons.

Yesterday I dined with Bruce Anderson at Greens. There is no longer any balls of my getting into the Cabinet – even the H of L project has diminished; a certain amount of 'you'll miss the House of Commons …' Well I don't think I *will* much. As I trod the Pugin patterned carpets yesterday, popping up to the Members Tearoom to get some fruit cake to bring down to the cafeteria, I thought 'really I've had quite enough of this …' Stale and fetid, etc. I know I can't go back, and I may regret it. The real problem is: I'm still active; bags of energy, keen mind, good health and appetite (now with an 's'), sleeping, stamina. It will be depressing feeling this atrophy – reading Ann Fleming letters,[4] she (and practically everyone else) seems continually to be ill – terminally ill in the sense that they were degenerative conditions that left you older and weaker and nearer the grave

---

[1] Julian Amery, served Conservative Prime Ministers from Churchill to Margaret Thatcher.

[2] John Browne, MP for Winchester since 1979, had previously risen to the rank of Captain in the Grenadier Guards.

[3] Godfrey Barker, *Daily Telegraph* parliamentary sketch writer, wrote that AC 'gave a lesson in how to cope with trouble from all sides. After a speech which was vivid, thoughtful, historical, witty and ad rem, Mr Clark complained that he was "amazed at the docility with which the Labour party has received my remarks … a caricature of what happens to a party when it has absolutely no policy, just a great gulp of crocodile tears" over any changes that had to be made. And to attempted trouble behind him from Mr John Browne: "I can't give way to everyone".'

[4] *The Letters of Ann Fleming* edited by Mark Amory and just published. Ann Fleming was the widow of Ian Fleming (creator of James Bond) and had been twice married previously, to Lord O'Neill and the second Lord Rothermere, proprietor of *Daily Mail*.

even when 'cured'. Only Nico Henderson[1] has emerged unscathed from the *Galere*, still preening and striding.

Yesterday I committed a massive solecism going into the Lords and sitting down on the steps before prayers. I then sat through Craig's introduction[2] (inflection of the voice-print still the surest guide to class). Haven't seen one of these since my father – how cross I was on that day, being reminded of it again by the objectionable 'for life' peerages.[3]

VC10 to Akrotiri   *Wednesday, 6 November*

For the first time am on an abroad journey in a state of pleasur-able exploration. The VIP VC10, lots of space, food, service, crew of five in the cockpit, as far as I can make out. First stop Akrotiri, then on to Dubai for the air show, then to Diego Garcia (nature notes), then Malaysia. The kind of trip that would have had me out in boils ten years ago, but now is an adventure, a comfortable adventure.

All this year I have been neglectful of my papers, have been unable – it seems – even to find time to concentrate my thoughts, think strategically (as the P.M. would need to do, now, I suspect, over his successor). I will be sad and depressed to be out of office. I ought to be S o S, but only a miracle can bring that about, and 'that's enough miracles' – Ed.

Poor little Alison is longing to fight the next election as my 'Campaign Director'; I dread breaking the news to her. I can't face it, so just hope something 'turns up' (Another miracle!).

I feel that 'x' and I may be approaching a consummation. But

---

[1] Sir Nicholas Henderson, former British Ambassador in Warsaw, Bonn, Paris and Washington, had been seriously ill.

[2] Former Chief of the Defence Staff, Marshal of the RAF, Sir David Craig, had been made a life peer following his retirement.

[3] By 1969 (the year of Kenneth Clark's barony) life peerages had become the norm. There would be very few exceptions in the years to come.

how the hell is this handled? When? And then what? I can't actually leave Jane now, although I must admit there were times when I did contemplate it. Could I risk it for a couple of weeks, ten days? Could I get my wish – a double life? Again, it's a miracle that's needed.

But I must record, I'm happier than for ages. It's hope that counts, always.

Diego Garcia[1]   *Sunday, 10 November*

This morning I was determined to bathe *privately*. Much of the charm of this place is spoiled by the constant surveillance of officials (the Commission is about as bad as Peter Watkins[2] who is adhesive in his silent quality), yesterday at the old plantation manager's home, a Somerset Maugham setup on East Island, I realised what Royalty must feel like. But this morning I rose slyly and stealthily, let myself out – yes, there was the Commissioner moving across the grass quadrangle. He said something to the very pretty (dark, lovely bones, ultra discreet/shy) WRAC whom I noted, and scored by calling, 'Doreen'.

I was aware of the fact that the Commissioner wanted to follow me, or call out, but couldn't quite. I walked in light, delicious humid rain to the edge of the beach. Low tide, lovely pale green ripples slapping the sand. The water was delicious, like silk. To Ascension and the Al Bustan I have now added Diego Garcia. My morale uncertain now, though not as bad as when I bathed at the Al Bustan in May. On my return I saw a little polished crab claw on the sand and pouched it. I don't know what power it will have, but it will be a reminder of a curious voyage when pain is still around, uncertainty is everywhere and the terrible incurable infatuation has one in its grasp afresh.

---

[1] British Indian Ocean Territory and a military base with access only to military or civilian contractors, and the occasional visiting British Minister.
[2] Peter Watkins, Head of AC's Private Office at the Ministry of Defence.

Saltwood   *Sunday evening, 15 December*

I was cheered by a letter from Charlie Allsopp saying the Gainsborough was 3–400,[1] which eases my mind about the pending arrival of the C-type.[2]

Poor Jane has had a 'blip' from Tom Bates this time, sending something along to be analysed: 'my secretary will be in touch in a week's time …' – what bad luck!

I feel myself continuing to lose standing and attention in politics. Work in the department has wound right down – I seem to spend much of my time shopping for, or tidying B5 in its new 'naff' form. This is going to be 'very successful'. It had to be done, and the boys will be pleased, although I don't want them using my bed. But ironic that it should be complete, and a place for people to come back for drinks – or even eat – at the very moment when I am about to retire and don't need it. Because I now feel increasingly that the likelihood of my going to the Lords is *very* small. Or, at least, going immediately, which would give the continuity that I want.

This morning at EMT Jane and I discussed her anxieties and finality of 'standing down'. I *dread*, of course, telling Alison, the admission, that for both of us, our professional relationship is over. A certain cowardliness, too, in telling the [constituency] Association. But we both agreed that you have to go out while they are still calling for more and anyway (my own dread) I might *lose* – worst of both worlds.

Will I then get very 'slow' and change my appearance? We'll see. Christmas first, and Andrew's young lady, and most important of all, the result of Jane's test.

Never seem to have done any shopping this year.

---

[1] Gainsborough's *Going to Market*. Charles Allsopp, chairman of Christie's since 1986.
[2] AC paid £360,000; it arrived in time for Christmas.

Saltwood   *Boxing Day, 26 December*

I'm very depressed – not from hangover, as had drunk little, though Christmas lunch was always lovely and I consumed (sic) three glasses of Stolichnaya with the caviar, then more Roodeburg than Andrew with the turkey and pudding. (His young lady Sarah, was a success.)

I'm concerned, somewhat profoundly, at the recandescence of my nose place; my sexuality seems to be diminishing again. I'm dust off the dial in terms of political insignificance – Bruce Anderson no longer makes contact, but he wouldn't 'chuck' like this if he thought I rated. Also, of course, I'm miserable about dear little 'x', away in some French ski resort while I mope around here trying to get old cars to start and splitting firewood. That's something else that is going to come to a head this year (if it hasn't done so already).

Well it's no good moping.

I must pull myself together … I will 'hold the line' at the Department – might even get in a couple more jolly trips. Then it's cutting peat in the Highlands and the fallow period of editing the diaries[1] and inventorising the contents and dispositions.

I wonder how long I've got? I have this nasty feeling that things are going to go so badly this year that I will be 'on the way out' next Christmas. My hair is white in certain back lighting. When I'm 65, sadly, I will actually look 65. Shopping for Jane on Christmas Eve I 'happened on' a ski shop in Folkestone's main street, thought to buy her an anorak and also found myself buying a ski suit for myself. It made me feel ten years younger. Oh if only I could really regenerate!

---

[1] Rather than memoirs, AC had now decided to see if he might emulate Chips Channon, Harold Nicolson *et al* and publish extracts from the diaries he kept while an MP and Minister.

1992

I've been 'lying up' here since Dai Davies[1] on Thursday. An expensive affair since I had it 'in theatre' in order that the path lab could pronounce it 'clear' (sic) on the (nose) spot – which they duly did. I don't know how long any disfigurement will last. Sometimes, these last days, I've got frissons of impending ill health and demise.

Wednesday, 19 February

I am in limbo at present. The major hurdle – telling Alison that I am not fighting the election – is over.[2]

Thursday, 20 February

Yesterday I had a great 'triumph' on my last occasion at the despatch box, pleasing the House and teasing the Labour Party. I had forced Jane to come up, and sit in the Gallery. 'A "last" is always important,' I told her, 'and you can compare it with the Lords.'

Whether I will 'make it' there or not, I don't know. Of course that is fundamental to the success of the scheme. 'x' and I wrote out the 'best' and 'worst' case scenarios on a napkin. She is so game, she's really trying now to see the bright side. Is it going to mark that episode which she identified in her letter of 'final' separation? Although I pretend that I wouldn't mind

---

[1] London-based consultant, who removed AC's 'nose place'.
[2] Nearly four years later AC reflects (17 December 1995): 'How well I remember being parked outside the entrance to the General Post Office in Plymouth with the letters of resignation in my hand. Alison begging me not to – as she had in the train coming up.'

that much I know that there would be the most awful period
to get through. It could last for months, it might diminish me
for ever.

For periods I can become 'serene'. I would, indeed be entirely
reprehensibly serene if I wasn't worrying about 'x'. Even last
night she was out dining with some friends I started fretting
after 11.15, because she hadn't phoned me. When she did – after
midnight – we talked for 3¼ hours.

MoD   *Wednesday, 26 February*

Left out the traumas of the 'Final decision'. The 'statement'. The
deceptions and hesitations. Got a *very* good press. A nice piece
in the *Mail* followed up by a 'commission' to write four articles
during the election.[1] Fun! I sent a reproachful *handschüd* to
Simon Jenkins[2] and he responded with a glowing leader in
today's *Times* trailing oh so subtly the idea that I might 'continue
my ministerial career in the Lords ...'

There lurks, of course, the pang of a final parting with 'x' –
how ironic that it should be Chile again, which signals this.
But she is being so vile at the moment, interrupting with
pointless and offensive remarks about my conduct, family etc,
that in a way it makes it less painful. This time, for the first
time, I am strong enough and determined enough not to
plead.

---

[1] Gordon Greig, the *Mail*'s political editor, wrote that AC 'who has amused and
shocked his party over the years, leaves it just three weeks to find a replacement
candidate.' 'Personal reasons' for his departure were mentioned by the Sutton
agent, to which AC riposted: 'I never said that. "Personal reasons" usually means
there has been a scandal, and I can assure you there is nothing of that. It's just time
to go.'
[2] Simon Jenkins, editor of *The Times* since 1990.

Tristar. Bermuda-Panama   *Wednesday, 4 March*

A short stay in Bermuda.[1] Lovely colours pleasing architecture,
winding streets and friendly black servitors. But hunka-munka
food. Everyone, it seems, so old, and certain things like driving
fast, and dogs, effectively banned. The food is disgusting. US
muck. The interim discards of a Brixton tenement. Couldn't
even get yoghurt, or pasta. We did fit in a bathe though – to add
to Ascension and Diego. Quite chilly. St Austell in July.

VC10K to Santiago   *Friday, 6 March*

Last leg of our flight with the RAF. The trip great fun, and Jane
played the part to perfection, and really enjoyed it. We had a
'loose' day in Ecuador, because a special battery change (would
you believe it) was needed for one of the Tornados which was
stuck at Bermuda and wouldn't start. Really! So the Nimrod
flew back from Panama where we offloaded it from the Tristar,
and we then went on to Guyacil, Ecuador with the Harriers.

Dirt, rats, rotting refuse, puddles, sewage open, incredible
battered pick-ups and buses – but great vitality and a sort of
contentment. The Hotel Oro Verde, owned by a Swiss company,
a little oasis. But the last day I was sulky and tired and avoided
food at the *longueurs* dinner. The Air Attaché, a common little
man, attitudinised me much as the chairman of a strong ward in
the Association might – knowing I didn't live in the constituency and didn't come down enough and held certain
'extreme' opinions. The Consul, however, was impressive. A
caricature of an Englishman, like someone out of *White Mischief*[2]
– tall, brylcreamed hair, moustache, caricatured manners. But
had made a great success of his business, which he started as a

---

[1] AC's final ministerial trip, flying the flag on behalf of defence exports to South
America.
[2] James Fox's 1982 account of the notorious Erroll murder in Kenya.

breakaway salesman from ICI and I felt guilty at not sparkling. I would have liked to talk more with him.

The next day (yesterday) we went for a drive 'up-country' in the Embassy Range Rover. A military road, new and wide, that took us to 'Chimbo' in 3–4 hours. But in *Cholera* time (and Guyacil had much of *Cholera*[1] about it) this would have been the great pilgrimage of Fermina Deza after her father had sent her away following his discovery of Florentino Ariza's letters. The township was pleasing. More than a little of *Black Rock* (as in bad day[2]) but sans menace. A memorial in the centre of the square, very much Highgate Cemetery school dated 1899. How remote it must have been in those times! On the way, through terrible slums and swamps. Children bathing quite literally in sewage pools. But much colour and much greenery.

Ferme Hotel   *Saturday, 7 March*

Arrived at this very peculiar, somewhat sinister place for a late (2.30 p.m.) plein lunch. A long drive, ending with about six miles of unmade yellowish gravel road and an antiquated iron bridge. The room, at ground level is dark, cool, and (in my opinion) cancer fetid. A bad night is in prospect plagued – I expect – by insects. I tried to Venice train after lunch, but wasps and marsh mosquitoes.

It's a strange clientele. Children – largely unattractive – and very elderly people hobbling about. Oh old age is so awful. How can I avoid it? Can I choose my moment as deftly as I did my exit from the Commons? I'd like to outlive Pin and Colette,[3] though. A fine parrot, or macaw (another link with cholera) sits in a giant green cage in the centre of the grass-covered patio.

---

[1] AC, encouraged by Jane, had read Gabriel Garcia Marquez's *Love in the Time of Cholera*.

[2] *Bad Day in Black Rock*, classic American film (1955) with Spencer Tracy.

[3] Colin (known as Pin, Col) and Colette (Celly), AC's twin siblings.

The following morning

We had a good night, after a long, but not objectionable 'banquet' at which I drank slightly too much and was giftedly 'amusing' to Richard (attaché) and Andy. We made love this morning, then drowsed, then had a long carbohydrate breakfast. I am much calmer. My God what a dance 'x' has led me! I think I must just relaxedly let go, resign myself to its ending or, at least, going into abeyance, because as far as I'm concerned it can never really end. When I'm strong enough I can write up all the nice episodes, like the piano duet. But right now I'm detached, serenely sated, philosophic. (Even so I must admit, I wonder if/what she should suddenly walk through here and across the patio and come up to my table where I am writing this.)

Well now the 'holiday' part of the jaunt is nearly over. HE is demi-hovering to 'go through points' for tomorrow's meeting. Pasta this evening. Air show all day tomorrow. Tuesday more meetings. Jane has really enjoyed it; been lionised by the RAF crew as well as doing nice characteristic things like collecting seed pods. God has really been kind to us. And she is really so good and sweet. That's what makes the situation so impossible. I mean what do I want? Certainly not to leave her and cause her pain. And yet as she herself admits 'x's appearance has revived our sexual tension by all the jealous cross-currents it arouses.

Lord Clark's Study, Saltwood   *Wednesday, 18 March*

Immensely serene. I must record that I am settling down very calmly to a pleasant detached existence with so much to hand in the way of diversions and accoutrements.

Just talked to Alison who is going down to Henry Bellingham[1] for the 'campaign'. Gosh, I'm glad to be out of it![2] It's delicious

---

[1] Henry Bellingham, MP for North West Norfolk since 1983.
[2] The general election had been called for 9 April

speculating, with just the right amount of access through the *Daily Mail*. But the polls this morning are bad, *very* bad, each showing 5% Labour lead. I don't particularly mind, even a touch of schadenfreude if it weren't for my lost peerage, even my lost 'K'. Although, intriguingly (sic) the lunch yesterday with Alastair Campbell[1] opened, just by a chink, the possibility of a semi-alignment with Kinnock – 'the other side'. Whew!

Saltwood   *Wednesday, 25 March*

Appetite and sleep perfect. I dozed between 6.30 and 7 and dreamed that I was squinting through the internal window into the Chamber. David Wilshire[2] was going in *in a shirt*; Robin Corbett came out and said something to me, like 'you can't go in there any more'. I thought, 'silly ass, it's only a dream, of course I can'; then woke up and the dream was reality – I never can again. I was sad and thought I should have been in for the Dissolution, heard all that mumbo, bowed to the Speaker and so forth. In a sort of dotty way I think I might still go back, a crash adoption for a safe by-election. ACHAB

Friday, 27 March

Last night we dined at the French embassy. My last Ministerial. Beatty's old house in Regent's Park, a pleasing dwelling with, unusually, Nash getting the proportions just right. Jane looked pretty in her turquoises, and slimline black dress, well holding her own over the French ladies. On the way back Pat[3] drove

---

[1] Alastair Campbell, political editor of the *Daily Mirror* since 1989.
[2] David Wilshire, MP (C) for Spelthorne since 1987; Robin Corbett, MP (L) for Birmingham Erdington since 1983.
[3] Pat, Ministry of Defence driver.

sepulchrally. Earlier he had agitatedly told me the MoD was investigating his 'prudent' overtime claims.

Car (M20)   *Tuesday, 31 March*

This my last (or last but one) trip up to London in the official car, with Pat driving. My appearance seems to have altered, my nose nob won't go down any more. I am feeble and drowsy after an interrupted night (stumbled down and took two Redoxons). Eva[1] is poorly, though sweet-natured, and the vet yesterday could find nothing (though stopped me bidding for the 'Bentley Box' at Sotheby's[2]). Jane shellacked me at tea for ringing 'x' 'behind her back'. Said I am 'not a minister, even an MP, nothing any more'. Bruce Anderson just chucked me – said 'Once you're out of Election politics, you're dead ...' I'm not so sure. If I was in the Lords at least I could say, 'I fought five elections, and never lost one of them.' So what's my vote?

Paddington train   *Wednesday, 8 April*

Well, now the era has ended. I am in the Paddington train; warm, comfortable, porridge breakfast; so evocative of jolly journeys with sexual tension high, and delight at being in the loved one's company. I will never be able to afford this again. £38 one-way from Exeter, and that with an OAP reduction card. Briefly back to MoD for farewell calls. Then load up carpet and clock and sundries and leave Whitehall – for ever, as it now looks.

   We were in Plymouth yesterday. Practically no posters at *all*.

---

[1] Eva, the Clarks' dog, a Rottweiler.
[2] AC remarked in his day diary that he was 'livid' not to acquire it.

A strange, dead feel to it. Jane said canvassing would be 'very heavy going'. Damn right it would. I simply wouldn't know what to say. A very disagreeable protracted experience, with no certainty as to the result – a nasty count, etc. And even then – what? If I was defeated I'd just disappear; none of the accolades of early March. If I scraped back it would be to a low and miserable House (although the whisperings would be fun); a hideous prospect of being permanently unpaired; a certainty of being 'eased out' by the constituency before the October election. The whole summer fraught and ruined for nothing. No I think I 'Houdinied' it as well as could possibly have been expected.

On the way back to Bratton I stopped and climbed to Brentor. It seems a long time since polling day in '87 when I asked for help after my 'gaffe' on the Channel Tunnel.[1] Periodically since, when in torment, I thanked God for a wonderful additional grant and all that incredible life-enhancement. Even if the total dream – the sword in the lake – has gone, I still feel that there is quite a bit to unfold. Although not, I fear, in my personal life. The wonderful, excruciating, highly dangerous 'x' 'affair' has burned itself out and, to my utter nostalgic depression we are now only, and I fear never again can be more than 'good friends'.

That charming sheepdog appeared the moment we arrived at Bratton last night. Jane brilliantly remembered the basket in the pump room and we lined it with felt and he settled down in the back porch after a fine meal. This morning he wanted to come back with us, and jumped bravely into the Discovery. He was so good and intelligent when I said 'stay' in the front garden. I do hope no ill befalls him.

---

[1] A reference to an interview which AC gave during the election campaign at which he had poured scorn on the Channel Tunnel project.

made me hope briefly that Hamilton would also be chopped, and for the sake of continuity, they'd keep me on – but from the Lords – my original scheme. I even went so far as to visualise the Black Turbo B from P. & A.Wood[1] for Pat; the Minister's room with red leathers and the computer; Alison back as my PA while she also doubles at another job at Westminster. A reunion dinner at Wilton's; in the Smoking Room – for the first time really since 1974. Wouldn't it be luvverly ...[2] As it is I suppose I will have to subliminate into asceticism, restoring order and the journals.

I drove the C-type last night and ended up at St Leonard's. It was locked, and I got the key from the Rev Wood. In almost complete darkness I tried to pray a bit, to little avail. The whole 'x'/Jane affair made a block last year of course. Now I am worried that by standing down from the Commons I have *wasted* the advantages He offered me.

Tuesday, 14 April

Here I am, in my office at the Garden House – how very nice, warm, bright and silently welcoming it is when one owns the key and even at 9.30 in the morning – *en retraite* at the age of 64 (exactly). There were two mini-moments yesterday – at MoD when Carol returned to me the portable '... in case No 10 want to get in touch with you', heightened by rumours in the drivers' room that 'Lord Arran's office were shitting themselves ...'[3] Then called by Peter Watkins, strangely distant in the morning, almost calling me 'Mr Clark', and later ringing with a message that 'there will be a ministers' meeting in the (tomorrow/today) morning: you are of course entitled to attend,

---

[1] P. & A.Wood, Rolls-Royce and Bentley specialists favoured by AC.

[2] AC's own footnote is in the form of musical notes (*My Fair Lady*).

[3] Lord Arran had been Parliamentary Under-Secretary of State for the Armed Forces, MoD, since 1989. In the post-election reshuffle he had been moved to the Northern Ireland Office.

but there is no expectation that you will ...' Then particularly, briefly, rallied by dear Tristan ringing at about 8 p.m. and saying '... any news?' *Why?*

I am doomed now to the wilderness, to awaiting 'tidings of men and events ...' It's difficult to keep one's hand in. I find to my surprise that my hunger for politics now causes me to buy *more* newspapers. I am going to ask Tristan to send me Hansard. On second thoughts I think I shall subscribe myself. (I paused for a second and thought that 'if nothing happens' I will wait a month or so and then write to Richard [Ryder] saying how awful I feel.) But things were put into scale, in a most alarming way this morning at EMT when Jane told me that Andrew had said that James had said, phoning from Eriboll, that he was so depressed. Made me feel very spoilt and grumpy. I am going to write him a long letter this morning.

Many full and lovely days lie ahead. But curiously, directly I shy away from 'holiday' planning – the magic months of June to September – I only notice how triste and dejected I have become when I taste, very briefly, the exhilaration of thinking it might still 'happen'. Because I still think – perversely for one usually so realistic and cynical – that if I were there as Minister of State I would inevitably get S of S – *even though a peer*.

Ah well, although we are nearly half way through this year it still seems only to have started. *So far* it hasn't been as painful as the past four months of last year were. But the future is a blank – and not a specially reassuring one.

Sandling train (!)   *Tuesday, 28 April*

A fortnight since the last entry. Withdrawal symptoms only flare periodically, but a lot of suppression is going on. So in subconscious it festers. I dream of reviving Commons privileges, tearoom, reference library and so on which I wake and realise are closed to me for ever. In the daytime I have to close my mind to

the full extent of my depression. I am 'put out' by my friends
ignoring me. Especially wounded by Richard. I did think that he
was a friend, and I a confidant of his. I am filled too with distaste
and resentment at all the new Conservative MPs and some of the
new Ministerial choices. But there's no point in dodging it,
when you're out you're out. The people who are *in* simply don't
have time to waste on someone who, however 'amusing', is not
au fait with the daily round of gossip, of 'men and events'. I
suppose, if I were to get my peerage promptly I could still 'catch
up', swoop into the tearoom, mob around. But notification for
the Dissolution Honours has passed, and so – almost – has that
for the Birthday. I guess it will be like the PC and take at least
two years longer than postulated (sic).

As for life at Saltwood – well it is pleasing, more so in some
ways than I had anticipated. Delicious food (too much indeed,
I'm putting on weight, am 11.7+ and at intervals get it at 12
even when dry).

Friday, 8 May

Very low and 'muddled'. Yesterday had nasty blows (3 if you
count Bertie Arbeid[1] saying that my 'historic' *lippen* spot 'we
should keep an eye on it'(!)).[2] A dramatic pathetic encounter
with 'x' and a hopeless parting; followed by an extremely disturbing, and unsettling phone call from Tony Fanshawe which
interrupted my scrambled egg high tea, telling me Tristan G-J
had been instrumental in the Robert Cranborne transition;[3]

---

[1] Bertie Arbeid, the Clarks' dentist.

[2] A spot in the form of a blood blister on AC's lower lip.

[3] No wonder AC was upset; any remaining hopes he might have entertained about
speaking for the government on Defence matters from the Lords were dashed by
the transition of Robert [Viscount] Cranborne, heir to the Marquess of Salisbury,
who had been 'summoned to the Upper House, as Baron Cecil of Essendon in
the County of Rutland'. He became Parliamentary Under-Secretary of State at
MoD, in effect government Defence spokesman in the Lords.

then, even more alarmingly, that 'a few peers' were complaining that my 'abrasive' style, while fine in the Commons, might not go down too well in the Lords, put people off a bit, and so on.

When I phoned him, 'people like who … Francis?'[1]

'Kimball'.[2]

Yes that figures totally. He has always been deeply antipathetic to me since we were on the same corridor at 'Waynflete'. Said no chance of being on either of the two coming lists (Dissolution and Birthday); must aim for January 93; don't bother to see Richard *now*, wait till they come back 'in September', i.e. October 'have it out' with him then.

All very depressing, only redeemed by a nice note from Soames.

Saltwood   *Saturday, 9 May*

I have been wrestling with the lawn in the Inner Bailey. We bought a new ATCO and it cuts crazily well so that even a half stripe needs its large plastic basket emptying. But the lawn remains obstinate – resistant to striping and with ridged 'bare marks'. The garden is relentless in its demands on time. Not only is the lawn like the Forth Bridge, it needs restarting as soon as you finish, but there is scything of nettles and use of the tractor in the arboretum and the wood, and a few 'artist's touches' in the Garden House.

I have a mountain of paper. The far end of the Green Room seems to have about four running white boxes in it, while the Summer Office has simply been evacuated, like the old battlefields of the Somme, and about 300 separate filing items lie around.

---

[1] Possibly Francis Pym, MP for Cambridgeshire 1961–83; Cambridgeshire SE, 1983–87; Foreign Secretary 1982–83, a life peer since 1987.

[2] Marcus Kimball, MP for Gainsborough, February 1956–1983. AC's Eton contemporary; a life peer since 1985. Part of their mutual antagonism stemmed from Kimball's devotion to fox-hunting whereas AC was totally against.

The cars – far too many of them – have overflowed the accommodation, they need drastic culling, but I seem not even to have time to write up a favoured culling scheme. Jane has a good amount of spare cash, and I want to work out an investment scheme for her – but that, too, needs time and care. Perhaps even more importantly, I cannot get *in* to the diaries, although many (namely Michael Sissons and George Weidenfeld are pressing me for them).[1] Never mind, today is foul; wet and gusty, and I may get some preliminary order. I am taking a year's sabbatical – slightly under – and hope that this will leave me next summer 'off' before the die is finally cast at the July or September reshaping of the Government. It is a huge waste of my talents that I am not in. Partly self-inflicted, I admit. At least I jumped, *really* jumped I mean, off the deck, before people even got round to thinking about it. But we dined at Aspers[2] the night before last, and I sat next to Barbara Amiel – attractive, intelligent but not (as I said to Jane) 'my cup of tea'. Conrad Black's mistress,[3] but writes well. I tried to sparkle – perhaps did a bit – but was conscious throughout of my diminished status. Today I read in the papers that the Government is going to bail out Olympia and York by taking a huge amount of office space at Canary Wharf. How I wish I was in the House to ask the Chancellor:

'Does he share my distaste at the proposal to bail out the property developer Olympia & York? Does he recognise that this – if he allows it – will be just the precursor of a giant "demand" from "Sir" Alastair Morton[4] – surely now the

---

[1] Michael Sissons, AC's long-time literary agent (Peters, Fraser & Dunlop); George Weidenfeld, who had published one previous book of AC's (*Aces High*), but also AC's favourite diarist, Chips Channon.

[2] John Aspinall founded a series of London clubs beginning with the Clermont in Berkeley Square. AC and Aspinall had first met at Oxford. In these diaries he is usually referred to as 'Aspers'.

[3] Conrad Black, Canadian-born newspaper proprietor (including the *Daily* and *Sunday Telegraph*, *The Spectator*) and Barbara Amiel, noted journalist, were soon to marry.

[4] Sir Alastair Morton, chief executive of Eurotunnel since 1987.

President Emeritus of the Delorean Club for a huge cash injection into Eurotunnel which never has and never will make a profit?'

There. Quite fun composing that, though sad.

Tristan rang yesterday. He was reassuring, but non-committal. Said he would try and have a word with Richard soon; with the PM in the summer when he stayed with the G-Js in Spain. Agreed that there was plenty for me to *do*, but I needed a 'perch'.

Tuesday, 12 May

I am having my 'quiet' hour and slight (nervous) indigestion/ wind and mild AF wondering if the phone will ring. PMQs on television. I watched them all sitting on the front bench and thought – barring a most unusual and improbable miracle – I can never again sit there. All made me a bit depressed. Progress here is *so* slow, haven't even mock approached the diaries extracts yet. The 'white boxes' have taken over all the top shelf space in the Green Room. I seem to be terribly stiff and creaky; I suspect I'm quite a few pounds overweight, and I have a weak prostatic trickle if I pee in the night (which I don't often do, I must say, and it's normal in the morning). I don't even partic-ularly want to go to Scotland this weekend, as there is so much to do here. Yet last year, when I was a Minister, one recharged over Whitsun. We are totally victims of Parkinson's Law. If you look at the wall-chart May–June are now full. And July and August fill me with some apprehension, because I believe they [James and Sally] are going to make a trial separation. Never mind. I must keep up my letter writing.

Wednesday, 13 May

First day of the 'heat wave'. I get waves of terrible depression, but not as bad, really as last year this time. Last year, I know, I would have been phoning in. And I must say when I think of the House of Commons in June, Finance Bill Committee stage, long whipping, even the beloved access to the Terrace doesn't outweigh the preference for being down here. Now that there appears to be a severance with 'x' I don't really see any reason why I should go to London at *all*.

Garden House   *Wednesday, 20 May*

The whole place burgeoning beautifully, and the last thing I want to do is go to London and on to Oxford to make a speech at the Union. Started filling the pool yesterday and I had a p.m. splosh in two feet of water. The wall-chart is totally blocked out, it seems, for June; worse than the DTI already. So we're back to 'observe' Parliamentary recesses. Altnaharra for sale for £7m. Can Marcus [Kimball] really have got in that deep? It was an idyll for me, even at Eton when he talked about this, and his blue Chevrolet. I wrote him a (guarded) letter of commiseration.

Garden House   *Monday, 25 May*

I am very tired. We made love in Courtneys in the afternoon. It always leaves me with nostalgia and wistfulness. A strange punishment, so packed with irony. The total melancholy of my relationship with 'x' is itself almost an attraction.

Eriboll   *Saturday, 6 June*

Very hot day, and I have 'caught' the sun. Delial is the *only* thing
that really protects and I left it behind. There is a tiny, spreading
mark under my nose nob, and I'm mildly concerned about the
'poached egg' on my shoulder – although admittedly this has
scared me on and off for years. For the last four nights (with the
exception of Cromlix, 10.15) I have been in bed after midnight;
so sunlight and bathing (Hope and Eriboll today, immersion
only) have made me feel – and look – very weary.

Yesterday we came up via Hope and I forded the river and
walked from Cashel Dhu up and over the Creaggan. Two hours.
And was quite delighted to see my little brown pup terrier
waiting and expectantly peeping for me so went and had a little
chat with her. The real *treat* of being in Scotland in June,
without obligations or commitments. Jane is being slightly
distant and not looking particularly attractive, as can sometimes
happen when her hair has been badly 'done'. The place is
terribly dry, dust (the first time I have seen clouds of dust at
Eriboll) and I am worried that many of those expensive little
trees will die. Also, there is so much to do here. One could fill
the day just as usefully as at Saltwood. On my way over the
Creaggan yesterday I thought a lot – about 'x'. And the more I
thought, the more insoluble it became. Perhaps the simple fact
is that I'm just too old and getting older. But certain key dates
do approach and give me a light AF *grippe*. Notably the summer
holidays. I am now so frightened of Jane. I can't do anything at
all with 'x'.

Reading yesterday about the man (an Army Captain, needless
to say) whose girlfriend killed his wife. They had sexual intercourse under water; and also about Charles and Diana: 'their
separate marriage'. How odious the Palace is. Nearly 30 peers in
the next two lists, including, apparently, six new 'working peers'.
Richard has not kept to his part of the bargain.

Saltwood   *Sunday, 14 June*

It's ridiculous, really. I sit here, on a hot Sunday, cloudless but
hazy, and round me the Bailey is, *passim* Bruce Anderson (now
never heard from), 'one of the loveliest places in the world'. The
cistus are out along the border, and many of the roses. The
honeysuckle by the pool, and a particularly fine 'French' geranium
fills the 'plinth'. Tomorrow is *not* 'Dave at eight', although we may
be going up for the Gilmours' garden party,[1] so I ought to be
relaxed, creative. In fact I'm not so much depressed as oppressed.
I've been out since mid-March, and made no impression on
files, or cars. No order in day-to-day affairs (except start of ledger);
barely keeping pace with day-to-day correspondence. Will just
hold the garden in check, and make some nice potential
development in the wood.

But my 'sabbatical' has really got nothing to show for it,
except, perhaps, the beginnings of a familiarity with the word
processor. And the DTI wall chart is now full. Every day seems
to have something on it – and one 'thing' will actively blight and
distort a whole day. But what has really depressed me is the list
of 'working' peers. I mean Hayhoe! How ghastly and mediocre
– the archetypal safe Tory politician – can you get? Stewart, little
Stewart and dear old Bill Clark (which will cause problems if I
ever get there) and they were all knights, so my exclusion from
the 'K' list doesn't mean anything.[2]

---

[1] Lord [Ian] Gilmour, former MP (Norfolk C and then Chesham and Amersham),
Minister, editor of *The Spectator*, and his wife Caroline; at their home by the
Thames at Isleworth.

[2] Barney Hayhoe, MP for Brentford & Isleworth 1974–92 (Heston & Isleworth,
1970–74); Bernard Stewart (who took the title Lord Stewartby) MP N Herts
1983–92 (Hitchin February 1974–83) and William Clark, MP for Croydon S
1974–92 (E Surrey, 1970–74; Nottingham S 1959–66).

Saltwood   *Tuesday, 23 June*

We went up to London for Enoch's 80th birthday.[1] A ragbag of a
dinner, ill assorted – wives and husbands sitting (as I had predicted
to Jane) together, and so on. There were some eminent people –
George Thomas,[2] Robin Day,[3] Mrs T etc and a lot of strays. This
mix never works very well, although I was glad to have a word
with Portillo.[4] Jane was in a good cache of politicians, said little
Budgen[5] was very chippy, 'I've only got two friends ...' he said
maudlinly at one point. 'I'm not surprised,' she said.

Speeches were *de profundis* in seniority terms – old Salisbury,[6]
George Thomas, Enoch, combined ages 243. All rather lowering, particularly the number of people who sort of accepted the
fact that I was now 'out'. 'Write a letter to *The Times*,' said John
Biffen.[7] On the way back in the car I complained to Jane about
this, but she wisely said, 'No. You're still ahead.' Budgen, typically,
had said that there wasn't the slightest reason why I should get
a peerage, reckoned it highly unlikely, and Robin Day, who was
listening, didn't demur.

We had run into Andrew and Sarah on arrival and were having
tea in the Albany sitting room when the phone rang. I went
through to answer it in the bedroom and it was 'x'; she always
sounds specially sweet and hesitant when *she* is initiating the

---

1 Enoch Powell and AC had known each other for more than 25 years. In December
  1972 Powell made what AC called the 'prophet's visit' to Saltwood. They shared
  many of the same views, particularly on immigration.
2 George Thomas, Labour MP for various Cardiff seats from 1945, a celebrated
  Speaker, 1976–83, when he was created Viscount Tonypandy.
3 Sir Robin Day, broadcaster and author, a noted political interviewer.
4 Michael Portillo, a rising star in the Conservative Party. MP for Enfield Southgate
  since December 1984; Chief Secretary to the Treasury since 1992.
5 Nicholas Budgen, MP for Wolverhampton SW since 1974. Powell had been a
  Wolverhampton MP.
6 The 6th Marquess of Salisbury had been president of the Monday Club, which,
  as Simon Heffer, Powell's biographer, has pointed out, was in the 1960s 'self-
  appointed Praetorian Guard of Powell and the Powellite interest.'
7 John Biffen, MP for Shropshire North since 1983 (Oswestry November
  1961–83); Leader of the Commons, 1983–87.

call. I had to dissimulate, and afterwards, and all evening, I felt that I had betrayed her. How many times am I having to do this sort of thing, how often can she stand it?

Saltwood   *Friday, 26 June*

Yesterday a sort of horror day. James (who else?) played a major role. Full depths of horror never plumbed without a James intervention. Wanted to talk about Sally; tried to put him off, and he broke down. I had to ring Sally, who was cool and wary etc etc, anyway her little dog was dying. All this against a background of Gay and Nigel Harris, Sarah's parents, arriving and being fluffed, and to whom I had to pay attention.

When, finally, I disentangled myself to go to bed I got upstairs to find the bed 'stripped', and had to 'make' it, the biggest bed in the house, at midnight.

Garden House, p.m.

Very melancholy and fatigued. I wish it wasn't so fine. All the plants and baby trees need water. I got all the cars (except Loco and XK) out of the Long Garage this afternoon and the Ghost was incredible 'for' Nigel – started on five cranks of a quarter turn! But *all* the cars need LCA. I seem to have no time at all; the Green Room is as usual a mad jungle of paper on flat surfaces, and I have three speeches to write while James's visit overhangs us. This is the only place where there is any tranquillity. But even here reflections can induce melancholy. I dreamed, again, of the House last night. I was in flying kit, the Secretary of State was somewhere around, but I couldn't gain access, and Jane was keeping me waiting.

Garden House   *Saturday, 27 June*

Gloomy this morning. Still terribly hot and dry. I worked a little nearby and thought how pleasing to have a pace of life when one can do this, and two hours at the word processor in the evenings, and play with the cars a little, inventorise, propose. There is a *sort* of fallow period opening up in the [late] autumn, I suppose. I was pleasurably anticipating the rest of this year, and its uncertainties. Now I'm not so sure.

Garden House   *Sunday, 28 June*

Went on to Aspers, very late, and had a good solitary dinner (Conrad Black and Barbara Amiel had chucked). He is now wise and majestic, in his old age. Though like so many he's been very ill – typhus (?), rheumatic fever, cortisone, chronic leukaemic condition. I'm lucky to have evaded that sort of general ill health. But whether I shall continue to do so now that both political and sexual adrenalin have been withdrawn must be doubtful.

Perhaps just as well I'm not in the House, although I feel it could in fact get tremendously interesting. JM now putting it about that he will resign if doesn't get Maastricht through.[1] Then could in fact be a very interesting period of 'factionalisation', just as I predicted. Will I get there in January? (*passim* Harold Nicolson).

---

[1] What became known as Maastricht began as an idea of Jacques Delors, President of the European Commission since 1989, for an International Governmental Conference on European political and monetary union. It was swiftly to act as a lightning rod, polarising the pro-Europeans and the Eurosceptics. The key issues became the ERM – exchange rate mechanism – and EMU – European Monetary Union. The conference led to a Treaty, which had to be ratified by each EU member.

Monday, 29 June

Private Office came down yesterday evening and gave me a tree. Very sweet of them. Perhaps gifts should have been 'exchanged'? Carol told Jane that it was an endless 3-line whip and Jonathan[1] was never allowed away. 'AC couldn't stand it.' But as I sit here, in oppressive heat, too-hot-Henry condition, almost the only thing I can do is 'amend' the dictionary on the word processor. But I wish, in spite of it all, I was in the Commons, stirring all this 'M' stuff, using the underground car park. Oh dear. I'm very low at present.

Tuesday, 30 June

Yesterday, after writing that entry, I trained up in the great heat to London (2 hours – dozing off and waking with a start – only Marden and Headcorn). I had Indian tea, having gone through the usual cycle (vide) of total dejection, rising towards paradise, then being disappointed. I set off for Chris Patten's Durbar Court farewell party[2] parking my car – actually Andrew's Audi – in that side street beside DE. I walked to FCO, Clive Steps, passing St Stephens Tavern where officials hang out. *Very* hot, dreamlike almost. I was in a suit, still a perfect Minister, but ethereal. Orphée. I could do nothing, give no instructions, penetrate no sancta. The Party was the following day, a lone custodian informed me. And I walked back – like a masque – and set course for Saltwood.

---

[1] Jonathan Aitken (MP for Thanet South since 1983; Thanet East February 1974–83) had succeeded AC at Defence as Minister for Defence Procurement.
[2] Patten was leaving UK politics to become the last Governor of Hong Kong.

Garden House   *Sunday, 5 July*

Tristan had rung Jane with a rumour that I was to be the next editor of *The Spectator*. That might be quite fun, too. Let rip!

Garden House   *Monday, 13 July*

A grey day. A time for planning. We really should operate to a timetable. Things that must have black lines set aside for them (not necessarily every day) are:

(a) house work in Garden House – cleaning kitchen, hanging pictures, plugs on lights etc
(b) word processor – already 7.30-8.30, provided this is working after KK. 7.45–8.45?
(c) Filing in summer office – *at least* one hour per day
(d) Cleaning cars   } possibly alternate?
(e) Scything and forking?
(f) SUNDAY FREE

I must look up old timetables.

Thursday, 16 July

I gave the 'RAF' lecture at the RUSI yesterday. Quality good audience – but I suffered from not having a typed-up text. Afterwards I ducked out of a dinner at the House. I just did not want to go into the Strangers Dining Room until I'm a Peer. People ask me if I miss it. 'Yes, dreadfully,' I say.

Garden House   *Wednesday, 22 July*

So little to actually *show* for the last 12 days. I am low, and *serene*
– almost Lenin Stadium with a feeling of total emptiness at the
groin, as if I was a man of eighty. Page yesterday, and casually he
said he'd send my blood for the Prostate Cancer Test as well as
a testosterone count. I said surely if I had it I'd know? He said
oh no, 80 per cent of postmortems show 80% of people over 80
(that's enough 80s! – Ed) or more do have it. 'It can be dealt
with quite effectively.' But I know how I'd deal with – by
chemical castration. There are worse things, I suppose, like going
blind. But it's bad luck on little Jane, after this lovely year – for
which eternal thanks. Would it have to be 'allied' with chemotherapy so that all my hair falls out? The effect has been to
devastate me utterly – combined of course with the fact that it's
now nearly six weeks since the last injection. And so much to
do. The diaries, the inventory, the files, the 'dispositions'. I've
been aware that my looks and general stamina (I seldom want to
do weights and press-ups) are much less than last summer. What
a long 'Indian' summer that was!

                                                  Saturday, 25 July

We bought the huge Sidney Cooper for £110,000[1] – which
makes things very tight. I will have to sell a little modern art, but
what? The 'chair' perhaps?[2]

---

[1] Nineteenth-century painting of Saltwood Castle.
[2] By Cézanne – but not sold.

Garden House   *Sunday, 26 July*

I was so depressed and hopeless. Almost I feel as if my life is over now. Just a few months to establish order; lay down some 'guidelines' which my successor can follow. It's such a wrench being out of the Commons. The papers are full of articles exculpating Mellor ('the mood has changed', all that)[1] and saying how wonderful and powerful and reclamé MPs are. On Wednesday it's the Quintons's[2] party on Lords Terrace and I hardly know if I dare go to it, the nostalgia will be so acute; and after that a 'farewell' from the Chief of Staff. I suppose, if my 'tests' are ok, I can just chat and get through. If not, well that *is* it, and this entry is just a preface. My symptoms are not imaginary. I am very low on energy – for instance in the old days, however hypochondriacally I felt, I would take a terrific walk after tea. Now I just enjoy a drive and the nostalgic thoughtfulness it brings (today the DS Chapron). I have an intermittent sore throat – traces of – and I break out into sweats from time to time. In the morning I don't wake 'refreshed'.

I feel the biggest mistake I ever made was to 'walk away' from the Commons.

Garden House   *Tuesday, 28 July*

Yesterday, no more than 50/50 confident of good 'tests', I don't see my way out of it. If I have to submit to treatment – strange tubes and probes and chemotherapy, well, I won't. I'll accept my sentence – of a few weeks or months, then go in my prime, as from the House. At that decision, I felt much better and stronger.

---

[1] David Mellor, MP for Putney since 1979 and Heritage Secretary since the general election had resigned following saucy tabloid newspaper revelations about a sexual affair.

[2] Anthony Quinton (life peer, 1982) and his wife Marcelle. A philosopher, he was not long retired as chairman of the British Library.

Then, when I got to Albany, there was Page's letter marked on the front: <u>Personal, Medical and Confidential</u> – an invitation to snoop if ever there was one! 'No trace whatever' of PreCan, testosterone right down, everything else ok – he sent me print out – except for cholesterol, about which I could not care. Can now revert to thinking demi-clearly about the summer and autumn. I must organise a proper car cull.

Last night at the Chief of Staff dinner at the Tower I was demi-lionised. Only person to be mentioned in Dick Vincent's speech, both he and Moray Stewart talked to me at length. Ken Carlisle[1] said 'we miss you dreadfully. You are a real H of Commons man. You could always make the House do what you wanted ...' More nostalgic thinking.

At one point Lady Arran said – well what do you want? I said 'to be a Member of the House of Commons and a Minister in the Government.' 'Would you swap with Tommy?' If, well, that was another matter, and I didn't give a proper answer.

Garden House   *Monday, 3 August*

I'm depressed, and slightly rattled today.

My interview with Graham Turner – although it read very well (for a connoisseur) – contained objectionable, i.e. that to which objection could legitimately be taken, research about poor old TK, and also about 'The Royals'.[2] It has been taken up, and *distilled*, in the *Express* today and will, I suspect, disqualify me from any 'perch'. BLAST. The photos that accompanied the Turner article were unflattering, particularly the one with Jane. Even she said I looked 'cortisoned'. I have become a little bit too

[1] Kenneth Carlisle, MP for Lincoln since 1979; Parliamentary Under-Secretary, MoD 1990–92.
[2] In the *Sunday Telegraph*. The piece began with AC on Tom King: 'He was ghastly, an awful person to work with – indecisive, blustering, bullying, stupid and cunningly cautious, even when he didn't need to be.'

heavy, off the old dial and standing at 12 stone. So I am stiff in the joints and a bit lethargic (But if I don't eat lunch I get sleepy and faint). I'm my most *en retraite* at the moment, as I often get with 'unfortunate' publicity. Just want to hide.

Shore Cottage   *Sunday, 16 August*

Watery August sun directly through the sitting room windows at 8.30 a.m. I am a little uncertain. Curiously, now that I can spend as much time (figuratively) at Shore as I want, I feel myself to be less keen on it.

I had an indifferent night (not a total submersion) peeing 4 times – but not at all prostatically. My first worry was dear little Meg, who greeted me specially. I won't be able to get her back this time as we are in the Jaguar and Jane is dropping me off in London, but I will reassure her; and next time we are up will prepare her kennels here, so she can live with us for a little while before the trekking south.

James, though, touch wood does seem much better. He's back in charge of Saltwood and got 'Ruby' going. Incredible!

Garden House   *Thursday, 20 August*

Exactly a year ago we set off for Zermatt. Private Office got me, literally at the airport gates and said Gorbachev has been overthrown. So what? We went on, and had a lovely week.

Then I came back, and made a balls-up of a lot of things.

Now I'm weary, creaky, 6lbs overweight, back pain.

I can't sell any of my cars and seem to have used up all my money. I'm 'out' of things, although I have a short 'flash' life in prospect until the diaries are out.

What I really need is a holiday, a proper one.

I said to Jane – a hut by the beach, Club Med type. White sand that gets between your toes, lapping water, a deckchair *in the shade* with six or seven books (*passim* Richard Ryder to whom I spoke on Thursday and is off to Corfu) and delicious meals available at a central dining room. She said, 'If anyone took a tape of you, they'd think what a really *awful* man.'

Garden House										*Monday, 24 August*

I walked into the Garden House this morning. The light is fading earlier and earlier and we have got a fire in the Green Room. I thought, when there was last a fire in this grate the election was on, and I was in high hopes for 'value' and (at least) administrative achievement this year. But nothing. Just 40 pages of diaries and a lot of unanswered trivialities. James's arrival has imposed some strain – but he has been incredible with the machinery; 'mending' the Westwood, the XK120, 'Ruby'. But I am the weak link. Selfish, moody, de-energised.

Monday, 31 August

David Owen has got the Euro-rep at Yugoslav Peace Conference job. So he's back in the stream.[1] Julian Critchley[2] writes in the *Observer* that I was the kind of MP (person in – sic – politics) who had style. I am pleased by this. But I don't see my role. I am OUT not IN and I notice the difference more and more.

---

[1] David Owen, MP (Labour 1966–81, SDP 1981–92; Plymouth Sutton 1966–74, Plymouth Devonport 1974–92) had been appointed European Union Co-Chairman, International Conference on Former Yugoslavia.

[2] Julian Critchley, MP for Aldershot since 1970 (Rochester & Chatham 1959–64) and author, was commenting on the *Sunday Telegraph* interview with AC.

Garden House   *Tuesday, 8 September*

I was a *mauvais relations* with Jane yesterday. She made me cross
by questioning me about *why* I was going up to London. I
thought I'd been so 'good' for four months that I might be
allowed a day off. But no, it was you haven't been to London for
ages and now you suddenly want to go to London. I want to
know why. Was clearly thinking/said, either I am going to meet
'x', or lunch with some tittles of a journalist, or have a hormone
(sic) injection. Sex, actually, is all women think about when they
don't know an answer. This made me cross. And it was unfair. I
had twice admired and complimented her on her appearance
and all she said was that I was like Frank Bough (whom I had
always thought ghastly, long before he got caught in a 'sex den'
– or whatever it was). I really do *not* resemble Frank Bough.[1] It's
most unfair.

But actually, I suppose, there is no reason why I still go to
London at all – ever, really.

B5 Albany   *Thursday, 17 September*

A very bad night. I woke at 1.20 – rather less than an hour after
putting the light out, with complete insomnia. Could have
made tea (*did*, in fact, after padding down to a night porter and
collecting some milk) and driven the Little Silver anywhere.

I dined with Jonathan, Ryder was there, Tristan came in later
(I'm glad to say, because he wasn't as much fun as the other two;
showed his limitations). Jonathan told me that Conrad Black had
told Moore to pay *anything* to ensure that he collared the diaries,
and Richard said that Jonathan Holborow[2] was a great fan of

---

[1] Frank Bough, television broadcaster, who specialised in sports reporting, had had
his sex-life exposed in a tabloid newspaper.
[2] Two newly-appointed editors, Charles Moore, of the *Sunday Telegraph*; Jonathan
Holborow, of the *Mail on Sunday*.

mine (seemed surprised, *why?*). But I felt *out* particularly when they started talking about the new MPs, and their disorderly behaviour, 'the hunger for the soundbite', as I put it.

Shore Cottage   *Sunday, 20 September*

Yesterday evening I spoke to Max Hastings.[1] We talked about the Government turmoil and how *bad* they all were (including the P.M.).[2] Max said he had threatened Norman Lamont[3] with implacable liability if he didn't resign. Max had lunch with Ken Clarke[4] (it's really too awful that the choice of alternatives should be Michael Heseltine – still – and Ken Clarke) who had ruefully said that, in Thursday's emergency debate, the Government couldn't admit that it had neither an Economic nor a Foreign policy.

I drove very slowly back down Eriboll Street in the (nasty) Range Rover in the dark and realised, almost with panic, just what I had thrown away by 'standing down'. I suppose I should have continued to trust in God, that He would give one the opportunity for the sword in the lake. Essentially it was selfish, opting for a quiet and comfortable life; sidestepping humiliation. God has given us self-determination, too, and of course if we are determined we can reject his gift.

---

[1] Max Hastings, journalist and military historian, editor of the *Daily Telegraph* since 1986.

[2] The twin causes of the turmoil were the Maastricht Treaty, which had caused twenty-two Conservative MPs to vote against the government, and Britain's membership of the European exchange rate mechanism (ERM). Sterling had crashed, and on 16 September, swiftly dubbed 'Black Wednesday', interest rates were raised temporarily to 15 per cent and British membership of the ERM was suspended. In short, the government's economic policy was on the ropes.

[3] Norman Lamont, MP for Kingston-on-Thames since May 1972; Chancellor of the Exchequer since 1990. At this point he did not resign.

[4] Kenneth Clarke, MP for Rushcliffe since 1970; Home Secretary since the general election and a rising star in Conservative circles, even though AC would immortalise him as a 'pudgy puffball' when *Diaries* came to be published.

Garden House   *Wednesday, 30 September*

Adrian Lithgow down this morning to 'help' one with a second
draft of a 'conference' article for the *Mail on Sunday*. Neat,
saturnine, 'slight' and cigaretting. An easy way of earning £2k,
you could say. I don't know how it will look, but I remain
restless and discomforted at being *out* of the House. Pat
Kavanagh has failed to improve on the *Mail on Sunday*'s offer of
£200k for the serial rights.[1] But half paid now and half on
publication so let that sort a few things out (but not, I fear the
Turbo R Cont). Then next week, agreeably, all those hardback
contenders of £150k are going to make 'presentations' to
ingratiate themselves.

Brighton   *Wednesday, 7 October*

On the way over here I parked the car, got out in the moon-
light, and walked along the Downs to a 5-bar gate. I spoke to
God. I apologised for having avoided Him for so long. The
muddle of guilt and lust over 'x' had blighted our contact for over
a year. Now I had to make penance – first for hurting sweet Jane
over 'x', and for still harbouring sinful, muddled thoughts there;
second for having discarded the special advantages He had given
me, to *get* me into Plymouth Sutton so late and so old, without
consulting Him or taking his permission.[2] Now the moment
had come, at last, when I could do something. But how could
He give me another chance? If He did, of course, our relationship would be impregnable. But could He? Everything is
possible of course. But nothing works out so easily.

---

[1] For the 'Diaries of a Junior Minister' as they were provisionally titled; Patricia
Kavanagh, director Peters, Fraser & Dunlop, AC's literary agents.
[2] See *Diaries: Into Politics*.

Garden House   *Sunday, 11 October*

It's drizzling and the long Park Ward 4¼ [Bentley], almost my favourite car, is getting spoiled as it sits outside the towers, where it has been since the grey 4½ arrived, waiting for 'Barry' (classic car transport driver). The contract people are roaring and thrashing in the level-crossing field, even though it is a Sunday, which is always unsettling. Poor dear Eva is in ever-sleeping decline. I don't think she'll last another fortnight. And yet so sweet-natured still. Jane will be shattered. I am a long way behind with my page schedule for Weidenfeld,[1] and 'one' for *The Times*, a review of the Schwarzkopf book.[2] I must quickly draft out, also, an article on how 'social policy' is catching us up.

Oh to be back in! (and *not* as a peer).

Garden House   *Monday, 12 October*

Poor 'E' is now in terminal decline. I had to carry her off the bed and down the second flight front stairs today. I could never have done that in the great days of the 'room fighting'. For the first time she is herself really low, and hangs her head as in the last minutes in the bullring. Thank God for the long break in Scotland, where we have a lovely picture of her, beautiful in the heather.

Garden House   *Sunday, 25 October*

I'm so depressed. Sunday papers go on and on about how awful

---

[1] Following the 'viva' of the hardback contenders to publish his diaries AC had chosen Weidenfeld & Nicolson. His editor would be Ion Trewin.

[2] The memoirs of the US Gulf War general, Norman Schwarzkopf, *It Doesn't Take a Hero*.

the Government is. But there is no leader on the right – like me all having left the House. *I* could be doing it. Of course there are endless imponderables. It was only after I left that I realised how much I had been appreciated; but would I still have been in the government? Probably yes. And if I were – would I have had the guts to resign before the parity debate? (I broke off for quite a while, composing and reciting a marvellous speech in the House of Commons that would have called on John Major – yes, there is work here for two Parliamentary terms – to think radically.)

The Old Bailey   *Wednesday, 4 November*

Testifying in the 'Matrix Churchill' trial.[1] Day wasted, though I get £70 for an ITN interview at lunchtime on 'John Major leadership' (Maastricht vote today, but the dignitaries have sold the pass – George Gardiner, Rhodes Boyson etc – presumably because they realise there's no one to take his place).[2]

Yesterday I met VH [Valerie Harkess] for a drink, not looking bad, really. Well-preserved. V good 'bust', and *very* restrainedly dressed. She said I would have been leader, 'got the leadership' if I'd still been in. It didn't need saying. I said 'it was the most catastrophically bad decision'. We walked up Piccadilly and parted outside the Park Lane Hotel, past two clubs where – in bedrooms, in the Ladies, etc we'd coupled. I said to her (which

---

[1] During his period as Minister of Trade (1986–89) AC had a meeting with machine tool exporters who as a result thought that the British government would turn a blind eye if they declared that exports to Iraq had general engineering rather than specifically military applications. The trial of the Matrix Churchill directors accused of selling weapons to Iraq, what became known as the 'arms-to-Iraq' affair, had begun on 12 October.

[2] Sir George Gardiner, MP for Reigate since February 1974, a council member of the Conservative Way Forward group, and seen by the party hierarchy as a key rebel where Europe was concerned; Sir Rhodes Boyson, MP for Brent North since February 1974.

is true) 'I have never felt the same degree of sheer physical desire as I did with you with any other human being.' She was pleased. She said I'd never given her any (sic) money. '£10,000', I said. 'Do you think I'm worth £10,000?' 'Well,' I paused, 'if you *can* quantify it, I'd say you were … "worth" £450,000.'

Went back to Albany. Curiously desexualated. Left a message on 'x's phone, did the flowers. Left, saying I'm going to Brooks's. But no sooner had I got to the Club than the Porter said she'd rung. Must have done so immediately she got it. I was delighted by this.

Garden House						*Tuesday, 8 December*

And what about testifying to Scott?[1] Last night Detective Inspector Lawrence phoned, asked for an appointment 'after Christmas' (brain washing to wreck in the holiday) for a meeting 'with my solicitor' and a 'statement'.

'I have nothing to say,' I said. Well could I put him in touch with my solicitor … etc.

'I don't see why I even need to pay a solicitor.' He was puzzled.

'Come and arrest me.'

'It's not an arrestable offence.'

My only choice is to 'clear my name' with Scott.

---

[1] The Matrix Churchill trial had folded on 10 November, following AC's answer to Geoffrey Robertson, defence counsel, who had remarked that a statement attributed to AC – 'that the Iraqis will be using the current order for general engineering purposes' could not be correct 'to your knowledge'.

AC: Well, it's our old friend being economical, isn't it?

GR: With the truth?

AC: With the *actualité*. There was nothing misleading or dishonest to make a formal or introductory comment that the Iraqis would be using the current orders for general engineering purposes. All I didn't say was 'and for making munitions'. Sir Richard Scott, a Lord Justice of Appeal since 1991, had been appointed to chair an inquiry

Garden House   *Friday, 11 December*

We buried dear 'E' today. She looked lovely, literally asleep with all the tension gone out of her body; and we put in 'Squeaky', an American bone, and some other mementoes and Jane's headscarf.

Last night she was so collapsed and intermittently crying in pain, even when I picked her up she couldn't stand. I went down to fetch Carlile (nearly missed him, not at Sandgate etc). A massive (x 4) overdose of anaesthetic and her head dropped into Jane's hand immediately. Jane could feel her last breaths. That morning, Jane said, she had gone out into the yard, the Bailey, just looked around – for the last time – and turned back. Thinking to the past I recall her doing 'last' journeys to so many familiar staging points – Lord Clark's Gate, the Long Garage, the car park field gate – separately, on different occasions. Right to the end she smelt beautiful, and had a lovely expression and smooth head.

Garden House   *Saturday, 12 December*

I had a tiny stroll with Jane. She said what an annus horribilis it had been for everyone. Only want to escape. Saltwood is such a mess, so distressing, absolutely nothing 'to hand'. I would like to be minimalist. A south sea island, a Club Med hut, some decent books and a 2CV. Perhaps, after the 'publication' [of the diaries] I can escape, totally?

I am lucky, surely, still to have my health and energy. 'No warnings'. But how long have I still this dispensation?

Garden House   *Monday, 14 December*

I have just finished transposing the entry for 20 September 1984.[1] Should have been much less cliquey, widened my circle of friends, never let my boredom threshold show. I should have entertained, in cycle, members of the 92, little dinners. Pressed on. I didn't realise, until too late, the prestige I commanded. I thought that they would think I wanted something. I should really have had a dinner every fortnight.

Now, in this dead and dingy and aimless parliament everyone would be talking about me.

I SHOULD NEVER HAVE LEFT THE HOUSE OF COMMONS.

---

[1] In which AC describes a letter from Julian Amery ('you stick out like a red poppy in the hayfield of mediocrities surrounding you ...') after surviving the reshuffle (*Diaries*).

1993

Never[1] have I contemplated the end of the holiday with such gloom, and headhung pressure. I am under *such* pressure with these *Diaries*, and my eyes are going red-rimmed. Piccolo row yesterday after my (very well-written) piece in *The Times* on 'Winston'.[2] No more writing now, until the end of the *Diaries* (whatever I write people will always look for the ooh! 'controversial' bit).

At EMT we agreed first half of the year *choked* (up to 'The Wedding'[3]) then blank. Keep it that way.

Did a broadcast at 1 o'clock [Radio 4's *World at One*]. Quite good-natured, with Andrew Roberts and Jim Naughtie.[4] But 'Charleston' of *Western Morning News* rang and said W Country MPs (none of whom liked me) said my article 'sour grapes' because I was out of things; and Bruce [Anderson] rang, congratulating, to tell me of a piece – very chippy – 'social misfit' etc by Cameron Watt in the *Standard*. *Guardian* wants to do an interview/profile; bound to be hostile, but must do my best to be bland. But *think* (as I said to Jane) what will happen when the *Diaries* come out! There's so much jealousy about. 'People' will

---

[1] AC's own footnote: 'not for a long while anyway; since European Bill Committee'.
[2] Inspired by John Charmley's about-to-be published biography, *Churchill: the End of Glory*, 'the most important "revisionist" text to be published since the war', said *The Times* on its front page. AC's thesis, which would even be called 'ludicrous' in the pell-mell that followed, was that Churchill by refusing to make peace with Hitler in 1940-41 betrayed the Commonwealth, lost the Far Eastern empire and shattered the British social order.
[3] Andrew Clark would be marrying Sarah Harris later in the year.
[4] Andrew Roberts, historian, whose first book, *The Holy Fox* (a life of Lord Halifax, 1991) had been highly praised, was at work on a series of essays that would be published as *Eminent Churchillians*; Jim Naughtie, former *Guardian* political editor, had recently transferred to radio.

really have something to fasten on to then. I will (ideally) be in the Alps, wrestling at the wheel of our Silver Ghost.[1]

Ups and downs. But one just takes consolation from the fact that the intensity of reaction is usually a good yardstick to the effectiveness of a particular quest.

Sunday, 24 January

Crazy spastic headline in today's *Sunday Express* – 'Yard moves in on ex-Minister'. Really! I am dutch, though slightly put out.

Sunday, 31 January

Only a month left to finish the *D*. I am lack-lustre and particularly depressed. Without hope, now, of 'x'. I'm in purdah for the next four weeks.

Wednesday, 10 February

I am back from London, desperately tired and low, having been 'lionised' at lunch with Jonathan Holborow, Dobbie, Angus McPherson and the definitely attractive Caroline Michel.[2] Why oh why (sic) did I leave the Commons? They more or less agreed that I could be leading the Right. I fantasise, sometimes,

---

[1] The Rolls-Royce Enthusiasts' Club Alpine 93 (hereafter called the 'Alpine' by AC) in June in which AC would drive his Silver Ghost, to mark the twentieth anniversary of the previous RREC Alpine, in which Alan and Jane had taken part in 1973.

[2] The *Mail on Sunday*'s bid to serialise the *Diaries* had been accepted; Peter Dobbie (long-time political writer), Angus McPherson, members of Holborow's team; Caroline Michel, marketing director of Weidenfeld & Nicolson.

that I could be *called* back into the Commons … But I need so many miracles. I fear my potency is waning.

Garden House   *Saturday, 20 February*

I am very unhappy. None of the old standbys that used to calm me are working. The Garden House – so warm and enveloping; so many little touches. The badge-room, the 'workshop', to fiddle with the cars, the archive room. I now see, of course, that they were only delicious when one had the position to fall back on. Now they are just 'hobbies in retirement'. I don't *want* to retire. I don't feel like retirement at all. My mind races, I am hungry for news and gossip, resentful at John Major, Richard Ryder (shameful), Aitken – how *could* they? Although, of course, the cruelty of politics is its attraction

I have come over here to write and to pray, for my 'game plan'. Could God give me just this one more chance? Since my last entry Judith Chaplin has died suddenly at Newbury (a very bad seat).[1] It would have to be ACHAB – as never before or since.

Is the sword still there, though now at the bottom of the lake?

Monday, 22 February

It was good. Clear, assured, moving. I looked compos and in my 'prime'. Many people saw it. All were enthusiastic. Today acres of coverage in *The Times*.[2] Particularly valuable was a compliment

---

[1] To call it a 'very bad seat' seems on the face of it surprising as Judith Chaplin, former political secretary to John Major, became MP for Newbury in 1992 with a majority of 11,057. But it marked a crucial electoral test for the government following sterling's ejection from the ERM the previous September.

[2] This first extract from AC's contribution to Channel 4's Opinions series of lectures, was spread across two pages under the heading 'Bold surgery needed to cure our once-great nation.'

from Bob Worcester.[1] He said I (not a CCO template twerp) *could* win Newbury. Hugely excited, I rang Peter Stothard at *The Times*.[2] He made a good point when I asked if I could 'enlist his help' – said the candidate would really be chosen by Major and Fowler.[3] They would have the choice of winning with me, and losing with a centrist – they'd probably prefer the latter. But how smoothly everything seems to be running at present. Almost creepy, down to the little note in *The Times* Diary (where from?) that I may be 'standing' at Newbury. Shades of 1968.[4] Later this afternoon Michael Cockerell rang, very appreciative, professionally.[5] *Deo volente* at present.

Tuesday, 23 February

Complete and utter dejection now. Everything gone. Nothing in *The Times* except a kind of play-safe piece by Peter Riddell.[6] No one has really noticed. So my 'game plan' has failed. But, at least, I said my piece – *and I said it well*. I poured out my heart to Jamie last night and he was encouraging. But I am blighted too, horrendously so, by the fickleness of my minx.

---

[1] Robert Worcester, founder of MORI, a leading political pollster.
[2] Peter Stothard, who had not long been appointed editor of *The Times*.
[3] Sir Norman Fowler (MP for Sutton Coldfield since February 1974, Nottingham S 1970–74) had succeeded Chris Patten as chairman of the Conservative Party.
[4] *The Times* Diary had run early stories about AC's political ambitions (*Diaries: Into Politics*, 14 June, 1972).
[5] Michael Cockerell, BBC political journalist, was making a television profile of AC, called *Love Tory*.
[6] *The Times*'s political analyst.

Thursday, 25 February

I am in limbo. Ten days to complete delivery of *Diaries*.[1]

But everything is overshadowed, made slightly *unreal* by Jane/ Bates, need for slides and tests. I can't believe it. But hope the ju-ju hasn't gone wrong somehow. I feel slightly depersonalised, almost demob happy by all this.

Would almost have forgotten about politics, were it not for a call from Jonathan Holborow and a full political fix. Apparently Richard R[yder] is going to be eased out to be Minister of Agriculture, and David D is to be chief [whip].[2] Which will be good. But where do I fit in?

Garden House   *Sunday, 28 February*

A series of little extra pieces fall into place. On Friday evening Dobbie rang me and asked if I would do a piece backing Paul Keating's attitude to the Royals.[3] 'Look, if I'm going to fight the Newbury by-election, the last thing I want is an anti–Royal article.' 'Cor, Alan, you're having me on …' etc. This just covered me, as it turned out, because the very next morning, in *The Times* leader 'Newbury die' I was named twice!

So this morning good friendly coverage in Black Dog (top),[4] and v reasonable in *Sunday Express*, thanks to dear Bruce who is coming down for lunch, and wants to be my campaign manager.[5] Perhaps more importantly and *complimentarily*, my verdict on JM in Graham Turner's *Sunday Telegraph* piece 'I have a high opinion of him …'

---

[1] As they had finally been titled.
[2] Turned out not to be so.
[3] Paul Keating, Prime Minister of Australia since 1991, had, typically, been making some provocative remarks about the Queen.
[4] *Mail on Sunday* political diary.
[5] Bruce Anderson had suggested AC to Richard Ryder as the candidate who would do least badly. Norman Fowler, apparently, thought it a crazy idea.

It all has a strange, magical quality. Almost as if I, and other forces, was willing it. Could I really bring it off? A year's sabbatical to assuage Jane, get the *Diaries* done. And then back to the second serious phase. And the lights of AC1800 in the garage, and the big party in the Jubilee Room, 'to celebrate the result of the Newbury by-election'.

Garden House   *Thursday, 4 March*

Still the accumulation of events. Yesterday Jane's 'tests' proved *negative*, and thus a fresh boost as the overshadowing lifts. Then Matrix, DPP 'cleared' me, good TV coverage – 'vindicates' etc.[1] Spoke to Gill Shephard[2] – she very indiscreet, said, 'You must put in' and (without telling Jane) I now intend to 'take things one stage further' today. Then, after Ch 3 [lunchtime ITN] news, phone rang and, rather quiet and sorry for himself, Richard !! It's all so impeccable, the timing. Polling just before the book comes out; and also the lawyers suggested excisions [to the *Diaries*] made it much easier to sanitise without upsetting the publishers.

Am I really contemplating the humiliation of a selection process, and then the Campaign and the bad polls, and then the count – and then ... I can get wild AF, yes. But until I am *stopped* it would be a derogation of responsibility and doubt 'to pull back'. The sword is on the surface of the lake floor.

---

[1] AC had feared he might be charged in connection with the Matrix Churchill case.

[2] Gillian Shephard, MP for South West Norfolk since 1987, Employment Secretary.

Saturday, 13 March

What I will never know is whether in fact I had any chance of being 'seen' at Newbury or not *before* little Sarah Sands' interview in the *Standard* yesterday.[1]

I suppose it was a mistake – led astray by a pretty girl, as usual.

Terrible row with Jane followed. All I wanted to do was step into a hole.

Trouble is this was really my last 'window'. Because once the book is out – with its crazy indiscretions and element of romping – I will no longer be taken seriously.

I am *not* released. A bit apprehensive of bad publicity. Heard from *Daily Express* (typically) that 'down to 18' and not on list. Very flat and depressed. I slept after tea on the floor of the Green Room. I am tired and aimless. I must also try and restore the body a bit more. I have been drinking too regularly, taking very little exercise. I am creaky and fatigued ('ravaged' in appearance – Sarah Sands). Strange though for three miraculous weeks it all seemed to fit in such a pre-ordained way, climaxing with the Matrix Churchill acquittal.

Garden House   *Monday, 15 March*

It is a beautiful spring day, and the lawn looms. One needs really a *continuous* week to get the lawn 'under'; at the moment it seems always to be 'getting on top of one'.

Last night I was doing the Runes – *very* pessimistic, started with the Ice Rune – nothing; then 'prediction' – but reversed, then the Black Rune – death.

Nobody in the papers rang at all. I am a non-person. Just that

---

[1] Sarah Sands, feature writer, on London *Evening Standard*, had interviewed AC at Saltwood, where he was indiscreet about the forthcoming *Diaries*, about affairs and much else.

last spluttering of the candle. Nick Budgen rang and said would I stand as the Referendum candidate at Newbury. Talked for ½ hour. Then rang again in the evening. But Jane got the perfect word – 'floundering'. You can't really stand against your own party.

Garden House   *Thursday, 18 March*

I have a very heavy heart. Took in the last pages of the *Diaries* today, and a long session (the 3rd) sorting out editorial queries. Now it is out of control, and the date approaches when 'serialisation publicity' starts. Jonathan Holborow is going to spend £½ million – and God knows what they will be saying. I will have to go 'into hiding'. Any idea that I can sign books and 'show' myself is ridiculous; I will be a figure of fun, like Mellor. It signals, too, the end of my career in serious politics; and the end of any hope of, even, a 'K' (the only thing I thought I might have 'hooked').

Sunday, 28 March

Walking down to the Long Garage this evening I felt something on my nose, right-hand side. Asked Jane, she said it was a 'little melanoma'. That's how the last nodel began, a little black dot. But in the mirror it's more of a line. Strange and depressing.

Garden House   *Friday, 2 April*

First of the galleys – to 1985 – arrived today

I'm not so sure about the book. Is it really very *slight* indeed? I am nervous and apprehensive. I have been going through a phase of hypochondria about my melanoma and my right shoulder. It is certainly a worrying shape, a configuration rather, but not large. But my real problem is that there is this huge void – between policies and frivolities.

Zermatt   *Wednesday, 14 April*

I have arrived here, now an OAP, and my hair is really quite white on my left side. I have a headache and my eyes aren't working very well. I feel completely desexualated. On my bed in the dressing room a PLO scarf was spread out, and a note of 'present' for 'the Minister' from Andrew. I thanked him, then expressed quite a little shock when he said he had left it there last year. It's eighteen months since we had our 'momentous' summer hiking stay. I've made mistakes in the period. Bad ones.

Suddenly, Zermatt like, I have had the most wonderful sign. I opened the drawer of Mme Piper, and in the violet shirt were my *candidate links*[1] This opens many doors.

---

[1] AC's speech at the Plymouth Sutton selection in 1972; 'Mme Piper' was a chest of drawers; the cufflinks, of lapis lazuli, had been given by Jane to AC, who wore them the night he was selected at Plymouth.

Garden House   *Saturday, 24 April*

At last the 'filming' is over.[1]

In the last days I became quite tetchy with them all – too much repetition 'if you could just do that again, Alan' etc. Much hanging about, intrusion on meals etc.

But now that is past, and the galleys are delivered. Nothing to do except dodge (or under direction accept) interviews until the serialisation starts. Time is incredibly congested. I am in a state of acute dejection and find it difficult to concentrate. Instead, I just come over here and mope, and relive agonies from the past.

What is my role? Christopher Silvester interviewed me today. Not specially sympathetic, somehow. He asked me who were my friends in politics. I mentioned Rhodes James, Garel-Jones, Soames.[2] 'But aren't they all much younger than you?' Yes, I said, thinking that my contemporaries are all buffers.

But audiences, as raised by Nick Wapshott and the Greenwich Defence 'students', all kind of expect one to 'go back' into politics.

It's not really possible, is it?

But ACHAB.

The second half of the year is a void. I fear the worst. I have to get over May 10 (*always* bad sexually for some reason), then, a Knight for the Tamar estuary and – Keith Douglas again –

The next month, then, is a window
and with a crash I'll split the glass.
Behind it stands one I must kiss.
Person of love, or death
A person, or a wraith?
I fear what I shall find.[3]

---

[1] Michael Cockerell and his camera crew had been filming AC (and Jane) for his BBC *Love Tory* documentary.

[2] Sir Robert Rhodes James, historian who edited the Chips Channon diaries (1967); MP for Cambridge (December 1976-92). He and AC were (friendly) rivals.

[3] Keith Douglas, who died in Normandy in 1944, was a favourite poet of AC's. These lines are from 'On a Return from Egypt'. He also quotes him at the close of *Diaries*.

Garden House   *Monday, 26 April*

A dreadful day. Jane is ill, and I sent her to bed (freesias and
Ribena, fluffing the pillows). I was got off the loo today to be
asked 'Nick[1] wants to know how long it takes to get here from
Gatwick' (!). I've had to scrape, scrape the barrel to pay for
Andrew's house. Jonathan Holborow will not now even restore
me the balance. And 'US rights', if there is such a thing, I will
not sell to Harry Evans.[2]

I really wanted to escape today – just go with books and a
deckchair to the sand – or perhaps to the châlet. But I finished
cutting the Bailey, and I thought how beautiful Saltwood
looked. I sang *Die Soldaten* and wondered what all might have
been and what (if anything) is in store.

Garden House   *Tuesday, 27 April*

Walked from Sandling [station], darling Jane had made a balls-
up of the arrival times and gone to Folkestone. London had
been blocked solid. And now I return to find Jane is being
bullied by Bates again and he's taken *twelve* slides. Uncertainty,
complete, prevails.

Saltwood   *Sunday, 9 May*

A week, much filled, but little achieved.

The flat surfaces in the Green Room are choked and towering;'key' letters like RREC Alpine and LPF[3] are still unattended

---

[1] Nick Beuttler, Jane's brother.
[2] Harold Evans, former editor of the *Sunday Times*, now President of Random
House, the New York publishers.
[3] L. P. Fassbender, the Clarks' accountant.

to; the yard and workshops are a shambles and the lawn is never quite fully under control.

Jane was forced by Bates to undergo an operation – a 'lumpectomy'. We were in silent abjection (I will always remember, though not as vividly as if it had marked the end of an era, answering his phone call to say it was a bit 'suspicious' after I had (demi-randily) my first after-lunch rest for ages, a Bank Monday – which had to be bad). But it turned out, on Friday, to be 'all right'. He splendidly rang me at supper. So I feel free to restart again, so soon after making or implying all those promises in St Leonard's where I had repaired after reading the interview which made me feel so sad and proud of her. But her being away is appalling. The pups[1] are a delight, but needlessly demanding: the weather is foul, with a high wind blowing all the time. I get up at 5.30, but still have only just got the kitchen in order, pups fed and walked by 7.

I am faced with difficult times. My instinct is to hide. Not even read the papers, just baste them nimbly.

But that was a lucky break at Newbury![2]

Garden House   *Tuesday, 18 May*

Today the first day of the hols. For I don't know *how* long, we came back from taking Pam[3] to Gatwick and just collapsed by the pool. Exhausted in our bones.

Saltwood is so lovely in May, each year one forgets how high

---

[1] Two Rottweilers, sisters, to whom the Clarks gave names with German association: Hannah (Jane's, after Hannah Reich, Hitler's test pilot) and Lëhni (AC's, after Hitler's favourite film director, Leni Riefenstahl).

[2] AC was indeed fortunate: the Conservatives were mauled at the by-election held on 6 May, with the Liberal Democrat candidate, Old Etonian David Rendel, overturning the Tories' general election 11,000 majority to achieve a LD victory by over 12,000 votes. As for the referendum/anti-Maastricht candidates, together they polled fewer than 700 votes.

[3] Pam Beuttler, Jane's mother, who was returning home to Benalmadena in Spain.

and sensuous enveloping is the Queen Anne Lace and the yellow-green foliage.

Garden House   *Wednesday, 26 May*

I feel very tired. The 'pressure' of all those interviews, publicity, serialisation, never anticipation of *disappointing* sales, plus need to really do quite a lot of paperwork before leaving. I pine for Eriboll, the long May light, where James is enjoying wonderful weather and no one can badger me.

Albany   *Friday, 4 June*

I feel I have now reached a point in my life when certain directional signals can no longer be ignored. (And by me not welcome.) I am up here alone and unsettled. I hate sleeping the night in Albany, being badly affected by nostalgia and a sadness, vestigial recollection of earlier torments.

Today a signing in Hatchards. Then lunch with Diane.[1] As I noted at our first meeting she is *very* sexy, legs and figure. Had the face, but not unattractive with blonde hair and specs. But just not interested. Slightly embarrassed if anything. The *Daily Telegraph* man rang with silly questions about Frankie Holland,[2] said she said I was 'avuncular' in my interest. Then an article I read about HRT for men, 'poor performance' etc has actually *made* me impotent.

Tip has finally failed Staff College, poor darling. He's such a good soldier. Fucking stupid system. I just spoke to James in Eriboll. He's not as close as he used to be. But if he is content that's something.

---

[1] Diane Rowley, publicity director, Weidenfeld & Nicolson.
[2] 'I'm madly in love with Frances Holland ...' wrote AC (*Diaries*, 5 June 1983). She was his 22-year-old Labour opponent in Plymouth Sutton at the general election.

Garden House   *Sunday, 13 June*

The last Sunday here for some while.

When I am back the days will be shortening, and the peacock feathers will be all over the grass. I am relatively tranquil. The 'worst' seems to be over on the *Diaries*, thanks to Michael Cockerell's film and Jane's attractive performance (relegating me to 'best supporting actor'). I don't yet feel quite as I should. My energy is down and the special thrill of plunging into the pool seems less this summer. I suppose each year now I will get a little older.

But the 'Antique' is a joy now it's back from Scott Moncrieff, and I am kitting it out for a (sedatory now) *Randonée Alpin*. I just hope it holds together, and I have time to brood and philosophise, as well.

B5, Albany   *Tuesday, 15 June*

Up for a 'round-up'. A 'long' envelope at Brooks's; and I know what that means. I am desexualated, too. No night E's any more, only very feeble half ones on waking. But I shouldn't really complain – I have had such a wonderful life; and all the bad decisions have been my own.

I woke too early for *The Times*, and read Chips. So interesting on Nazi Germany,[1] his trip there in 1936 (the best year for everything from Miro to the 4¼ Bentley). Chips will be remembered for his diary, and so will I. But I have one already over Chips – I'm still alive! – so ACHAB.

---

[1] 'Hitler was coming and he looked exactly like his caricature – brown uniform, but not grim look … I was more excited than when I met Mussolini in 1926 in Perugia, and more stimulated, I am sorry to say, than when I was blessed by the Pope in 1920.' – *Chips*, 6 August 1936.

AC achieved his ambition and drove his Silver Ghost S1914 Ch 59 TW, otherwise known as 'The Antique', in the second (possibly harder, he thought) Alpine Commemorative twenty years on, organised by the Rolls-Royce Enthusiasts' Club.

Schönbrunn Palace Hotel   *Saturday, 19 June*

Goodness knows what will happen.[1] A challenge, of man and machine. Is this my last solo adventure? I hope my dear 'Antique' holds up. Strange, a bit of catharsis, almost. It's not that I can't believe I will from July onwards, be a 'buffer'.

Vienna to Salzburg   *Sunday, 20 June*
Solo. 257 miles. 7 a.m.–7.45 p.m.

The Antique was parked in the Schönbrunn gardens. Looking very 'macho' (as 'Dan' Meyer said) beside all the shiny show-offs. But I was secretly uneasy about the clanking or *clonking* noise. Alan, who was scrutineering, seemed dismissive of it, however. In colonial, thundery heat I blundered about unpacking and reloading. Duncan Dickinson and 'Tony' stood about helpfully. I had a great dish of venison and noodles and retired, to wake just before the 4.50 (3.50 UK) alarm call. I virtually missed breakfast due to 'losing' things in the bedroom – particularly RayBans which seem to have gone irrevocably – and dashed swearing and carrying four pieces of luggage to load up.

Typically, and an ominous precursor – I would guess – of what was to follow, we stood thummingly in line outside the

---

[1] Part of this account – taken from AC's motoring journal – appeared in *Back Fire*, a collection of his motoring journalism (2001), but only when transcribing his 1993 journal did the editor of this volume discover additional entries. Here AC's complete account of the Alpine is reproduced for the first time.

Palace for some forty-five minutes before moving off. I soon became impatient, and by double-parking and out-accelerating people (not difficult as I weigh 35 cwt only) I soon caught up with John Kennedy in Radley's old blue 'Eagle' R587 and a nameless in a red Ghost (also quite quick). Quite soon we started to misfire, or rather *hesitate*, which deteriorated into a full misfire. My spirits sank. Was it ignition?

At one point it seemed to recover when I jiggled with the Adjust-Retard lever. She was unhappy, though just firing on all six on the long straight out, where the Austro-Daimler cars used to be tested, and the hobgoblin in the red Ghost – slowly drew ahead. In a moment of recovery, at the start of the scrutineering, I surged past them exiting a hairpin; then she stuttered hideously and audibly as the cut-out was open. I was thoroughly out-of-sorts. But I filled the tank and (over)filled the radiator. Thereafter, fingers crossed, she gave no trouble and behaved beautifully, triumphantly when I swung out and passed Radley, at the very outset, and had the satisfaction of him getting smaller and smaller in the mirror. As I overtook him he did *not* acknowledge, but muttered to himself as we swept ahead.

Was in buoyant form as far as [Wels?] (arrived in rain) en fête. But reasonable lunch in marquee – ruthlessly barging to get ahead of queue. But after lunch rained very disagreeably and continuously. I stopped to put on more and more clothing. Got to Salzburg by the back route (unchanged) refuelling at the autobahn junction and getting angst about her restarting. Dodged an obviously pointless civic reception, and arrived by luck at the hotel to park in underground garage with all the other Ghosts. Triumphant at the high mileage, and glad of a rest day tomorrow.

In Salzburg   *Monday, 21 June*

Fiddled with the car a bit. Drove (late) to a boring reception outside the Civic Centre, peasants gawping. Car was leaking water massively and afterwards I found 'Alan' who greased the water pump hugely – and cured it. Early start tomorrow. The engine 'clanks' objectionably, but Alan is calm. The car is really lovely to drive.

Salzburg to Toblach (Tirol)   *Tuesday, 22 June*

Left, in drizzle. Some difficulty and hesitation stops getting out of Salzburg. It's very hard navigating solo, and several times I overshot, had to reverse, left the indicator going on restarting, etc etc. I know that if we could do the Tavern (long and steep) then she would do the Katschberg (even steeper, but shorter). Refreshed in Mauterndorf, poured in a lot of oil, but no water needed, thanks to Alan. Timed start, and she swooped off going splendidly though baulked by that slightly suspect Irish group going spastically slowly.

Palace Hotel, Merano   *Thursday, 24 June*

A most incredible day today. Comparable to the final four hours of the 1955 Le Mans or the closing laps of the 1959 Nurburgring 1000km when Moss overtook the Maseratis after the delay caused by Fairman 'I spun the car'. John Kennedy (with whom I now have better relations) offered me a seat in the back of his beautiful Alpine Eagle (although I noticed that the gearbox was rougher than the Antique) to ascend the Stelvio. Christ! What a pass! 9,500 feet. An endless series of Ghosts gamely ploughed on, sometimes having to reverse on the lacets (a 'K' turn big fat Dan Meyer called it).

Quite spectacular and exciting – although I was rebuffed by the little BBC 'Top Gear' girl, whom Johnny H had tipped me off about, and got fearfully *chilled* – after getting *soaked* yesterday for the third day running – and am now unhappily drinking *thé limone* with a lumpy sore throat, blazing cheeks and pulse of 84 (just taken it) and a temp of 99°. I do hope I'm not going to be thrashed, as I really would love to complete the Alpine now, best of all meeting Jane in Venice.

Saturday, 26 June

Was a little better yesterday; but this morning *stress* mark on forehead (perhaps due to the slow deterioration of Antique's performance and reliability factor – now hates starting from hot).

Sitting in gardens in shade of cypress trees by the pool, but blazing cheeks, tight chest, pulse 81 (fluctuating) temp 98. No appetite. Periodic nose blowing. Voice seriously diminished. I was ?heavily nostalgic driving here.

I talk to Jane and she is tired and fussed. I'm not apologising enough. I'm worried, too, that the pups will have forgotten me.

Jane told me that it was terrible watching Heseltine[1] getting out of his wheelchair to get into the helicopter, white-coated attendants still carrying the drip. The old lion in decay. Five days in a Venice hospital, and no boxes. Yet lean, didn't drink or smoke. And Hughbugh[2] has gone – from lung cancer. We've got his very last letter.

Wien [Vienna]   *Tuesday, 6 July*

Back at the Schönbrunn. I can hardly believe it. The Alpine went *incredibly* – after a catharsis in … when Andy Wood[3] changed the coil, and Alan cleared the switch points at the bottom of the steering column.

---

[1] Michael Heseltine had had a heart attack in Venice.
[2] The 6th Earl of Cawdor, Hugh John Vaughan Campbell, an Old Etonian, but four years younger than AC.
[3] Andy Wood, of P. & A. Wood.

A rest day, after a desperate drive yesterday in great heat to get 'first over the line' accolade. Tonight the ceremonial dinner – *longueurs* but I'm used to that. I'm going through a *lippen* scare (the blood blister of many years standing that Bertie Arbeid suddenly 'worried' me about).

Now for the final trial (who knows, perhaps the most arduous of all?) of the long drive home. A great thunderstorm is building up. I do hope we don't have to drive through blinding rain tomorrow. But what a triumph to drive home back through the Barbican gates! At least, we have done the great rally – and acquitted ourselves brilliantly. Jane has had a lovely three days, too, and a 'break', and a feeling of being needed.

Saltwood   *Wednesday, 21 July*

A dreadful cold wet July, intermittently 'muggy'. I bathed, one length, this morning and cleared a headache (almost a hangover headache caused, I would stress, by that 'Lido Hotel' wine which tasted good, but is clearly full of antifreeze), but the water is the same colour as the moat, and smells of vegetation.

Yesterday we went to the [Buckingham Palace] Garden Party, calling first at Andrew's dear little house in Farnell Mews. He was grave, though beautifully handsome. I felt tired, and lost interest. Opposite was the ideal mews flat and garage, 'under offer' at £210,000. But I no longer have the liquidity, and any-way I have too much *on* to take on more commitments. At this rate I will be dead before I've done the basics here; but my major works priority must be to open the moat and arch of the Barbican bridge. No one else has the vision to do this.

I had interviews with two high cards at once. First Mrs Thatcher, rather unmade up, blonde hair not usual etc. Denis looking ghastly, thin, grey, though cigaretting massively. As always she doesn't actually engage in conversation, but states propositions and concepts. But no ill-will there, in spite of all the innuendo and interpretation in the hype. Then bumped into (literally) Geoffrey Howe[1] in the cake queue, and mobbed him. He came and sat with us, talked about Scott, and the Commons. As I said to Jane the mafia band of politicians in the same party is such that we really can't bear grudges, it's not worth it.

A cheery little fellow, ludicrously badly dressed in a pale grey morning suit came over and sucked up to Geoffrey; knew my name and introduced his wife. The new MP for Blackpool.[2] A mild pang; as also when talking to Tony Grant[3] who looked very fit and fresh (must have a mistress).

Garden House   *Friday, 30 July*

The opening of a new volume, in which events are likely to be lower-key – a gradually declining trajectory.

I am remarkably creaky and de-energised. My morale is down and I am more than a little scared of the *lippen* operation on Monday. At the back of my mind, I suppose, lurk fears of image mutilation. 'I think perhaps we better return to this under a "general", radiotherapy etc.'

Last night I slept from 10.40 to 7.10 without waking at all – 8½ hours. I had been incredibly tired yesterday after Soames's end of term, when we stayed up drinking until 1.30. Soames looked ill, sweated a lot and at one point very splendidly *took his temperature* (it was 98, having been 102 earlier in the day). He's had his gall bladder removed and I remember from my tonsil operation that one does suffer afterwards from violent

---

[1] Lord [Geoffrey] Howe, former Chancellor of the Exchequer and Foreign Secretary during Margaret Thatcher's government.
[2] Harold Elletson, MP for Blackpool North since 1992, and his wife Fiona. Elletson was forty years AC's junior, but also an Old Etonian. He held the seat for only one parliament.
[3] Sir Anthony Grant, MP for SW Cambs since 1983 (Harrow Central, 1964–83).

fluctuations in fever and depression. The boys were genuinely friendly, and tired; but I sensed, as I wrote afterwards to Richard, the 'gossamer curtain' between those in power and those who are OUT. Jonathan, so thoughtful and wise, asked me what I would say if Faust offered me a miraculous translation straight back into the Commons – Government or back benches as you wish – at the price of surrendering the *Diaries*. Initially, I suppose, one says 'no'. But always there is the heavenly recollection of the sword, now on the floor of the lake's bottom.

However, all that seems much more remote than it used to at, say, the time of the Newbury selection. I no longer fret, the way I used to, about going into the Government again (although a pang yesterday talking to Peter Watkins – on how I did enjoy myself drafting a response to Scott's 'discussion' paper and zapping Muttukumaru[1] and talking to Robin Butler).

This morning we went to Ashford market, the Hobbs Parker sale of agricultural oddments. A lovely atmosphere of de-escalation, and I bid for some of the old tractors, none made more than £500, all were running and the little Ferguson Diesel with spindly wheels made £320! Much of the stuff 'on offer' was really just scrapings from Bob's Room. The 'Poet' (I can't recall his name at the moment) appeared and talked knowledge-ably. He is a habitué of such functions. He told me that the Channel Tunnel people had acquired the site – why? With what powers? To build a supermarket and the auction was going to be moved to a 'green field site'.

I have been very nostalgic and homesick for Scotland these last weeks and days. And I privately pine for a de-escalated existence, playing with old machinery, no pressures.

---

[1] Christopher Muttukumaru, lawyer, secretary to the Scott inquiry.

Garden House   *Monday, 2 August*

A delicious 'cleared' from the youthful, but impressive locum at 55 Harley Street, took 11 seconds to say 'no, no' (as opposed to Whitby's 'oh ho!'[1]).

I must work on my speaking schedules and topics for the autumn, and how I am going to phase that in with an image build. I really don't know how I am going to evolve (because I *must* still evolve, even if it is only into de-escalation) this next year.

'Diarist, a Political Savant' I have been saying. But Jonathan said 'book a safe seat, get back in' (to the Commons); flattered that he should still think me youthful enough to do this. In a way it is lovely to be free and independent, and (semi) sought after. But I must try and improve my fitness.

Shore Cottage   *Wednesday, 17 August*

Was it only yesterday that I welched on the Los Angeles trip?[2]

It seems like weeks. I think it has done me considerable damage, the inner ache of *another* bad decision. The young had 'booked' Jane in to dine with Heather Gow [owner of the adjoining estate] last night. If I'd known that it would just have tipped the scales and I would now be expectantly waiting on delicious room service breakfast in the Biltmore [LA hotel] before going out with Charles and Uta for a good tyre-kick and a deep 'taking of the temperature'.

As it is, I'm only slightly what-of-it? here; thinking of the mass of paperwork, and already 'tentatively' planning a date for

[1] Whitby, doctor in Hythe.
[2] Charles Howard, friend and dealer in classic cars, had suggested the trip to hunt out interesting classic cars, but Jane had countered: 'All you've been saying is how much you want to get away to Eriboll; now the moment you get here all you want to do is leave.'

our return to Saltwood. Yesterday I hung around while James very slowly (it is a nightmare of complication and trial and error needing a forklift with 1 ton capacity *and* a hydraulic crane) adding a section to his RAF shed – which is very nice quality and beautifully made of Oregon pine from Canada, part of the RAF expansion programme of 1938/9. Then in the afternoon we met for a 'stumble' in the new plantation at Arnaboll turning back before the rowan grove; and after that I went to Whales Corner and brought back three loads, a 'caulk' (which I had to trim with the saw) and two heavy 2" planks. Slept continuously until woken by the dogs at 6.20 or so.

The trouble is, this kind of idealised EARTH existence is only truly enjoyable (just as open peaceful days at Saltwood for which I used to long when in Parliament) if the other life is there ready to be embraced, grasping at one almost.

I need BOTH. Said to Jane I was going to LA because I was 'bored'. I wish I was there, talking to one and all, spotting new self-styled experts in the 'movement' and filling my reservoirs. Then, on return, I could savour the low pace and the cleanliness of the Highland tempo. I am still more restless than I thought, I suppose. Or is it the consciousness of the days left reducing all the time in number? So that one which goes by without anything to fill it is a waste? Unless of course it is occupied by *rehabilitation and recovery*.

I hardly think of 'x' any longer.

Green Room   *Thursday, 16 September*

Yesterday evening I finished putting on tape the *extracts* from the book [for an audio cassette] and came to the passage (penultimate on the tape) when I contemplate my exit – February 1991. There was over a year to go before I announced it. And indeed I had been just as decisive in 1985. But of course then it was to leave the Government, not the House. Yet, I think if I had left the Government then Plymouth would have got rid of me in 1987. They would have struck as soon as I stopped being a Minister.

If I am really honest with myself I dreaded the General Election because I thought I *and* we were going to lose. I was very unhappy torn between 'x' and Jane; and I suppose Richard must take some of the blame for half-encouraging me. But oh, how I miss it. It was all right during the summer as the great benefice – the wonderful utterly memorable Alpine rally – would not have been possible.

Yet now the hour is gathering 'Conference' first, then the temperature rises. This is the second conference I've missed. I will be forgotten by the rank-and-file. Yet I remain active, interested, consulted ('a natter', *passim* Michael Howard).

B5, Albany   *Tuesday, 21 September*

I have been walking about London, somewhat *désoeuvré*. Tomorrow a snoop on 'Scott'.[1] Poor JM under screeching pressure – in Tokyo, of all places – and in Brooks's, extempore, I drafted a note to send him.[2]

---

[1] AC's only comment afterwards was that he 'quite liked Presiley Baxendale', counsel to the inquiry.

[2] Major was leading a party of senior UK businessmen to Japan, but before leaving Britain there had been leadership speculation, possible stalking horses for a contest in November; Norman Lamont, now the ex-Chancellor of the Exchequer, writing on the first anniversary of Black Wednesday, had criticised the Prime Minister; and on the flight to Tokyo Major had been indiscreet to the press party on his attitude to the Eurosceptics. AC eventually sent his note to Major, 'trying both to cheer him up and ingratiate myself.'

Garden House *Tuesday, 5 October*

I should be calmer. The 'new' Ghost, 20UB, has arrived and is ultra pleasing. I really want it here so that I can play with it. And this morning I had a nice letter (a poignant letter, you could say) from JM, which made me feel calmer in myself.

I hang around the Garden House thinking how lovely it is, how peaceful and enveloping. It's a great tribute to my father's good sense. Would he have been better, or less effective, if he hadn't been rattled so much? I used to think it was my mother who rattled him, now I realise it was guilt.

Saltwood *Sunday, 24 October*

I had sat down to write a passage, a couple of days ago, in the Garden House, but was interrupted by the urge to write a note to Richard Ryder (following my lunch with Willie Whitelaw) at Mrs T's Foyle[1]). I asked him to set up a Defence Commission with me as Chairman.[2] Naturally he didn't reply ('Alan goes mad every so often and wants to get back in, last time it was a week before the Matrix trial'). It was strange that lunch. Sweepings really. Is that really all she could manage in terms of distinction, being between the Indian and the Hungarian ambassadors?

But I still want to be a *player.* Thing is – on *Question Time* I had a heavy time. Peter Mandelson said, 'you're still so young.' Peter Sissons [chairman] talked sensibly and confidentially to me about broad trends and JM's PR men, and so on.

---

[1] Foyle's, the booksellers, had as their guest of honour at a lunch Margaret Thatcher, whose memoirs, *The Downing Street Years*, were published the previous week.

[2] On the opposite page to this entry are a series of rough notes under the heading 'to RR'. The main thrust is 'the security of the UK' with participants to include Lord Lewin (former CDS), the historian Sir Michael Howard and John Keegan, defence editor of the *Daily Telegraph* and historian. AC added a sub-heading, 'Social points' – where the commission should meet – 'the dining room at Saltwood is out of commission' and suggested for a final dinner 'the oval room at Brooks's'.

I can't quite settle down. Although the lure of de-escalation is delicious I am under heavy financial pressure. Can't see prospect of fresh earnings ('new money'). I am going to have to cull both cars and pictures.

In the meantime I am copying out (opposite) the great list of (pre)occupations from an envelope in the kitchen, together with the objectives for the next six months.

<u>Jane and Alan Clark</u>   <u>September 1993</u>

Stately home owners
Classic car connoisseurs and enthusiasts
Public speakers
Essayist and author
Keen gardeners
Shrewd investors
Collectors of paintings and other pleasing artefacts
Alpinists
Nature lovers and crofters
Political consultees
Television personalities
'Famous persons'
Artists – and much, much more.

<u>The Struggle for Order</u>   <u>Late in October 1993</u>

Bank statements
Car files
Resurrect ledger
Summer Office
Press cuttings (headings)
Photos and albums
Garden House (motor mags; shape up)
Archives and the archive room (to be plastered?)
Winter Office
Headings for, and subsequent entry on, computer

Saltwood   *Friday, 29 October*

When I got home I pottered in the Long Garage, realised I didn't actually want to sell *anything*. Earnings won't cover everything owing – anyway near – so will have to do it from Art. Why not? The cars are a collection – bit of 'Applied' rather than 'Fine' – Art. It is the full moon, Halloween tomorrow. Unusual combination.

Of course, £350 for the Mask[1] would do very nicely thank you, but I'm glad I resisted that. It must work spells for me, because I saved it, will have to make other sacrifices.

Saltwood   *Sunday morning, 31 October*

Woke, and shrank instantaneously with thought of pressures – financial and paper. But we went for the 'w' and the trees were so beautiful, a perfectly still morning of late autumn so early that no one was about, and vistas and colours that you get only once every three or four years. I was worried about the bark on the great oak – it must be done next month. But the walk – the dry leaves were so lovely and calming, that we both felt better.

When we got in, Jane said, 'we've got everything, and yet we don't enjoy it.' So true, so very, very true. But she said it in good humour.

If I could get significant liquidity then I could plan out a schedule for *The Struggle for Order*.

Later, p.m.
I am so old and creaky in the afternoons, and generally.

I like just to sit in my chair by the bookcase, not always even listlessly turning the pages of an old mag, a car directory.

---

[1] The Torres Strait tortoiseshell mask, bought by Kenneth Clark, once owned by Picasso. Charles Jerdein, a dealer and friend of AC's, had offered $450,000 for it ten years before (*Diaries*, 9 May 1985).

And yet, if I look at the schedule etc of barely a year ago there, at midday, was Gossie. I seem to have aged at too fast a rate. My face looks more crumpled on TV, and when I run my hands over it I can feel folds of skin around the eyes and the dewlaps.

Of course, in London, I barely ever drank at lunch. Today I had two glasses of Sauvignon, two of '70 Palmer, and two of '83 Palmer. I know it's meant to stop heart attacks, and in the evenings (less so) I will still do it. But from now on I am going to drink at lunch only on Saturdays and Sundays.

Monday, 8 November

A strange dream last night. I was looking after Tom, and he had lost his lead, but I was making do with bailing twine. In a kind of way he was muddled with the dreadful, harrowing story, dribbling out day-by-day in the courts, of the cruel 'walk to death' of Jamie Bulger. After he got demi-lost a few times we ended up in College Green. I realised that I could not cross the street to get into the Palace of Westminster. I reflected that my life in Parliament really divided into three phases (1) as a backbencher, much boredom, relieved by backgammon. Time wasted, in the main, like early years at Oxford. (2) As a Minister before, and (3) after 'running into' 'x'. The further stage I eschewed – the 'respected backbencher'. But I think best of all the factor that forced me into this, it was my bad relations in Plymouth that was the principal one – just as it was they who cramped my style in the very early stages.

Garden House   *Thursday, 11 November*

A lovely fine still day. At the eleventh hour, of the eleventh day, of the eleventh month we walked, almost by chance, to Lord C's

Gate and were seated there when the Western Front fell silent. A good moment to put things 'in perspective'.

I started the morning (after an intermittent night, waking and rewaking with those damned sums going round in my head) by walking to the dump on the Seeds. I thought how I longed to back off, have just two weeks before we go to Scotland grubbing about here, tidying and adjusting. I have taken on far too many engagements – usual feature of the autumn; one fills up the diary during the summer doldrums. Yet each one is income, of course. I have written two articles this week, each at £1000, and tonight go (unpaid) to the Cambridge Union to debate – press impartiality – I'm in favour of it – with Max Clifford (!) and Simon Jenkins.

I would feel myself, just, capable of handling this – even the boredom, but this morning managed to get a hand-mirror to illuminate this strange spot at the top of my head which looked sinisterly dark pink, if not red. Special hypochondria cramp set in. Now I have to go and collect my things for a drive to Cambridge via Andy Wood, for the Union debate.

Garden House   *Monday, 29 November*

A very cold, clear day. Our undulant 'virus' is still around, and Jane coughed continuously for the latter half of the night. Our sex life is somewhat dormant at present. *That* was the true miracle – and to think that at the time I couldn't really recognise it! Last night, watched the second half of *To Play the King*. Ian Richardson so good[1] ... the scenes in the Commons made me wistful and nostalgic. 'You can never go back,' Jane said. But how wonderful just to walk into the Chamber after Christmas. Can *anything* happen? Yes it can. My energy *is* down. And I am

---

[1] Ian Richardson had earlier played in *House of Cards*, also by Michael Dobbs and also with a Westminster background.

creaky. But nowhere near 'par' for my age yet of course. There is still enough potential to respond to a boost.

This coming year I had planned on, virtually, a sabbatical. I don't know if I would just get fossilised. But such a relief to move away from deadlines and 'engagements'.

But in the familiar phrase, 'I can't afford it.' It's not just the pressure of tax demands, but it is simply grossly irresponsible to pass up £300,000+.[1]

Just down here it's a full-time occupation, never going to London at all, to keep my cars reasonable; 'polishing' them one at a time (at present I am working on the Buick); and the garden – especially over here – reasonably under control.

So next year we must keep sections 'blocked-off'. It will be the only way. So as to accommodate both 'work' and 'recharging'. It is a bore, the Jimmy expedition,[2] as it blights the start of the year, but it is necessary I fear.

Saltwood   *Tuesday, 30 November*

I went over after tea to shut the drive gates of Garden House, and on the way back I looked at the dark outline of the Mains, the Santé wall. My open prison. I am not ready to stand back yet. But I am nervous of *using up time* – even when, e.g., 'polishing' the Buick – because I dread that suddenly, I may 'go'.

Saltwood   *Saturday, 4 December*

Blustery and soaking. When I woke up the first thing that came in was the failure of the 25/30 to sell at Brooks's. Cars are just unsaleable – quite soon they are going to be unsaleable at *any*

---

[1] He had been offered this sum for the book and newspaper serial rights to a second volume of *Diaries*.
[2] Sir James Goldsmith, 'founder of industrial, commercial and financial enterprises', had invited the Clarks for a holiday on his Mexican estate at Cuixmala.

price, like 'yachts' (scope for an article here, tying in with 'buying value' for restoration that will never be undertaken again). Yesterday I went round Sotheby's giant Christmas sale – a large Turkey farm, I said.[1] Really the only nice car there was the 12/50 Alvis 2-seater. Some incredible black Mercedes 7-series – you could visualise them sweeping up the foothills of Berchtesgaden – but totally 'what's the point?' unless you are buying 'input'. But a certain nostalgia emanated from the great planes: the Lancaster, of course; and the Lightning. Did I see a TSR2 there? (Never forget what he did, Denis Healey, posing as affable and bluff, actually a nasty old thing.[2]) And of course the V-bombers Victor and Vulcan. I watched, by chance, the film of the Vulcans taking off. We seem to have come down an awful long way since then. Another quarter step downward from the heyday of the Spithead Review.

And last night with news of the Princess of Wales, so enchanting and clean and emblematic, 'standing down'.[3] Forced out by the rival and relentless pressure and undermining of 'the Prince's Party'. I put a call through to Andrew Neil – he was abroad, didn't respond. Then spoke to Jonathan Holborow – he totally agreed with my line – it's the end of monarchy. The Queen Mother will be dead in five years' time – who will we be left with?

Shore Cottage   *Wednesday, 22 December*

Christmas marks the end, and the beginning of 'our' year, and already since getting here I have been 'unwound' and contemplative.

---

[1] Taking place at the RAF Museum, Hendon, north London.
[2] Cancelled in the April 1965 Budget, when Denis Healey was Defence Secretary in Harold Wilson's government. AC considered the TSR2 a British warplane that was in advance of anything else in the West. Two prototypes survive, but not at Hendon.
[3] Princess Diana, her marriage to the Prince of Wales in tatters, announced that she wanted a break from the stress of public life.

A pleasing journey, with just the right amount of 'challenge'. I ended up in the ditch just out of Altnaharra pine woods on the Tongue road. How? Most odd. I took my eyes off for one second, laughing and joking with Jane and next thing I know we were bouncing about on the verge, snow going in all directions. Jane screaming.

A kindly fisherman (*most* providentially) soon put in an appearance in a Japanese 4WD and pulled me out backwards (with, thank God, a very slight gradient) and I was none the worse except for a broken or bent o/s wheel trim. We still managed, just, to get to Eriboll before the light faded.

The first part of our journey was mainly, to all intents and purposes, *under water*, and we were one hour behind schedule at the 'Welcome Break'. But held to the old times thereafter and v pleasing at Gleneagles (now preferable to Cromlix) with room 302, a black pianist at dinner who played 'Stormy Weather', 'Smoke …' etc.

Boxing Day

Very cold, all the roads have frozen hard, in to its ridges and the puddles are solid translucent grey. We went beachcombing from Whales Corner and, unbelievably, bathed in the glass-like loch, in the low sun (we have bathed from there before in the summer).

I have now been here five days and each day have taken two hours on the hill – in one form or another – and then one fine evening meal, an early night and 10 hours' sleep.

Something cautions me away from *Diaries II – Towering Inferno II* etc. Also I'm not quite ready to get locked into the Great Work[1] preferring to pick, still, and read round it (greatly enjoying *Beaverbrook* by A.J.P. Taylor at present). So my considered

---

[1] What would become *The Tories: Conservatives and the Nation State, 1922–77.*

favourite, at present, is to take up Jonathan Holborow's offer and try and make something of it.[1]

It will be hard work; discuss Tuesday morning; lunch every Tuesday at the Beefsteak, to get the atmosphere. Reading all the papers. First draft Wednesday morning. More Thursday and usually Friday (are faxes portable, by the way?). Allow six weeks' hols – two at Christmas, two at Whitsun, three in August. To some extent I will be on call, which I don't like.

Tuesday, 28 December

Sleety and gales in the night.

I set off up the Creaggan at lunch. I thought briefly, I can't tell why, of 'x' and sadly – though philosophically, not achingly as on previous visits. It is over. And I became sentimental and composed a letter, which I doubt that I will ever send.

Then I said a prayer to God. How rare it is to do this nowadays! I thanked him for 'seeing' me through; said that I was still ready, if it was possible, to make one more try to fetch the sword from the lake's bed. I prayed for him to keep me fit – as so manifestly I still am – and also for a tiny heir, before I am too old for the 'generation gap' to be happily bridged in their early childhood when I can impart wisdom. I must face the fact that I will be seventy now, at least, before I can really start talking and playing; and that I may die while they are still at school.

On the way back I stopped and spoke to James – somewhat *désoeuvré* around all his great machines. We talked of weapons and the incredible concession for the very big guns, and tank armour. His knowledge is so extensive, his recall so immediate. It makes me sad that, really, we did so little together while I was at Procurement. One more sadness at being excluded from the House as it reassembles, warm and enclosing in the great interior of the Palace of Westminster, which 'never sleeps'.

---

[1] A weekly political column in the *Mail on Sunday*.

Shore Cottage   *Thursday, 30 December*

For the first time this holiday I am not tired out in the evenings.
In spite of fiddling around with wooding in the Jeep etc most
of the day and ending with 1 hour helping shovel out the gravel
into the trenches around 'Jane's shed'. Ready now to move back
to the Mains and start tackling things. (Peggy's 'envelope' arrived
this afternoon, so thin that one thought it had been sent empty.
Only the faxes enclosed as 'too many cards to decide which to
send'. – *Really*!! The epitome of primitiveness. Pure domestic
servant 'left in charge'.)

I am reasonably calm about the year in prospect. But yet a
little uneasy when, flicking over the pages of the green diary I
come upon August. Supposing things are 'no better' then. Will I
just be that much older, that much further removed from the
centre of things?

One of my great preoccupations remains to put off old age. It
has started to show – very slightly – in my hands. The cross vein
remains in place, and several pale death spots are appearing. My
neck is sometimes really quite embarrassingly thick – even
between the video of the Alpine and the start of the books-of-
the-year interview with Jack and Jill.[1]

Up here, at least, I drink very little. Nor do I want or need to.

Shore Cottage   *New Year's Eve*

I am now fully 'programmed' to return on Sunday. My mind is
rambling round tasks and preoccupations and objectives and I
am neither so sleepy (in spite of walking the Arnaboll round
today, starting by going over the ridge) nor so easily relaxed/

---

[1] AC means John McCarthy – held hostage in Beirut – and Jill Morrell. Their joint
memoir was called *Some Other Rainbow*. The three of them appeared together on
the Sky book programme.

comatose. We have been here ten days, and much fabric has been repaired. But if we stay longer we will no longer be on holiday, not even 'crofting' so much as 'in residence' with all the cares and duties that then start to close in on one.

Some things make me sad – I've always felt sadness at Eriboll, though really nothing like the dreadful Highland melancholy of '85, '86, '87. Julie, Jane and I were standing round the church, talking of how to protect and refurbish it; there was mention of a christening. That evening, helping James with his 'bucket' for the Hymac [digger] he said he would be 34 next year (in two months). Sadly I realise I will never (unless God is exceptionally kind) live to see my grandchildren marry. Will I ever have any? We have this slightly unnatural existence at the moment, Jane and I. The boys grown-up and (in theory) settled, but no Grandparental duties.

1994

A day spent with chores and various, before heading south on a great drive tomorrow. There is always so much to do at Eriboll. Some things have been left undone for six, seven years. And the *Maid of Morwen* still lies on her side, her entrails slowly rotting.

Just as the light faded I walked with Jamie, to Birkett Foster.[1] He is much, much better. And sensible. He might get married this year, to Julie. Laughed when I said, 'breed, anyway'. He was realistic about the onset of old age, concurred with my analogy of the hourglass triangle.

I have been less affected by depression than ever before on this sojourn. But tonight I am low.

Thursday, 20 January

Today, in contrast, I woke fresh and felt reflectively confident on Indian tea in the kitchen. Why? Nothing has really changed except one's mood. What has caused this? A good night, I suppose, and waking with an erection.

Everything seemed to come to a head today.

I'm completely impotent – *why*? I'm sitting in my 'romper' suit; all I've had is Indian tea and a piece of shortbread. I don't seem to have done anything at all and it's already 12.30+. I took calls from Dobbie and a very long one from the BBC about a programme on the Windsors.

---

[1] AC owned a small seascape by the Victorian painter Myles Birkett Foster, with rocks like those at Eriboll.

This piece for the *Mail on Sunday* hangs over me; it is a permanent blight, from which there is no relief (except, I assume, in August when everyone else is 'off' and the weather is hot and foul and muggy and one becomes strangely ill). I am so short of time; and yet I do nothing, it seems with what I have got. The endless pressure of paperwork – now totally out of control again, as I 'cleared' the Green Room table and dispersed the various piles into either/or the dining room or Green Room.

Accounts, Taxation and VAT, i.e. the very core of paperwork, are in total confusion. I appear to be in an identical situation to that prevailing (say) ten years ago when Jane and I would have great convulsive sort-outs – grading things by year, all the Kafkaesque brainwashing of 92–93 is *called* 93–94 (or is it 91–92?). Pile after pile after pile. On top of this, and having no secretary or even will have a secretary, I have to do all the other stuff about *Diaries*, speeches, toadies writing about how much they admired my father etc etc. Only interesting thing that still surfaces and, I suppose I must admit, gratifies me, is that I don't get any 'hate' mail.

Small wonder that I am strained to shrieking point. Jane said I was being really awful, never been worse. As for income, typically, it never matches outgoings. Yes there is a new contract for *Diaries* II, but for some reason Sissons has negotiated only a £25 on signature instead of £50,000 as last time.

I'm still owed driblets and droplets from past contracts and welchers, but it's an endless labour 'chasing' them.

Yesterday I had lunch with a 'tittles', Julia Llewellyn-Smith.[1] Really rather nice, long clean fair hair, *no* eye make-up (is this the new thing?). I was greeted – without giving my name – by the maître at the Savoy Grill (as last time with Jonathan and Dobbie), which is good for one's ego. I've no idea what 'tittles' thought, although she conversed giftedly. But I was irritated by the way she seemed to have had lots of boy-friends (her age 17). Just like 'x'. I've had it.

[1] Julia Llewellyn-Smith, feature writer on *The Times*.

The previous evening as I drove over Westminster Bridge and saw the Palace I felt so depressed. So utterly abandoned. Like when I see TV shots of a crowded chamber.

Only mildly cheering thing was David Dudley speaking about RREC matters; said he'd been given my *Diaries* by his son – familiar pattern – and was angry at my continued preoccupation with growing old – 'someone as fit and athletic as you ...' This sort of remark gives me encouragement.

Saltwood   *Friday, 28 January*

A clear cold day, with the high winds dying down. The great sheds are going up. At last we are getting enough *covered space*. I am brushing them down inside and cleaning the window panes. Wood is the only material for sheds and these have wooden floors also.

I am depressed at being excluded. You only really know what's going on if you are inside the Commons. Although I suppose as a peer I would have access. I miss it dreadfully. When I was there living on physical reserves, I spent these, all but, but accumulated a huge intellectual bank. This is slipping through my fingers fast and in a year's time I will be left with nothing. If 'Scott' clears me, and if JM survives I suppose there is a faint chance of New Year '95. But after that I'd have to wait for the next Conservative government even for the offer of a 'K' – at the age of 76.

Saltwood   *Sunday, 30 January*

The wretched JM is under appalling pressure still. Right across the front page of the *Sunday Times* a terrible photo of him at the Leeds dinner, hands clasped behind his head held over the plate.[1] Could have been doing a Bush in Japan. And the usual row – extended now to include total non-starters like Redwood[2] – of leadership contestants. What *did* I do? Why did I not consult and reflect? Jane did give me a let-out when she said it's really almost too late ... (to serve notice). My calculations were entirely justifiable – not included in Government, boredom of being in opposition, funking losing seat, drainingness of hung parliament. Could be last chance to 'book' peerage. But if I had really got away, walked, talked with my voices I suppose that the sword in the lake would/might have held me.

Saltwood   *Thursday, 3 February*

And now Pin[3] has got cancer. Of the prostate. Perfectly ghastly. How long have I got? It's hard to know what is right – straight into the hands of surgeons or hold out – and when it comes just GO. Force yourself over the edge on the Creaggan. I fear the latter is probably right – but would one have the courage? It would be like turning the gas on, or pipe from the exhaust; it's no good changing your mind when you get drowsy. Then it's too late.

---

[1] John Major was speaking to the Leeds Chamber of Commerce. Whatever the photograph *appeared* to show, Major was particularly relaxed that evening. Anthony Seldon, in his study of the Major government, wrote, 'The audience appreciated his spontaneity and his wit, and he spoke well ... at one point later in the evening he doubled up and was photographed head in hands, an image to be endlessly recycled in the press thereafter as evidence of a man at the end of his tether.'
[2] John Redwood, MP for Wokingham since 1987; Welsh Secretary since 1993.
[3] Colin Clark, AC's younger brother, also known as Col.

Saltwood   *Friday, 4 February*

I was slouching in my chair, suffering from toothache. Both my back wisdom teeth have disintegrated into blackened stumps or stalagmites, they hurt at intervals, but Bertie Arbeid is always within reach. But in Mexico ... I dread some agonisingly expensive, strange dentist, AIDS-infected needle, the pressure of a long return flight. Ergo, I must contact Bertie on Monday. The phone rang, and it was Dobbie dissatisfied – inevitably – with lack of 'impact' in article about Special Relationship. The money is wonderful, but their demands. The 'jar' in journalist is going to make it impossible. We'll see.

Then I thought I ought to help Jane clear out her studio, the old sewing room. We came across a cache of photographs, everything seemed so much fresher in those days and we all looked young and vital. Max/George [jackdaws] was teeny, Tom was teeny (I am worried for Tom; he is slow and down on energy and sleeps an awful lot. Then, too, the Mexican trip hangs ...). There are photos of the Yeos, and Mrs Cloake, and Peggy looking so smart at 'Teas', and Christopher and Geoffrey[1] coming down in the Cloud III. Also my first, and I think, only 'letter to my constituents' between elections in 1974 with a photo on the cover taken from election night that February when I must have had the highest quotient of adrenalin ever running through my veins.

I suppose I will be remembered for the *Diaries* (*still* at No 2 in the *Evening Standard*).

Jimmy Goldsmith's, Cuixmala, Mexico   *Wednesday, 16 February*

In the swimming pool pavilion, with its straw roof, by Jimmy's pool, itself drained and refilled with salt water every day.

---

[1] Christopher (aka 'Daisy') Selmes, a friend of many years standing, who had made a fortune in the City, and his boyfriend Geoffrey; both were to die of AIDS.

Everything is oversize, mattresses, deckchairs, urns, parasols. Lovely chevron clay tiling on the pool floor. The staircase down is pure Alma-Tadema, out of Port Lympne, with many a coign of vantage and beautiful pots of blooms so bright and vulgar that, as Jane says, you need acrylic to do them justice and the delicate box of water-colours is inadequate. The whole level of sumptuocity is magnif-icent – separate 'villas' for the guests cunningly sited within the flower and jungle hillside of the condominium. Makes Jeffrey Archer's 'apartment' look like a journalistic bolthole.[1]

Jimmy is magnificent, a philosopher-king. Eloquently he expounds on the devilish dangers of the GATT, the indignities of Maastricht. Also staying are Ed Epstein (writer and critic)[2]; Nancy Kissinger (beautiful and attractive style); Toby (Jimmy's keen young gofer in Hong Kong), Michel (?), president of the Bradley Foundation and his *much* younger wife Mary-Jo. He is just a little hunted-and-shunted in manner; she is a sporty young gymnast/swimmer.

Last night hit it off again with Kissinger[3] – but a sad moment. He was talking about my 'getting back in'.

'How old are you?'

'65.'

Incredulous. Spluttered. '55?'

'No, 65.'

Just stared, in silence. I am always delighted when I impress, and K made it clear that he thought I should be active in the Conservative Party, 'which is so short of strong men'.

But of course for most people 'age 65', it isn't just difficult, it's unthinkable.

Ah well, we'll see.

---

[1] Jeffrey Archer, author, former MP (Louth) and deputy chairman of the Conservative Party, had a high-level flat with panoramic views across the Thames to Westminster.

[2] Edward Jay Epstein, who made his name for himself with a study of Lee Harvey Oswald; currently at work on a life of Armand Hammer, the oil millionaire.

[3] Henry Kissinger, US Secretary of State, 1973–77 (under Nixon and Ford); and Nancy, his second wife.

On Friday evening young people turned up, with a coal-black band imported from New Orleans. They were *so* chic they were virtually incredible. 'Chamber music,' I said – which for some reason went down badly.

An attractive young American blonde was seated beside me. She was intense, so politically correct it wasn't true. Got into a 'state' about Bosnia etc, especially the way Muslim women had been raped.

I had a great scare the following day when (after taking off from the grass strip in the Merlin, just, JUST, our flight attendant frequently consulted not only the map, but the manual (!)). At the BA desk in Mexico City a stylish rather classier version of 'x' materialised 'to look after us'. We hit it off immediately, and she started to 'audition'. Jane, naturally, was livid, and put on the special strained expression she wears when she knows I fancy someone nearby.

Saltwood   *Sunday, 27 February*

Just put the phone down talking to Pin.

Poor Pin! It's too awful, the slow Chinese torture of the big cancer operation – like Lloyd's, but with your life, not just your fortune at stake. He says the surgeons are 'so good'.

'How do you know?' I asked.

'They are so confident.'

'Well Ronny Cornwell[1] was confident, when he was selling insurance, doesn't mean a thing,' I said.

There is so much to do. I shone the torch over the SS100 (moved up into the new shed today) and got a quick evocation of Oxford, the Morris Garages where the cars were lined up on opposite sides of that great shed, and I used to go and wax it

---

[1] The father of David Cornwell (the writer John le Carré) had been revealed as a confidence trickster by his son in the novel *A Perfect Spy* (1986).

most evenings, and a canny Irishman with black curly hair
offered to drive it in the TT for me. And I thought then I had
absolutely nothing to do or read or watch over. I was waiting for
the next edition of the *Autocar*. Now I really don't think I will
finish it all before I die. It's part of getting old, is it, accumulating
more and more pressing memories?

Garden House   *Friday, 4 March*

Fine and bright, though cold wind. Spring now due to arrive
any moment, with all its demands out of doors, and no progress
whatever in interior management. First task in less than three
weeks, which means dining room, top landing (Jane's 'studio') all
cleared, Great Hall spruced and garden – or Bailey at least –
reasonably orderly.

I am demi-listless. Last night the 'paperback' publication
dinner at the Groucho – itself low-ceilinged and dirty-carpeted
– and I was sub-lionised. I sat next to the manager of W.H.
Smith. Pleasant, intelligent, spoke sensibly about books, my
book indeed, and why le Carré was so much more 'the real
thing' than Jeffrey Archer. He was luke-warm though about
Diaries II (as indeed was Roger at Waterstone's). Said, 'Don't do
it. Go back in, instead.' When people say things like that it makes
me really wistful. Driving up last week I had a nostalgia/fantasy.
Get adopted; fight a really wild campaign, just win! 'If he can
win a by-election, then he will win a General Election.' The
point being, there is *no one* with my charisma and intelligence
whatsoever in the House of Commons at present. I have all the
experience I need; I am good, now, at the bar. Confident and
level-headed. In 18 months it could be mine.

On Tuesday there was a letter from 'x' at Brooks's. Began 'Dear
Alan'. Not friendly, but long. She's made a real study of *Sir
Gawain*, and how apposite it was!

Saltwood   *Monday, 7 March*

Incredibly tired after a whole day consumed ('wasted' one could almost say) by Walden.[1] Car came at 10.20, didn't get back here until 4.40 – nearly six hours.

I sparkled. They got rid of Tom Clarke and Alec Carlile[2] and we gossiped, Brian, the editor and the producer and I in the upstairs corner 'Hospitality Suite'. Brian is still, of course, a manqué politician. He knows the real thing. And once again I thought 'if only' and 'I wonder'. 'Well, who can lead them? Who *is* there?' Jane kept saying at breakfast. I nearly said 'Me', but didn't. A little later, in the correspondence section was a note saying 'Alan Clark should be Prime Minister'. This evening I thought really my only chance, I suppose, is for Michael Howard to die, and for me to *force* them to let me take his place. ACHAB.

Garden House   *Tuesday, 15 March*

I am not in good shape. I am sleepy and my bones – joints ache. Poor old Peter Harding has resigned, just walked into it and Bienvenida Buck setting things up.[3] Every week a 'scandal'. But it, and the comments, and the letters all remind me of a time that is past. I will never again have a mistress. I could have had a huge rapport (which we both knew and Jane did also) with the 'hostess' at BA at Mexico. But I will never have the opportunity now. Ministers' room in the Lords, directors' ante-room in

---

[1] Brian Walden, TV presenter and journalist (*Weekend World* and *Walden*), previously a Labour MP for two Birmingham seats 1964–77.

[2] Tom Clarke, MP (Labour) Monklands West since 1983 (Coatbridge & Airdrie, June 1982–83); Alex Carlile, Labour MP 1983–88; Liberal Democrat since 1988 (Montgomery).

[3] Marshal of the Royal Air Force, Sir Peter Harding, Chief of the Air Staff since 1988. Bienvenida Perez-Blanco had briefly married (as his second wife in 1990, marriage dissolved 1993) Sir Antony Buck (MP for Colchester, 1961–83; Colchester North 1983–92).

Lloyds PLC (*that* was a short-lived fantasy). Archer living on his own, with secretaries, just doesn't get 'around'. And if it means you have a frightful nemesis at about 82–84 *so what*? Better really to 'go out' than become a figure of pity.

Then all my 'friends' have abandoned me. Only dear Soames was on the answering machine this morning, and still keeps in touch. Jonathan [Aitken] is having me at his dinner for Richard Nixon on Thursday, but is correct on other topics.[1] Richard – silent; the PM – silent; 'Tristan' quite openly trying to shift the Scott blame on to me as the 'direction of the Inquiry's finding starts to emerge', and winding up toadies like Bruce Anderson to say as much.

Politically, I'm now really a non-person. And at least half of me wants to go North – for good. 'Care and maintenance only.'

I've been driving different cars, and enjoying them. The 1914 Ghost – so lovely; how incredible it would be with the 'Nicholosi' body on it! And then the Buick Roadmaster – the Todd Buick. Quite extraordinary and unworn. The only new car I've got except the Continental Turbo R. But I can't do this until the place is orderly, and inventorised. So that when I (or anyone else) come back I have only to stretch out my hand and find it/pick it up.

Finally there is the problem of dear Tip. He is determined to leave the Army, which formerly he loved so much. Got down by the new tendency – the bookkeeping and being wankily career conscious, sneaking a 'late luncheon', going 'classless' etc. He's no idea what he's going to do … 'travel'. Won't get a pension or a golden handshake. But his face is a little crumpled, and unhappy. Today Malcolm Rifkind is going round – with David Hart (strange ménage).[2] They are looking at it[3] to see about selling it

---

[1] Jonathan Aitken had published a well-received biography of former US President Nixon.

[2] Malcolm Rifkind, MP for Edinburgh Pentlands since 1974; Defence Secretary since 1992; David Hart had been an *éminence grise* among special advisers, originally to Margaret Thatcher, now to John Major and soon to Michael Portillo.

[3] The headquarters of the Household Cavalry.

off, to Jews, to make into offices. Andrew, partly because he is
marginalised and out of favour, is deputed to show them the
men's bedrooms. Don't despair, I said, that's all politicians are
interested in.

I asked, what about the horses? How can you move out of
those lovely stables? Ah no, a 'report' is being prepared at the
moment (by a *sailor*) on possible 'options' for reducing the
cavalry strength – or even getting rid of it altogether.

This, as so many things at present; the toadying to Delors, the
impossibility of getting offences against the person punished, the
politic and contemptible appeasement of Ireland. With each
fresh atrocity they get up and bleat about '… will not alter our
determination to …' (now 'search for peace'; formerly 'crush
terrorism').

It is an extraordinary interlude, the Thatcher decade. Now we
are back with Mr Wilson, or worse. The moment will come
when I have to say this (so to that extent I am fortunate still to
have the column in which to say it) – but not just quite yet.

Having been loyal through thick and thin, all the scapegoating
etc, what will finally cause me to turn is that they are leading
the Party into a barren defile where it is going to be *annihilated*.

Saltwood   *Tuesday, 29 March*

Jane has gone on a 'massive' shopping round – Glass Co,
Geerings, possibly Canterbury map shop. It's really rather
pleasant and relaxing being left in the empty home.

I would like to get out and play out-of-doors. But here I am
two years out of retirement and chained to the paper, and the
desks, more than ever. (Just reread an interview with Robin Day
who has said on the difference between capital and income –
'with high capital you are a free man; with high earnings you are
a slave'.) And tomorrow the Coutts team are coming down –
like tea for the IMF.

Garden House   *Thursday, 31 March*

I am low, and feel that things are slipping away from me.

A re-run of November '90, but without, of course, the platform or perch.

The week's papers have been blazing – Major finished, end is nigh, not a friend left, sooner he goes the better. Sterling crisis – you name it.

Jonathan H talked for an hour on Tuesday. He'd had lunch with Jeremy[1] who gave him 'the whole thing is over' spiel; then that afternoon JM did poorly in the Commons and Marlow bagged a headline with his you-must-go declamation. Dobbie got more and more apocalyptic – finally calling at 9-ish p.m.

I booked a meeting with Richard – 'the Chief Whip will come and have tea at Albany at 3.30 p.m.'

Later in the evening Soames phoned – part II – and said it was a shambles, Baker was taking people on one side and saying 'JM was dead in the water' etc. I asked him if he wanted to be chairman of the Party and he said yes. Why anyone wants that job beats me, but anything can happen ... if I could afford it myself I'd grab it.

But (later) when I put this to Richard he said 'Nick who?' 'Oh, give him a director-general to pay the wages,' I said, and got the only real chuckle of the afternoon. RR was reasonably communicative. Admitted that the only real danger would be a Cabinet welching; a 'difficult' meeting at which one or more people expressed reservations.

Quite.

Richard was amiable, almost Gow-voiced in his insistence on a 'dinner' soon after Easter. But of what clout does he actually dispose? At one point I said, 'You must find something for me to do.' Did he even acknowledge? I will return to this next time.

---

[1] Jeremy Hanley (MP for Richmond & Barnes since 1983), currently Armed Forces Minister, but in the summer Cabinet reshuffle would succeed Norman Fowler as chairman of the Conservative Party.

But this morning I have been trying desperately to keep Jonathan Holborow from 'plunging in'. Apparently M. Heseltine was imploring Dobbie last night to take his side – 'on his knees'. Perhaps mistakenly, I said to Jonathan, *you* see him; make your own mind up. You're in the strongest position of the Sundays, not in anyone's 'camp', not concerned with personalities.

They put the whole thing in place immediately. So that while I was talking to M Howard (he, too, took my call immediately!) – also very splendidly said, 'tape the interview and run that.' It may have been a miscalculation; Jonathan H could be overcome as he is still, in one sense, politically *naïf*. At present I've got calls in to Bob Worcester (the polls are crucial in this) and David Davis. Tristan is no longer friendly, and I see no point in showing my hand.

My handwriting is terribly disturbed.

Garden House   *Sunday, 3 April*

The papers are full of Heseltine – ludicrous, this, nearly four years on. No mention of me anywhere except at No 2 in the paperback lists. I'm not interested in the book, in writing, at the moment. I don't 'return calls' from Orion. I am desperate, though, for peace. I came over here, and it's not bad, but too many cabinets and dog-earedness and dust. The great rug, which I had on my floor in MoD and which David Franzes[1] charged £700 (I seem to recall) to clean is fading fast.

While it is true that I can't bear being OUT, it's also true that I seem to be wasting my time so much here so that if I *did* 'get' anything there would be a mountainous backlog. If I can just establish the infrastructure then I can leave a framework of instruction – a recommendation to my successors, a note for my

---

[1] London dealer.

literary executors. How old was Papa when he was fussing about this – 74, 75?

Now too late to book the Buick in at a discount to train up to Eriboll. *Why* is May so dreadfully congested? Poor Col sitting in a chair with a rug on his knees. Was quite funny about the Prince of Wales whose Aston broke down in the Brompton Road – 'this kind of thing always happens to me ...' and 'just my luck'.

'He's a prince, for God's sake, married to one of the world's most beautiful women, with two lovely boys, what's all the whingeing about?'

Garden House   *Easter Monday, 4 April*

Today, I think for the first time, I actually found myself accepting the reality of defeat.

The old analogy – with the Reich in 1943–5 – is less valid than Vichy France in 1940. I have now to go through a Pétainist period. Really quite hard to see what will extricate me. No one rings any more – except people who want to pick my brains on the cheap, or also want to put me on their programme and lift its status – for £35.

Anyway I am going to get everything in order – and then I will be free. I can walk out – but without going to 'another woman' (although, of course, it will be suspected that I have). Where do I go to? I would really prefer Scotland, but I suppose it has to be Bratton, as that's the only place, absurdly enough, that belongs to me. I might start in Zermatt, in fact.

During the night there were *five* interruptions: Tom (urinated twice on the white carpet); then Lëhni urinated in my bathroom, went out re-Thompsoned; then Tom had to go out Thompsoned; then Hannah met me on the stairs, took her down – she Thompsoned. Finally Tom hyper-ventilated, looked into the Yard briefly, settled for the Green Room.

Jane, I may say, made absolutely no effort whatever to cope with any of these episodes except the first when she ably removed most of the stain using rubber gloves and Jif.

So this morning I am utterly exhausted. Had to come straight over here after EMT to type some letters. Now I'm back here, very depressed, nothing on the machine, and will spend 40 minutes or so 'Windolening' the plate glass before shuffling back across to the Mains.

Garden House   *Tuesday, 5 April*

I was over in the Great Hall study with Jane, looking for some of my father's articles which I need for 'Michael Delon' (sounds quite scholarly in his approach). I came across some tiny pocket engagement books of my grandfather,[1] *very* sparingly entered: 'out', 'shooting', 'Inverary', 'Mrs MacArthur to lunch'. Some are clearly future engagements, clear (if the word can be considered applicable) records.

In August of 1914, the week of the great seismic tilt, when the earth plates buckled, they were sailing off the west coast of Scotland – 'Oban', 'Poolewe'. About the 14th, they took the train to Euston, spent the night in their London house (visited v rarely) in Berkeley Square (come to think of it, all the satinwood stuff must have been bought for this, from Malletts – just round the corner) the next day took the train to Sudbourne.[2] Stayed there (shooting) all through the Battle of the Marne. What a style! Three large and expensive houses (plus the lodge at Poolewe and the villa at Cap Ferrat), the yacht, hordes and hordes of domestics.

My own structure still shadows it – but with no support whatever. Like the Royal Navy in the 1970s, compared with the Grand Fleet.

---

[1] Kenneth McKenzie Clark, who inherited wealth and enjoyed it to the full.
[2] The Clark estate in Suffolk.

Garden House   *Sunday, 10 April*

This is, as it were, the birthday-boy entry – next week is 'a horrible' and I won't be back here Thursday morning.

Recently I have been thinking about an escape plan. It goes like this:

Put Saltwood on 'care and maintenance' ('it is already on care and maintenance', Jane says.)

Reduce the contents virtually to modern museum level – bare, clear walls – except for the Red Library and the dining room (in mothballs for 'crash' meeting). Garden House ticking over warmly for a visit when necessary.

Look for a low 18th-century stone house with nicely proportioned rooms in Perthshire – 200 acres for wintering the Eriboll flock, a good chunk of hill and a nice black-spate salmon river for Jane to fish in. Plenty of outbuildings. I even fantasise about getting Bill Holdings to put up one of his sheds there. That way we would be near enough to James and Julie, especially as they are now talking of 'winklers'. It would mean selling Seend for Tip.

I've always said I'll never move, and probably won't. Lord Astor sold up Hever, went to Scotland and died of cancer very soon afterwards. It would mark the transition into an old man I suppose from (*passim* today's *Sunday Times*) 'much-missed in the corridors of power'. A final abandonment of the sword and helmet. Even as I write that I realise I can't do it. But pleasant to fantasise.

Albany   *Monday, 11 April*

Although cold at Saltwood it is warm and springlike here; St James's Park burgeoning with yellowy-green buds. Why does this always make me so nostalgic? In recent years, of course, because I have associated it with 'x' 'going off' somewhere (I think no agony compared with the agony while I was on my second trip to Oman in May of '91). Also because I have habitually likened it to the preference of *not* being able to enjoy the countryside. Now, although free, I seem to have completely filled May, again. This must never be allowed to happen in the future.

As I crossed Westminster Bridge I felt the usual agonies of being banned from the precincts. Then I walked into Wiltons – in 'Grunge' – and there was Franko[1] sitting on the bankette. I lunched with him and we gossiped. In came Heseltine (!) and a PA who was *all over him*. He was in a brand new dark grey suit, white silk shirt, hair coiffed (I mean Teasy-Weasy coiffed) from behind. Loathsome.

Frank is intelligent and, doubtless for that reason, we depressed ourselves. Then walking out to go to Chatham House library I ran into Bruce Anderson! He was fluent and radical. Make David Owen Foreign Secretary etc etc. He doesn't give Major much chance. But it emerges Tristan is still 'seeing' him (and giving bad advice).

Saltwood					*Wednesday, 20 April*

Fearfully beleagured by pressures – which have 'got to me' that I feel extremely tired and don't see any sunlit uplands. I sit at the table in the Green Room – absurdly laden, now, with the various trays. Behind me several Pisa towers of sundry newsprint, car sale catalogues, important incoming letters interleaved (I don't doubt) and every kind of unexpected document I've beside my chair and on the bookcase.

The speaking engagements are disorderly. Some acceptances lurk, unrecorded on the chart. Fresh-faced undergraduates

---

[1] Frank Johnson, deputy editor of the *Sunday Telegraph* and former parliamentary sketch-writer.

telephone 'to confirm'; what's the use of that? I appear to be simultaneously double-booked (sic) for CUCA and OUCA, just as tomorrow I am double-booked for Simon Heffer and David Evans.[1] Tonight I allowed myself to be booked for a 'Five Alive' show that I ran a pilot for Alastair Campbell.[2] At the time I thought I was to be booked on to a panel (say alternate weeks). Boring, because from the hours of 12 to 2 a.m., but maybe £4000 for 6 weeks? But it has already degenerated into a *chat* show (without even Alastair chairing it), which I have vowed not to do.

I had a bad night, or at least woke early, worrying about funds as much as anything. 'Where are the jobs coming from?' I hung around in the Lodge for the youths on bicycles who have been emptying the milk bottles. Caught some and photographed them, though was not cool enough. Now I feel sickish, terribly congested, and for some reason my toothache in lower left has returned.

Yesterday evening, after [dog] training (which did not go well; I was distracted by a pretty young woman with a nervous Alsatian), I walked down the valley in fading light, which I used to when I was living here and before going away to Rye. I thought: I suppose to a detached observer at least, my life in terms of potential, is over. But instead of pleasing open days I have in front of me a Matto Grosso of paperwork and filing which I must try and get in order before I depart.

Nixon had a stroke today. 81. He can understand, but he can't talk. The worst of all, because so soon they start talking about you in the room, in *audio oblique*. The days are lovely now, longer daylight than in August. It would be so lovely to be meandering about outside, like one used to at Seend. Will one ever be free of *will we ever*?

---

[1] Simon Heffer, deputy editor *The Spectator* since 1991, about to rejoin the *Daily Telegraph* as deputy editor (he had been a political and leader writer there previously); David Evans, businessman and former chairman of Luton Town football club, MP for Welwyn Hatfield since 1987.

[2] AC recorded at the time (February 1994) that the panel included Tessa Jowell, 'who is apparently a Labour MP [Dulwich, since 1992] but I thought was a "liberal" Conservative'.

Monday, 9 May

Absolutely blind with tension pressures. These last two weeks I haven't even filled in the day diary – never mind the journal. And all against a background of *The Heseltine Assumption*. Poor JM getting in more and more difficulties.

My own schedules are even tighter than in the halcyon days of being a Minister of State at DTI (MDef blighted of course by the angst of my 'double' life). Flailing with the earnings – but no more than a treadmill, just keeping the 'limits' at bay.

Tomorrow up by train to see [Charles] Jerdein at 3 p.m. about selling the Mask (his *client* is raising his bid), which I can't really do.

Sunday, 15 May

I just dare not accept Jerdein's offer for the Mask: $100, plus £265. Would solve all debts. But if I keep it, it will go on generating its protection, I believe.

Albany   *Monday, 16 May*

I had to stop the car (Big Red) in the lay-by just as the M20 ends and nap for 15 minutes, and when I got here I thought – I'm emerging now from my pining for public life. It took a very long time, just as it did to emerge from 'x' with each trough followed by a blip, then slightly lower still until – almost – the yearning is extinct. Helped, I suppose, by thinking that perhaps after all Labour (Blair) will now be the next government. I will, finally, be relegated into the older generation, which I have for so long avoided. Do a full switch, into historian, and do the Tory Party book.

Ritz dining room, Paris[1]   *Sunday, 29 May*

Just drank a delicious glass of orange juice. A very good hotel
(except no tutti slippers in the bathroom). Staff – unusually for
French – courteous and obliging and I had a lovely room on the
6th floor with double windows and balconies looking out over
the roofs.

Oy! What cramped and nifty writing ... A bit apprehensive, I
suppose, though basically dutch, at the Harkess 'story' which has
broken – manically – in the *News of the World* and been, gleefully,
I don't doubt, picked up by the *Sunday Express*. Jane is gamely
meeting me at Manston and I may have to ride from Sandling
to Saltwood in the boot of Big Red.[2] It's really too boring. I
don't enjoy this kind of 'publicity' at all and it has been running
on and off now for a year really. I suppose it may sell some more
books, but expect Orion won't be able to provide demand, just
use the 'subject' to clear their stocks.

A *very* painless way of getting around. About as effortless as
being minister (and without the *longueurs*). Jimmy's plane from
Farnborough; met by a fleet of 'stretched' Mercedes and drove
to the Ritz with Annabel[3] (still great fun, and voluptuous) and
their incredibly bright little son Ben-Ben.

Saltwood   *Tuesday, 14 June*

A lovely evening of high summer – longest day (how quickly it
comes up on one) next weekend. Then it's shedding tail-feathers
and quieter all round.

---

[1] AC was in Paris for Jimmy Goldsmith's 'L'autre Europe' party.
[2] AC arrived in the Goldsmith private jet at Manston. Jane had forced her way
through journalists outside the Saltwood gates, saying she was just going off to do
some shopping. She returned, with AC indeed in the capacious boot of Big Red,
drove straight to the Long Garage; AC did not emerge until they were safely inside.
[3] Lady Annabel Goldsmith, third wife of Sir James Goldsmith.

A certain sense of peace – 'at last'. But there is much talk of a reshuffle after the disasters – but not *that* disastrous – Euro elections.[1]

This is my first *contemplatif* for over two weeks. I was under some pressure – all those journalists and questions [over Harkess]: '… are you going to answer the charges (sic)?' actually assume one's guilt. I couldn't even fill out the Green Diary day-by-day.

I suppose the tide actually turned on 'the' Wednesday. Tristan rang that evening (welchly late, as I said to Jane, but an indication that we had made 'if not port then the lee of the shore').

If there were turning points I would say, Richard Littlejohn aside, *The Times* leader,[2] the *Daily Mirror* dope on Joei and finally the Judy Finnegan show which showed them – thanks to Judy and her husband – *in a poor light*, culminating in a vote when the score was 72–28.

I may even have 'come out ahead' having sold at least another 20,000 paperbacks and, ludicrously, been approached to go into a 'National' Police advertisement scheme (I'm still doubtful about this) with an appearance fee of £25,000 plus (!).

In my present form all really I want to do, though, is to stand back and become a guru-sage.

Wednesday, 22 June

The seat by the moat after EMT. Mid-summer, the anniversary of Barbarossa. This time, fifty-three years ago the whole Eastern Front was ablaze and the YAKs were smouldering carcases,

---

[1] 'Disaster', in hindsight, is too strong a word: the Conservatives held eighteen seats, more than even the most optimistic had forecast. However the Tory share of the vote was the lowest achieved by a major party in a national election in the twentieth century, and in five constituencies Tory majorities were less than 1 per cent.

[2] 'With his *Diaries*, he has written himself into the life of our times with a panache and candour that ranks him next to Boswell or Pepys.' (*The Times*, 10 June 1994).

wing-tip to wing-tip, on the Soviet airfields. But only three years later it was the collapse of Army Group Centre (always one of the strangest failures of nerve of the magnificent German army) and the 'rush' into Poland.

Things have taken a turn for the better for us. So far this week I have been a 'triumph' (*passim* Paul Channon[1]) on *Frost*;[2] then a call from Cdr Aylard[3] saying how interesting the Prince of Wales had found my piece in the *Mail on Sunday*. Selina Scott wants to include me in her next series with Clinton, Murdoch, Pavarotti etc – 'from a woman's point of view'.

We went up to Jimmy's great party. Lovely fun. Everyone was there. And Princess Diana turned up 'for the coffee', looking incredible as always. Isobel Goldsmith sat on my left wearing the most beautiful necklace. 'Do you deal with the Nortons?' I asked. Of course she did. It had come from Nicholas.[4] Opposite me, on Conrad Black's right, sat Jane Wrightsman[5] gone from being blonde to being gypsy black; with tiny birdlike movements of vain, elderly women who are trying to conceal their age.

My 'approval' rating remains high ('four times that of the PM,' as Charles Moore giggled) and people as varied as William Shawcross (who he?[6]) and the doorman – who was a Serb, wonderful people – came up to 'shake my hand'.

Jane drove me back in the Big Red and I lollingly dozed. Slept like a top. Strangely, I don't think I have been happier, or more fulfilled since Seend – and perhaps first being made MFT. And I thank God.

---

[1] Paul Channon, MP for Southend W since January 1959, succeeding his father, Sir Henry ('Chips') Channon.

[2] Sir David Frost's Sunday morning 'sofa' show, as AC called it, was required viewing for politicians. Frost had come a long way since satire shows of 1960s.

[3] Cdr Richard Aylard, private secretary to the Prince of Wales since 1991.

[4] Nicholas Norton of S. J. Phillips, jewellers in Bond Street.

[5] Jane Wrightsman, widow of Charles Wrightsman, American oil billionaire.

[6] William Shawcross, journalist, author, married to Olga Polizzi, daughter of Charles Forte.

Sunday, 26 June

A lovely hot still day and we rose early and sat breakfasting by the pool, then afterwards in the long chairs by the fig tree reading the Sundays. Publicity – I get it. Absurd really. Only cloud is little Page who came in when I was having an injection, said I should have a check-up. Wouldn't have minded so much if it hadn't been Col's doctor who said, 'Your brother should have a PSA test.'[1] So this hangs over me. But I am much calmer now, and seem none the worse (dare I say it, slightly better for the whole experience).

Great Hall Study, Saltwood   *Sunday, 10 July*

Last night we went over to Sissinghurst, arriving early for dinner and walked round the gardens. Lovely, and no public, and very redolent of Harold and Vita and 'Miss Niggeman'.[2] 'Cleaned up' as NT properties always are, but one could still imagine the old boy driving back from Tunbridge Wells station (old Austin taxi, of course) and thinking about the countryside during the Battle of Britain and then, much later, shuffling out of his study in the tower, and collapsing. 'Is this where he collapsed?' I rehearsed in the car going over, and Jane had a *fou rire*. At dinner I was lionised. Marvellous to be compared to Byron, Shelley and Pepys in one's lifetime – and by such good judges. Stephen Spender and Elizabeth Longford[3] quite effusive, Natasha Spender, whom I remember as being dark and voluptuous and rather frightening still very attractive, at 70+, with short blonde-dyed hair and lovely eye ditches.

---

[1] Protein Sequence Analysis for early detection of prostate cancer.
[2] Kent home of Nigel Nicolson, author, former Conservative MP, son of Harold Nicolson and his wife Vita Sackville-West, who restored the house and its gardens, now in the hands of the National Trust; Elvira Niggeman, Harold Nicolson's secretary, 1938–65.
[3] Sir Stephen Spender, poet; Lady Longford, biographer.

I sat next to Rebecca Nicolson[1] and she and some ambassador[2] gave me a bit of 'when are you going to take the helm?' treatment. All v gratifying, but frustrating also. Phone and fax silent all day.

Next week the result of the 'test'. Will I be 'cleared'?

Talking of which, little Archer[3] again in trouble over 'insider trading'. Every week a new scandal.

Saltwood   *Wednesday, 13 July*

We have had two days of very great heat – 86° and more in London. On the Monday we drove (in the Jaguar, as Big Red has gone away for part exchange[4]) to Highgrove. HRH very magnetic – greatly to my surprise. I took a liking to Paul McCartney, saw a few other notables (little Gummer[5] notably unfriendly). A slightly bizarre grouping. But at the close we were escorted to the car park by Richard Aylard, to whom I talked giftedly and recklessly.

Highgrove is terribly nice, really organic. But the place was incomplete, without a woman.

Saltwood   *Saturday, 16 July*

As I walked back from the Garden House, having finished my *Mail on S* 'column', I saw the mother hen and the little black baby bantams under the beech hedge and went over to talk to

---

[1] AC 'tried to get off with' Rebecca Nicolson. She was flattered, but refused.

[2] Michael Pakenham, British ambassador to Luxembourg; son of Elizabeth Longford.

[3] Archer had been accused over Anglia TV, where his wife was a director.

[4] AC was exchanging his present Bentley for a new one, identical in colour, also called Big Red.

[5] John Selwyn Gummer, MP for Suffolk Central since 1983 (Eye, 1979–83, Lewisham W 1970–February 1974), Environment Secretary since 1993.

them. On the other side of the moat one of the moorhens was busying itself. I was deliciously at ease, not having drunk anything at midday, felt marvellous. In the late afternoon drove with Jane in the KGV car to collect some of her framed pictures from the Evegate Art Shop and then on to get petrol at Tesco. Tea with black bread and pepper salami (only a croissant so far today) and then I wandered up to the top of the house to open the tower playroom door for the swifts. I found an old, very old Bartholomew cloth-backed Ordnance Survey map of Sutherland (Tongue and Cape Wrath, sheet 26) possibly even Victorian as it showed the Creaggan as fully driveable, two ferries across the Loch, one going to 'Port Eriboll'. Then I hung on the bar without ill-effect. On the way down through the upper floors I fantasised about ways of 'doing them up' and realised what lovely things there still are here. A day of real contentment and tranquillity, unchronicled for a very long time, and thanks be to God.

In the Volvo at the Creaggan peat workings   *Wednesday, 10 August*

The ninth day here, but – unusually and sinisterly – I am very much not 'a thousand per cent'. That little spot on the tip of my scar has turned into a basal, I'm sure of it. Irrevocably it enlarges and hardens. My rear lower wisdom is aching intermittently – and for longer at a time. How can it? If the nerve has been taken out, how can it hurt? Everyone away (naturally) until September has prescribed antibiotics. But why/how should/could there be an infection there at all? Jaw cancer is always one of my great horrors.

I am really fit – do a lot of scrambling and walking, out practically all day. But I am not unwound. I dread the journey back – I suppose we'd better grit our teeth and try and do it in a day.

I am unsettled by all the boring things I have to do in

Sept/Oct/Nov. I cancelled poor Selina. She was so sweet. But would it have worked? I think not; it would have been *Love Tory* II. We have cancelled *Diaries* II, because that wouldn't have worked 'out' either.

I still contemplate cancelling everything, and just concentrating on my book, TNS[1] and periodic reviews, but if I am to keep up the column then I suppose I need periodic nourishment. What do I actually want? Soames replied to my letter of congratulations immediately; Cranborne after three weeks; Aitken not at all.[2] But I'm not *inside*. My burning determination to get back in and scare them is slowly dying down. I'm sublimating it, I suppose, in the great work. But I am not yet at ease with myself.

Looking back I think the only *really* happy day I've had, quite perfect and utterly memorable was the day in July of last year when Jane had just joined me and we drove along some lovely Slovena valley, bathing naked in the river pool while the other Ghosts wafted by above us, and got to our hotel, made love and walked in the town listening to a wedding choir and then praying in the Catholic church (or have I compressed two days? No matter).

Although to be fair last Saturday here was lovely, also. But I am so unprogrammed.

Shore Cottage   *Saturday, 13 August*

I have massively overdone it physically. Must have shifted 2–300 bales of hay – but not as decrepit as I might be. No time to walk *long* (I had wanted to go to Whiten Head – might make a recce

---

[1] Also referred to in these diaries as 'Big Book'; what AC saw as his magnum opus, *The Tories: Conservatives and the Nation State, 1922–1997*, eventually published in 1998.

[2] In the summer reshuffle, Nicholas Soames had been made PPS at Department of Employment, Lord Cranborne Leader of the House of Lords, Jonathan Aitken Chief Secretary to the Treasury (the latter two joining the Cabinet for the first time).

tomorrow), still have to write – although ideas for the Tory book ferment pleasingly. I am a bit apprehensive at intervals, occasionally almost Lenin Stadium and indirectly about the congestion of the nose-place op, and all those bloody speaking engagements.

As Jane said last night – 'We're going to head south for a complete rest.'

Actually for the first time today I can contemplate the going home. As always at Eriboll we've banked a lot of stamina.

Garden House   *Sunday, 28 August*

It was sensible of me to go on to 'Mr Page's rooms' as I had suffered a setback and Dai Davies[1] who had settled for 'a cyst' (it wasn't, having a tiny core of basal cells) etc etc. Then on to Page for blood tests and a discussion about whether this is affected by men on HRT. Page says don't know.

Saturday, 3 September

It is fifty-five years since Chamberlain broadcast the declaration of war, and we were staying at the Hare and Hounds Hotel at Westonbirt (oh so near to Highgrove) and that afternoon (or the next day) rummaging in some stables/shed looking for a 'secret package' when Mr Ashmore (or Ashmole) appeared, surprisingly, and said that the *Courageous* had been lost and to my private dismay I could not remember what class of boat it was.[2]

Now I sit at my desk in the Garden House, very depressed. I have so little time left. It is so precious. There is little enough until I actually die – even less before my 'powers' fail.

---

[1] Dai Davies, specialist.
[2] An aircraft carrier, actually sunk by a U-boat in the Bristol Channel on 17 September.

Saltwood   *Thursday, 15 September*

This morning I read a little of Julian Critchley's book.[1] So light and pleasing a touch. A charming and witty fellow looking (until very recently) younger than his years and most unsuitable for a whole range of reasons (some of which he shared with me) as a backbench Conservative MP. But when he writes about the 22,[2] and personalities in earlier times, I felt so wistful. It took me almost to the day when I first wanted to go in, under 'Uncle Harold'. Like sex, I wasted an awful lot of time, yet, as it were, 'finding my way'.

I wish to goodness I hadn't taken all those speaking engagements for the autumn. I suppose I thought that could I still ingratiate myself with a constituency? ACHAB. And you could say it keeps me 'in touch'.

Monday, 19 September

It has been very wet and cold – almost underwater conditions all day today, and dark. We are due to fly from Gatwick tomorrow for the Hamilton rally. It seemed a good idea at the time – lots of expensive sports racing cars hustling along D-roads in the Lot region driven by rich spoilt amateurs. But as the weather faded and faltered we decided (I think brilliantly) to quickly commission and despatch (also) in the truck the Citroën ('always used on holiday' – qv). Prospect, ideally, of idling, one hand on the wheel, as the Chapron effortlessly keeps up with a lot of expensive trash, some of it pre-war like all those 2.3 Alfas, in swishing rain and *nids-de-poule*. It may not work out like that, though.

I think it *very* unlikely I'll be doing the column again next

---

[1] The memoirs of Julian Critchley, *A Bag of Bottled Sweets*.
[2] The Conservative 1922 Committee of backbench MPs.

year (I may not even be invited to do so) unless offered pointless extra. I suppose for 120 I would have to say yes, but I would really rather be free (it was delicious last weekend being at Saltwood yet not having to concentrate on Friday evenings/ Saturday mornings and just do the odd TV and book review).

On Saturday night we went to dine with the Howards. The Lamonts, MH and Sandra, Jane and I, Aitken and Lol. One passé, one in jeopardy, one OUT, and one in ascendant. Aitken was again disagreeable – said something on the lines of '… for those of us in the front line …'(i.e., not you). I thought he was rather giggly and high-pitched. 'My goodness, you're dark,' I thought as we were introduced. Jane said he must be dyeing his hair and sure enough there were discreet henna 'lights', up market *PropinoMilanese*.

On getting home that evening, I was depressed.

Rosemary L (rather likeable now) said was I looking for a seat, and got excitedly inquisitive when I said 'yes'. But I know better. Only *just* tolerated at Uckfield; interest more prurient than approbatory.

How long have I got? I'd settle for another ten years – but can't realistically expect this. Fair? I would be wise (as I am) to get the books done, be a granpapa, and a semi Howard Hughes. I think it is this knowledge that there isn't all that time left that makes me so irritable when a day is being wasted.

Thursday, 29 September

As I pottered about Garden House this morning I thought how lovely to have a whole year – see the seasons round – without a single engagement. But can I afford to chuck the *Mail on Sunday*? And can I resist invitations? My problem is that I can't really relax unless there is a *clear run* ahead. But if there is a clear run, however short, I fill it up (like paying off an o/d, and then 'taking advantage of the facility' again).

Thursday, 13 October

My very last Party Conference — short of a miracle. It must be all of 20 years — could have been '69 or '70 when I went to Blackpool nervous about being, as it were, *visually probed*, been keen (how little I knew then) to find and suck up to chairmen. Now most of the cheeky-chappies, 5' 8" high and with 'waisted' jackets and exact templates/candidates of the kind that were all over the place then, and saying the same things. CCO standard issue.

I comment[1] shrewdly and drawlingly at the start and end of sessions. But glimpsing myself in the monitor at the end of the day's session with Huw (Edwards, I think?) I thought how old I looked. Earlier in the day the sweet little make-up blonde was getting friendlier and friendlier; expressed sympathy at the idea of 'going for a walk on the beach'. But when I asked her, she said, 'You mean take off our shoes and walk barefoot in the sand?'

'Yes, yes.'

'I don't get a lunch hour.'

Was she mocking? She didn't turn up all afternoon.

I walked along the beach alone …

Portillo and Heseltine 'clashed'. Portillo got the better ovation. The first time anyone has beaten MH for years (except, of course, and by rote, the PM).

MH, also, looked old at times. Almost 'Mr Chips' in his half-moons. And last night as I worked the conference hall it was so clear that people were unhappy, and longing for a lead. They cheered Hanley,[2] but only a kind of knee-jerk — because basically he was *low*. You can get laughs, and 'affection' that way, but it's not leadership. (I must say, though, that I did get a pang

---

[1] The BBC had employed AC for interpretation and summing-up.
[2] John Major had made Jeremy Hanley party chairman in his summer reshuffle, believing that Hanley with his easy manner might do for the Conservatives in the mid-1990s what Cecil Parkinson had done for the party early in Margaret Thatcher's time as Prime Minister.

when Malcolm Rifkind, introducing his front bench, pointed out that the entire previous line-up – Aitken, Hanley and Cranborne – had all gone into Cabinet.)

I went to two fringe meetings. Little Lamont, making the intellectual case for complete withdrawal from the EC; and less publicised, but colossally crowded, the Goldsmith-Tebbit meeting. A lot of Cuixmalan freeloaders there – Aspers, Taki, Ed Epstein, Greville Howard[1] – playing at politics. Brian Hitchen – first time I've seen him in the flesh – bright red and taut with over-weightedness.[2]

On the way back I was waylaid by the *News of the World* gang and had an open-air negotiating session with Piers Morgan. Quite engaging (high flown, aet. 29). Offered him a clear run for £25,000 – including my costs. Very generous.[3]

Garden House   *Monday, 24 October*

I took a train up to lunch with Ion at the Garrick. 'Have you seen anything of "x?" I said to George thingummy in the bar. 'Yes, I went to the wedding.' It was like some terrible surgery on flesh-wound administered through a huge local anaesthetic. I can feel the knife entering, but only barely the pain. I suppose that the real blow will be when I hear of her child. Strange, but in a curious way half encouraging (or do I mean comforting) that she couldn't tell me.

I explained to Ion that I am going to take a sabbatical – a real sabbatical – starting on (effectively) 18 December. Eschewing

---

[1] Lord [Norman] Tebbit, a mainstay of Margaret Thatcher's Cabinets, later Conservative Party chairman; Taki Theodoracopoulos, Greek-born social columnist; Greville Howard, Norfolk gentry, chairman of Fortress Holdings and a member of the council of the 'Europe Yes; Euro No' Campaign.

[2] Brian Hitchen, editor of the *Sunday Express*; AC added a later note – 'at last a crazy illustration of the medical term "hypertension".'

[3] Following the *News of the World*'s serialisation of the Harkess' story, AC was threatening legal action; Piers Morgan, the *N of W*'s editor.

the column? Speaking? Occasional journalism? 'Yes – all of
them.' It will cost me £200,000 minimum.

Replete with a kind of melancholic loathing.

I am almost revelling in the idea. 'Alan Clark is dead.'

'No he isn't.'

'Yes he is … I'm sure he is.' etc.

Saltwood   *Monday, 12 December*

I am back now in the Tower Office, having been driven out by
the sheer height of the piles of paper in the Green Room. I am
quite out of kilter and made extremely thoughtful by poor
Eddie having had, a couple of days ago, a mini-stroke.[1]

He is 'muddled', and frail and – I fear – a write-off. I called
on him this morning and felt moved by how sweet-natured and
loyal he was – 'I'll be back shortly, just do a few odd jobs, get
some wood in …' etc. But apparently when Peggy came back
from the farm he told her that he had fed Pepper. She found that
he had taken the back off the wireless and put the batteries in
the dog's dish (a quite dream-like surreal sequence). And there
is an unhappy look of fear, almost of panic, in his eyes.

The ramifications of this are enormous, and uniformly unwelcome. We can't go away together, and leave the dogs. How
can we leave the dogs? So no Zermatt together, no rallying, no
(unless we can persuade Andrew and Sarah down) Mexico. Even
when we go to Scotland for Christmas and take the dogs we
will have to lock up the whole house, take potluck over (a) a
burglary (b) a fire (c) an appalling leak.

Then there are so many odd jobs he did – already a leak that
needs bitumising in the workshop; a Yale lock on the back door
of the wooden shed. The top border. Oh dear. I suppose we
must take consolation that it will force our hand into searching

---

[1] Edwin Wilson, groundsman and gardener of long standing at Saltwood.

for a 'Treasure' or couple.

Also a timely reminder of how suddenly 'it can happen'. I have high blood pressure myself, this is known. 'At any moment I can be eliminated by an assassin or a lunatic'(Wolf). But how awful not to be eliminated, but just drastically crippled. And you always get another within three years of a stroke – often less.

Shore Cottage   *Tuesday, 20 December*

Arrived in the afternoon, very wet lying, but light beautiful and Julie had got the croft in shipshape order. James had made a really beautiful strong bench for me and sweetly had stuck a red ribbon on it – my Christmas present.

Shore is simply divine – needing only a porch, a little decorating, a deep freeze in the cold larder and a double bed (new) and oak bookcase in my 'study' and I could 'work' here for weeks on end. Even now it is a most wonderful refuge – completely away from the telephone, rentaquote, newspapers, howling peacocks, M-way roar, calling out, engine noise, television etc etc.

Yesterday we came up the Great North Road, leaving two minutes later than 'bogey' time and alighting in Gleneagles car park at *exactly* the same time (2.46 p.m.) as on the previous visit. Heavily laden (with the – quite cheering – cockatiels[1]) in the new Discovery which is quieter, even more economical, slightly better handling, but quite a little slower than the old one. I must say that at Gleneagles dining and after tea (I was too exhausted even to read) I did get a most wonderful sense of relief.

An 'open' – relatively – year stretches ahead. And, absurdly, like the last weeks before a reshuffle the anticipation is agreeable.

---

[1] As at Saltwood the cockatiels took up residence in their cage in the 'warmer kitchen'.

Shore Cottage   *Wednesday, 21 December*

Detached myself at midday and went up the Creaggan, low
sunlight, but the air quite still. Thought of many things, and
quite content really, although I have not got long enough to live
for all that I need.

I returned and joined Jane in a meander along the shoreline
and on the way back saw 'the young' and I upbraided Andrew
for having chosen the 'wrong' Range Rover (the diesel instead
of the V8). Jane said his face crumpled as I shouted and sneered.
Why do I do this to those I love? Almost immediately after it
emerges that it was the BMW diesel – a most interesting
comparison. I tried hard to make it up. I do so adore Tip, and
hate to wound him.

Shore Cottage   *Friday, 23 December*

First entry at my desk in the panelled room. Eddie's tubular
heater makes it incomparably more congenial than the 'sitting
room'. Right height. I look out at the shed and the bank, hear
the stream running. Yesterday I fiddled with the cars (James
came down in the evening and got them all going in one
burst!). Meandered along the foreshore, spotted driftwood. In
the evening the young all came down for supper which we held
in the kitchen at Meecee's table – v successful, except for dear
Tip who is a bit quiet and overshadowed by (a) James and (b)
Sarah. Sarah said, quite insouciantly, that 'everyone in Zermatt
says what a bad influence I am on Andrew: he used to be such
fun …' etc etc. Poor dears. I do hope things work out all right
for them.

I am heavier than in previous years with a 'pot' that needs
controlling. But I sleep, eat and Thompson satisly and my cock
is fine. Senescence is indicated by getting sleepy and passing out
at moments during the day, and by poor recall (having said to

Andrew: 'Did you hear what Tom did – locked himself in the car – ?' 'Yes, I was there'). But my mind still runs freely and actively around the future.

Shore Cottage   *Saturday, 24 December*

It is a truism that any holiday only lasts three – or possibly four – days before some jarring episode or reminder changes the atmosphere and arrests the process of unwinding.

At EMT Jane and I were sitting this morning, still utterly comatose and uncoordinated. She was dressed, and after a bit decided to take the dogs, starting ahead of me while I Thompsoned and dressed. Quietly, ruminating on the loo with *Three Years of War in E Africa* (first time this hol)[1] I thought I heard shouting, rather Saltwood-like. Thought no more of it, then unmistakably Jane SCREAMING hysterically. Rushed out naked, barefoot in wellingtons with only a Jaeger dressing gown on. The dogs had attacked a sheep, forcing it in and out of the stream. Poor darling, she was white and gasping; hit Hannah fiercely with my stalking stick. This made me deeply gloomy – can we never let the dogs off the lead – much less free range – again? It's hard enough to get her to come to Eriboll, still less to stay here for any length of time …

Later I went to gather driftwood in the jeep and Andrew got it at a really dangerous angle above long beach. It then suffered fuel starvation and I went back on foot to the byre, noting at the same time how very fluently and fast the young walk (rather like the Charles Moores).

---

[1] By Captain Angus Buchanan; another Eriboll favourite.

Shore Cottage   *Monday (Boxing Day)*

We went to midnight carol service in Tongue. As always, ahead
of a 'function' felt comatose and reluctant. But it was pleasing.
All the good tunes, and perfectly sensible message of reassurance
about the resurrection, a good audience (including some in
crew cuts and bomber jackets) and not one mention, from start
to finish, of the Third World or the need to 'combat' racism or
homelessness or poverty or any of that crap.

Now it is hailing and with a cold wind and I sit at my delightful
study window and at the Seend gratis desk and ponder.

Saltwood   *Thursday, 29 December*

Back here and in a high state of nervous readiness (quite the
reverse of nervous randiness). We 'did' the post (nothing from
John Major or the PoW), caught up with a few cards and I sent
off £5800-odd worth of cheques.

Our journey back was comfortable. Incredible, surpassingly
beautiful light as we drove over the Moyne, and across Crask.
Several times we stopped the car and looked over the snow-
covered moors to the peaks of Loyal, Klibreck, and Hope from
the eastern side.

More and more I incline to the view that in art it is the
representation of light that ranks above all else. 'Form' is a poor
second, cubism all that. Cézanne is colour, that and light – just
a mess, really, of splodgings vaguely evocative of sans illumina-
tion. Monet, Heade, Church, the 'luminists'. And what about the
distant horizon in, e.g., the little Rousseau of the Becs[1] before
'cleaning' away, for ever, the pale lemon dividing streak between
sea and sky.

One has only to write these all down to see that it is not

---

[1] A picture owned by the Clarks.

simply a matter of going back refreshed and tackling things with vigour. The whole day, like the flat surfaces indoors, is impossibly congested. 'Discipline,' Jane says. Yes, that would help. But the sheer scale of the task may force, in the end, 'its own modification'.

1995 – so hard we must strive. (Followed, perhaps, by 1996 picking up sticks.)

Am I also going to be able to concentrate enough on the problem so as not to make 'a bad decision' of cutting back? I do have too many cars. I really can only manage three (H) classics. And while I get great pleasure from going into 'the smart part' at Saltwood will it ever really be used again? There is masses and masses of wealth scattered here. There, too, one can draw up a retrenchment plan, a *cuvée privée*. But, of course, once the Mains is stripped, or demi-stripped, it could never really be filled again.

Later

This had come to me very forcibly the previous day. Quite late in the afternoon I took the old Volvo to Whales Corner and walked along the shoreline and past Grassy Knoll. Jane I left on the long strand searching for seashells and watched slate blues and blacks and pinkish backlighting; as the storm clouds changed, by the minute, I did reflect a little. I am excluded now, I suppose, from political prospect (though, endearingly, James told us on the last night that, demi-in-his cups, Tip-book said that he wanted to go into politics). While I am in Scotland I wanted to stay there, to go *en retraite* after this year, last 'stint' with the *Mail on Sunday*. Timing just about right, I suppose, as by then either we will be 'picking up' or the Tories will be doomed for ever. This year, too, I should be cleared by Scott, and so will, in the autumn, demand my dues (or perhaps better leave it until November/ January though this could be tricky as JM could be ousted in November). But once I am back here, read my mail – all favourable – the papers, talk to Dobbie and Soames, I feel I still have a lot of activity left.

Saltwood   *New Year's Eve*

More and more I am convinced that the most precious commodity in the world is TIME (was it not the clip of my father
comparing himself to the White Rabbit perpetually looking at
his watch that moved me to tears in Michael Cockerell's film?).

Today I just squandered it. The 'piece' for the *M on S* (written
yesterday and looking quite good on galley, although I had my
doubts about it) was done, and I repaired to the Garden House
to do my correspondence. Only managed three letters – one of
them completely unnecessary and will make bad feeling, on
Jeffrey Archer's personal number plate to the *Guardian*,[1] and still
not typed up the new setup for BB. Was in a vile mood, no food
except a digestive biscuit and two cups of Darjeeling at 7.30.
Rotten post, and the Honours list.

It really is too much, Hosker (Treasury solicitor who 'allowed'
– sic – certain documents for the Matrix trial – admitted it to
Scott) got a knighthood.[2] Also Rocco F[orte].[3] The line-up of
the 'businessmen' looked even lower, scruffier and more venal
than the politicians. I have simply been bypassed. And once
'bypassed' it is virtually impossible to get 'streamed' again. Why?
Scott the excuse, of course, but when I am 'cleared' (a nice
Christmas card from C Muttukumaru cheered me up) it will be
too late. The excuse will be my 'private life' – even though that
was known to the Cabinet Secretary and the PM before I was
appointed to the Government.[4]

---

[1] The *Guardian* diary ran a competition when Archer crashed his car. The number
plate was blanked out in the photograph and readers were asked for suggestions.
AC produced a cutting, from the *Glasgow Herald*, with the original number plate
clearly visible. He also disclosed a second Archer number plate, a 'low-digit Exeter
registration … at present (one assumes) on a retention certificate'. The *Guardian*
diarist made AC runner-up.

[2] Gerald Hosker, Solicitor to the Department of Trade and Industry (hence his involvement over the Matrix Churchill matter) 1987–92; then Procurator General, Treasury
Solicitor and Queen's Proctor.

[3] Rocco Forte had risen in the eponymous restaurant and hotel chain founded by
his father, Lord (Charles) Forte, whom he succeeded as chairman in 1992.

[4] See *Diaries*, 24 June 1983.

I didn't get back here until 1.30 and then ravenously ate some macaroni cheese and chutney. Slept (for 15 minutes) in my chair then collected the battery charger thinking I would try and start the Porsche. Went to the archive room to collect some boxes – the '95 boxes for categorised paper – and was diverted by some material on Upper Terrace.[1] God! What wonderful rich stuff there was in that house! Practically nothing left, it seems except the Renoir jugglers (which I would sell if I could) and the great painted Blenheim bed.

Next I went over to 'Woolletts Garage'. Totally predictably the Porsche battery was undetachable; the spanner did not have the room, due to the curvature of the front wing, to attach to the terminal nut. I fiddled and fumbled for hours, it seemed, sometimes just resting with my elbows on the wing looking at it dejectedly. Then moved sideways to try and start the Barnato car. Pump trouble (naturally). I forgot that when I put it away there had been some problem with the Mitsubas getting choked. Got back here again just in time for a not very comfortable tea perched on the edge of my chair and the fire in the Green Room starting to smoke viciously. The photos of Christmas at Eriboll are dreadfully revealing of me. Red-faced, thick necked, something almost of Evelyn Waugh ('all right then, Grandad?' Jane said). Something of Tom King and Marcus Kimball – who was portrayed stoutly *Jorrocks* in the saddle in *The Times* yesterday. He's hung up his riding gear, poor Marcus, for ever. One thing after another closing in on him.[2]

So it has been a very frustrating day. And this pen, which seemed so nice, is actually foul and making my already disturbed writing disagreeably – as opposed to codedly – illegible. I can't remember a New Year's Eve when I have been more tense, and frustrated and restless. What it boils down to, I suppose, is that I am afraid of dying before I have done the things I want/need

---

[1] Upper Terrace House, Hampstead overlooking the West Heath, a post-war home of the Clark family.

[2] Marcus Kimball had been joint master, at varying times, of the Fitzwilliam and the Cottesmore Hounds.

to. Irrevocably the mathematics illustrates this. Divide the time it takes into the time left, and it 'won't go'.

Supplementary note
I've resolved not to answer the phone – at all. Just listen first to the message.

No more 'quotes'. Don't get caught by journalists.

I must get stuck into Big Book.

Last year I had the prospect of enormous tax demands, but was calm. Somehow, they were 'coped with'. This year there are the huge Lloyds-like calls on Big Red. Again I am calm, although it is only two weeks away. Why? How?

Sometimes I get so cross about the cars, the way I can never get at them. It always seems (and always will seem) as if I am 'playing' when I should be doing something more virtuous – like, today, cleaning the greenhouse windows.

But every car I think of (even the green Buick, which I am now contemplating using for the Polish rally) has a reason. Even though, if *force majeure* were to supervene I would be quite content to be left with 3 (+1).

1995

Dined with Richard Ryder at the Berkeley. He told me Churchill wanted Tommy Dugdale to succeed Margesson as Chief Whip,[1] but was 'talked out of it' – who by? It's a colossal task, to complete Big Book in the two years left. January has got off completely 'on the wrong foot' with all three 'pieces' and book reviews. Will pull in about £1500, plus £3000 from TV. But today I signed the first of the cheques for Big Red (looking identical – what's the point?) and then funked ringing Hoare's to tell them. I went back with Richard for the 10 p.m. vote so that his driver (Janet) could take me home. A strange, sad evocation as we passed all those cars double-parked on a wet night, for the first 3-liner of the New Year. First time I have seen them like that for over two years, must be nearer three. I feel older and sadder, and somewhat more convinced of the impossibility of return.

I think I have only a very short time left to live. I am desperately worried about finishing Big Book, which could/will be so good. A possible 'researcher', Graham Stewart, came down this morning.[2] I took to him almost at once; good mind, sympathetic attitude, we think alike on the main subject. Oh so lucidly and giftedly I took the entire drive from Sellindge to Albany expounding, got quite hoarse. But made a convert I suspect.

---

[1] Captain David Margesson, very much Neville Chamberlain's man; Churchill did not trust him. Dugdale had been Stanley Baldwin's PPS.
[2] AC was looking for a researcher to help him on *The Tories*. Graham Stewart, who studied Modern History at St Andrews University before going up to St John's College, Cambridge, was at work on his first book, eventually published as *Burying Caesar: Churchill, Chamberlain and the Battle for the Tory Party*.

Saltwood kitchen   *Saturday, 11 February*

How delicious is 'the quiet hour'. There are few more agreeable (intellectual) conditions than a pot of Indian tea, a nice pen (earlier I was fussed because I could only find a biro) and a blank page. I find it impossible to do this if first I sometimes glance at a newspaper, so it is critical to start before the papers can have arrived (and that is why the entries are so much smoother, and better written, in Scotland).

I had lunched with Alastair G[oodlad].[1] Something especially pleasing about entering Sibyl's house at lunch-time – although of course while remembering the geography I never (or did I once?) came as a guest in my own right.[2]

I thought the lunch went, on the whole, 'well'. Clockwise from my left: Soames – lovely as always and jollily responsive though fussed about his diabetes so that he dieted spastically and ascetically (though without, it seemed, any effect on his weight). Magnus, nice quiet intelligent son of Alastair. Charles Moore, came in late, not much to say for himself – but of course never good at mixing it in a shouting chorus. Richard R[yder], looking amazingly young ('on work experience', as Jane says), Jonathan A[itken] whom stupidly I allowed to half cut me upstairs and with whom there is now a clear froideur. Paul Johnson, now senior, and permanently cross.[3] Alastair benign and alert. Robert C[ranborne] – also unchanged, lovely company. Then between me and Robert, Tristan [Garel-Jones].

What is it about Tristan that now makes him something of a bore? I suppose that once he was removed from the epicentre of power and intrigue his *raison d'être* disappeared and all that was

---

[1] Alastair Goodlad, MP for Eddisbury since 1983 (Northwich February 1974–83); a former Whip, he had been a Foreign Office Minister since 1992.

[2] Sibyl Colefax had lived at Argyll House, King's Road, Chelsea until the death of her husband, Sir Arthur Colefax. She moved to 19 Lord North Street, off Smith Square, Westminster, where she entertained famously. Given its location, it was a particularly desirable London home for a Member of Parliament.

[3] Paul Johnson, historian (*The Birth of the Modern: World Society 1815–30*) and former editor of the *New Statesman*, whose political views had moved to the right.

left was the camouflage. So he's now simply a kind of raconteur, almost down to the '... and do you remember when ...?' level. T said he never went into the House, except to vote, now. 'You'd hate the tearoom Al, not a single person you'd want to sit down with.' (Misunderstanding completely, of course, why I want to get back in – which is to motivate and galvanise those boys who are leaderless and unsettled.)

That evening T rang me at my desk in GH. Earlier, talking to Jane, he had said, 'Al's his own worst enemy; people say "how can you like that awful man?"'; there never was any chance of him getting to the Lords.'

Speaking to me he said he was going to have 'that' luck himself – it was 'magic', etc etc (a crash gymkhana). But then, rather irritatingly went on to try and commiserate – 'don't repine', all that. Made it pretty clear that I had no hope of getting into the Lords – or anything else (quite different from talk of 'condign recognition' and 'we must find a perch for Al' in 1992).

When I got up to leave no one followed me out (the 'journalists' had already gone; much later I began to suspect that they had been discussing me/real stuff '... now that the journalists had gone').

Continued Sunday, 12 February
This was confirmed by today's *Sunday Telegraph*, which led off with a spastic item 'Alan Clark to "mourn" Jill Phipps', clearly 'placed' at behest of Aitken/ G-J (or was Moore acting on his own behalf?).[1] Frightfully depressing, somehow. This endless search for the *disreputable* angle. I just want to hide. A *Daily Express* reporter rang, and I tried to give her reasonable and measured answers. I could sense her getting impatient. 'Haven't

---

[1] Jill Phipps, a 31-year-old mother, was a member of the campaign protesting against what she – and many others – saw as the cruelty of the export from Britain of live veal calves to the Continent, a campaign AC actively supported. A fortnight before she had died after being run over by a cattle truck that she and other demonstrators were trying to prevent from entering Coventry airport. Many in the Conservative Party disapproved. In May AC reports a call from Tristan Garel-Jones saying he was being considered a 'loony' for his animal rights activities.

you left it rather late to talk to Jill Phipps's mother?' etc. So I am very tired, very depressed, very beset by 'engagements' and demands – and by shortage of money, too; I can't settle the car cull. I caught sight of myself in the window of Andrew's jeep this afternoon. I am puffy and lined. Last empty week coming up and I will show discipline, by (a) not drinking, (b) taking a walk (Gossie or M-way) each day.

I wish I didn't even have to do the column. I'd rather pay back my advance to Weidenfeld,[1] clear the debts and be a recluse (I wish, too, that I could get even with my 'friends'. What debt do I have (sic) from them, anyway? No recognition – companionship of any kind – just kicked out).

Tuesday, 14 February

Back from a long day (though the journey was smooth) to Coventry to Jill Phipps's funeral. I had hoped for a pilgrimage, a Mecca, a mullah's funeral. But although the Cathedral was respectfully full, it was nothing like at capacity. The Sutherland altarpiece is incredible, magnificent, and one of the most impressive works of art I have ever seen. The size of Saltwood towers inner façade, perhaps even a bit under. The lady priest (deaconess?) was lovely, attractive and with a lovely clear voice, looked not unlike Presiley Baxendale. The service, with some nice blessings, none too awful in even the new English – and then an address, quite an ordeal for him, I suppose, by 'Justin' thingummy. (Jill, who clearly was attractive, was hop-picking in Kent four years ago!)

---

[1] AC was annoyed that his agents, Peters, Fraser & Dunlop, were representing his brother Colin for his diary, *The Prince, the Showgirl and Me*, and that to compound matters Weidenfeld & Nicolson had offered to publish. In the end it was published by HarperCollins.

Wednesday, 15 February

Splitting headache and paralysed by paper pressure.

When it gets to a certain level you can't start, dread starting on account of what it may disclose. An example, the KGV garage doors ('workshop') were left open about a week ago. Since then it has rained every single day and blows viciously. I've just left them open. Why not shut them? Why not, indeed?

I woke this morning and realised that at my next birthday I will be 67. Now that figure, actually, is OLD. 62 (say) seems quite cheeky and youthful. Not only is time running out, but I am not using what I've got left properly.

I *must* clear the decks for Big Book.

Finance and Trusts need attention (money-raising and cars selling).

On the way downstairs teeny Tom, so game and bonny, foolishly fell on the corner flight and squeaked. He just crouched there paralysed, like a praying mantis. I had to carry him into the yard, where he could pee (because couldn't balance), later he slunk back into the 'kennel' cubby in the kitchen. Later he climbed out of it (while we were dressing) and rallied and then sat by the Aga.

I carried him down for the 'w' and he just managed two Thompson blobbets on the first bunch of snowdrops.

Sunday, 19 February

On Friday the little yellow cockatiel died. Poisoned by that sprouting seed-corn which I had brought in from the silage dump by the level crossing and put in their cage. She was so bonny and curious and alive. I felt awful. The grey one is going to die tonight, I know. He is just a few days behind her, being more cautious and discreet. I talked to him, softly. Told him that he was going to the rainforests where there would be sunlight and warm and shoots and leaves and roots that would keep him well and happy. I am, to my surprise, even sadder about him – because it was he who found us; was frightened by the dogs and then returned, of his own accord, to the yard. Had a miserable time in a tiny cage, then came into his own in the big cage, spread his wings so beautifully at breakfast time and particularly enjoyed the apple stump with its many perches.

My tongue is sore on one side and I am tired and low.

Saltwood   *Wednesday, 22 February*

In London yesterday. We went to the *Guardian* party for Richard Norton-Taylor's book on Scott,[1] then to the National Gallery to see our little Zurbaran[2] hanging extremely well besides the other Zurbaran which was very shiny and restored. The following morning I found myself having a kind of catharsis. The Conservative Party is doomed unless it really pulls itself together. This faffing around, making jokes at Party audiences saying it's all going to be all right when the economy picks up etc, is not on any longer. I'm going to switch my tack to we have to face facts, take risks. The Party can no longer delude itself.

By chance that lunchtime Roger Scruton[3] came round – in complete agreement, wants to start a 'group' to meet regularly. I was mildly irritated about an article by Henry Porter (I'm still waiting to get even with him) about the 'young historians' – also 'the group' – Andrew Roberts, d'Ancona[4] etc. Nucleus of the 'Resurgent right'. But all these people are waiting for the defeat revamp afterwards. Useless. We must try and do it now.

---

[1] *Knee Deep in Dishonour: the Scott Report and Its Aftermath* by Richard Norton-Taylor, Mark Lloyd and Stephen Cook.

[2] A still life, *A Cup of Water and a Rose on a Silver Plate* by the Spanish Baroque painter Francisco de Zurbarán, 1598–1664.

[3] Roger Scruton, writer and philosopher, Professor of Philosophy at Boston University, Mass., since 1992; a tenant of the Clarks, using the attic above B5, Albany.

[4] Matthew D'Ancona, assistant editor, *The Times*.

Henrietta Royle rang. Lately I have – I just don't know why – been thinking about Chelsea as being the ideal constituency.[1] Albany resident, garden parties at Saltwood, safest seat in the country, etc. She told me that they had booked the meeting for Chelsea HQ and were advertising it in the Chelsea newsletter! Suddenly I thought – could this be a sign? I know Chelsea are considering their vacancy, how far have they got? I don't want to know. All I do know is that – for all my fatigue and listlessness at intervals when surrounded (as now) by paper I am still driven. I just feel that something may happen. After speaking to Henrietta I popped over to the Great Hall and said a prayer at the long table where I composed my speech for the Sutton selection twenty-three years ago.

Senator Dole, I'm glad to see, is the leading character for the Presidential Election in two years' time and he is already 71.[2]

Albany   *Friday, 24 February*

Woke at 3 a.m., figures going through my head. My debts are £350,000 (Lloyds[3]), this, after a bit, made me tinkle. Couldn't get back to sleep and waiting for alarm, set for 5 a.m., so as to allow me to 'beat the traffic', get to Christie's viewing of the 'model' sale (James wanted me to go) and then Bertrand (sic) Arbeid. Thrashed, and 'took cover' for a bit, but no use (why am I going to a sale when I can't even write a cheque for the Heal's repairs to the mattress?). 'It's the giant sell-off,' I said to darling

---

[1] Following boundary revisions Chelsea (MP – Nicholas Scott) and Kensington (MP – Dudley Fishburn) were merging to become Kensington and Chelsea. A safe Conservative seat by any standards, the selection of its new candidate guaranteed a seat in the Commons at the next general election.

[2] Senator Robert Dole, Republican Senator (Kansas) since 1968, had just become Leader of the United States Senate, as well as a contender for the Republican presidential nomination.

[3] AC was not a Lloyd's 'name', but often used the analogy when discussing his financial situation.

Jane. She doesn't worry about debt any longer (or at least doesn't mention it), she doesn't do the correspondence. Yesterday Mrs Frowd[1] told her she had potential 'heart' trouble. So unlikely, but her grandmother, father and mother all did.

Went into the larder to get some organic digestives for my coffee and saw all those lovely entries on the doors. So happy and tranquil: 'Sir Sydney Cockerell[2] died peacefully in his house' etc. Might transfer them to the great ledger and notes with inventory.

Albany   *Thursday, 2 March*

(One of the few advances in recent months is that I have at last got into the habit of writing my 'a's' more legibly.[3])

I am still extremely rattledly congested with tasks. I ought, for example, to be presenting a beautifully polished, balanced paper to the Staff College this morning. But I only started it on Tuesday night – set it out in skeletal form, will have to infill verbally. Partly, I suppose, it is an aversion. Why was I not Secretary of State? Partly because the subject is uncomfortable, at least in its conclusions, but largely because I have so much to do that the system has become less efficient. I glaze over, can't prepare, defer until the blinding urgency of 'the last minute'.

I'm lunching with Portillo on Monday (every day next week is pre-empted). I'm slightly getting cold feet about the address to Chelsea.

---

[1] Mrs Cindy Frowd, Hythe reflexologist.
[2] All the Saltwood cockerels were named after Sir Sydney Cockerell (1867–1962), museum director and bibliophile.
[3] Sadly for his editor, it didn't last.

Saltwood kitchen a.m.   *Saturday, 4 March*

I've been waking early; this morning 4.30-ish and nagged –
though not nearly as much as (perhaps) the situation warrants –
by total exhaustion now of liquidity. Wasn't even able to pay the
quarterly interest charges on the various overdrafts – all, at their
different banks, at the limit. I was a success at Camberley. Almost
at the point of frivolity, but not.

Saltwood   *EMT, Friday, 10 March*

Last night dined with Andrew Roberts. Expensive flat in Cadogan
Gardens, quite nicely fitted out with lovely library shelves. The
Hamiltons (Neil)[1] – he a little pinched and nervous; she very bossy
and almost Miss Newman[2] disapproving. That evening a somewhat unguarded interview by Rory Knight-Bruce in the *Standard*
in which they said they were 'dining with Alan and Jane Clark'
(demi-boring for Andrew and Camilla) and Christine H then
went on to say, 'I do wish Jane Clark would do a bit more to stick
up for herself.' Andrew's neat little fiancée [Camilla] is Welsh
(it turns out) and her mother also. Attractive, both of them.
Conversation didn't quite mesh, somehow, at dinner. Disparate,
and too many guffaws. But I had a pleasing pic with Andrew in
the library afterwards. Much journalistic gossip. Not many people
seem to get more than £100 a year. A.A.Gill was mentioned.
Apparently I am being considered as literary editor of the *Sunday
Times*. Would I like this? Yes, for a five-year contract I suppose. But
Big Book must not suffer any longer.
    The night before I had been to Eton. Distorted, at least in its

---

[1] Neil Hamilton, MP for Tatton since 1983, a junior Trade Minister, 1992–94, and
his wife Christine. Hamilton had issued a writ against the *Guardian*, who in
October 1994 had alleged that he (and a second Tory junior Minister, Tim Smith)
had taken money to ask questions on behalf of a lobbying company.
[2] Miss Newman, a Clark family governess.

approaches, by traffic. And seeming much smaller, everything closer together. The Provost, Acland,[1] was his usual diplomatic self, benign, but reserved. The boys polite and effete. 'Thank you for being so entertaining' said one of the wives. I was tired, and couldn't drink. Just adequate, I hope. The names preceding me in the book were Aitken and Jeffrey Archer! Earlier I had done a teeny home movie on 'Eton during the war', masterminded by a boy/beak team. And was disconcerted at how thin were my memory and recollections.

Saltwood   *Sunday, 12 March*

The sunshine hot on one's face for the first time this year. 'Edward' came down from Danny [Mews], and the Ferrari 340 Mexico started at once. We all drove it, and later pitted it against the C-type. Pleasing, and a hint of the *douceur de vivre* of the old Lartigue album. It went magnificently, handled uncomfortably (transverse-leaf front suspension). When really pressed, over 5.8 or so, it belched smoke, and this also came into the cabin. But when I went in the dear 'C' – so smooth, flexible and balanced – I realise how dangerous 340 actually is.

Tip and Sarah went off, having bought some tropical finches at the garden centre. Next week Sarah is going to Thailand and Oman on her own. She is a character. They are a modern couple. While James and Julie, really, are old-fashioned. Much more like Jane and me.

It all reminds me of what is to happen to Saltwood, and the family Trust. We are in limbo, until the grandchildren are born. I still feel ok, in some ways. But moving about this morning at midday I felt rather old and feeble. Was I 'dying' for a drink? I certainly feel much better with the first two glasses of M. Goisot.

---

[1] Sir Antony Acland, diplomat (Head of the Diplomatic Service 1982–86; Ambassador to Washington, 1986–91) before becoming Provost of Eton in 1991.

It's strange this condition I'm in. It is almost as if I am sedated. Five years like this (72), eight with the grandchildren (80) and five or whatever God gives me I'm a sage. Just feasible.

I am almost drinking too much at the moment. Not quite, but almost. But we have given up sweets for Lent.

Saltwood   *Tuesday, 21 March*

Occupied myself with an exchange of correspondence with Max Hastings over Scott (useful to have heard from him that the Prime Minister was trying to persuade people to accept me as a 'burnt offering'). I tried my hand at composing a letter to the PM which combined grievance of not getting any 'recognition' with veiled menace at what Max had told me of any role I might play in the coming leadership and General Election. All may be altered of course as there is talk – yet again – of Heseltine taking over in a snap poll. But when? Unless JM stands down voluntarily it would mean calling it in December, which just not likely.

This morning a row with Jane at breakfast as the tablecloth had been laid over crumbs. The one thing I can't bear are 'previous' crumbs on a table when you sit down to a meal, even in Zermatt this upsets me.

Looking at how teeny this writing is – and compare it with the clear, balanced hand when I was at Shore Cottage.

Albany   *Tuesday, 28 March*

Drove up in the Old Ministerial, very flat and quiet.

Walked along Whitehall, noting the new smart gates outside the MoD, past the 'new' building entrance, an official car was coming out of New Palace Yard.

At St Stephen's entrance I 'shot' the queue and a policeman called out, then recognised me and was amiable. The pretty policewoman ditto, and asked me to take my cap off. I walked up, past the benches noting that the tiles have degenerated even more, like the hall at Chenonceau; the first time I was in that corridor, I suppose, was with Malcolm McCorquodale[1] – thought it all so boring. It was agony. I wanted to tinkle, thought how easy it would be to dodge left into the one at the end of the Members' cloakroom – MEMBERS ONLY. Standing in the Central Lobby I watched MPs scuttling across to meet 'delegates' whom they had kept waiting – 'so sorry', 'hul-lo' etc etc. Before I turned into the gate I had briefly fantasised about slyly going in that way after winning the by-election. I was half in a dream, half awake.

Met up with Frank Pakenham, lunched with him and Fr. Seed.[2] I don't wholly dismiss all that, and will read Newman over Good Friday.

I still cannot wholly surrender. ACHAB – and I know if I really asked, *really* asked, it would happen. Is it that I am afraid of the price?

Saltwood   *EMT, Sunday, 2 April*

I can't really face the idea of turning back the clock, 'nursing a constituency' etc etc. Yet, curiously, I don't pine for the Lords now. It's the death sentence (deferred), the nailing down of the coffin lid. From then the next step really is the grave.

---

[1] Malcolm McCorquodale (1901–1971), created Baron 1955, later chairman of McCorquodale & Co., printers, a National Conservative MP pre-war and MP for Epsom, 1947–55.

[2] Frank Pakenham, former Labour Minister, in his ninetieth year, who succeeded his brother as 7th Earl of Longford in 1961. Father Michael Seed, Roman Catholic priest, credited with a number of high-profile conversions to the Catholic faith.

Garden House   *Tuesday, 11 April*

Yesterday I was frantic with frustration and pressure and then, on top of it all (sic) I was phoned to ask if I would do a leader-page piece.

'How much?' – 'Pound a word.'

I laughed. 'Not nearly enough.'

'How much do you want?' – 'Two.'

'Done.'

So all afternoon I was locked into the little white computer room. Not sure I got the tone quite right, and *eleven* phone calls of different kinds including a lady (Jane Gordon (?)) doing an article on mid-life crisis ('I've been enjoying one for the last 40 years,' I said) and then, portentously, Graham Stewart, to talk about his installation in June. So I was an hour late filing, and walked out of here leaving the French windows open all night.

All based on my brief crack on the *Today* programme. *Today* is like *Breakfast with Frost* – everyone listens to it. I said that whether a government of celibates and train-spotters would be any different from what we've got … I didn't know.

In the meantime Jonathan Aitken went demi-bonkers and staged a press conference in Central Office.[1] Certain fatal (*Hello*-type) cliché 'the fight-back starts here …' etc.

On the 'early evening news' I saw that Senator Dole had got the Republican nomination – at the age of 71. This cheered me up immensely. A classic example of ACHAB. All (sic) I need is, somehow, to get back into the Commons. The Lords I'm no longer really bothered about.

I walked down to the Long Garage; too late to go for a drive,

---

[1] Jonathan Aitken was yet another Conservative involved in 'sleaze' allegations. He was suing the *Guardian* for defamation over their allegations of improper commercial relationships while Minister for Defence Procurement. His statement included a phrase which would enter modern dictionaries of quotations: 'If it falls to me to start a fight to cut out the cancer of bent and twisted journalism in our country with the simple sword of truth and the trusty shield of British fair play, so be it. I am ready for the fight. The fight against falsehood and those who peddle it. My fight begins today.'

something drew me to look on the side towards the rowan and I wondered if – *if* – I could call on God for a miracle. The moon was almost obscured but I waited, it got virtually invisible, then quite rapidly cleared and shone metallically bright. Strange, how mercurial my miracle can be, still.

Easter Monday, 17 April

How I long for solitude and tranquillity! This must be one of the most pressured Easters ever – and yet I am 67 and 'retired'.

We did the whole lawn yesterday. Tomorrow night I set off for Eriboll with sundries in the Discovery (sit-down mower, enamel sign, iron chandeliers for the chapel, etc) on probably the last Motorail journey ever.[1]

Monday, 24 April

How am I ever going to get out of this?

I can buy 'space' I suppose, by letting the Degas[2] go. But as I said to Jane late afternoon it's really Saltwood – the whole ethos of the great curtained room almost unchanged into which I can wander, and reflect, go back 20-30-40 years and play the piano. I have never left the Music Room without feeling stronger. And I remember the pain of selling the bronze (so fortunately recaptured).[3]

But time roars past, an absolute mill-race. There is far more to do; I am far more behind than when I was a Minister. Yesterday evening I had a full attack of Sunday evening blues. Something

---

[1] The Motorail service from London to Inverness was being withdrawn.
[2] *Femme s'épongeant le dos* (see March 1991).
[3] The dancer bronze (also by Degas) was sold and then bought back.

I swore I would never get again once I had 'stood down'. This great block of paperwork I have to tackle before I can 'stand back'.

EMT, Tuesday, 25 April

Many entries at the moment – indicating unsettlement.

I am most heavy-hearted at losing the Degas. Go up and look at her often, at different times of the day – and last evening sat there, on the facing sofa for quite a while talking to Jane. Jane is 'definitely uneasy' about it. But is it not the practical solution? We can't really 'freeze' everything – Mask, Zurbaran, Moores[1] (cars, 'C' and Big Red etc etc). That would be so unbalanced. And to make up the cash from lesser items would involve 'stripping' (which both boys have objected to and warned against) to a far greater degree. But now, just as I notice and remember the hip of the dancer only in Crowe's office, I notice so many extra colours in the whole picture, that reddish around the basin; shadow on towel?

Sunday, 30 April

Yesterday it was pressure, pressure. Finishing the 'piece' (not a very successful one on Ashdown) and clearing up for the Americans (coming today) and 'Little' and – 'Littler' – his partner.[2] They'd hardly been in the place five minutes before I wanted to say to Jane 'these guys are just a couple of bull-shitters'. 'Little' probed me about the Degas, which I had originally mentioned no more than in passing as the reason for

---

[1] Kenneth Clark and Henry Moore were friends, and the Clarks had a number of Moore's works.

[2] Two London dealers.

trying to sell the 'Coptic stuff'.[1] He said he could get his 'big client' straight on to the case, wouldn't hesitate. Lyingly said I had been guaranteed £800, wouldn't, couldn't deal under 1.5. They prowled about, 'Littler' peering at everything – Burne-Jones Angel, 'torchères' in the Great Hall (known fakes) up a ladder to look at the Alexander the Great tapestry etc. Afterwards there was a long courtesy recital of travellers tales ('3-card trick', as Jane pleasingly called them), half Jewish, half just straight Mews.

Saffria, 'Charles Cates' (who he?), Lord Wimborne, of getting … 'my big client' Saffria again (who strangely put 'Little's' back up by walking into the showroom and saying to 'Littler', 'I like you, we can work together'). 'I can think of worse things he might have said,' I suggested and Jane giggled, but they didn't. This went on for too long and was too circular. A cursory look at the carpets, clearly they didn't want them. 'A rug like this, Alan, would be 70-90-100 if it was in good condition.' 'Surely in this condition it would be 35 then?' I wanted to say, but didn't. Off they drove. Later the phone started ringing. We had been working all afternoon in the Great Hall and were exhaustedly lying low in the Green Room, left it to the machine. Hung up a few times then finally 'Little' soft-spoken with a message to ring a number (which I had already checked out on 1471). His 'client' – I can't believe this – is ready to buy the picture unseen. But was it in the book? Jane and I had a long, but unsuccessful time, rooting about in the library and various sources of books including the package I removed from the Garden House. Never mind, an 'Art Critic' called Sylvester (never heard of him)[2] was coming down *today* at 2 p.m. – naturally coinciding with the US visit – to look at it. Nothing will come of this, because he will spot the two worm holes, and all rich people bother about is 'condition'. But all quite fun.

---

[1] Framed tapestry fragments.
[2] The art interests of AC and David Sylvester obviously didn't coincide. Sylvester's expertise included Moore, Magritte, Bacon, Spencer and Giacometti.

Saltwood   *EMT Friday, 5 May*

During the day I had been constantly recognised and hailed as I walked about London; sat in café in Marylebone Road waiting for the GLR programme and a blonde appeared, smiled, walked on; a 'gay' got into a 'boo-hoo-I've-had-the-sack, too' conversation (sat while they waited, at my table). An American woman came up and said 'you don't know how much we admire you…'; going back up the street a Rasta, a Brian Classic lookalike, AN Other etc all acknowledge me. Earlier a mulatto lady in jeans.

I walked to the Beefsteak, sat next to little Hague.[1] Cagey, like all people who have a great future ahead of them … Mark Lennox-Boyd[2] came round at the end of the meal and said that 'Alison Young' was working for him.

I sit here, on a lovely fine still May morning; but I funk ringing Henrietta Royle and asking if Chelsea has yet 'chosen'.

The carpetsellers, after much phoned bull-shitting put in a pointless demand – for the Christie's guarantee – the 'client' obviously thrashing around for a way out. I said piss off and Christie's, a week later, are collecting it. But at least we are through the psychological hurdle of selling it and Jane has made that incredible, inspired copy.[3] I will now attempt to force the pace and continue with cash-raising: Broomhayes, R Cont, SS100, possibly Zurbaran for $1m with Feigin.[4]

---

[1] William Hague, MP for Richmond, Yorks, since February 1989; Social Security and Disabled People Minister since 1994.

[2] Sir Mark Lennox-Boyd, MP for Morecambe and Lunesdale since 1983 (Morecambe and Lonsdale 1979–83).

[3] Jane Clark, an accomplished painter, had never previously worked in pastels. She measured the picture, studied what she thought it might have been painted on, the nearest (some brown laundry paper), and set to work. Looking back she says she was inspired. Her reproduction has fooled experts. She did though refuse to replicate Degas's signature. AC marvelled at what Jane had done: 'her brilliant, spooky translation' (27 May 1995); 'Jane's miraculous substitution' (19 September 1995).

[4] An American art dealer and friend, Richard Feigin.

Garden House   *Monday, 8 May*

Frightfully tired and glazed. Almost last engagement this evening – colossal longueurs at the Savoy for the AT&T book award. That £5000 fee, which looked so tempting has actually worked out at about £20 per hour – less than a 'daily' in a posh bit of Hampstead what with reading 150 books, four judges' meetings, general hassle and a 5-hour award ceremony.[1]

Yesterday in absolute despair. Randyish, so sexual frustration and self-pity mingled as I talked to myself a great deal – whingeingly. Fiddled with the 'Webb' [mower] in the morning. But really no achievement until interrupted by the answer-phone p.m. and a Count (nearly – a Duc in fact – de Magenta) (which I thought a bogus, or trade name) to deliver the wine I had ordered. He was handsome, distinguished, beautiful manners as only the very grand French have, but tottery. His wife, I couldn't at first believe it was his wife, was at least 45 years younger. English, but quite attractive. He expressed deferential curiosity, hovered around the Barbican gates. The dogs, demi-baleful, impeded progress. 'Go round behind me,' I said, legs astride them both and holding their neck scruffs.

Jane arrived and called the dogs and I put-putted (it's on one cylinder at the moment) them both sitting on the Mehari with all the wine; she hesitated on the slope up to the Bailey gates. Showed them the Great Library. At very end he produced his own 'brochure'. The moated Château de Sully, with the largest Renaissance courtyard in Europe! For some reason this cheered me up, and I drank some of his wine at supper – quite delicious – Montrachet-ish, and I was drinking from the chef's bottle.

We went up to the battlements for the VE-day service, and I cast my mind back, thinking that 50 years ago I did assume that I would be the Prime Minister. Expected it.

---

[1] The £25,000 award went to Mark Hudson for *Coming Back Brockens*.

Saltwood   *Friday, 26 May*

Will the Tories lose? Now it really feels as if they might be
going to; I would still like to be there, if only to play a part in
the succession. An elder statesman in the corridors (but *not*
in the Shadow Cabinet). But has the opportunity finally gone
for 'this is the way that Britain can recover her former
greatness; and I am the person to do it'? Read this morning
at EMT for the first time for many years Rauschning, and
where I marked it.[1] Germany was perfectly structured for
Hitler, of course, who simply used the old Freikorps cadre to
impose compliance on an essentially capitalist structure.
Quite different from Russia where communism depended on
a huge urban/agricultural proletariat and all its latent waste
and incompetence.

All v lonely the thought of these dreadful Islingtonians getting
in. (I was more put out than I care to admit by little Juliet
Stevenson[2] being nasty about me and my book, in that special
implacably humourless way that the PC adopt.)

But what do we offer as an alternative? Mawhinney?[3] And a
vast army (soon rapidly to disintegrate) of template PR speciali-
sation and 'researchers' without substance and conviction of any
kind; or commitment save to their own self-advancement.

Can anything happen? I need to retreat, and think
uninterruptedly for a little.[4]

---

[1] Herman Rauschning, author of *Hitler Speaks*.

[2] Juliet Stevenson, actress (*Les Liaisons Dangereuses, Death and the Maiden* etc).

[3] Brian Mawhinney, MP for Peterborough since 1979, Conservative Party chairman
  since 1995.

[4] On the next page AC has started a draft of a letter to John Major, which begins:
  'Dear PM: I haven't written for ages, and I feel you must need this explanation of
  the access to which Privy Counsellors are allowed. I am now, for the first time,
  just a little bit worried about your safety ...'

Thursday, 1 June

Ted Heath[1] spoke in the Bosnia debate last night. His voice now rich (I said). Jane: 'no, it's gone.' Voice timbre is so indicative. My own is at its peak; will decline, I suppose in my seventies. Seventy-five is when it goes off, the last thing really except for sight.

MFS, Great Hall   *Wednesday, 7 June*

On 27 May (less than two weeks ago) I said that I needed a sign. Three days later, or so, Nick Scott 'crushed' a pushchair when reversing his car after a 'party' in his constituency, then shambled off 'to a friend's house', but was pursued, breathalysed positive, and arrested.[2]

Well, of course, for some reason (I forget its origins), perhaps the Henrietta Royle initiative, the agent's own invitation to speak next Monday at their 'garden party', I have had my eye on Chelsea for these last months.

Took a cab, to Chelsea, ostensibly (sic) to talk to the agent about arrangements for Monday. On the way the cabman – who had shown no sign of recognition – chatted.

Self: 'Fucking King's Road always blocked; half these fucking people ought to be at work' etc.

He got going on the Tory Party: 'John Major all right, but what he wants is a bit of panache (pronounced 'panarsh'). No style, too apologetic' etc etc.

---

[1] Sir Edward Heath, Father of the House, MP for variously titled Bexley constituencies since 1950, Prime Minister 1970–74. He and AC had not always been on the best of terms.

[2] Nicholas Scott had been MP for Chelsea since October 1974 (Paddington South 1966–February 1974); his career in government had culminated in seven years as Minister of State at DHSS (latterly Social Services). The episode AC refers to led to a series of cliff-hanging reselection and selection processes over the next eighteen months.

'Well,' I said, 'who do you fancy?'

'Do you really want me to tell you?'

'Yes.'

'I'm a bit embarrassed ...'

'Oh, really? Go on.'

'You.'

It was a real sign. He was serious and I was serious.

I spoke to Tip on the phone this morning.[1] He was serious, said huge numbers wanted me, 'scaffolders etc, as well as upper classes'.[2] I went for a walk and my fantasy developed, even down to choosing the government, the first night in Scotland: 'You've a PM and a Chancellor who are Scots – I doubt if you'd get better than that even with full independence.'[3]

As I walked around the huge rape-oil field opposite to Hobbs's farm, I noticed this very difficult wadi that protected Summerhouse Hill. If the entire Luft Jagl Division, all their Ju52s, had regrouped after Eban Emael, landed on the dunes behind Folkestone *as Dietrich promised*, we'd have gone. Illustrated how quick a roll will work if you take every opportunity as it comes up.

But (I explained the whole thing in a backgammon illustration to Tip) I must throw 4×4 to get any pair 'free'; then $3 + 1$ to imprison his sole straggler; then 5×5 twice to get ahead on the runner.

But I almost half know that, if I allow myself to become possessed, submit, it can't work. Exhilarating, really. I took out Wolf's portrait,[4] and put it back in its place. First time since leaving Parliament.

---

[1] Andrew and Sarah Clark were living in the constituency.

[2] Elsewhere AC recorded a constituency big-wig asking, 'where is the Wellington?' AC mused, 'Something in his manner made me think he wanted me to say, "it's me"; or he wanted to say, "why don't you do it?" I didn't answer.'

[3] On the opposite page of the journal, in very faint pencil, AC picked his government: 'OUT – Hurd, Clarke, Howard. IN – Owen, Rifkind, Mayhew ... Eric Forth, S of S Scotland.'

[4] AC kept a signed portrait of Adolf Hitler (Wolf) in the Saltwood safe.

MFS GH   *Thursday, 8 June*

Yesterday was fantasy, euphoria. Today plunged into gloom, apprehension and accidie. At EMT Jane drew attention to a lesion on my left shin, and lower leg, about 23 mm across, brownish, circular and sandpapery rough and v slightly raised. Not 'angry', no 'rolled-up' edge. Not (yet) a melanoma as too pale. Could it be a squamous. Very depressed and drained over this. 'Needs watching' was the verdict, so I watched it the entire time.

Reading the papers later, Andrew Neil *again* on the demoralisation of the whole Tory Party – 'Michael Heseltine will be in No 10 by Christmas.'

Then the little duck, which had done so well, and is so composed and amiable, was again terrorised by the dogs – which deliberately turned round and went back while we were fitting the handle (not wholly satisfactorily repaired) to the KGV car. I thrashed them both with Hannah's collar. But I fear it can't take two goes of this. Terribly depressing. We failed with the baby blackbird, then with the duck, next with a baby jackdaw that is hanging around outside the kitchen, signalling that he 'needs help'.

Then a phone call from David Leppard of the *Sunday Times* to whom I was offensive – but discursive. God knows what he will print.

I am low, rattled and apprehensive. How things can change! But can change upwards, too, of course.

MFS GH   *Tuesday, 13 June*

Yesterday we went up to the Chelsea Garden Party. I was apprehensive; I was not fully prepared and did not like the idea of speaking out of doors in a garden off the King's Road. As we passed over Westminster Bridge I saw that canopies were out, and felt a terrible pang. I am driven, which is why I am so unsettled.

In fact the meeting was a success. The chairman introduced me as 'the most interesting politician since Lloyd George …' – to some titters (because, presumably, of Ll G's goat-like tendencies), but I was delighted. People were friendly, and appreciative (except for that strange, handsome, groomed man whom one often sees at Party conferences – is he something to do with Central Office?). A young bearded, in company with a pretty girl with bad chin – acne – and a chinless boyfriend – said to me, 'I'm not into politics at all, but that was a really good speech. It meant something to me.' Then, in spite of the intense cold there followed a number of amiable and interesting questions. Dear old Nick Scott *was* there – looking quite fit I was sorry to see – and we put on a show of camaraderie. Also that berk who was on the Swinton course with me and held up all the traffic on the M1 on the way up. 'Do you want to go back into the Commons?' he asked as were leaving. 'Yes,' I replied; and the agent – Barbara Lord, with whom we – thanks to Jane too – are by now on better terms, pricked up her ears, and sought to confirm.[1] So I need a/*the* vacancy. I know I can do it. Because if the vacancy occurs it means I am meant to do it.

Bet for a by-election in September. A blazing Conference speech, and then back in the House 'introduced' on the first day back. After that ACHAB. Half of me actually sees it as inevitable. So strange.

It blights everything else. I still write well (a good piece in today's *Independent* about Mrs T) and was calm and handsome on the *Frost* programme on Sunday (this helped to give me 'confidence' for Chelsea).

But I am totally becalmed in paperwork.

---

[1] Barbara Lord, agent to the Chelsea (and later Kensington and Chelsea) Conservatives.

MFS Gt Hall   *Wednesday, 21 June*

It is midsummer's day, and the year half gone, with nothing, really, to show for it. Except earnings just keeping pace with expenditure – the treadmill.

Last night my programme on *Myths*. Good I thought, voice excellent, particularly the VO. It clashed with fresh turbulence over the Scott leak. First the substance of the leak itself – which I rode blandly. Then it degenerated into a rumour (presumably Tristan had something to do with it) that *I* was the source of the leak. This panicked me briefly as I have lost some of the papers and anyway hadn't read them properly. However, after a lot of phoning to Mike Brunson,[1] the Tribunal staff, etc etc, I was cleared. Might even, as can sometimes be the case, have come out 'stronger'.

I am still so restless politically. Something must be going to happen, I feel. Some sign will manifest itself. So everything is still secondary to that. As a result paper worse than ever. The whole system has broken down. Will the Degas sell? I hardly care. All I want to know – PM's Questions on TV drives me frantic – is how do I get back into the Chamber?

The pool is only now filling up – but heating rapidly (already over 66°). Even the swallows, so sadly few this year, have perked up and begun to chase each other; although their dawn chatter is restless and curtailed.

MFS, GL   *Saturday, 24 June*

How I love Saltwood – for all its pressures and 'claims'. After EMT I went into the front part to wind the clocks. It is peaceful there and still quite timeless. I wonder how long the boys will

---

[1] Michael Brunson, political editor, ITN, had gained a draft extract from Sir Richard Scott's report, which appeared to implicate several ministers including AC.

maintain it, and felt a pang (I am getting these more often lately) at not being able to see my grandchildren. The Degas is coming up next week – but I am resigned to it not making its reserve (which I will come under pressure to reduce, and won't). But if it sells I will *just* be able to set up another Trust, and slip 'sideways'.

Big Book has been totally neglected since (I suppose) February.

Here I am using, in my father's old study, the far side of the Great Library, the only remotely clear flat surface in the entire complex, and the great Adam long-case clock ticks readily (one per second) as the jackdaws chatter busily and unbeknownst outside the windows.

Really my diary is my only true solace.

I am wrecked, *wrecked* by my impotence at the turn of events.

John Major has offered himself for re-election,[1] and the television shows the blue door (another blue door this time in Cowley Street) of his headquarters, people scuttling in and out. But somehow, transposed 1939 to an old 1918 shot.

Yesterday I went to Gordon Greig's funeral.[2] Sensibly choosing Big Red at the last moment so that I was 'on the phone'. Jane rang to say Douglas Hurd had resigned![3] Correspondents hanging about outside the doorway. As I arrived, though, slit-eyed David Hunt[4] said, 'You should still be in the House, Alan. Then you could put your hat "in the ring".'

---

[1] John Major resigned the leadership of the Conservative Party, immediately offering himself for re-election. This was his offensive against what he called 'a small minority in our Party' who opposed him, undermining the government and damaging the Conservative Party. 'I am not prepared to see the Party I care for laid out on the rack like this any longer.' John Redwood immediately resigned from the government and announced that he would also be a candidate.

[2] Gordon Greig, long-time political editor of the *Daily Mail*.

[3] Douglas Hurd, Foreign Secretary since 1989, had told John Major some time before of his intention to retire at the next reshuffle; he had turned 65 in March.

[4] David Hunt, MP for Wirral West since 1983 (Wirral, March 1976–83), successively Welsh and Employment Secretary, then Chancellor of the Duchy of Lancaster, 1994–95.

Earlier a man in the car park had approached me, said how much he enjoyed the TV programme. Simon Heffer said, 'you should put in for the leadership – you don't have to be an MP – just a member of the Party.' Paul Dacre[1] said, 'We'd use him, but he belongs to another paper.'

A little later Alastair Campbell said, 'Why don't you come over?' I said I might leave the Tory Party if they put in Heseltine. On the way back I stopped for petrol in the Tesco car park and a big man – demi-loony, or was he drunk? – started shouting. Unintelligibly, but on the lines of 'give you thirty bob for your car, must use a lot of petrol etc etc'. After filling my tank I walked over to him in my what-the-fuck-are-you-on-about? mode. 'I'm so sorry I can't hear what you're saying.' He shook my hand, 'You are the only Tory with any balls' etc.

Is it any wonder that I can concentrate on nothing? Over here this morning I was on the point of making my appeal. I spoke out loud to God, apologised for my frailty and hesitation, always making excuses. Soon I will. Very soon.

MFS GH   *Tuesday, 27 June*

That pleasant feeling after a giant tour (50 NADFAS from East Sussex) when Saltwood breathes easily again and everything is so hot and tranquil and summery; and the leaves and the greens are so magical.

I swam a couple of lengths in the pool now only one week full but 67°. At such a time, and in this season, the pool at Saltwood is 'one of the loveliest places in the whole world'.

But this year, perhaps, there is a pervasive nostalgia, a certain mild *courant d'air* that trails a sea change. Normally, as in previous years, it is the pre-reshuffle time. Except for my first years at DE I was not apprehensive, but anticipatory. It will be better for me

---

[1] Paul Dacre, editor of the *Daily Mail* since 1992.

than for some, and the hols lie ahead. Now there is a reshuffle with a capital 'R' under way – and I have no part in it – except as an extra.

Very early this morning I was on College Green, and behind me the House so bandbox clean in its yellow sandstone – but *terra prohibita*. All those other MPs, Irvine Patnick,[1] little dapper 'boyish' Alan Duncan,[2] could just walk straight in. And yet – I am demi-lionised in the Millbank office, and a dark girl in a tight white suit greets me. When I parked the Porsche at 7 a.m. there in Great College Street was a stooping white-haired old gentleman walking his dog, with a peevish expression on his face. It was Peter Walker,[3] younger than me, the Great Hope and Rising Star – thwarted and done down by Margaret (one of her – not few – personal mini-achievements). 'Good day, Peter,' I shouted. He mumbled. 'Enjoying it all?' He didn't respond.

The previous night I had dined with Gill Shephard at Wilton's. To my surprise she had accepted at three hours notice on a phone call from Saltwood. I was worried about the whole party going into meltdown. I can't believe that Heseltine would get it by default – but to be sure of that there must be someone from the centre-right to come through. And, as I have often said (including to her) I think Gill is that person. She is keen, did some – but not too much – personal boosting. Expressed her irritation with the chaps' atmosphere at Major's headquarters and when I raised the question of who might inherit his organisation if it went to a second round said she thought it could be Ian Lang.[4] She is a tiny bit too short. Has lots in reserve and I think would be good against Blair in an election.

---

[1] Irvine Patnick, MP for Sheffield Hallam since 1987. Knighted 1994.
[2] Alan Duncan, MP for Rutland & Melton since 1992.
[3] Peter Walker, Lord Walker of Worcester (MP for Worcester 1961–92), member of Heath and Thatcher cabinets.
[4] Ian Lang, Scottish Secretary since 1990, MP for Galloway and Upper Nithsdale since 1983 (Galloway 1979–83).

Saltwood Tower office   *Sunday, 2 July*

A great psychological cloud lifted by letting the Degas go at 515 so can now (a) keep Big Red, which Jane really likes, and (b) set about Trusts.

By the pool, Saltwood   *Sunday, 6 August*

A great sense of well-being pervades me. The dinner party (15 people as Mary Archer asked herself *en supplement* at the last minute) was an enormous success. There are no functions left this summer, and an 'awayday' next Wednesday 9th when we go up to Bisley to see the Howards (Charles having had another heart attack, his 3rd – or so I was told by Bartosik[1] in the room at Brooks's, while actually *at the board*!).

Picking systematically at paper and files before heading north at an early hour on Thursday, 17 August. Confident-in-the-knowledge that there is precisely 500 on deposit in Coutts money market.

As to the autumn – a friendly letter from Angela Rumbold;[2] made me realise how incredible if I could pull that one off. Graham Stewart is more amiable and discreet than I had anticipated. And I am at peace with my cars. The only one I feel I ought to let go is the SS100 (but there was little Mrs Ben How coming up to me on the Albany/Royal Academy traffic island majestically and saying 'How's my car?') Probably also the R type Cont and the Todd Buick? Would raise 85, 60, 16 (XK 140) and 24, so not far off 200 (and what's the difference?).

A note about the dinner: we worked – myself intermittently, Jane continuously – for nearly a week; 'Duke of Norfolk' getting the whole 'ceremony' so that it went through flawlessly.

---

[1] Sam Bartosik, backgammon player (see *Diaries*, 27 October 1983).
[2] Angela Rumbold, MP for Mitcham and Morden since 1982; DBE 1992; writing in her role as Deputy Chairman of the Conservative Party.

Shore Cottage   *Wednesday, 23 August*

On Sunday we had left Saltwood at 3.30 a.m. – bathing before, on Jane's initiative, and I had (*for the first time*) a wonderful and perhaps never-to-be-repeated experience – swimming on my back, frog-legged, and looking up at the stars. We made good time to Scotch Corner in very light traffic, then headed on through the Border country and the Buccleuch estates – simply beautiful. Jane did most of the driving as I was comatose and she triumphantly delivered me to Gleneagles (where, as always, the dining-room staff were efficient and the food delicious, but the bedroom was poky, an old staff bedroom classed as '1st class' and costing £400).

The next day after the massive and nourishingly delicious breakfast – sitting somewhat apprehensively at Mrs McTavish's table – we cruised along the A9, took the Hope Road and, on impulse, and fully loaded – three dogs, and the old 'yellow' Hermes computer and screen as well as some lead for James's weights plus God knows what else, and two crates of drinking water – took the ford at Cashel Dhu!!

Slept again for eleven hours; woke with slight sinus headache, still v feeble.

I suppose if one did this for 2½ weeks – no alcohol and 'rest' alternated with writing and physical – one should show results. 'Feeling' better though comes before improvement in appearance. It takes longer – three months rather than three weeks – to reduce sacs of fluid and build up muscle tone. I should be encouraged by Tom, who is now 115 and his back legs cause him to stumble quite a bit – he fell into the burn yesterday after failing to recover from rolling in something – then he goes up and down the banks sorting out the burrows and led the way along the shoreline to the 'Great Burrows' before turning and separating from me to return to the croft. This morning he did a most wonderful prancing leap over a broken rung in the foot-bridge. As so often in the first days here I simply let my mind stray, I don't look at the papers, we have no radio and I don't rootle in my briefcase. It is all I can do to send postcards.

Shore Cottage   *Monday, 28 August*

Back this afternoon from a 'break' at Pait Lodge.[1] Practically everything was as one had anticipated – but nicer.

The people were old, but not as old as we expected; boring, but in a congenial way, not-yer-herr-herringly so.

The Lord-Lieutenant, Burton, a stooping man with white hair and the mien (deceptive it would appear as a tale was told of his 'short' temper, and slamming the car bonnet down on the fingers of some individual who was trying to effect repairs at the bottom of the drive – dodgy behaviour, surely, for the Queen's representative?) of geniality. On thinking it over, he looked something of a mix between Maurice and Jo Grimond,[2] having the 'old school' high table style.

Perhaps it was this (although neither he nor his strangely fey wife, a former demi-beauty *en deuxième noce*, now dressed unaccountably from head to foot in black, stayed the night) that induced in me an overpowering access of nostalgia. In the late afternoon Jane and I took a walk up the glen, it was intended to last an hour or so, but we were out for more than two and a half hours.

We were escorted by young Richard Hamilton, a charming lad, immensely athletic, who had *run* up several of the Munros,[3] and disconcerted me on our return – there was only just time to take a bath – by saying that he was going to 'fit in' his press-ups. 'How many do you do?' 'A hundred'.

But the whole experience was steeped in Buchan – as Richard's innocence (it is curious how this can be combined, as it was in Buchan's time, with witnessing the most dreadful scenes – he had seen a man beaten to death on a train in China)

[1] Pait Lodge, the home of the Clarks' friends, the Stroyans.

[2] Sir Maurice Bowra, Warden of Wadham College, Oxford; and Jo Grimond, Liberal MP for Orkney & Shetland 1950–83 and leader of the Liberal Party, 1956–67, May–July 1976.

[3] The Munros, the highest of Scotland's mountains, 284 mountain tops named after the man who first catalogued them, the Victorian mountaineer, Sir Hugh Munro.

and his asceticism. And the furnishings of the lodge ('Sapper's' *The Final Count*[1] was by my bed) all bought en bloc from old Lady Stirling who used to knock her pipe out in the butter dish, in the early sixties. Tongued and grooved pine, and enormous jug-and-basin washstands.

John Macnab.[2] And the Royal Navy on station around the globe. In Belgrave Square the great town houses are August-silent and dust-sheets over the furniture.

As the boat took us back down the loch I underwent a strange inducement of feeling. Those great Munro's falling into the water, utterly remote and free of human imprint. Far glens and slow curves and the shoulder of distant Coires. At the time I was absorbed and brooded on my own destiny. But now I wonder if I shall ever see it again?

At the pier on the Monar side two stalkers' ponies were waiting, fully saddled-up, with a ghillie leading them.

Saltwood   *Wednesday, 27 September*

What should have been a delicious *désoeuvré* day, free of obligation, and with choice, soon evaporated. On came that tricky little prick Sebastian Shakespeare.[3]

'Always a pleasure to talk to you.'

'You may not think so this time ...'

Asked me about putting in for Chelsea; I referred him to the agent. 'People are saying you wrote your CV on House of Commons notepaper' (Gaaah!). I explain I'd paid to print it myself. But what a lesson in how everyone is just waiting to fault-find. Whispering he mentioned something about the 'Matrix Churchill scandal'. Silly little runt.

---

[1] The last of Bulldog Drummond's four rounds with arch-enemy Carl Peterson.
[2] The eponymous gentleman poacher of Buchan's novel.
[3] Sebastian Shakespeare, editor of Londoner's Diary in *Evening Standard*.

Saltwood kitchen   *Friday, 29 September*

Still very unsettled. My jaws ache (both sides) and I have split a back molar on the right due to avoiding (funking) Bertie Arbeid for the last three weeks. Naturally he's away until next week.

Quite a friendly piece in today's *Independent*: '... allowed his name to go forward.' That's more like it – just the phrase. So far I'm managing to keep this out of Jane's notice, as it's still 50:50 that nothing at all will come of it. Alastair Stewart[1] wants me on Sky TV – but I'm not so sure that's wise at the moment.

What is really irritating – but totally 'serves-you-right, Alan' – is that – muddled and fatigued – I refused Carla's[2] dinner for Jimmy [Goldsmith] last night; all she could say is that Redwood and Jonathan A were going to be there. I didn't specially want to see Redwood who I think slightly loopy.

But now it turns out to have been a really interesting conclave. Conrad Black, David Frost, Alexander Hesketh, John Patten, Evelyn de Rothschild[3] and many others (including Jonathan A). I could have made a real contribution. Then today, p.m. Jonathan H[olborow] rang softspoken. Stewart Steven has resigned from the *Standard* and Max (of all people)[4] has taken over. Key question, therefore, who is going to get the *Telegraph*? Jonathan wanted me to approach Conrad. I couldn't, left a message, but hasn't called back. If I'd been at the dinner last night it would have been so much easier. Why did I duck it?[5]

---

[1] Alastair Stewart, newscaster and TV presenter previously with ITN.
[2] Carla Powell, wife of Charles Powell, private secretary to the Prime Minister 1983–91.
[3] 3rd Baron Hesketh (various ministerial appointments in the Lords, also a Whip); John Patten, MP for Oxford W and Abingdon since 1983 (City of Oxford 1979–83), Education Secretary, 1992–94); Evelyn de Rothschild, chairman N. M. Rothschild & Sons Ltd.
[4] Stewart Steven, editor of the *Evening Standard* since 1992, *Mail on Sunday*, 1982–92; Max Hastings, editor of the *Daily Telegraph* since 1986.
[5] Charles Moore (*Sunday Telegraph*) succeeded Hastings; Dominic Lawson, editor of *The Spectator* since 1990, succeeded Moore.

Saltwood   *Saturday, 30 September*

Very heavy-hearted now that I know I'm (barring a *total* miracle) finished. I think all my 'public speaking', TV, column, phoning, lunching and dining with colleagues – Portillo, Gill Shephard, M Howard, the rest – has been in the context of assuming/hoping/fantasising that somewhere somehow I would be offered the choice of a constituency and a return.

Up through the members' cloakroom, the big staircase (or the little front one by the loo) along the corridor, past the big octagonal writing table in a bay window and into the Members' Lobby – through the door that only Members can use, so that as they swish open any waiting journalist will know that only an MP can be coming through. Then a glance at the telephone message board (perhaps a 'badge-messenger' handsome in their white ties and tailcoats) will spot me and shout 'Mr Clark' and bring a letter from the message board on the other side. Perhaps look into the Chamber, see what's up, how full it is; stand 'at the bar' for a minute or so. Then down the tearoom corridor looking in there, or on into the library; drift up past colleagues busy at the various desks – Nick Budgen, Enoch always in his traditional place (last time I was there) and on to the No-Smoking and the Silence room (where if people talk too loudly you can call out 'ORDER') and slump in a chair there to read the *Spectator*, or something more esoteric.

Yes, all that still mesmerises me and for three years I used to dream about it, half certain that I would return. But now that Chelsea (which, somehow, so much seemed pre-ordained – the speaking invite, Nick's accident, the audience reaction etc) won't even see me, I realise that, in fact, it is hopeless.

So I might as well pack everything in. No more columns (I'm just starting to get a wee bit stale and repetitious); no more appearances, public speaking and soundbites. If I'm around (but see below) perhaps the occasional nicely crafted review to help pay for 'petrol'. In theory I become bookish, concentrate on Big Book.

But this afternoon I begged Jane to come on a long walk with me and help me think things through. It was a failure. We started by bickering; she just didn't comment at all on my dilemma except to say things like 'you've had your chance'; 'you (by implication) failed, flunked it …' or whatever. Never far below the surface the 'you've been undone by women' accusation. A good deal of stuff about how absolutely impossible I am to live with. I suppose I am only making her unhappy (still). Then on my return from Patel in the Bustard I left the Barbican gates open – only for such time as it took to put the car in the garage, come in and phone Patel. Although the dogs don't, in fact, wander she was concerned I had let them out, got into a fearful state. I drove off in S16 in case they were loose in the street. Naturally they were not, and when I got back (having been buttonholed by a nice lady who wanted me to revisit Dover docks which I must do next week) they emerged from the undercroft. But yet more damage had been done, and we sat in total silence all through tea.

I really feel I must get away. Really away, I mean – *Eothen*. Just do a Stephen Fry.[1] I can't, of course, until I have got some order so that, at least, she doesn't have debts to banks or other unfinished business. This can only be done by selling cars – but which?

My solace at the present time is to drink even more deeply from the Buchan nostalgia. That way of life '…and the Grand Fleet was stationed around the globe'.

Saltwood   *Tuesday, 3 October*

Went over to Garden House. My phone had twelve messages on it – goodness knows when it was last cleared. Among them a

---

[1] Alexander William Kinglake's *Eothen*, or *Traces of Travel Brought Home from the East*, first published anonymously in 1844, ten years after the journey it describes had been undertaken. Kinglake (1809–91) was an Old Etonian, who went on to Trinity, Cambridge. Stephen Fry, the actor, had recently disappeared after opening in a play in the West End. On his return he admitted to having suffered a breakdown.

perky-sounding Barbara Lord. With thudding heart I returned the call (perhaps mistakenly starting by saying '…I assume it's bad'). But no, she was just apologising for the piece in the *Standard*. We had an amiable conversation getting down to twenty before Conference – interviews afterwards. I felt wonderful – lifted. But now as I write this I fear it means that 'notices' will go out before Conference and so if I'm not in the twenty I will be thoroughly out of sorts (again). I went to the Great Hall (by chance as I left the light on there) and sat at the long table. God told me to ask for serenity and balance. If I didn't make it – well, decks are clear. Because contemplating being back in, delightful though it is, consider the implication of enchainment until old age or death. In spite of everything I said, I will become a buffer – or quasi-buffer – in harness. Easier to commute to Saltwood, of course. And I know how to 'swing the lead'. But I would be turning my back on will-we-ever?

MFS GH   *Thursday, 5 October*

I was all day at P. & A. Wood having the new steering wheel fitted to 'Big Red'. What a luxury! Raises it to the level, almost, of 'the ultimate driving experience.'

This evening I pottered over here because the Executive is sitting in Chelsea deliberating the twenty. Am I, actually, a 'front runner' – *passim The Independent* – or is the whole thing ridiculous? I prayed at the long table. And drew some strength from the fact that it may not have been a bad idea to 'stand down' in '92. Because in the last three years I have become a FP – my status may work in my favour; may not. But it helps me to become philosophical. If I lose at Chelsea then I will become a sage.

Zermatt   *Thursday, 12 October*

Arrived here to find the whole place unchanged, undisturbed as usual. The new block of flats behind really quite tasteful – very little sense of oppression, though one needs some kind of *blocken* trellis to protect the back wall along the terrace going up to the house and the backgammon-room chimney.

We came in the Discovery (having earlier wavered between the Citroën or 'Big Red'), recording extraordinary fuel consumption figures and enjoying James's green *Ausweis* on the windscreen which – inestimably convenient – allows one to drive the whole way to the 'Parking'. En route, quite late in the afternoon when we were looking carefully at the signs on the autoroute, Jane spotted the name Colombey-les-deux-Eglises. For a second I thought no; no time to make a detour; but then *of course*. Because what-is-written-is-written we drove through ineluctably French countryside and villages. First (due to unnecessary diversion) coming by way of the memorial – an extraordinarily powerful erection; a croix de Lorraine about 120 feet high in granite bits, pinkish in colour with a very slightly parabolic contour and against the lower wall just the letters (in forged bronze) GENERAL DE GAULLE.

No one about at all. I spent a little time there, went to the shop – noting the General's Quinze ('Big Six') Citroën which he had used until 1958 – bought and sent postcards to, inter alia, Soames, Ryder and Goodlad.[1] We then went down to the Boiserie. A 'homely' low-built house covered in Virginia creeper, heavy white gravel, garden rather contrived, rather Ascot-like. But the beautiful view of distant forest-covered hills so unforgettably mentioned in his memoirs. The interior also quite confined: the dining room intimate, you could not have sat down more than eight. The salon also, and the General's library and bureau in the ground floor of the turret and his desk

---

[1] Alastair Goodlad, newly appointed government Chief Whip in succession to Richard Ryder, who returned to the back benches.

looking out over the countryside. There, too, was the leather armchair, nicely stuffed, where he had died. 'So important to die at home,' Jane said.

I fantasised a little, nice to absorb atmosphere, but not very successfully. I am too wound up with the last charge of the Royal Guard of Charlemagne – as it is. But I am glad to have visited the place; and like almost everything else in this extraordinary saga the timing is uncanny.

Because at the weekend after the short list had been chosen I was on the *Today* programme with my 'essay', and *Breakfast with Frost*, where I drew the extraordinary compliment from Michael Foot. 'I always think Alan Clark articulates what both on the left and the right wing of the Conservative party feel better than they do themselves.' We'd hardly been here an hour before Sheila Gunn was on the phone saying how (truthfully or otherwise) the Chelsea constituents at conference had 'enjoyed' my CV.[1]

Monday, 16 October

Yesterday, another bullish signal. I rang the Kensington–Chelsea paper to find out about back issues, giving my name. 'Oh, uh, Alan Clark? … You're going to be the next MP for Kensington and Chelsea.' This from the News Editor herself! Greatly boosted I started putting my speech into shape, and running it through the tape recorder. A useful trial – as seemed far too slow at first. I can't decide whether to use the jokey opening or not. But there is no doubt that the Scott extract works.

---

[1] In *The Times*, Sheila Gunn, one of its political staff, wrote, 'Not many rate his chances ahead of less colourful figures.'

Sunday, 22 October

After return from the selection committee.

A curious experience – seemed to go well; almost too well? Barbara Lord said to me, on the way out, 'you were marvellous.' But then went on to say, 'I think ... [hesitation] what will tell against you is your age ... If they do decide to replace Nick it will be with someone much younger ...' I was bland and understanding, though hiding it. 'But ...who can tell?' she added. Did she mean *on the night*, or 'today'? The nice fat girl who gave me a map of the constituency said the calls would go out 'about 5.30' which is what it is now.

I ought to welcome release. Three and a half years later. But I am really tense (this morning in Albany mirror I had 'stress stripes') which mean the let-down will be dreadful. So many signs were good, all the way through.[1] *Waiting for the phone*. One of the great ordeals of modern politics.

Great Hall, Saltwood   *Monday, 23 October*

I suppose that I knew last night by 7 o'clock that it was over – for certain by 8 p.m. when I went sadly through to the kitchen. Nothing this morning save some probing gloats from the *Standard* and the *Independent*.

I set off for a great walk, it being such a lovely autumn day. As I rounded the corner, looking across to Saltwood church nestling in the fields, I felt a dreadful pang. No longer the profound, paternalist, nostalgia of 'this is the country I am defending; for which I am responsible'. Because I am no longer responsible, and never can be again; for if age was the cause of my rejection that is a condition that worsens every day.

---

[1] In a brief diary note on 19 August following 'a trail in Black Dog (*Mail on Sunday*)' about the Kensington & Chelsea selection process, AC remarked, 'all the angst, tension and (probably in the end) humiliation.'

I walked up the Down to the great cattle grid looking down on Beechborough. Sat for a minute and tried to pray. I search for a formula for some kind of serenity. Reflect utterly is the best; lie low while 'transitionalising into a sage'. Financial penalties, of course, but a certain guarded self-containedness. Practically never leave the walls, more and more eccentric, saveable now only by a miracle.

Can the mind overcome this reversal? The mind can do anything, even reverse a malignancy, if it is properly programmed.

Only consolation is that Franko is back as Editor of the *Spectator*.[1]

Saltwood   *Wednesday, 1 November*

Dinner at Bucks where (ludicrously) I was 'guest-of-honour'. Poor old Robin Day was crotchety, parodied himself to the point, almost, of discourtesy. Ronnie Millar[2] also, very frail and queer. Could almost be 'sickening' or 'fighting', but softspokenly asked for my phone no, a lunch at Brooks's soon. (No thanks, I think, for a bit.)

Donald McIntyre[3] walked me back to the Albany shutters. He is curious, but supportive I think, about both Scott and my search for a seat. We talked for some time about the former. As to seats, when I said I was also putting in for Mole Valley, Horsham, Arundel, 'Oh, so you really are serious ...'

This made me feel better, and I still thought about it when I woke just before my alarm call at 5 a.m.

---

[1] Frank Johnson succeeded Dominic Lawson, who had been editor of *The Spectator* since 1990, with Lawson becoming editor of the *Sunday Telegraph* where Johnson had been deputy editor.

[2] Ronald Millar, playwright, but best known latterly as speechwriter to Margaret Thatcher and John Major.

[3] Donald McIntyre, political writer on *The Independent*.

Saturday, 4 November

Very depressed. Ticky little agent at Mole Valley wrote with 2nd-class stamp saying 'applications closed' on 26 October.

I went for a walk, to get out of the place, as Jane in foul mood. (Although as well as doing my piece, I also lit fire, laid breakfast coffee, rolls etc, she was black as thunder, didn't comment.)

Came back, said a prayer in a dimly lit Great Hall. 'Do something' – swimming pool or House Colours, though not so intense of course. The message was stay calm, await the moment. It may yet come if you don't give up.

But then, during tea, Soames rang from his car. Bellowed away – quite funny, he told the Mole Valley dinner, 'You owe it to the nation to choose Alan Clark ...' I gathered, though, that this didn't go *all* that well. I slumped and brooded. Later, found myself a glass of Dôle from the Migros bottle I brought back. And as I walked in the moonlit outer Bailey I thought back to the buffet at the Bahnhof in Brig. The blind beggar playing his accordion and my early, as I often did in those days, tête de veau vinaigrette. And the Simplon pass which I knew well in those days, not much used as people preferred to take the tunnel. I always intended to do it once in the Bang Bang (now parked outside the Long Garage, dead, perhaps it is that which subliminally triggered it). That was all of thirty or more years ago. Before even my first rejection at Weston-super-Mare.

But, strangely, I am not yet finished. An interesting lunch with Phil Hall.[1] Pleasant, but *naïf*. Needs me on the paper to advise and consult about politics, write leaders at intervals ... Rupert[2] himself is putting the pressure on. Jane is totally opposed (but I have fixed her reward). Alastair said 'grab it'. Jonathan Holborow I am dining with on Tuesday. I hope he doesn't offer a lot more money (Phil has already gone to 125) as I think I am better 'standing back' from that anyway. But he won't be pleased.

---

[1] Phil Hall, newly-appointed editor of *News of the World*.
[2] Rupert Murdoch, the owner of *News of the World* through his company News International.

Wednesday, 8 November

Dined (modest dinner) with Jonathan Holborow at Wilton's. He is keen for me to stay at *M o S*, is 'reorganising the paper round you, Alan ...' Has said he will be faxing his 'offer' today. We got on well; my only slip-up, when setting out the 'generous' terms which Rupert (alias Phil H) was offering, was when J said, 'He's not offering you a seat on the main board ...?' 'Oh, no, I wouldn't want that.' Perhaps that was what J was going to work up to?

It is a difficult decision. Associated are (marginally) more congenial to work with – but I don't see how they can match Phil's 125 (+25).

EMT   *Friday, 10 November*

Last night was the Chelsea selection. Am I strong enough to recognise that this has to mean the '... end of that particular road' – *passim* Ted Heath at the Party Conference?

Albany   *Wednesday, 15 November*

I was at the Garrick, in the bar, prior to lunching with Ion and (asked himself) Sissons. On the way up in the train I had found among my mail a very pleasant acknowledgement from Nick Scott of my 'a thousand congratulations, good luck with the Rozzers', etc note. And there he was at a table with a dignitary of the Kensington and Chelsea Association ('you are such a success that the chairman let it run over by popular acclaim') and an Iranian 'businessman'. Point being, just a whiff of Tammany there – and good luck to him – lots of people had an interest, in the Nelson sense, in helping Nick *en poste*. Plus the old biddies of course.

Even so as I walked back, though, that phrase of Nick's, 'you still hear the drum' haunted me.

Then, somewhat unenthusiastically, I went across to Wilton's to meet Bob Balchin.[1] Just as David Davis had predicted – almost high camp. But we got on better and better. He was not discreet (although we both drank water), tipped me off about seats; told me to redraft my CV; said, 'no, no, get on with it' with *N o W*. So the whole day, the little Charles Addams boy, and the medicine.

Saltwood, EMT   *Tuesday, 28 November*

Still very mild, and this morning a (somewhat faltering) dawn chorus. At least one blackbird, or a thrush singing prettily. I found myself touched by a wistful nostalgia. The dawn chorus in late autumn. A year gone. While in May, of course, it holds all the promise of a major summer – sunlight and well being.

A false dawn with Chelsea (I genuinely thought it was *written*). Now it has to be a miracle. Tunbridge Wells at the last moment. I must stay in there, and bet. But what I hope, quite firmly now, is that the Tory Party is smashed to pieces and a huge number of people lose their seats. Then, at last perhaps, my particular brand of radicalism can grow.

Saltwood, EMT   *Wednesday, 29 November*

Jane lay awake last night for two hours (she told me this morning) in a mood of depression so black she could have killed herself. My fault, I suppose, because I had 'bitten her head off'

---

[1] Bob Balchin who via David Davis had offered to meet AC and, if he approved, to introduce him to constituency party chairmen in search of the right candidate.

yesterday morning when she brought photocopies of the typescript of my piece on Scottish independence when what I wanted was the copy of the piece in the paper itself – the cutting. And at dinner last night after being compelled to apologise, which I did – I don't doubt it seemed – with my usual ill grace I set out my own grievances.

Saltwood   *Saturday, 16 December*

The tail end of flu hangs on, and makes me depressed and lassitudinous. This afternoon I just stood in the Long Garage, defeated by the fact that the Bustard battery lugs had screw attachments not 'female' post sockets.

Had a sardine tea, but with the orange cake I got 'dyspepsia'. Cancer scare again as I had a sudden aversion to bacon this morning at breakfast. May be an element of 'nervous stomach' as I now realise that my Christmas holiday is also going to be 'filled out'; because James-Julie are here until 30th and KK [labrador] for a month after that. My first column for *News of the World* not until 21 January and I was hoping to use the vacant period for a last assault on the paper. We waste so much time looking for things. If that could be aggregated into tidying time we'd be so much better off.

So all in all, I'm in (8 days ahead of normal) standard pre-Christmas depression; and frustration, too. Jane is happily whistling and singing in the hall doing Christmas greenery. She really loves Christmas; and I am such an old Scrooge and wet blanket. Twice in the last two days to Canterbury, and everyone so busily bustling and rich. Coats' are going down which always puts me out of sorts.

The vein across my hand (particularly left hand) is permanently bluely raised – as I used when a child to notice in people of '60' (i.e. old people). My face has become so crumpled and jowly that it is irreparably downgraded. Still more muscle tone lost. Only eight days in Cuixmala can cure this. And as I write I realise that of course the presence of KK makes this impossible in the only free period we've got. Oh dear. No wonder I have a slight tension headache, and wind.

My recuperative powers are, or need to be, excellent. But they do need a 'kick start'. I somehow feel if I don't get on in the first two months of '96 I will suffer a downward step.

Saltwood   *Sunday, 17 December*

Helped Jane erect the (lovely and big) tree on an empty stomach. I had felt awful on waking – stiff, tired, de-energised – and was in the 'siren suit' over my pyjamas. Then I drove off in the green Continental to post some last-minute cards and collect a *N o W*. Tom had escaped (through a gap in the 'Roman' wall, involving a long glissade the other side – how's that for activity at age 17, '119 human'?). Walked over to the farm, collected him from Ann.[1]

Darling Jane was decorating the tree. The lights were fixed and I – 'watchman', most ceremoniously – lit them. Lovely. But the whole thing so *hollow* somehow. How many are we going to be? Four; five with Julie's mother. Later we looked through the window and it looked so lovely. 'Why aren't there children scampering about?' I asked sadly. I will never live to see my grandchildren marry. And what worries me is that I will now be old; shaky and selfish, when they have difficult passages between the ages of 9 and 18. Sex, drugs, shocks and bikes. Later we watched that (excellent) film on the Labour Party. Poor Kinnock – too much himself. Fatal in politics. Lessons, most of them melancholy, for the Tory Party in its present condition.

---

[1] Ann Felce, a friend and owner of Grange Farm.

Saltwood   *Saturday, 23 December*

One pleasing thing has happened. The Yeats 'Rose in a Basin' has actually come back here (cum expenditure of some £21,000 in legal and sundry expenses).[1] I never really thought that would happen. Now, of course, I look at it more closely just as I did those Yeatses in the room at the National Gallery in Dublin (incredible, so strong). Interesting, and satis because yah-hoo to 'McCann' (the thief) and his solicitors Stephens Innocent (sic).

Otherwise – not good. The Zurbaran is still in the USA with Feigin. Next year my own earnings will plummet catastrophically. I can't really live in present style and level of activity without £1.2m in the money market. So cars will have to be sold – but which? Even the SS100, which I feel rather warmly towards. Really the whole lot, I suppose, should go, leaving just the Alpine Ghost, the XK and the New Bing, plus one other (summer car or 'little Black').

---

[1] The picture, by Jack Yeats, had been stolen from AC's stepmother, and turned up in Ireland.

1996

It is only a week since I started on the Winstons.[1] But the tendrils had been moving below the surface for so long … (no, a poor analogy; I should say the material was all tinder-dry in my brain so the fire spread at colossal speed). And have done sixteen pages plus, in spite of being up in London on Thursday.

Big Red up and down. What a magnificent vehicle it is. Virtually no fatigue factor. Every mile a pleasure, and comfortable-in-the-knowledge-that … but cars are going to have to be sold. It's very sad, but at least 300-worth needed really.

I have one more year of this high earnings – from which no savings will be makeable, all directed to debt and taxes.

I must try and get Zermatt sorted out this year, too – and that requires a substantial sum (preferably in US $) on deposit and a kind of treuhand [trust].

James reported that Andrew – who has already claimed Broomhayes much to the indignation of the other couple – is complaining about my affairs in disorder. What happens when Daddy dies? … etc. (This must be the first time the young adults are starting to worry along the same lines as I used to.)

I was planning really to devote myself to the Winston this year. A long haul. Fired by progress I talked to Ion about length. We agreed at 450pp. That's 40 pages a month (allowing for holidays and wastage) or 10 per week. At this rate I'm ok, just. But plainly it is unsustainable. The timing is going to be perfect – for Tory conference 1997. But I'm sure others will be doing the same thing. 'Spoiler' operations.

Last night I had a talk with Tony Benn.[2] He was the only person even half-right on the subject of North Sea oil. And how

---

[1] One of AC's many names for what will become *The Tories*.
[2] Tony Benn, devoted MP for Chesterfield since March 1984 (Bristol SE, November 1950–60; August 1963–83), a radical, a parliamentarian, a diarist, and a minister in the Wilson and Callaghan Labour governments (including Postmaster-General, Industry and Energy).

fascinating he is to talk to! His mind so quick and versatile – but the loony prejudice (and this of course the motivation that keeps him active) never far below the surface. 'We want an Asia economy so as to be like Singapore – with its penal code' etc.

Politics still consumes and fascinates me. But I am conscious of being a little slower (at last). Somehow I can't always remember a name. And I am too tired/lazy to master policies in detail. This matters less than many think, but – *passim* E. du Cann and Jane's comment twenty years ago – you need it a bit or its absence shows. Watched John Major on *Frost* this morning v compos – greatly superior to Blair. But lined and strained and his bad English handicaps him.

And am I still capable of returning? The Thurber moth of course, but I just feel a tiny bit less alert than earlier in the period (even the last year). John Preece [from Plymouth], whom I have always liked, rang a couple of nights ago: 'you'll make it. Just keep trying. A lot of people down here have a lot to say for you' etc.

Do I still *burn* enough to do it? I have aged, quite suddenly and noticeably.

Kundan   *Thursday, 11 January*

Up in London – goodness knows I did not want to leave the Mains this morning – for two TV 'shows' and tomorrow a BBC *Kaleidoscope*. On a (virtually) empty stomach spent 2½ hours with mustard keen Mark Fulbrooks of Parliamentary Services, preparing my CV.[1] And my gosh he knows his onions.

And although I thought for the first time, I am too old for this, I've lost it. I don't want to get on a constituency interview list. The last time I have really experienced this sensation, all at once anyway.

---

[1] AC felt that a professionally massaged CV would help in his quest for a parliamentary seat.

But after Jon Snow – Channel 4 News (watching the Lady's 'domestic' speech) then being door-stepped by the little untidy-haired but lively BBC *Breakfast News* interviewer *I smelt powder and flint.* The special exultation, a version of which I felt after the first friendly/apologetic call from Barbara Lord at Chelsea. I am good on TV. So important. Who knows?

Saltwood   *Friday, 12 January*

Got back this morning, picking up a thin and unappetising-looking mail. Opened a letter stating something-something Sevenoaks Conservative Association. Almost before I got to the end of the paragraph I skimmed ahead, as it were, simulta-neously to an invitation to 'put my name forward' (!!!). And from a vice-president association treasurer for five years: 'I write in my personal capacity, but feel I am confident I have the support of many of my colleagues.'

So in a state of total euphoria. Second, really, only to Chelsea from the point of view of convenience.

A new roll has started. How lovely life is, and thanks be to God.

EMT   *Wednesday, 24 January*

I feel terribly tired today. And over the last 2–3 days I have suffered very brief spasms of 'Norwegian Embassy' – which I haven't suffered for several years, plus a very tight lower back. It's all too silly, the way I am still at SD (Standing Down) plus four years hemmed in by pressures and obligations.

This morning, briefly on the back doorstep by the asthma rail I smelt the crisp air from grass and water as the sun gets up on a winter's morning when the light has started to lengthen. Why was I not just pottering about out of doors – wooding or polishing? Then meandered in here and cast my eye over Big Book fragments – just scholarship. Again, tranquil and tempting.

Various clouds on the horizon. Scott: ought to be all right and am steadfastly refusing to comment, but occasionally wake in the night and think of the ultimate nightmare – Henderson (and all the other Matrix C directors) suing me under the direction of little Gilbert Gray.[1]

Saltwood   *Sunday, 28 January*

Bitterly cold. Yesterday I came back from Grantham, where I had been to deliver the Ernest Bevin memorial lecture to some trade unionists. The place got snowed-up and I had to take a cab from Grantham to Peterborough. The A1 was unrecognisable; a hesitant black-ish streak wound, down one lane, with barely a vehicle in sight as we crept round the double roundabout at Blyth so crowded and busy in the summer when we are heading north (or, return, south).

At Bertie Arbeid on Thursday to have a fantastic 'bridge' fitted (v successful; laughingly in the mirror I answer difficult questions at a press conference).

Saltwood   *Wednesday, 31 January*

After cup of tea at Albany went round to No 10. JM came to fetch me from the little reading room – so boyish and jokey. Really immensely attractive and in good form. He has had a

---

[1] AC worried that if he were criticised in Sir Richard Scott's report he might in some way be open to legal action from the Matrix Churchill directors represented by a QC of the stature, say, of Gilbert Gray, a Recorder of the Crown Court since 1972.

magnificent weekend[1] and is buoyed up by it. 'I'm beginning to think you might make it,' I said. Delighted, he agreed.

Saltwood *Friday, 9 February*

Nothing like the peace of mind after 'filing'. I have now really got into the hang of the *N o W* column. Although this evening, just as I was talking to Bob Warren[2] – very surprising cultivated 'suit' – he said a huge bomb had gone off in Canary Wharf.[3] And now the IRA has declared an end to the ceasefire. (So I have to rewrite something for it.)

Do I really want to 'put in a bid' (*passim* the Italian newsagent at Sevenoaks) for the various seats, Guildford, Arundel? It really is going backwards – and Simon Hoggart's interesting article – on the barrenness of the chamber was off-putting and sad. No more F. E. Smith and Baldwin.

Wednesday, 14 February

New cares, literally countless, weigh me down. Is it (light) alcohol poisoning? Oh-so-foolishly I told a reporter last night (ridiculously I don't even know who it was) that I was going to Mexico 'on behalf of *the* PM'. Extraordinary, this weakness of mine – and just as I thought I had it under control.

---

[1] The PM had given an upbeat interview to the *Sunday Telegraph* that weekend, which concluded, 'I like elections, and clearly we are within fifteen months of an election, so I am beginning to sniff the wind and feeling much happier about it.' AC had an audience with the Prime Minister to mark the start of his column in the *News of the World*.

[2] Bob Warren, of the *News of the World*.

[3] The IRA ended eighteen months' ceasefire by trying to destroy the new symbol of a resurgent Docklands; two people were killed.

EMT   *Thursday, 15 February*

Two punches landed yesterday. Clydesdale suddenly wanted their money back – 45 – all of it, at once. And Coutts wrote to say o/d is just over 60 (how *can* it be? I nearly always keep rough tallies in my head and thought it was about 35-40 at most). Rattled by Scott build-up[1] (some stupid Scotch wanker rang last night about the Al Habobi missile 'when you were defence minister'. 'When was that?' 'In 1986.' 'I didn't go to MoD until 1989.' Curiously rang off at once).

Later
Strange how one can feel better – more confident, ready for adversity and exploitation (should read 'opportunity', but exploitation sounds better, no double '-ty') after three cups of EMT. Caffeine is a stimulant, alcohol a depressant, isn't it?

Le Bourget   *Friday, 16 February*

In the (chocolate and cream painted) 757.[2] Not very imaginatively fitted out. Rather Arab with the seating arranged in grouplets – no private snuggery, but the loos are sumptuous. A taxi-driver had, or so he claimed, waited for three hours, took me to Le Bourget. Still cost £20. Now a long flight in prospect. Fellow passengers not v appealing; a mature lady in black – 'groomed'. A little Italian professore-type, muddled and anxious to please (*later:* actually the cook). Jimmy skulks unhappily in his bedroom in the tail – Howard Hughes!

---

[1] Sir Richard Scott's report due to be published that day.
[2] The private jet owned by James Goldsmith. AC joined a house party put together by Goldsmith for a few days at Cuixmala, his estate in Mexico.

Later

A v rich, but ill-looking Jew in young middle age with a pretty unbleached blonde wife. A French 'gentleman' ('not comfortably off' – Jimmy's phrase, but 'keeping up appearances' with chateau outside Paris). The illish-looking passenger is No 2 in, and heir to, the whole of Lazards, £200m+. But what's the point? Manners – simultaneously insecure and un(successfully) assertive. Jimmy is being charming to me. Speaks brilliantly on USA (high opinion of Pat Buchanan,[1] naturally) and French campaign of Michel Noir[2] now finally in total trouble – 'a write-off'. I wish BLJ was with me.

Cuixmala   *Saturday, 17 February*

4.0 p.m. English time. It is 9.10 a.m. here? I'm muddled. But slept well and had a delicious Cuximala breakfast. Spoilt only by the fact that my return here, Thompson pressing, the tiny maids (amiable, but 4 ft high) are encamped. And I know from experience that they will be here for at least another hour. Oh for three years of war in East Africa.

I just so wish Janey was here. The blooms and trees have grown vastly since we were here exactly two years ago. There is cloud, patchy, and the sea is less angry. A breeze, humid and gentle refreshes. I am in Ed Epstein villino and contemplate the rough, almost Cornish, coastline of the eastern Pacific seaboard; with reddish rock outcrops sparsely covered in vegetation and breakers foamily dousing them.

I am already feeling better. Although still worried-ish about sexual mechanism, problems building up in UK (are papers

---

[1] Pat Buchanan, right-wing Republican, aiming to get his party's nomination for the next US presidential election.
[2] Michel Noir, former Mayor of Lyon, who had been supported by Goldsmith in his attempt to become French president.

bothering Jane?[1]) and certain sign of age — particularly random memory failure.

We talked about Aspers (has got leukaemia, but 'under control'. Had a dreadful abscess in his mouth necessitating a double operation as 'they left some tools in' — eh? Uh?). Politics: Jimmy told me, most relevantly to the work I am reading up at present on the two '74 elections, that Heath had sent him out to Brussels to inquire of Christopher Soames what he wanted as price of desisting — apparently he was in cahoots with Peter Carrington — from furthering their plot to deseat Ted (illustrating, but I must look this up in Campbell's biography,[2] Ted's obsession with 'heavyweights' — just like JM's notorious phrase 'we've had a very good Cabinet' — and ignoring the electorate, in this case the parliamentary party). Soames said he would lay off if he got the Foreign Office in the next government. But there wasn't going to be (this was between the two elections) 'a next government'. Presumably he was talking about the 'Cabinet of distinguished people of good will outside party politics'. When I pointed this out to Jimmy he said — old Mexican political adage — 'in politics assurances only bind those who receive them'.[3]

In the night I was gloomy. I thought, what, at all, has been achieved in the two years since we were last here? A high profile, but even that seems to be going off a bit. How right I was not to do or say anything pre- or post-Scott. Apparently it

---

[1] Huge row over the Government's handling of the Scott report, but AC was exonerated.

[2] John Campbell, *Edward Heath: A Biography*, 1992.

[3] AC researched this account further. It was not quite as Goldsmith related in Cuixmala. In 1974, Jimmy, whose father had been a Tory MP, was already rich and wishing to make 'rapid ascent within the Conservative Party', he joined, on an unpaid basis, the Conservative Research Department, where he came to Heath's notice. Heath used him as his emissary to Soames.

As AC relates in *The Tories*, 'Yes, Soames would endorse Heath, align himself firmly if a squall blew up. His price? The Foreign Office. Heath knew that Soames still fancied himself as a possible Leader of the Party. He had been exerting massive pressure in Central Office to "find" him a parliamentary seat. "He'll ask for the Foreign Office," Heath told Jimmy. "Tell him 'Yes'."'

is still being puffed in Britain. But they'll have to do it without me.

Bernard [a French guest] said – when Jimmy was trying to explain the 'scandal' – 'I hope you made a lot of *monnaie* ...'

Jimmy, like me, sometimes looks like my father in his stooping movements and expression. Last night he escorted us to the villino, and I was worried by how old and shuffly he looked.

At breakfast he said he kept no papers – none. Because anyone in the USA can sue you, and hard disks are impossible to wipe.

Cuixmala   *Wednesday, 21 February*

Happy to be going back. I have missed BLJ so many times. Not specially worried about the flight – only it is always disagreeable suddenly waking from a catnap and realising one is over the Pole. Also I don't like all those people in the back of the plane spewing germs into the system.

I am returning (barring major and specific crises) to press attacks,[1] financial pressures, correspondence (even five days) backlog. Funny about James, Andrew, why no grandchildren? Humiliation at Sevenoaks. Days just being frittered, however good one's intentions may be. Breakdown of discipline. And until one masters discipline nothing will ever happen.

Jimmy meanwhile is recovered from his brief malaise (he is congenitally manic). He bubbled with enthusiasm. I note that he does sometimes forget the place in mid sentence, almost Hiram-like.[2] On Monday, just before lunch and down by the pool he suddenly said, 'What's the time?' 'Five to one.' 'I must go and have an insulin injection.' He walked round to the car park, went up in one of the FWDs; I'm lucky not to be *on* anything.

---

[1] The aftermath of the Scott report.
[2] Hiram Winterbotham, a mentor of AC and taught him to drive. A specialist in Georgian domestic architecture, he was a friend of Kenneth Clark and responsible for AC becoming a Governor of St Thomas's Hospital in 1969.

EMT   *Tuesday, 27 February*

Walked out into the Bailey this morning with T.O. and pink
sunlight on the Great Library wall, through traces of mist. The
grass white with frost and 6-8 ducks waddling about on the far
lawn.

These last two days I have managed to get out for an hour or
so, perhaps more, in the middle of the day and 'pull' brambles. I
am working on 'The Bank' (corner of) below GH.

Jane said she is still stressed, couldn't get to her studio. I
pointed out that at least the Webbs[1] were now installed and the
dogs had taken to them. She said it was because I wasn't working
on Big Book. Quite right. I did eleven letters yesterday, all
ullage, and easy for any competent secretary. Another sixty to do.

Later

I am in strange, if not 'poor' shape. I walked the Giorgione,[2] half
draped in a suit bag, half wrapped in bubble-plastic, to Emily
Black at Sotheby's. She is very pretty, with grey eyes. Unimpressed,
'too badly damaged', N. Italian, 'Putto with apples.' 'Really not
worth very much at all.'

'It's a matter of complete indifference to me what valuation
you put on it,' I smiled.

'£4-600.'

When I told her, she (actually claiming to know Jaynie
Anderson[3]) held her ground. 'How do you know?' etc.

Next I went to Christie's. Here it looked better propped up
on a chair. Unfortunately the atmosphere was slightly rarefied

---

[1] Lynn Webb, who became housekeeper at Saltwood, and her husband Ken.
[2] *Cupid in the Guise of an Angel*, a fresco fragment acquired by Kenneth Clark from
the Ruskin picture collection in 1931. He identified it as by the Renaissance
artist, Giorgione, from the Fondaco dei Tedeschi, the German customs house in
Venice. AC had even attempted some restoration on it in 1972, and, as a result, his
father observed in a letter, 'a certain amount of it has come away. But there is still
enough to be of considerable interest.'
[3] Jaynie Anderson, art historian, who was writing the *catalogue raisonnée* on Giorgione
(not published until 1997).

by the receptionist recognising me and calling me 'Lord Clark'.
So when Ben whatisname looked at it he realised 'there is
something important here'. Thrashed about, though getting that
it was a fresco transferred to canvas, and declared it at £2000. I
tried to get Charlie H[1] down to look at it, but he was tied up in
a mega-deal.

I came back to Albany. Drank five cups of tea, etc, Danish
pastry and fell (deeply) asleep. Woke up not knowing where I
was, hyper-chesty and with a pulse-rate of 82. Found a
thermometer, but only 97°. Strange. I cancelled any thought of
going to Pratt's.

EMT   *Saturday, 2 March*

I sit here and, after a few pages of Jim Lees-Milne (I am
dabbling in *Caves of Ice*[2] at the moment) I felt calmer and more
reflective.

But in fact I am showing classic signs of diarrhoea. Last
experienced on this scale in September in Zermatt; Jane said it
was nervous-stomach ahead of the Chelsea selection. Now the
timing (ahead of the Sevenoaks selection) is almost identical.

Let this, at any rate, be catharsis. The agent (Ann Barrow) is
pleasant. I am to see her on Tuesday. My 'contact', Kenneth
Miller, is probably less doddery than he seems. He has asked me
to lunch at the Carlton on Wednesday week '... assuming you
get through the interview ...' (uh?). If we can't bring it off here
then I will have 'done my best', and will settle for being an
academic. Three months will have been lost. But with Graham's
[Stewart] help this is still reparable.

---

[1] Charles Allsopp, chairman of Christie's since 1986, had become the 6th Lord
Hindlip in 1993.
[2] *Caves of Ice* was the third published volume of James Lees-Milne's diaries.

When I wake I groan with the sheer – self-inflicted – pain of how I am expending my time.

Yesterday I went over to Sevenoaks. The agent Ann Barrow dark, pale, unmade-up, in black, was pleasant, mildly cynical sense of humour, seen-it-all.

There were two members of the selection committee there fussing about with papers. Each, outwardly amiable (-ish), plainly were working their own schemes. She took me through the set questions. All matters of policy – concerning which, of course, I am completely ignorant. Also a good, not very encouraging and hard to memorise rundown of the wards. After a bit I just felt terribly tired and hopeless. Thoughtfully I drove back to Saltwood (after contemplating going straight on up to Smith Square to collect the briefings).

I rang the Research Department of CCO. A pleasant-voiced, but coolish young secretary would make no promises. I faxed a set of headings. I will drive up (in the Discovery of course) this morning to get to CCO at 11, then down to Sevenoaks to talk to the chief reporter of the *Chronicle*. This individual, like all provincial journalists, totally clueless about politics, very hack – asked what I was 'doing' now and then, 'I hope you don't mind my asking this – how old are you?'

As I said 67 it kind of came through to me how ludicrous this whole thing is. And yet Bob Dole (now doing well), Ross Perot, and the 'entire Chinese Cabinet'.

So I forced the pace, not knowing what the result will be; or even if it is favourable how much operational time I have left to me. I concentrate single-mindedly on this – to the neglect of urgent things like signing contracts (i.e. raising cash) for Nick K[1] and Ion. This Friday, ungetoutableof – I tried – my 'Stamford Bridge Before Hastings', the Macleod Society in Winchester.

---

[1] Nicholas Kent, head of Oxford Films, for whom AC would make a television version of *The Tories*.

Usual thing – M25 – on a Friday night. Exhausted all day Saturday zapping up. Sunday up previous in order to be at Sevenoaks (sinisterly Ann Barrow said I was to be greeted by Maj-Gen Pellerew who, so Kenneth Miller told me, thought I was too 'me-me'). Apparently I had also called Mark Lawson David until Ann Barrow tactfully corrected me. Also wrote down 'nursing', in list of policy headings. Had said, at the end, 'what does that mean?' 'Nursing the constituency', she said. Of course. We had discussed that at length. Then, that evening the coup de grace, or, conceivably, the stay-of-execution. If the latter, up to Ampleforth to pray, or to give me a lever with Father Seed to mobilise support in the seat. Executive reception, with Jane, plus speech on Tuesday. Final catharsis on Thursday. Then – more or less open skies except for 'police bail' – 4 April, fatuously the day before Easter.[1]

Saltwood   *Saturday/Sunday, 9/10 March*

Usual rejection syndrome. Very, very sad, but I must show resilience and 'class' even though now the lake is far, far distant. It's now 1.30 (I must have woken at about 1, and furtively took the clock *under the bedclothes* upon pressing the little button).

I looked out of the window, and saw a half/three-quarter moon over the woodland. God gave me the news/hope of a grandchild yesterday.[2] And just now I said that I would strive for constancy, and youth. That is to say I must retain my *tenu*. Not flag (*Spectator* articles etc). Take more exercise and drink sparingly.

I can now 'clear my diary'. I suppose I ought to have a blood test; particularly as I am now completely impotent, I need a heavy boost.

---

[1] Following a bomb scare close to the Albany entrance, parts of Piccadilly had been closed off. AC, who had the Giorgione with him, had driven the Discovery within a few feet of a suspect package that bomb squad officers were about to destroy in the aftermath of the IRA ending its ceasefire.

[2] Sarah, Andrew's wife, announced that she was pregnant.

EMT   *Wednesday, 13 March*

A 'full' day yesterday, but not wholly satisfying. Up to London by train (incredibly cold, knife-like, wind) and walked along the Strand – very much against the tide of pinched bustling office workers – to the Temple to hear Richard Scott on Matrix Churchill.[1] He is a splendid man – cool, clear-headed and witty. He was interesting – it was by and for lawyers – on case law. Lambasted discreetly Tristan Garel-Jones[2] and the whole deception of the 'response' document in the House of Commons Library.

(On the way back I glanced at the doorway of the chambers where I crammed successfully for the Bar Finals in 1955, a good discipline.)

MFS GH   *Sunday, 17 March*

I went up, somewhat against my inclination, but at Jane's prompting ('V-sign them') to Frostie. For some reason the camera stayed on me practically the whole time so when I wasn't speaking I could seem to be wanting-to-sit-on-my-tinkle-face and fidgeting. Also a weenie bit more mature now. Some shots good, some not so good.

John Redwood was there. More authoritative than formerly, less ready to smirk deferentially. Said JM's only skill was staying in office.[3] I wonder what he feels? There is a lot of talk now about a 'long' parliament, or a small Labour majority. I'm not so sure. I still think it could be very, very bad. (And of course finally, if I don't get back – which now seems virtually

---

[1] After his report was published, Scott gave a number of talks to lawyers and at universities.
[2] On the evidence of Tristan Garel-Jones, who had been a Foreign Office minister at the time, Scott called it 'risible'.
[3] John Redwood had stood against John Major the previous July in the leadership contest.

impossible – would prefer this. All those second-rate Tories just threshing around getting nowhere.)

On the walk we released a woodcock, which had got stuck between the two fence lines – always satisfying. But earlier I had been caused heartache by 'Cross Bencher' [*Sunday Express*] relating to the Sevenoaks shortlist – Stephen (ghastly), Fallon, Johnson[1] and thought of that note: 'You were in the frame until quite [sic] late'.

I suppose I really ought to concentrate on the BB. But it is the lure of the sword that agonises me. Will anything happen?

Tuesday, 2 April

As I write this date realise this is the 14th anniversary of the start of the Falklands war. When Jane met me at Sandling and I was making my plans to go lock-stock-and-barrel to New Zealand![2] (very odd). Later, though, I got into my stride. (Occasionally) wonder if I might have aimed at the premiership had I been made Navy Minister when Keith Speed resigned, been *en poste* when Notters had eased him out.[3] I would have been in rivalry with Cecil, of course. But at that time I was blacklisted on the computer.[4]

When am I going to get into Big Book properly?

---

[1] Michael Stephen, MP for Shoreham since 1992; Michael Fallon, MP for Darlington, 1983–92, who was ultimately selected as Sevenoaks candidate and won the seat in the 1997 election; Boris Johnson, *Daily Telegraph* journalist (whose route to the House turned out to be at Henley, where he succeeded Michael Heseltine in 2001).

[2] *Diaries*, 2 April 1982: 'We've lost the Falklands,' I told Jane. 'It's all over. We're a Third World country, no good for anything.'

[3] Keith Speed, MP for Ashford since October 1974 (Meriden, March 1968–February 1974), had resigned as PUS, Defence (Navy) in the early days of the Falklands imbroglio; Sir John Nott, MP for St Ives, Cornwall, 1966–83, Defence Secretary 1981–83.

[4] Elsewhere AC recorded '*spilling the beans* to an Inspector what's-his-name' after learning that a mistress was threatening to get some Italian Mafioso ('I've forgotten his name') to shoot him. 'A fine example of premature and ill-thought-out panicking.'

I simply don't know what to do about the cars. Am going over to P. & A. Wood this morning taking some nice stuff to be plated. Why? KGV car unsaleable. Ditto the Bustard; if I make an exception then why not x? or y?

MFS GH   *Easter Saturday, 6 April*

Foolishly and semi-drunkenly I broke the great terracotta pot by the swimming pool with the tractor. Jane was very cross and upset. On the walk she marched several paces ahead of me all the way. This morning I thought of the châlet – for the first time since 1960 no one has been there all through the whole winter-sports season. I'd like to get away – but I can't. Big Book is terrifyingly demanding now. I haven't any feeling of relaxation at all, [slight] workaholism. James rang to say that 'it's 78° at Eriboll', LLG and T-shirts. But here it is grey-cold, featurelessly light, and I must finish mowing the Bailey.

Easter Sunday, 7 April

I am getting intermittent toothache from lower-right. Why? The nerve is meant to have been removed and it's capped with a powerful gold-ceramic bridge.

Last night and again this morning we talked about a total Saltwood overhaul – lights, wiring, plumbing, decoration, the lot – £2 million? Need the Giorgione (or the Lottery?). Would have to be photographed first, then we move over to Garden House, precious stuff to Bank/Great Hall or GH. No longer feasible to contemplate for my 70th birthday.

Perhaps, too, fate would intrude, ficklely, and have me 'claimed'; just as the packing cases are full and the work started?

But the concept, now it's been given shape, homes in …

MFS GH   *Saturday, 13 April*

Already Birthday Boy; the year one-third gone and this notebook coming up to half distance. Rather more melancholy than
on previous birthdays. But oppressed, too, with the need for
BB to do its stuff, because 'its timing' will be spot on. SE
Staffordshire by-election and swing of 22%;[1] I don't see how we
can win the General this time so in autumn of next year the
Party will be 'trying to find itself'.

I have a perfect vantage point *in the wilderness* – but with just
this horrid dissatisfaction – I have no seat. Odious, every
prospect of being an elder, a senior knight of the shire. Only a
miracle can solve this.

I bought myself a birthday present (self-indulgently). A huge
royalty cheque came in, £78,000,[2] abolishing at a stroke the
Coutts overdraft. Almost within 12 hours I spent 40 on Core's
3-litre. On the way back from looking at it today I recherché-
du-temps-perdu at Hurstbourne Tarrant;[3] looked at the old
rectory, smaller than one remembered – as is everything when
one revisits. A planning application notice for converting old
stables (looked to me as if they had already *been* converted).

My mind wandered back, nostalgically. We were golden then.
Short of money, living at Rye/Bratton and envious of the
Grahams'.

I would like to write a where-do-we-go-from-here piece.
Must be over further to the 'right' – you cannot have two
competing centre parties. But never forget that Mrs T, who was,
suffered endless criticisms and ridicule for telling us where we
ought to be going up to '79. To leave the EC and simply to
anticipate its natural – and inevitable – implosion.

This ought to go in *The Times* – but can't (I will offer it to

---

[1] Sir David Lightbown, MP since 1983, had died. In the by-election Labour turned
a Tory majority of 7,192 into a Labour majority of 13,762.
[2] In particular sales of the paperback edition of *Diaries*, but also the ongoing success
of two of AC's campaign histories, *The Donkeys* and *Barbarossa*.
[3] Where Euan Graham lived.

them, though) because all they do is put Libby Purves, Bernard Levin in the prime place.

But first it must be written – when?

Right now I am going to work in the evening light, and pick at the badge room for goodies to fit on the 3-litre.

EMT   *Monday, 15 April*

I suppose that, technically speaking, I am in a pre-nervous breakdown state. I got up at 5.30; driven by pressing bladder (although had feebly urinated at 1.20 a.m.). But an hour and 20 minutes have gone past – and I can't do anything (just written these four lines). Look at my teeny crabbed writing. The last time I wrote even half legibly I was in Cuixmala. I have read Woodrow Wyatt – not much there really; they're better off with Al; M.Winner pretty cheap; the whole paper[1] is *so* tacky. But that's what people want?

Did fifteen letters, including a cross one to Clara[2] about the programme going to pieces – her idea to get Mellor and Edwina Currie (for God's sake) – and only just caught the post. As always, didn't quite have time to start up and go off in a classic.

Then went to start the mower. But although Ken had sharpened the blades beautifully – he had not re-tightened the belt, so the cutter drive shaft just rotated impotently. I went across to wash the Little Silver. Superficially an easy job, it is actually very time-consuming to do it properly. And, as frustratedly I worked, so did I get myself into a rage about the police stopping me yesterday on the M20 (where else?). Sure, the car was not taxed. But what caused them to check out the number? They couldn't have seen it. Sheer spite and aggression. You're worse off in a silver

---

[1] Lord (Woodrow) Wyatt, former Labour MP, chairman of the Tote since 1976; Michael Winner, film director – both fellow columnists in the *News of the World*.
[2] Clara Glynn, AC's director on the TV series based on *The Tories*.

Porsche than a black youth with dreadlocks in a BMW. In the latter case some of them, at least will be put off by the thought that they might get stopped.

Later the Webbs turned up and Ken tightened the blades. I cut the lawn until a late, late tea – 6.15 – as all we had at lunchtime, 2-ish, was some delicious smoked salmon and toast followed by *too much* of the unbelievable Doney's-like chocolate cake.

Thus it was already almost too late to go out in the Bustard, which, for some reason, fluffed a bit (very unusual) and backfired. But is still a beautiful example. No play in steering and springs at all. Wandered about in the gloaming, full of maudlinesque self-pity.

I am so rattled by pressure on time. I've been edged out of my office (early entries shows how important as a refuge) by Graham – which I knew would happen. And now Clara pre-empts the first of the week while the column forecloses Thursday and Friday. Saturday is always a particular scramble for the incredibly early (but useless, as it does not catch a Monday delivery) 11.45 post.

My time overdraft is even bigger than my financial one. This is real stress. It will be interesting to see how my blood pressure is when I have my tests (which I am funking).

Albany, EMT   *Tuesday, 16 April*

Mrs Frowd, sinisterly, asked me if I had any 'indigestion' – '*is the colon all right?*' This made me feel terribly low.

Once again, a lovely open evening – and it is 'to London', the night at Albany. Dined with David D (he has taken the place of Richard R as my principal *fix*). He said 'something-something your seat'; 'we did want to talk about …' I am dismissive and he didn't press the point.

He made some good remarks: 'MPs are different these days, socially and economically. They are a levy. And what happens when a levy is put under pressure? It runs.'

'Twentieth-century politics is the medieval warfare. The leaders are in the front line and the standard is what is important for rallying. The standard must be high, and it must be visible.'

And 'in' politics the natural (Darwinian) selection process for the larvae is quite different than that for the survival and advancement of the adult/leader ...

These are real aphorisms.

He was late arriving and while down at the end using his mobile phone to check with his office, Annabel Goldsmith came in plus Jimmy and Ben Ben (he now looking sinisterly terribly like Desmond Guinness at Eton with dark eyebrows and (as it were) striking bleached hair).[1] I had already drunk two glasses of the Wilton Puligny Montrachet and was 'silly'.

I ate six oysters, pâté de foie and toast, grilled turbot, and delicious crème brulée and raspberries, at least two-thirds of the bottle plus a glass of claret with the pâté.

In the night (2 a.m.) woke, felt uncomfortable. If I'd turned, or even moved, I 'could' (sic) have been sick. This morning I rose at 5.50 and again (finally) at 7.20. Looked dreadful – jowls sagged right down – and felt so old and creaky. In particular and looking back at the dinner I feel that I no longer have anything left in real politics. I must make my way with BB. But have I got the time?

MFS GH   *Sunday, 21 April*

To record a lovely day. These last two or three I have been low – concerned that I may have cancer of the colon ('any change in bowel habits should be investigated immediately'). And since Mrs Frowd – most sinisterly – had asked one about indigestion, and the 'colon' it seemed to deteriorate – so that I was convinced that I was not evacuating properly.

---

[1] Ben Goldsmith, James and Annabel G's youngest child.

However the sun shone and the air was lovely, still and clean.

I rose very early and looked at some texts for Big Book over EMT. Later I said to Jane ¾ of my stress derives from not properly addressing Big Book; I can feel the level easing off as I get near it. So much twist (or 'spin' as it is called) to put on this subject.

After breakfast we loaded the Discovery with stuff for the dump. Had our boilies early and only collected the papers on our way out. Dabbled our toes in the water at Hythe beach (Jane rightly pointing out a film of dilute sewage which lay on the surface of the LLG water). I finished cutting the Bailey and we had a pasta and salad, followed by mangoes and Belgian chocolates, which the young had given us.

No time for a zizz, but did a formal 'w' along the woodland (a fox by the stream bank now sojourns the day at the edge of his earth by the bottom tree).

Graham brought over an immensely polite undergraduate who is doing a PhD on the Manchurian crisis and I showed them round. A cup or two of Indian tea, and out for a drive in the Bustard.

Still light, and I'm over here to record 12 hours of almost continuous euphoria.

On days such as this I think – am I not fortunate to be an active academic (self-styled), living with a pretty and affectionate wife in 'one of the loveliest places in England', charged with a most fulfilling task and with two lovely sons and the prospect of a grandchild. How could I complain, or fret. And thanks be to God.

EMT   *Friday, 26 April*

The Party yet again in trauma. If you have no sense of direction ('no compass' in the current code) you don't know where you are going. This makes you vulnerable to attacks of panic and, particularly, mutual recrimination.

Of course it all makes me regret so sadly not being in the House. Not just for the gossip; but because I believe that I *could*, just possibly (certainly I could now with the acquired experience of knowing what to do), have been urged to take the helm myself. Anyway for the fourth, or is it the fifth, time in this Parliament the Party is in turmoil – this time over Jimmy.[1]

It starts with the feeling that seats are threatened – threatened more than is usual that is – then a feeling spreads – why not? There is talk of major figures (*passim* Redwood and Lamont) insisting on a referendum now, declaring a splinter Conservative Party and forcing an early election with all the Goldsmith money and campaigning zeal getting behind them. It could be valhalla of course.

But if between now and the local election results, JG gets serious, plans a campaign and this means saying what he will do in power, there could be a creditable freshness for the second stage. This means getting in professional campaign managers, a chief of staff, and an analyst (all, I know, uncongenial to Jimmy who likes to be a solitary buccaneer).

Yesterday at tea I was looking at the atlas and my eye wandered over a later page that showed the Western and Central Highlands. I said to Jane that there is a will-I-ever scenario that has been plaguing (sic) me since Portland Place,[2] almost. When will I/why can't I load my tent into the old Buick and meander about, climbing ridges and photography? W. A. Poucher constituency at last. I could, I suppose, still do it at 70.

---

[1] Sir James Goldsmith had announced the formation, and funding, of a Referendum Party, which would put up candidates against Tory MPs who were pro-Europe.

[2] A Clark family home in central London close to Broadcasting House before both Upper Terrace, Hampstead, and Saltwood Castle.

MFS GH   *Wednesday, 1 May*

Over here in some trepidation. Is this my very last free weekend
at Saltwood? Several times in the past I have thought this, I
admit. Yesterday while talking to Jaynie Anderson about the
Giorgione – a slow-moving saga – with my feet up, as usual, on
the jamb of the 'Tinker' door, I felt a strange lump on the
tendon of my left knee. An unusual place, surely, to have a
malignant growth? Whitby away, so booked into Nick Page for
a grand slam on Tuesday next; will also be bringing up the
Zurbaran and going to Rosemary for 'oral hygiene'.

Later
I don't object to current affairs taking so much time; except that
– like trying to keep fit – what's it all for? The death knell finally
sounded at the Sevenoaks rejection. DD more or less said 'it was
my reputation, and they felt they couldn't run the risk'. Now I
no longer do the *Mail on Sunday* (Mr Crocket, the boiler man,
one of today's many time consumers, reproached me for this).
I'm scrawny; my weight is back at 11.3½, 3 lbs down. So really
(if God spares me) I'm doing little more now than 'working out
my notice'. But if Big Book works out, then I will be satisfied.

EMT   *Friday, 3 May*

The local election results. Has the tide turned? Or is it perhaps
'*on* the turn'? A 2-3 point recovery, no more.[1]
  I suppose for both selfish and nostalgic reasons I would
welcome utter defeat. I don't want to see all those colleagues
who no longer court my attentions preening themselves.

---

[1] With only 27 per cent of the vote, the Conservatives lost 567 seats, but CCO's
worst estimates approached 700. This allowed the Party spokesman to say that the
results were less bad than in the 1991 local election, which was followed a year
later by a Conservative general election victory. Would the same happen in 1997?

Quietly back to 'where we came in' – a Labour government and a long period in which to foster nostalgia and in which my book (oh the book, how good it will be – and how difficult it is to 'put it together') will be a guiding light. But the vox-pop session for Basildon made me uneasy. No one offered a reason for voting Labour – only about voting against Tory. I feel in my bones that there might be enough of a rally to produce an 'almost-hung' parliament. And what wheeling and dealing this would give rise to!

Last night I spoke on the phone with Francis Maude;[1] clipped and authoritative, not unlike Redwood in his own way.

Lovely in a way, like pining in love, this sadness that I can induce about here, going down the wide corridor from the members' staircase to the Lobby, past the bay window where Clay Freud[2] used to sit and work out his bets before diving into an adjacent telephone booth to ring his bookie.

Bank Monday, 6 May

Very low today. I should have gone to Duxford[3] for the anniversary rally of the Spitfires. But slept in, intermittently, 30 minutes at a time, and was/would clearly be late leaving. Wanted to hear the Merlins,[4] see Alex Henshaw and get him if possible to sign the Mew Gull para in Jane's [*All the World's Aircraft*]; tell him how I saw him win the King's Cup air race at Lympne when he dived under the little blue Pobjoy monoplane.[5] I felt a tremendous pull to this, and hated myself and my intentions for

---

[1] Francis Maude, MP Warwicks N., 1983–92, Financial Secretary to the Treasury 1990–92.

[2] Clement ('Clay') Freud, journalist and droll broadcaster; MP (Liberal) for Ely, July 1973–83; Cambridgeshire NE, 1983–87.

[3] Former Second World War RAF station in Cambridgeshire, now an outpost of the Imperial War Museum.

[4] The Merlin, Rolls-Royce engine that powered the Spitfire and many other aircraft of the period.

[5] In 1938, when AC was ten years old, Alex Henshaw, a distinguished air racer of the 1930s, was piloting a Percival Mew Gull monoplane.

shirking it. Totally frittered the day. Mainly spent helping Tip wash and clean S16 (which responded beautifully, I must say).

I just hope the Zurbaran which I am taking up tomorrow can be placed. Really one needs £1 million in the Trust to yield income, relying on remaining contents to 'protect against inflation'. I absolutely refuse to sell, but perhaps the grandchildren will thank me.

B5   *Wednesday, 8 May*

At the flat phone ringing – would I take a call from the Chief Whip? Paraphrasing Chips I said – 'I can never resist a Chief Whip', Alastair [Goodlad] – worried about David D. 'He's going to chuck it in …'(?) Had seen the P.M. on Thursday, was going to talk again to him that afternoon. What had he been like at the weekend, etc?[1]

That's my third call from a political notable in 24 hours.

I took the Zurbaran back to Christie's. Then I drove slowly home in Big Red as I tried to ring David D and counsel him to ask for what he wanted. Finally he came back, as I knew conciliation-wise he would – while I was filling the tank at the M20 BP station.

Somehow I got the feeling that the tide had turned. I got back, ate scrambled eggs and finished polishing S16.

Shore Cottage, Eriboll   *Monday, 20 May*

Slept last night from 10 p.m. until 5 – can't even remember turning over. Yesterday we were drowsing on-and-off during the

---

[1] Now a FO minister, David Davis was said to be disenchanted by the government's handling of the EC's ban on British beef following the outbreak of 'mad cow' disease, and by not being promoted in Cabinet.

day – usually this ends on our first or second day – and now at last beginning to feel better. Need at least another week. Could consolidate tonight, but promised to take the young out to the Creaggan.

On Saturday we went to look at the great Arnaboll Forest project. Could be incredible. Already the game are back in copious (*passim* Jane) quantities. Strange and unknown vitality in plant life, secret and long dormant mosses and lichens. From a rocky outcrop James showed us the contoured lines of the plantings that leave plenty of glade and open areas for the wildlife to congregate. As far as the eye could see, some seven or eight miles on and over to Cashel Dhu. In ten years' time it will be noticeable. I hope to come as a buffer, in my plus fours, with a stalking stick and stompily survey it, but even James will be dead in seventy years, when it comes to full fruition.

On the way back we looked at some of the foundations, some of them even pre-Christian of the original Arnaboll settlement. At the graveyard the children's headstones were in the main still standing. But some vandal had – most recently as a fresh apple-core was nearby – levered out the lead lettering, scratching the marble with his knife, of little Jane Mackay who had died aged 5½ in 1867 and had such a pretty gothic stone. Loathsome scrounger. I hope some ill fortune befalls him.

Shore Cottage   *Tuesday, 21 May*

Our last day. Bright sunlight, bit windy. And there are two swallows back in the long shed – though none, yet, in the boat-house. I am hating the prospects of getting back. Almost as bad as leaving Portmeirion for school in 1942. Speaking engage-ments, Clara, mail, police proceedings (unspecified); always the relentless pressure of the Mains, at the centre of whole vortices of claims.

Like the Wehrmacht, and the Waffen SS in 1944-5 winter, just enlisting any old riff-raff into the fight. I can't/daren't work out how little time there is until have yet more 'under my belt'.

Always when I come up here I think of emigrating. Saltwood in care and maintenance. Everything in trust. This is such a lovely little study. And it, too, will become outdated shortly after the General Election, when BB is delivered.

Saltwood   *Sunday, 26 May*

Jane's birthday, and she has been absolutely sweet all day since we had EMT upstairs and talked about things – children, car-culling,[1] possessions generally.

I did my ten letters, and we then attacked the 'slab' – dispersing the dust of 13 years – since, I would think, last public openings as a tiny packet of 'Cadet' cigarettes stuffed with butts smoked down to the filter was found in the old shell-case that holds the walking sticks.

But for much of the day I have been uneasy, almost to the point of AF. *The Sunday Times* was loathsome – page 3, and huge colour mock poster plus – needless to say pictures of Valerie and Joei, various actors – 'Clark gets cold feet' etc. Thank God, and due largely to Jane, I'm out of that. Phew! But of course 'damaging' like being summoned 'Minister faces jail sentence' just in time to wreck Reigate.[2]

Then at tea, Jane – unerring eye – chanced on a long article about someone who had appalling metastasised cancer starting with a melanoma. Like seeing a bad motor accident, it makes it

---

[1] 'Yet again we return to the car cull,' writes AC opposite this entry, and then lists, with his estimated prices in £(thousands): 4½ litre Bentley (100); SS 100 (110); New Bing (40); XK140 (15); Loco (45); Big Red (120); B'Bang (18); plus in US $ Buick (45).

[2] AC was having second thoughts about a dramatisation of the *Diaries*; AC's court appearance was imminent; Reigate Conservatives were looking for a successor to George Gardiner, Eurosceptic rebel.

practically impossible to drive/look at one's shin. I am willing myself to have this condition; like giving your opponent good dice at a crucial point in a backgammon game.

Just as I was going to join Jane on the 'w' Jimmy Goldsmith rang. Rightly said that 'Beef war' was the wrong battle. He should have been fighting on fish. Will see what happens – but outcome looks like peace-in-our-time over gelatin. Then ... 'will have to see what we do.'

JG quite interesting on world financial markets. Wall Street crazily over bought; prices have no relation to earnings. Pure tulip bulbs. 'Social conditions and unemployment etc likely to worsen in EC as Free Trade continues to bite in.' What should one be in? Government bond, gold, Swiss francs; US $? Even if the Zurbaran sells (most unlikely) will it be in time? Already, as I suddenly realised and pointed out to Jane, as we walked around in the dripping mist of the 'wettest Whitsun on record', we are already only three weeks away from the longest day. How infinitely melancholy.

MFS GH   *Monday, 3 June*

Still apprehensive, Jane this morning said, 'I'm frightened for you.' But the likelihood of imprisonment (slight, surely?) for obstruction ('they always go mad on anything to do with bombs', she rightly said) is not what is rattling me, but the strange silence on the Harkess book front.[1] Just behave with dignity, like Charles I.

---

[1] AC's court appearance, for driving through a police cordon in Piccadilly, took place at Bow Street; AC pleaded guilty, apologised, and was fined £650 plus £50 costs. But next morning headlines and photographs concentrated on the fact that he gave a homeless man (also due in court that day on a begging charge) £5 towards his fine rather than face a jail sentence. Meanwhile a Harkess memoir had been announced to the press in South Africa, Valerie Harkess's domicile. In fact nothing more was heard of it.

MFS GH   *Friday, 7 June*

A lasting feeling of complete disengagement.

A hot, hot June evening and because the shadows are so long and the light so persistent with all the full green foliage and wild flowers we could be in north Italy.

We went over today to Bromley – the 'Kentish Gadabouts' all over 70, it seemed. And I talked for 40 minutes without notes. Asked, of course, if I want to return to Parliament and gave a reasoned reply. Jane came, fluffed them impeccably and looked sweet in the white silk dress and pearls.

On our return I took a call from Mike White. We chatted. It wasn't either Redwood or Portillo. The AN Other should be me. I know that. History knows that. Apart from anything else I 'so good on television' *passim* Clara.

But for this to work only the very last combination of fortune will do. Reigate *and the by-election?* I went into the Great Hall and prayed, aloud.

Dear God

You have given me so much. A lovely family, wonderful possessions, this incredible place, and now, even, the promise of a grandchild.

So I don't like to ask you for things. Because if you give then you can take away. Which is demanding of one really, I suppose. But I want to go back to the House of Commons, because I want to save my Party. And only you can so order this. Because of course you can do anything.

I funked Sevenoaks, which you offered me. Have I learned from that? Whatever happens, I need you to save me from myself.

It is lovely to communicate. Please stay with me.

Saltwood, EMT   *Thursday, 27 June*

It is 7.10 a.m., and I have just read a little Chips to get in the mood to write.

Little Tom came in a second ago. He wagged his tail at me so pleasantly, and I let him out at once where he quickly did a giant tinkle. Alas, and for the first time, real old age seems to be troubling him. He is (rightly) cautious about 'ball-play' and uneasy beside the pool.

He stumbles when he walks (how he still goes up, and even more dangerously, down stairs I just don't know) and didn't quite get on net with 'Keegan' and the ball at the England-Germany semi-final last night. I couldn't bear to put him down so hope he passes away suddenly.

Albany   *Wednesday, 3 July*

Up today for Jimmy's Press Gallery lunch.

Greatly to my delight I was 'lionised' – might never have been away. George Jones said, '… and I see Alan Clark there,' or something of the kind; 'Thank you, George, and thank you for singling me out …' Hugh Pym spirited me away to some 'clips' on MPs' pay, the Somme, and the Referendum Party.[1] Julian Brazier[2] talked to me about the great homes row at MoD. Yesterday, after the sad news from N. Dorset,[3] I was even more determined to return. And at David Frost's party on Thursday dear Gill Shephard was specially encouraging.

---

[1] Two political correspondents, George Jones (*Daily Telegraph*) and Hugh Pym (ITN).
[2] Julian Brazier, MP for Canterbury since 1987.
[3] N Dorset, yet another possible seat in which AC showed an interest, chose Robert Walter, who had contested the Labour stronghold of Bedwelty in south Wales, 1979.

MFS GH   *Thursday, 11 July*

Flat and rattled. Trying to stay off drink. Took too much with Dobbie yesterday at the Savoy Grill (recognised by the waiter when I went back to and tipped £10); cut by Mawhinney who was lunching with Peter Oborne.[1]

Dobbie offered me – I genuinely thought he was an emissary – 400 for the serial rights [of *The Tories*] as 'pre-emptive'. This really did 'make it all worthwhile'. This morning, naturally, it turns out, or he claims, that he had no status at all.

Then, I cannot get rid of this dreary-sounding compulsion to 'put in for' seats. Angela R[umbold] told me that David Simpson, the regional director [of the Conservative Party] was against me (ageism). I thought of ringing and bawling him out. Don't do that, I was advised, ask him to lunch. I got him on his mobile (he was on his way to meet Mawhinney!). Was he not the person who came over when the two maidens from Blandford came to interview me?

But it's all such a drag. Nothing will come of it, I know. It's absurd, I'm 68. But I can't stop.

GH   *Saturday, 3 August*

One thing I must note – both welcome and unwelcome. I am almost an alcoholic. I 'have' to have my half (a generous half, often) bottle of wine, usually Burgundy red or white, in the evening. If I don't get it by about 7 p.m. I feel irritable and (similar to) hungry.

But, when I don't drink I feel much better waking-up in the morning (we never go to lights/bed before 11 p.m. now it seems). And, particularly, if I don't drink at lunch I feel much better at tea-time and in the evenings. Today, for example

---

[1] Peter Oborne, political writer on the *Evening Standard*.

although we had late salami-cheese lunch by the pool and it is a Saturday, I still would not slurp. Nor do I intend to drink tonight, although I would love, if I think about it, to drain a glass of the Marquise's Chasagne Montrachet. Champneys in August? It is only the second day. But not only do I feel better, but I feel more sexual. And my prostatic symptoms have completely disappeared. Strange.

GH   *Saturday, 10 August*

The cockatiels escaped. Jane brilliantly – how? – recaptured the little grey. But the yellow (maiden) is flighty – literally – and calls at intervals from different points around the Mains; venturing this afternoon bravely to the giant sycamore over the Long Garage.

Shore Cottage   *Wednesday, 21 August*

V low cloud, and fine, though penetrating rain. Doesn't worry me at all, though depressing for James as we noticed lovely piles of turned hay in the half-light as we approached yesterday evening.

We did the whole journey in one gulp and, I must say, it makes one incredibly tired (though very slightly less so, I must admit, after deferring to the Grampian police and driving at only 60 mph on the A9. Last night I could barely manage to get to the boat house. Jane and the girls streaked away from me. I slept round until 8.15 (having been briefly woken and licked by Lëhni scratching at the door at 4-ish).

Shore Cottage   *Saturday, 24 August*

Woke this morning both of us absolutely knackered, still, in spite of 10½ hours. Thought we would never recover. But in the early afternoon we went out in the little Pioneer with James to clear the lobster pots. Absolutely divine – the loch was like glass and the silent little Yamaha outboard throbbed reassuringly on tick over. An absolutely perfect hour of tranquillity.

Shore Cottage   *Saturday, 31 August*

We found our gravestone the other day – sent by God, just off the Birkett Foster bank. I will go out and look for it in a second or two.

Saltwood, EMT   *Friday, 13 September*

Short of miracles, this is the last charge. I went over there [Tunbridge Wells] on a recce on Wednesday. Recognised almost immediately by a charming man who accosted me and said how glad he was that I am to be 'the next MP'. The agent, Steve Owen, not just grumpy and rebarbatief, but slob-like; with shoulder-length hair and a beer belly. A dreadful ward official in his late sixties – the kind of organisation that illustrates the tenacity of the human body when exposed to carcinogenic factors – and common-voicedly talking to the agent. Ignored me; then at the end said, 'Hello, young man.' 'Hello,' I simpered.

Archie Norman[1] is the favourite. 'I hope he trips himself up,'

---

[1] Archie Norman, chief executive of the Asda Group since 1991, who had political ambitions.

indiscreetly said the agent. Mrs (sic) Fookes[1] is the dark horse, according to my contact, Kenneth Miller. I'm not so sure about him, either, now. He talks almost loonily – 'I seethed for an hour' when people said I was being interviewed for 'entertainment'; and is very keen on telling me people's objections.

As I walked about I got a somewhat Cheltenham impression. Could go in any direction. Then sure enough Bob Worcester's poll results came through. We are in a minority. 'New Labour' are second and a still very substantial Liberal vote.

The whole thing is too ridiculous. I am telling myself to fight a seat that is worse than Plymouth in 1992. Once this is out of the way then I really can revert. I think the odds against me must be in double figures. But it is possible – if I am inspired. Will K–C inspiration come?

By 'The Boy' [statue by pool]   *Saturday, 14 September*

A simply beautiful, still September morning. I drove over to Bob Worcester to get the (very expensive, £7+) MORI printout for Tunbridge Wells. He briefed me – on the inevitable Tory defeat. Even T–W, 42 last night is now down to 40! He has this theory that the Lib-Dems will actually benefit as a stop-over from switching Tories. I'm not so sure. Could be that all these SE seats split 40–30–30 for us.

But I still don't see how we can do anything but deteriorate. At present our majority is ONE. Are we actually going to *win* seats?

I said to Jane over croissant cheese and figs, which we ate deliciously by the Barbican, 'In 24 hours I will be free.' Almost like 1992. And yet, inwardly, of course, I want to win. And go on

---

[1] In boundary changes Janet Fookes's seat – she had been the constituency neighbour of AC as MP for Plymouth Drake since 1974 (Merton and Morden, 1970–74) – was disappearing.

being 'good on TV' and a 'personality'. It's just that my compensation mechanism is working hard.

I am leaving my *revision* dangerously late. I know nothing about Education, Hospitals etc. *But this is it, Alan ...!*

MFS GH   *Sunday, 15 September*

An absolutely beautiful still autumn day.

As the swallows, the remaining ones, dart about and feed their fledgling babies I wonder, in some gloom, what state I will be in when they return.

We will have a new government. Privately, I hope, of course, that it will be Labour. Sort those party toadies out. Eight years as 'shadows' is no fun. Agony, of course, if it is a 'hung' Parliament with Conservatives holding a balancing chunk. Jimmy is blank, incidentally. Quavering his voice on the phone 'just wanting a chat, nothing special'. Personally and unpleasantly attacked by Mellor in the *Mail on Sunday* yesterday. But it is, I fear, a rag-tag army, and he may well lose heart, and abandon the field.

Then, how will my own health be? Will I be a grandfather? Almost certainly yes. Will my affairs be more orderly? Will I have culled some cars, inventorised some structures?

Ahead of my disappointment at T-W I began to fantasise on the Venetian nobleman: he insisted on going up to the villa even though they had long closed it down; only the old man-servant, Mercurio, was evocatively in place. He plunged into the greeny semi-stagnant swimming pool – and had a seizure.

At tea yesterday I philosophised to Jane (who didn't pay much attention) cited the example of those old Venetian families who hang on to their crumbling palazzi, with their wonderful contents, and their archives.

I just want to be sure that Saltwood stays as an entity, even though the foci may exist separately – Eriboll, Broomhayes, Garden House etc. Just to walk through the rooms, with the lovely things, in the low summer light. Silent, and redolent of earlier regimes and generations.

This morning was so beautiful that I left Jane and the dogs. I walked over and back along the valley. So full the leaf on the deciduous trees. It could have been like nineteenth-century France. But it wasn't. It was England, my beloved England of *Our Island Story*, which due very largely to my own selfishness and impotence I am drifting away from.

Saltwood   *Friday, 20 September*

V convincingly Archie Norman 'walked' Tunbridge Wells. Same age as I was when chosen at Plymouth Sutton – a generation ahead I ought now to be calm and free – 'relaxed'.

EMT   *Tuesday, 8 October*

Drove early to Gatwick and at Geneva Airport lashed out at Caviar House, bought a medium-sized tin of Beluga, bottle of Fondant and sundries. Delicious picnic in Geneva train and took the supplement old-style coach on the Glacier Express (restored and not very comfortable – should have had period prints). The châlet at first seemed a little shabby and dated, but soon we are happily ensconced. Gamely we walked up to Ried – raising heartbeat to 140+ and fibrillations – and to a high tea and early night. The next day a lovely Zermatt meander in the morning, up to the Winkelmatten Chapel where I said a real prayer of thanks and back via the watch shops.

The day after our return we drove in Big Red to Broomhayes and found Andrew and Sarah had really settled in happily. After tea across the fields to the church and over the wall by the grave-digger's hut and found the Marley shed still with its

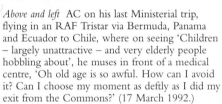

Above and left AC on his last Ministerial trip, flying in an RAF Tristar via Bermuda, Panama and Ecuador to Chile, where on seeing 'Children – largely unattractive – and very elderly people hobbling about', he muses in front of a medical centre, 'Oh old age is so awful. How can I avoid it? Can I choose my moment as deftly as I did my exit from the Commons?' (17 March 1992.)

Below The 1992 election photograph that was never used. AC had for a year contemplated retiring from the Commons, but only told his constituency three weeks before the deadline for nominations. Tom, the Clarks' Jack Russell, who was now nineteen, had been a feature of the Plymouth election campaigns since the beginning.

Above After the Gulf War in 1991 AC, as Minister for Defence Procurement, was despatched to the Gulf. At Oman he met Andrew (right), on attachment to the Sultan of Oman Armoured Brigade, 'magnificent, handsome, clear-headed and hugely popular with his brother officers'. (12 May 1991.)

SALTWOOD

'When we got back I "striped" the Bailey.' (2 June 1991.) But not as beautifully as mown by Brian the gardener in this photograph.

Weeding by the pool, with the statue of the boy, during a heat-wave in 1995.

'Private Office came down yesterday evening and gave me a tree. Very sweet of them.' (29 June 1992.)

'This afternoon the christening of tiny Albert. Afterwards we posed, the three males in line, beside my father's gravestone.' (8 March 1997.)

'The endless pressure of paperwork – now totally out of control again, as I "cleared" the Green Room table.' (26 January 1994.) Only purple teddy survived this particular onslaught. *Left* AC has moved to the dining room, watched over by TC, one of several jackdaws that became part of the Saltwood family.

'A great sense of well-being pervades me. The dinner party (15 people as Mary Archer asked herself *en supplement* at the last minute) was an enormous success.' (6 August 1995.) Jane surveys the table in the Great Hall the morning after. The other guests: Jeffrey Archer, Algy and Blondel Cluff, Jonathan and Vivien Holborow, Selina Scott, Nigel Nicolson, Fr Michael Seed, Sandra and Michael Howard, Sarah and Andrew Clark.

'Rang Andrew Roberts [right], said "come down" and he suggested bringing Dean Godson. Just what I like. We sparkled and enjoyed ourselves with a rosé and two Bourgogne Aligoté in their "sleeves". Jane adapted brilliantly with heavy-duty canapés.' (27 September 1997.)

Shore Cottage, with the new porch ("the wheelhouse") at Eriboll. 'One of the best-value expenditures ever, it is commodious – even room for the two Bulgarian straw chairs plus the "Army" work table, plus length for gumboots, heater, Julie's (return reluctantly offered) Canadian pew. Coat hooks banned. It really is a most congenial spot.' (Easter Sunday, 1997.)

'The Christening – so pleasing in the little candle-lit church and the Catholic ceremony – Fr John Maguire – much more significant. Afterwards we did pile into the jeep for the Christmas-card photo. The last occasion for some while, I fear, when we will all be under one roof. (28 October 1998.) With Jane sitting next to AC at the wheel, back row: James (with Angus), Sarah (with Albert); middle row: Julie, Andrew (with Archie).

Left AC on what proved to be his last visit to Eriboll in July 1999, with James and Julie's son Angus.

Middle 'Today a great walk all around the forestry plantation.' (30 August 1997.)

Below 'I see always the beautiful view of the shoreline from boat house beach and hear the slap of the wavelets.' AC swimming with Lëhni and Hannah at Eriboll. (5 July 1999.)

Top 'There is always so much to do at Eriboll. Some things have been left undone for six, seven years. And the *Maid of Morwen* still lies on her side, her entrails slowly rotting.' (New Year's Day, 1994.)

Above 'In the early afternoon we went out in the little Pioneer with James to clear the lobster pots. Absolutely divine – the loch was like glass and the silent little Yamaha outboard throbbed reassuringly on tick over. An absolutely perfect hour of tranquillity.' (24 August, 1996.)

Left James with Angus in an Orkney fishing boat named Katoomba after one of the Clark family's yachts

Relaxing at the Schönbuhl Hut in 1996, but to reach it – one of AC's favourite walks – required iron nerves as the path has vertiginous stretches. (8 October 1996.)

His grandfather's estate in Suffolk. 'Detoured to Sudbourne. The great house demolished ... I posed for a photograph, got on some disintegrating stone steps with a large cedar growing nearby. The whole garden now a wilderness and the lake grown over.' (13 October 1996.)

'En route, quite late in the afternoon when we were looking carefully at the signs on the autoroute, Jane spotted the name Colombey-les-deux-Eglises', synonymous with Charles de Gaulle. AC stands in front of his '"homely" low-built house covered in Virginia creeper, heavy white gravel, garden rather contrived, rather Ascot-like'. (12 October 1995.)

With Andrew and Albert, just six months and the youngest member of the Kensington & Chelsea Conservative Association.

'The Bailey in July at 1 p.m. was full traditional Saltwood. Beautiful, sunny, warm, hollyhocks burgeoning.' (28 July 1999.)

'We then did the "w", woodland as always. It always can make me sad, will I be doing this next year?' (22 May 1999.)

At Eriboll. 'How I wish that I could stay up here and just cure myself by God helping me to regenerate (as he has done so brilliantly up until now).' (3 July 1999.)

In the Knight's Hall before AC's funeral on 7 September 1999. 'A white damask tablecloth of Great Granpa's with Albany gold curtain over and then the shroud on its wooden base. Did the flowers, 2 large bowls. The white urns inside the blue pots – full of chrysanths, lilies, bay, rosemary, old man's beard and Russian vine and hops. We put our individual posies on Al – peace lilies from Hannah and Lëhni, mixed little bunches from all of us. Very pretty it looked.' (Jane's journal.)

'Felt very shaky, but hope I looked ok for Al, black plain linen dress, black stockings, black shoes, hair clean and loose. Only jewellery my diamond cross Al had given me, and my sapphire rings.' (Jane's journal.) From left, behind Jane: Julie, Col, James, Graham Stewart, Andrew and Sarah.

Lëhni sits on the stone that marks AC's final resting place at Saltwood.

windows intact, but besieged and entangled by brambles of wire rope.

On the way back via Seend Street ran into Peter Rogers now looking like a mildly corrupt senator from Oklahoma with a fine head of white hair, 'chiselled' features and dark eyebrows. Mrs Rogers amiably attractive still. And Wiltshire seemed very much as if (almost) one had never been away and delighted to have Andrew and a new generation there.

Saltwood, EMT   *Thursday, 10 October*

Back late last night, having driven the Little Silver *without glasses* from Bournemouth in 2¾ hours on 3 gallons of petrol (it seems). Slept like a top.

Conference, as always, left no time for anything. Lionised, still, but selectively. Middle-rank colleagues (except, interestingly those on the Right, like Townend,[1] Gardiner etc) are suspicious, don't want intercourse. Old mates – Ancram,[2] Goodlad ('love thy neighbour' was his elliptical parting shot) just as if I'd been speaking to them yesterday. Nellies, some of them up-market, are always friendly, and I am universally recognised by policemen. Some tough young 'graduates' (the best). Most of my time I seemed to spend in the company of ladies, Clara, of course, Jackie Ashley,[3] Sue Tinson[4] started me off on Tuesday evening. She saying 'you must see Major, he loves you … etc' (shades of 'she'll have him in the Cabinet if she can'). Bruce

[1] John Townend, MP for Bridlington since 1979.

[2] Michael Ancram, Minister, Northern Ireland Office since 1994, MP for Devizes since 1992 (Berwick & E Lothian, February–September 1974, Edinburgh S, 1979–87).

[3] Jackie Ashley, *New Statesman* political writer, married to Andrew Marr (former political editor, the *Economist*, editor *The Independent*), the daughter of former Labour MP, Lord [Jack] Ashley.

[4] Sue Tinson, DBE, associate editor of ITN since 1989 and its link with Number Ten.

Anderson also told me that 'it was JM who had said "put in for Luton".' Then at the dinner I sat between two fat ladies – both amiable and intelligent. Although I had thought it would be low-key, a second XI and was wary of Gary Streeter[1] and his hostile wife (who Jane told me had widely said to the ladies at a Plymouth function – 'If he's so exhausted why doesn't he just stand down and make way for somebody else?'). Actually, fortified by a late, giant gin and tonic with Sue Tinson and some champagne and red wine I deftly whizzed over and sat next to and mobbed/flirted most indiscreetly with Rebekah Wade[2] (!) who I was interested to see was a flame-haired lovely (and must in 1993 have been even more luscious).

To some extent my whole performance was bogus. I have no standing. Am I famous, or infamous? Sarah Baxter, looking very attractive, wanted me to be 'interviewed' for the Sunday Times. I was in two minds, but finally assented, mindful of the risk, but thinking it was quite funny that I should be the post-conference profile in the ST. Will see what happens.

MFS GH   Sunday, 13 October

I sit here in the gloaming (about 6.30 p.m.) The porphyry desk set, the faded leather and veneers of the giant 'partners' desk'. The John Adamson long-case clock ticks slowly, a giant tapestry covers the north wall. Everything over here is shabby, but romantic still and with a latent glow, awaiting burnishment.

I was pleased by Sarah Baxter's article – 'busy reinventing himself', a perfect formula. On the way back from Aldeburgh we detoured to Sudbourne.[3] The great house demolished, but wonderful stablings, and outbuildings still, although the glass

---

[1] AC's successor at Plymouth Sutton, a Whip since 1995; his wife Janet.
[2] Rebekah Wade, deputy editor of the News of the World since 1989.
[3] The Suffolk estate of AC's grandfather, Kenneth McKenzie Clark.

canopies for resting the cars and carriages are gone, like the huge greenhouses – although the walled garden perimeter is still intact. What a huge property! All the cottage ornée are untouched – almost vulgar, but my goodness they were well built. We wandered about. It is sad not knowing more about inventories and schedules and how many staff there were and so forth. I posed for a photograph, got on some disintegrating stone steps with a large cedar growing nearby. The whole garden now a wilderness and the lake grown over.

When we returned I got out the albums – everything so spick and span. But a vast undertaking. My grandfather went there quite a lot; taking trout in May, pheasants in October and November. In between to Scotland – on the yacht – and sometimes just for a night on passage to 25 Berkeley Square (!). Yet Sudbourne could never really have been kept on – which Shielbridge [at Ardnamurchan] could. Though both estates so vast that without perpetual supervision you were going to get ripped off. When we got back to Saltwood I wondered if, in ninety years time, my grandson would still be here and to what extent the estate/property would have been forced to yield.

Saturday, 19 October

A curious 'turn-up' on – as so often can happen – several different fronts at once. On 16 October at 6.31 little baby Albert McKenzie was born. 'King George VII' I call him mindful of the signature 'Bertie' in the Port Lympne visitor's book (though even as I write I realise that this would have been Lord Bertie – a courtier of some kind – as it also contains the signature in a round, juvenile hand – 'Albert').

We went to see him the next day at the very pleasing and brand new Chelsea-Kensington Hospital, built on the site of that gloomy St Stephens (was it?) next to Netherton Grove. Even as I write this I am reminded, one of those ineradicable memories, of that summer night (it would have been the summer of 1954, I should think) when I heard a child crying, crying, crying in an upper room in one of the houses – which one? – that backed on to the gardens from a parallel street. It was so deeply and entirely distressed that alarm woke, and a little knot of concerned people gathered in the street. But what could we do? Knowing now what one has learned about child abuse, and the like, I suppose we should have been more assertive. But we dispersed and, after many hours, from exhaustion I judge he (for it was male) fell silent.

I felt sad, curiously so, when I looked at the tiny baby. 'A page turns', I said, only half-jokingly, 'on to a new chapter of anxiety and heartache …' Curiously I found that birth gives one a sharper sense of one's own mortality than death. How seminal was that film *2001*![1] What a strange sensation and experience, to open one's eyes for the *very first time* ('He's nought', Jane said) in one's life, and take in the surroundings of a maternity ward.

I did privately notice that Nick Scott had barely improved his position by being 'found' collapsing face-down in a side-street in Bournemouth, and saw he had been summoned to his Executive Council on 4 November. Last night Soames rang, claimed to have been told that people in Chelsea who had voted for him once now going to vote for me. 'But don't do *anything*, Alan. Promise me you will say *NOTHING*' etc.

Largely fantasy of course, but fun. I mustn't think about it. But no doubt I am on a roll at the moment.

Garden House   *Sunday, 3 November*

Just took time off from BB to record how immensely happy I am. I must thank God, and do something for him – but I don't know how or what.

---

[1] Subtitled 'A Space Odyssey', and directed by Stanley Kubrick, 1968.

Albert is sweet and healthy; Andrew and Sarah are 'excellent parents'.

All is as well as can be expected at Saltwood.

Jane has 'passed' with Tom Bates just as I did a couple of weeks ago.

The Bustard has been sold for £125 (and they also want the Loco for 60/5 and the SS100 at 98).

The Zurbaran is plodding on, and will consolidate Zermatt and possibly start a treuhand.

The Giorgione is full of promise, and we may go to Venice on 23 November – think of that!

BB is potentially terrific. I am devoting more and more hours on it, and recovering confidence (and shape). A difficult passage, the Churchill-Eden government to Suez has turned out very readable.

And Nick Scott comes up (*again*) for de-selection tomorrow.

Garden House   *Sunday, 17 November*

I'm glad I made the last entry, recording how deliciously happy I was – because now I am rattled and disconsolate. All (or nearly all) a matter of mood, I suppose – but none the less real for that.

In the last six weeks I have become conscious of being much older. I am now so still and wobbly when I carry Tom downstairs in the mornings and I (excusing myself by 'stiff back') can no longer bound up the stairs.

Really resigned to the fact that even if there's now a vacancy I probably won't even be *seen* (re) by Chelsea. Also (perhaps because of this) it is all much more through-a-glass darkly now. That last draft of nostalgia. Now it seems remote, being desirable. A new miracle needed.

This is reflected in my standing. Many fewer approaches now. No Christmas party invitations. I wrote to JM suggesting a supper with myself and Simon Jenkins and Sue Tinson – no answer. Soames' own voice print kind of gives it away.

I must just concentrate on BB. But last night, v 'frail' and jumpy (I am lividly jarred when Jane bangs saucepan lids in the kitchen), I came over here to do a couple of pages on Ted. For some reason the machine went shifty and I kept getting 'You may not leave Winword' in a large oval white box after doing 'exit windows – ok'. In the end, livid, I switched it off and lost a whole evening's work. Ha!

Summer Bedroom   *Saturday, 23 November*

That delicious sense of relief and calmness that comes as one emerges from a filthy flu-cold. Yesterday I just lay here, eyes streaming, incapable, listlessly plucking at *Hello* or an Audi catalogue.[1] Ate nothing till the evening, then had a mini-craving for a piece of white bread and butter and a raw onion and knew that 'the crisis was past'.

Down at the gates this morning (the interior of the Mains is shabby with neglect – will it outlast us?) and thought how long have I got? Usual answer – '20 years'. But this is unrealistic. Ten, then? But I will/would be the same age as my father when he became doddery and feeble-voiced. And anyway, *ten isn't enough*. How can I say this? I am so fortunate, so much for which to thank God. It just is I would like three completely free, but still with some vigour, to enjoy myself with Jane.

---

[1] Jane Clark says AC never read *Hello*; much more likely to have been *The Field*.

Tower Office   *Monday, 2 December*

Nick Scott is clearly going to win his public meeting tonight (his *third* in tenure) – but in any case, no one remembers me any more. I've suddenly become, and look, 'too old'.

Saltwood   *Tuesday, 3 December*

Back from Julian Amery's memorial service at St Margaret's.

Little Winston's address quite good – don't know who wrote it – and reminded one of how long and rich Julian's life had been – though never with complete fulfilment. Mrs T let him down; just as she did today by not attending. And last night Nick Soames said, quite true, that he was weak at the base – though wonderful on his feet as a back-bencher.

St Margaret's was less than two-thirds full. Jonathan [Aitken] very splendidly intercepted us and conducted us to the centre aisle. I sat next to Lolicia [Aitken] and we were later joined by Richard R[yder] (now, as Jane observed, just a little accountant. Quiet, deafish and chetif). On the way out he scuttled away through a side door. Spotted little Budgen (unaltered and as chippy as ever); Pirrie Norrie[1] benign, but seeming to have put on most of Lawson's shed fat; Paul Channon – looked quickly away when he caught my eye – like so many of us had added to his jowl.

As Jane said in the car everyone seemed a good deal older (has it all happened in the last two years?), and she meant people like Richard Shepherd[2] and Mark Lennox-Boyd – but they/we are from a generation after Julian, he was our father. His death marks the passing, finally, of an era. We, too, have been shunted up a tier, and are now obsolete.

---

[1] Norman Lamont, as he was known by the Clarks.
[2] Richard (Rick) Shepherd, MP for Aldridge-Brownhills since 1979.

No one spoke to me much. Afterwards I did a quick bite for the *World at One* in the Millbank studio with a sweet dark Welsh girl with a slightly sideways face/jaw, as if she had had an accident some time. But absolutely no approaches or overture from Chelsea – which must be seething now.[1] Immediately after the (surprising) vote Nick Soames rang; some talk that four out of the six people he was dining with said they would vote for me etc etc. He wound me up – and we had a very bad night. I lay there unable to de-focus and mindful of the fact that yet again an empty period now looks like being filled and fraught.

Almost where we left off/opened the volume.

But as this last entry closes I must record I have personally had some setbacks. Blood in the urethra, attack of 'distorted vision', heavy eyestrain (glaucoma). No longer race up stairs, some strange AF attacks in middle of night, pulse rate 140 plus. Appearance rather cross and alarmed or apprehensive, with hair white and receding. Sexuality declined almost out of sight. Even so – lucky to be around, to have so much, sweet Jane and the little baby grandson.

Saltwood   *EMT, Tuesday, 10 December*

I am depressed. I am worried simultaneously about my health, my book (BB) and the state of the party/politics. My entire morale seems to have suffered, and it is only on the great Beechborough walk (slightly over two hours) that I feel better and freer (I can't remember when I last did Gossie – was it a true 'last'?).

On Sunday, having got a lot of logs in and pleasingly exhausted, I phoned the PM. after his broadcast. He was pleased

---

[1] In the latest round of a roller-coaster selection process, Sir Nicholas Scott, who had been MP for Chelsea since October 1974, found himself rejected by the new Kensington and Chelsea Conservative constituency association set up as part of the boundary reorganisation that would come into force at the general election.

and friendly, though seemed a little unhappy. What is happening to the Party? They are now a medieval army in the reign of King Stephen – pre Ironside – each one concerned to preserve their individual estates (constituencies) fragmenting into even smaller Margravates around dignitaries who may, or may not, be in a position to distribute favours and booty. Discipline has completely broken down, and they loot the countryside as they march and counter-march. It is the warlord syndrome. Harold and Stamford Bridge; Afghanistan, Mozambique. Am I half pre-empting disappointment at being rejected by Chelsea? Do I want to be back at the House – right back – in opposition and in smaller numbers, I would judge, than in even October 1974-79?

Sandling train   *Monday, 16 December*

Daily the assumption grows that we will be routed at the election. And there is the strange smell of 1938 in the air – of a massive, ill-disposed accumulation of power on the European continent. It can be appeased, concessions made – each one at a higher cost; or it can be resisted – almost an act of desperation and with consequences wholly unpredictable. And again, as in 1938, it is hard to find any leadership that exudes complete confidence. Major's intuition (like Neville's) was sound, but he is hampered by party political constraints.

Saltwood   *EMT, Saturday, 21 December*

Decks clear for Christmas! (Whatever that means.)

I am still somewhat blighted by my head (eye) ache. I have sat here at the kitchen table for nearly 40 minutes pressing my temples with fingers and trying – very occasionally succeeding – to defocus. Yesterday I forced myself to do one page of 'Heath

II' (BB) at the white computer. A brain tumour would be moving faster than this, surely?

K-C remains a mirage. I get little bursts of enthusiasm, but have suffered too many disappointments (I mean I really did think I was a shoe-in for Sevenoaks). But at Max Hastings' party (he had raging flu and a high temperature) I spoke with David Heathcoat-Amory.[1] Always an interesting, clever man. He said the whole course of history both of the Party and the country would be decided in conclave after the Election by who backed whom for the leadership.

Pirrie Norrie's party the previous day was a total frost. As Jane said coming up the stairs we realised there was no buzz. I was glowered at by some (as it were) Area Chairmen on the landing.

MFS Garden House   *Monday, 30 December*

I must set out a résumé – both 'where am I', and what has been.

Jane excelled (even) herself over Christmas; the whole house so beautifully, and tastefully decorated. Greenery everywhere, quite pagan, a calling out almost. But this time, first occasion for thirty years or more there was a *pram in the hall*! Nanny's great grey, which pushes and rides like a silver ghost, was wheeled down from the Rabies Room and, somewhat, admittedly under HE's-Reception conditions I Autosolvol'd the wheels and the dumb-irons, Simonizing the 'coach-built' body. Little Albert was lovely, changing each day. We all went to Canterbury for the carol service and he was a little starfish in his blue ski-suit, and quite placid. I carried him (v heavy) a little way in the aisle when we left – to approving glances. But how much of him, or of any brothers or sisters (or cousins) will I live to see? I am multi-hypochondriacal at present – after a sign of prolonged

---

[1] David Heathcoat-Amory, MP for Wells since 1983, Paymaster-General 1994–96 and before that Deputy Government Whip.

gestation. My memory has quite rapidly become atrocious. Can collect it up to a point, but now almost pre-Alzheimer. But my appetite is fine, weight 11.4½ (+) or so. I drink third of a bottle of wine every day.

Sunday Times Magazine did its usual gallery of people who died last year, aged 73-77. I can't believe that I have only about five years left, preferring to think that like Bill Deedes I will still be scrawnily around aet.88.[1] But I must admit that the likelihood of my going back to the House, even being interviewed for Chelsea does seem quite remote. It no longer seems realistic. A colossal effort of inspiration would be required although there are of course reserves which I can draw on if they will allow me to.

Paradoxically, if I were back in the House there would be more free time. I suspect because life is more orderly and compartmentalised, and much is done for you. I have been my own secretary now for nearly five years – and it shows.

If I could just get BB (and the TV show) out of the way this year perhaps in '98 we can choose.

1997 – could go back to Heaven

1998 – a lot less/more on his plate

So I simply don't know. I don't know if my health will hold up, or the book get finished, or I am finally excluded from public life. Or if by some strange and miraculous concatenation I return as a big player.

Garden House   *New Year's Eve*

The handwriting recently has been abominable. Is this poor vision, or 'nerves'? I went down to Hythe P.O. (long queue) to record the letter and CVs to K&C. Everybody slouching up and down the street absolutely flush, each person holding a plastic

---

[1] Lord Deedes was actually 83 at the time of this entry.

bag bulging hideously with merchandise. I called back here to make a note, of how it is HE's reception the entire time at the moment. I don't seem to see a clear run ahead (the best, actually was five years ago when I first 'holed up' here for the G. Election) – a switch-off fortnight as driven by the tyranny of the column.

1997

A little calmer, which is surprising, because the entire morning was spent 'doing' the top of the tallboy in my bathroom. But fortunately I 'forced the pace' and went through to the end – i.e. polish and rearrange the tortoise-shell objects, so that tiny sector is now 'clear'. But, as I said to Jane, Walcheron Island. Consumed the entire Canadian Corps from Sept '44 to March '45 and when it was over, and the Scheldt clear, so what? My eyes are better today. Last night I wrote a my-patience-is-exhausted letter to Goodlad. Eleven lists since I stood down, and no recognition of any kind.

David D rang last night. Said that Heseltine most likely to succeed in the post-election contest – between him and Michael Howard; at first round there will be seven or eight candidates. But whoever has their nose in front will win the second head-onner. Dorrell[1] probably won't stand. Ken Clarke might not, not wanting to get a tiny total (I don't believe this – Gillian [Mrs Clarke] will make him, anyway); and would probably let it be known that he was supporting Hes, having been promised Foreign Secretary. The Right, on the other hand will be a shambles. Portillo, Redwood, Shephard, Rifkind (dark horse – 52 votes)[2] and Howard himself. In between the two ballots Heseltine's supporters will say (a) a bandwagon is rolling; (b) 'he's really on your side, you know.' Not much fun leading in opposition – but Labour may 'get into trouble' early on – particularly over Euro-vote.

What an exciting House it is going to be! If I go back in there

---

[1] Stephen Dorrell, MP for Loughborough since 1979, Health Secretary since 1995.
[2] Malcolm Rifkind, Foreign Secretary since 1995.

I will die, or at least become impossibly infirm in harness. If I don't I will be a recluse; not at Colombey, not even at Elba, but at St Helena. How very melancholy. I am sad, and so apprehensive that sometimes my hands are improperly co-ordinated.

Dean Godson rang last night. He was grave, but, considering he wanted me to go to Hull[1] on his behalf (something which earlier I have refused) not optimistic.

EMT   *Thursday, 9 January*

At his invitation I drove over to Michael Howard last night. 'Congratulations on your part in ... helping the Chancellor to concentrate his mind on aspects of the single currency at Cabinet before Christmas,' I said – showing that I was well-informed (but *how* well?).

He launched straight in. Without telling JM Michael raised at November 30 Cabinet the need for a debate, said Ken Clarke should prepare a paper for the pre-Christmas Cabinet. Ken C blustered, said he didn't see any need for a new paper, but would 'of course' provide any Treasury documents, that 'colleagues' might want to look at. Somewhat disingenuously (more likely hyper-shrewdly) Michael claimed that he had not warned the PM so that he (PM) could say to Ken and Hes afterwards, 'I had no idea that this was going to happen'; also, of course, because five or six people in Cabinet who 'take PM's orders' (Lang, Newton, Freeman,[2] Dorrell, ?Goodlad, ?Cranborne, ?Gummer [AC's question marks]) would, if alerted, have talked it down.

The mood, expressed thus, was for a 'paper'. This didn't please

---

[1] Dean Godson, deputy chairman of Kensington and Chelsea Conservative Association 1995–98, was also Tory candidate for Great Grimsby. In his mid-thirties, he had been chief leader writer, *Daily Telegraph*, since 1996.

[2] Tony Newton, MP for Braintree since February 1974, Leader of the House of Commons; Roger Freeman, MP for Kettering since 1983, Chancellor of the Duchy of Lancaster since 1995.

Clarke at all, and a good deal of leak and counter-leaking began. By the time the 'paper' arrived JM had of course worked on his own placemen. But (in order not to give early warning) had not made approaches of any kind to the sceptics. So at the debate, very narrowly, lost 9–11.

The No 10 machine, however, did not leak a 'sceptics routed' story. Instead it indicated that Clarke had been told to go back and take another look at it all.[1]

Saltwood   *Sunday, 12 January*

Lovely and enclosed by snow/fog. The M-way is silent, and one is reminded how peaceful, magical Saltwood could be transferred to a position in, say, Herefordshire, or the Welsh marches.

David D down – talk at breakfast, then dinner. A clever boy, but like Major a little chippy still. Neither he nor Michael Howard says anything of the 'you're needed' type, and Soames hasn't rung for weeks. A quiet recognition that my time has passed. Well, that's all right if what is written is written – though I am still haunted by the fact that it is *my fault*.

Later

Jane pointed out that at least a gallon of water had leaked/ seeped from the Hen 3-litre. Did Guppy not put anti-freeze in? A 3-litre block would cost – at a guess – £4,000, water pumps and things still more.

Reading at the moment Thatcher account of the coup[2] against the background of the Gulf War. TK gets a favourable mention. I am too sharp/clever for Mrs T. Like Ian Gilmour, but without the polish. That was six years ago. Sometimes it seems

---

[1] AC adds a note: 'continued in BB'; indeed the story of the internal battle within the Conservative Party over Europe as related by AC has a definite insider feel about it.

[2] In the first volume of Margaret Thatcher's memoirs, *The Downing Street Years*.

like 18 months. Then followed by the miracle. Zermatt in 1991, and a lovely three years. Now the quality of my life has deteriorated. But it remains within my capacity to recover (most of) it.

EMT   *Thursday, 16 January*

On Monday, sitting quietly at the 'white' screen in Garden House, at 8 p.m. I felt so overcome by depression, sense of waste of being out *due to my own idiocies and weak character*. I love the history, the participation, the minutiae. But at the back lurks, too, the sword. And yet the *machine*, the pigginess of the Party, will not allow me ever to be seen.

The hour has come, and passed, when the call should have come through.

So I prayed – properly, but shortly. Thought little more of it. Patrick Hennessy for the *Standard* on the answering machine – presumably for a gloat. I was out-of-sorts. Doing paperwork with Jane in the Tower Office (she is so good at that, quadruples over rate). Then on came Barbara Lord. I was to be interviewed – I gave her the works; she very sweetly said she preferred me. I have got quite a good vote ('which surprised her' – compliment?) set out rules of secrecy. A huge wash of adrenalin *surged* through me. I went straight to Beechborough. What *is* written?

The next day she rang again – purposely to apologise for the leaking (as they had the whole list it couldn't have been me), but significantly said that Trish Sill Johnston[1] wanted to talk to me, tell me of a few local points. Now this (I thought) was significant. An overture from the Nick camp as well …! For the first time it seemed to be realistic. Sitting on the Green Room floor I got flu symptoms alternating with AF. Could it really be feasible? Jane, as always, was brilliant, though drily unimpressed. I had a baddish night, semi near the surface most of the time.

---

[1] Patricia (Trish) Sill Johnston, Secretary to Nicholas Scott.

Up in Big Red this morning to lunch at Marks (lost the way and arrived late) with Dean [Godson]. Intense, indefatigable, something of a young Isaiah (Berlin) about him. I thought he was a teensy bit guarded – but we have agreed to dine on Saturday and he will 'tell me the questions' (shades of Graham Butland).[1] I've got to come up on Saturday morning, that's quite clear, to 'walk the Borough', get to know local issues etc. And so there we are – the last offensive, April 1918, on the Ardennes.

EMT   *Monday, 20 January*

I must record the developments in this big eerily, crazy, half-tragic, almost incredible and possibly calamitous final charge. I had a *nuit cassé* on Saturday night. Went to bed with the speech unformed; a reasonable end paragraph, an opening formed on my long adrenalin-dispersing trek that afternoon before getting a cab back to B5 tea, and out to dine with Dean Godson (or Dean Whitter,[2] as Jane amusingly calls him) – but no third link passage about the majority party and social events. These sort of formed into shape in a two-hour half-sleepy period from about 4 a.m. But it was still far from solid. And untimed. Soft-spoken I 'rehearsed' after losing the place. Then parked, beautifully timed, on corner of Flood Street. Mini panic and demi-breathless arrival at '1a' (as it is now called) and ushered more or less straight in. Atmosphere very pleasant. Andrew Dalton hyper-smooth. They did, I must say, 'put me at ease.' Speech just got past; a couple of good passages. The first question from 'Big' Barry Phelps:[3]

---

[1] Graham Butland – at Plymouth Sutton in 1972 (see *Diaries: Into Politics*, 31 January 1982). Godson backed AC in the initial, but not in the latter stages of his K & C candidacy.

[2] Dean Whitter, as in the bankers Morgan Stanley Dean Whitter sometimes used by AC.

[3] Barry Phelps, local councillor.

'Mr Clark, last time you appeared before this committee and I asked you a question you delivered a prepared answer that had no relation to it whatever. This time would you like to give the answer first, or second?'

'Well, Barry, the committee should know that with your customary sensitivity to the feelings of others you have always told my younger son and daughter-in-law who are constituents of yours, that there was no point in my putting in for the candidacy as I didn't have a chance and I was just wasting everyone's time ...'

Great applause and laughter (in which he chiefly joined). Got me off to a good start. After that, not too difficult, could be statesman – giving my 'single-currency' answer.

Interrupted at this point: I was going to write about all those people on the committee who had rung last night 'taking out insurance' as I said; but Lynn spotted the fact that I sounded 'coldy'. I am snuffly, runny nose, eye-ache and pulse 84 (it only goes to 72–76 if just 'agitated'). Spoke to Barbara Lord and she said that every single person on the committee had voted for me! But what's the use? – flu for the final – I cannot believe it – McEnroe.

EMT   *Tuesday, 21 January*

Today the most tiresome bit. The 'Executive'. But 150 (!) of them so had to include a number who are opposed, and a mike necessary, which I hate and am unused (*Brideshead*) to.[1]

When I woke I thought so fondly of darling little Jane. I am putting her through this ordeal. She is so loyal. Doesn't, of course, want me to get through. And she is right, but I am driven by the sword. My stars are incredible. Everything seems to be

---

[1] AC adds his own note: 'Marquess's son unused to wine'.

falling into place. Is it to be 'all my life seemed but a preparation for this hour ...'? Or back here, having 'lost' 10 days which I can ill-afford, to be an academic?

I thought, too, that if I win I will immediately write Jane a long letter, not just telling her of my love, and my gratitude; but setting out my commitment to her and to regulating (at last) our life so that we can be 'Mama Paça' as well as FPs.

I am on this fantastic roll at the moment. What a let-down when it evaporates. But of all the meetings this somehow is the one about which I am most uneasy.

EMT, Albany *Tuesday, 28 January*

I should have made an entry earlier; at once, indeed on the Friday morning. But instead went for a full Beechborough. Jane let me out of the conker-tree gate where a single agency-photographer who 'knew the area' was lying in wait. Stumblingly he walked backwards down the rough and muddy path from the iron bridge; his red light glowed at intervals but like all cameras malfunctioned, and seldom flashed.

Soon I was on my own – utterly, ineradicably euphoric. Then, one last, magical sign. I was walking along the bank above the dyke before the valley curves round and a huge fox, lovely and orange like the one living in the tyre-shed at Broomhayes church. Loped very casually in front of me. For a second he stopped; and turned round, looked at me and then disappeared. I don't mean he ran off. He simply disappeared. Magic. I know what he was saying – 'we helped. And we understood what you had to do.'

As I crossed the bridge on the M20 I sang. A prayer of thanks, of total happiness. I don't honestly think I have been so utterly happy in my entire life as on that Friday morning. And I climbed on up to the cattle-grid where I have so often sat some-times in disappointment, sometimes in search of inspiration or to contemplate and speak to God.

This, though, anticipates the happenings, the agonies, the dry-mouthed soft-spoken, foodless, sleepless hours that ran on from the previous Tuesday. The Executive, as I had anticipated, the most difficult audience. Preceded by a 'cocktail' party (the glass of white wine most welcome) at which Jane was lovely and made 'a conquest' of the initially un-twinkly battleaxe who had been allocated as our 'minder'.

But I underperformed. I was carried away by my supporters. So although I came out top. It was done not by conviction, but by allegiance. Even the voice print of Andrew Dalton's[1] message carried the faintest nuance of uncertainty when, having slept exhausted but fitfully, I staggered down in the morning with Tom to switch it on.

So now we are committed. The last great offensive. In the afternoon of Thursday the reconnaissance. The Kensington Town Hall so red and soulless. The hall, and the gallery. At 6.40 p.m. we parked Big Red in some nameless, expensive street and made our way to the doors where a mass of hateful paparazzi and brutal reporters with mikes mobbed us.

'Why do you think K&C will choose you?' 'Aren't you even worse than Sir Nicholas Scott?' 'What do you think your chances?' etc.

'Well they can't be worse than 3 to 1,' I said bleakly. The press (literally) was frightening and hostile. I got separated from Jane – literally manhandled by Central Office officials through the doors to where a huge crowd of disapproving members were queuing for ballot papers. Most of them avoided my eye. 'Like the polling station at Leigham,' I said to Jane.

We were all confined to an underground 'green room', windowless, tableless with four bottles of mineral water (three of them fizzy, so liable to induce a burp when answering questions).

The other candidates all had something. Trish Morris – nice-looking, long copper-curled hair, vivacious, had wowed

---

[1] Andrew Dalton, chairman of Kensington and Chelsea Conservative Association.

conference earlier on the ERM.[1] Daniel Moylan outrageously camp, but a former president of the Union and with a high-profile record in local government; and Martin Howe, 'the Eurosceptic QC' with a pretty wife and a portentous manner. I was last. I found a make-up room with a flat-surface in front of a mirror and rehearsed, timing three lines through – being interrupted only once by a tiny, tubby Asian man who came in to urinate – what was he doing in the Ladies anyway? I was demi-transcendant, the space-craft was on course – collision, burn out, or triumph. Jane quite rightly came and fetched me out, knowing that I would be unsettling myself. Daniel had returned – frightfully funny and quacky about Elspeth Rhys Williams' intervention – and the atmosphere lightened. We all started to talk among ourselves, agreeing, naturally, how awful they all were. Daniel smoked eleven Camels. Longer and longer we waited. What on earth had happened? Then suddenly, Andrew Dalton re-appeared – I think he was actually doing what my mother called *priest*, dry hand-washing. 'Well, the contest is over …' making across to me, '… and Alan has won. Alan has won.'

I was incredibly happy. But also got a hint of 'all my life has been but a preparation for this hour …' Now almost at once, it seemed generally preordained. (It turned out that they had been counting all three ballots without telling us.) We went up the stairs to a loud cheer. I made a few anodyne remarks of gratitude; then congratulations, including lovely ones from Sarah and Tip[2] – and out to a battalion of flash bulbs and that most incredible sense of euphoria. Finally we were hauled away, followed Barbara to Jeanie Craig's house (all I wanted, desperately, was a pint of beer. I couldn't/didn't drink the champagne). Took calls, immediately, from David Davis in the car – *he* saw the point! – and then home at 2.30 a.m.

---

[1] Exchange rate mechanism, which at the time was rarely out of the headlines when the European single currency issue was being discussed.

[2] Andrew and Sarah Clark, and their 15-week-old son – 'the association's youngest member' according to *The Times*.

Albany   *Wednesday, 5 February*

Pam Churchill[1] has had a stroke in the Paris Ritz. Now they're trying to 'save' her. Why? What is the point of preserving the beautiful and vivacious courtesan as an old crone in paralysis?

As well as the sheer bliss of having the safest, nicest and most convenient seat in the country – and as a result of total victory in an outright, full-scale contest – there is the prospect of Big Book. Now I can dabble in this with real participating (ugh, oy! Etc) enjoyment.

EMT   *Sunday, 9 February*

I am sitting at the kitchen table; outside is dark and misty. Around me are spread all the constituency engagements, and the active election planning ... the old warhorse smells powder! Bogus of course, because hard to lose this one. In the night I worried if I might be assassinated during the campaign? I don't want to be paralysed, as politicians often seem to be after such attempts.

Albany   *Monday, 10 February*

Almost a fairy tale come true. This morning William Rees-Mogg in *The Times* – across four columns – 'Who will be the next Conservative leader? I suppose Alan Clark is too much to hope for.'

---

[1] Pamela Digby was the first wife of Randolph Churchill, Winston's son, and went on to marry the American theatre producer Leland Hayward and the diplomat Averell Harriman. She was sometime US ambassador to France. Her son, also Winston, had been MP for Davyhulme since 1983 (Stretford, 1970–83).

B5   **Thursday, 13 February (James's birthday)**

I am looking ghastly in the glass. Scrawny, jowls all too easily hanging. In the night I woke at 3.40. I had sweated (nothing new about this) and my faint, disparate, oculo-related headache 'came in'. I worry about my health and when it will perceptibly disintegrate. The headaches are related to inability to defocus/ relax.

Bruce [Anderson] at Pratt's last night said as choice for chairing the 22 committee I would be 'bigame', then the same word to describe my selection at K&C. 'You don't seem entirely at home', I said, 'with the Anglicised usage of what is, in origin, a French adjective.' I am lowered by the prospect of black, unproductive opposition. What I really don't know, and sometimes can't get to grips with, is the pace at which I should move. A pleasing remark last night from Bruce. 'Once they spot the skull-and-crossbones on your masthead they'll all be on to you ...' Jane said, though, that same evening, 'You must push yourself.'

Saltwood   **Tuesday, 25 February**

Returned this evening to find, and instantly, enter into, a state of deep depression. Lëhni's jeopardy is clearly not over.[1] Our advice is that she is protected by not falling into either of the two categories in the Dangerous Dogs Act – Designated Breed, or Out-of-control-in-a-public place. The moment I saw the text I spotted – but did not tell Jane – the catch-all clause, 'or being in a place, not being a public place, where it should not be' (i.e., on the other side of the asthma gates).

---

[1] The day after AC's selection at Kensington and Chelsea, Saltwood was besieged by the press. A BBC camera crew set up opposite the back door waiting for AC's return. Lëhni jumped up and grabbed the arm of a technician, tore his jersey and drew blood. The technician seemed unconcerned, declined an offer to come inside, said he would finish the interview and then use his own first aid box.

I've just refaxed Birt,[1] having basted his secretary earlier in the afternoon. BBC complete shambles; no one in charge, no one able to locate still less override 'line managers'. All they can say is 'Oh, I'm sure they don't want to destroy the dog ...' Fat lot of use that is. A totally worthless assurance.

The whole thing incredibly upsetting and distracting, which is sad really, because I had a most interesting lunch with Soames (35 minutes late, as I had to walk from Albany, got as far as Wilton Road – clearly not the place. Backtracked – still on foot and carrying my cases – to Wilton Street. Had intercourse with a policeman of the Special Protection Group (the only good ones left) outside a house – 'is this a restaurant?' (it had exterior carriage lights full on at 1.20 p.m.). 'No.' He laughed. Turned out it was Ted Heath's London abode. 'I'd better clear off then. He's not too keen on me'.

Finally caught up with the great man. And he is great, real Churchill genes, as he talked with such intensity and understanding. Full F. E. Smith, and streets ahead of dreamers like Budgen, or other has-beens or *déséché* remittance (of ideas) men. He was good advising me. Most sensible.

MFS GH   *Saturday, 8 March*

I am serene and contented. This afternoon the christening of tiny Albert. In the kitchen last night, horrified by the 'alternative' form, printed on a cling-film-coated card which 'Reg'[2] had handed the young, I went upstairs and fetched the little white parchment-bound prayerbook, inscribed by my father for Jane at the time of our wedding, and read to them the true form of service. I don't know what Andrew did, but most pleasingly Reg intoned the age-old phrases while the little

---

[1] John Birt, director-general of the BBC.
[2] The Rev. Canon Reg Humphriss, rector of Saltwood.

prince was humped and jigged by me, fretting just a little, on and off, but easily distracted by the stained glass. Afterwards we posed, the three males in line, beside my father's gravestone.

Thursday, 13 March

I had lunch in the 'Churchill' room [at the Commons] with Jonathan Aitken and Alastair Goodlad. It is glorious being back in the Commons. Everywhere I went I was hailed by staff; no one questioned my right of access (I put my luggage in a locker in the dining-room corridor). Dawn Primarolo[1] held a door open for me – or was it Tessa Jowell?

Saltwood, EMT   *Sunday, 16 March*

Depressed and out of sorts. Fatigue comes into it, of course, plus the oppression of every day filled with engagements. (Not all of those, I suspect, on the chart – like I had totally forgotten meeting the pensioners in Kensington Town Hall tomorrow – the first meeting I went to, on the wrong day last month.)

Last night at 3 a.m. precisely poor T.O. had, or rather started, a very long fit. He convulsed into walking movements, though lying down, defecated. I thought he was going to die – but he's so tough. We carried him outside, legs completely paralysed it seems, his ear cocked, but he slowly picked up. Back indoors he walked round and round incessantly, would not settle. We went back to bed and after two hours' sleep I went down – he was still pacing up the corridor through the top Green Room door, then back and round. He must have walked to Ashford. This

---

[1] Dawn Primarolo, MP (Lab) for Bristol South since 1987.

morning he is still muddled, but drank his saucer, went out as in routine. He's 18 years old.

So many people have come up to me to wish me well. Nellies in the street, the loony man from Wensdyke with his Cumberland accent; a sweet shy boy who stuttered slightly who walked all the way across the forecourt at Ashford Tesco. And yet, just as I knew I was going to get it – from way back, when Henrietta Royle first said, 'a lot of people from Chelsea may be there' (to the speaking engagement, my first entry to 1a) – so I also have the terrible feeling that I am never actually going to 'take my seat'. Ill health, crisis, personal anti-vote ... My despondency increased by a very poor performance on Jonathan Dimbleby's show this morning. The whole of Sunday demolished, and I was old, hunched, and out manoeuvred. 'You must be aggressive (sic),' as Jane said. TV finds you out, and I was slow and stooping.

Just occasionally I ask myself – especially when threatened or worsted, what's the point? There are all those brambles in the woodland; and the Hen–Bustard hood-irons still to be blacked, and the early spring surge in the Garden approaching ... 'Are we all mad?' (Chips).

Summer Office   *Tuesday, 18 March*

Last night we dined with Daniel Moylan – and a cocktail party first. The smartness, and the sophistication! 'You'd never get *one* of these people in a normal constituency,' I said to Jane,' – never mind a roomful.' But is it all doomed to ash? Personally, I mean. Nationally, indeed, we are on the verge of annihilation it seems. Polls this morning show Labour 26 points ahead and the *Sun* has turned.

I haven't had a normal pulse for ten days.

Sandling train   *Thursday, 20 March*

David Davis interesting – cool as always. Said Cranborne and co were 'a cloud of parasites looking for a host on which to settle ...' Wanted to fix everything first; 22 Executive elections etc. Suggested that they would probably prefer Tom King as 22 chairman. Key thing is to get Major to make a statement immediately that he will ask 22 chairman to convene an election before the summer recess – doubting that we could extend it to November. JM himself may anyway not stand; but would have time to test the water and recover.

MFS GH   *Saturday, 22 March*

I hate elections. This one hasn't yet started; but already I want to fast forward. I have had bad experiences already – Jonathan Dimbleby; and the pensioners (most notably reported in the *Kensington Times*), the Lympne postmistress said to me, 'There are a lot of discontented people about ...' I am always susceptible to hostile press comment (as must be everyone who habitually enjoys being preened). Complete meltdown is possible. My own majority is far from secure because of a personal anti vote which is solid (the lady with a spaniel and head scarf from Swan Court) and my fan vote is fickle.

MFS GL   *Tuesday, 25 March*

Poor old Allan Stewart[1] forced to resign – instantly – today as PPC because of his 'association' with a woman he met at an alcohol-dependency clinic, even though his wife is 'standing by'

---

[1] Allan Stewart, MP for Eastwood since 1983 (E Renfrewshire 1979–83).

him. It is really preposterous, this kind of witch-hunt. There is now a total blurring of the lines between personal (sexual) conduct and personal (financial) conduct.

And I know, I can't say why or how, but I just know that something awful is going to happen to me and I get AF thinking about it.

Shore   *Easter Sunday, 30 March*

Really, with the possible exception of the balcony at the villino at Cuixmala I don't think there can be any more pleasing site for EMT – particularly, and most inexplicably, on a 'rough' day – than the new porch at Shore. We can't go past without popping in. One of the best-value expenditures ever, it is commodious – even room for the two Bulgarian straw chairs plus the 'Army' work table, plus length for gumboots, heater, Julie's (return reluctantly offered) Canadian pew. Coat hooks banned. It really is a most congenial spot; the wheelhouse of the *Hebridean Princess* with views down the Loch and up Eriboll Street to the Lodge and the Creaggan, opposite the Long Shed and the 'Gossie' bank. Truly panoramic.

The dignitaries in the Party are going down like nine-pins. Since we came up here Allan Stewart, Piers Merchant, and now poor Mickey Hirst – on the point of getting (Stewart's) seat – has 'crash'-resigned in the face of 'charges' of a relationship with a (male) researcher.[1] As Jane said, 'are the Labour Party made up of 200 virgins?'

---

1 Piers Merchant, MP for Beckenham since 1992 (Newcastle-upon-Tyne Central 1983–87); Sir Michael Hirst, Scottish Conservative and Unionist Party chairman since 1998.

Shore   *Easter Monday*

Am I relaxed, confident, beautifully turned out, one of the few 'real' Conservatives, historian, authoritative, high-profile media figure: to be returned smoothly to the new 'difficult', 'interesting', etc House of Commons?

Or am I shaky, nervous of crowds, with incipient prostate, bowel and basal cancers; demi deaf in one (right) ear, completely non-functionally impotent with a limited lifespan and an enormous crowd of ill-wishers waiting for me to fall over?

The next month is critical. But it is April; my 'lucky' month.

MFS GL   *Saturday, 5 April*

More apprehensive and ill-at-ease than I should be. Was it only yesterday that the *Evening Standard* came out showing that I had a 6-point advantage over the Party average in London(!). I am really chuffed. The hottest currency in politics. Then (in all probability) blew it by telling stupid little Michelle Stephens, who was trying to set up an 'open' debate between me and Robert Atkinson[1] – fired by his 'triumph' with the pensioners he thinks he can parade local issues around which is, of course, all a 'local' paper wants. Were they interested in my 6 points? – not at all. Foolishly, in explaining it, I lost my temper and said the 'Royal Borough is bloody lucky to have me as a candidate.' What a headline! Fool, Clark, fool, etc.

---

[1] Robert Atkinson, Labour candidate at Kensington and Chelsea.

B5   *Sunday, 6 April*

I wrote this with a ball-pen (which I dislike) that has cost me
£233 – the price, including tip, of a two-bottle lunch at the
Berkeley with Soames (splendid, but illish-looking) and Ancram
– grinning and compos. Jonathan A, somewhat diminished as
Soames and I – not for the first time – agreed, had given us
champagne at Lord North Street, but was depressed, almost
chetif.[1] We had come from the Candidates Conference in that
very low-ceilinged room with its strange overhead pipes, like
the ward-room of an escort carrier. Some pleasant young boys,
friendly and fresh-faced, who were going to be cut to pieces by
the *jagdstaffel*; some old warhorses (everyone looking quite a bit
older, I must say) and some sharp and indeed Semitic-looking
template figures who presumably had taken the best seats.

Mrs T spoke fantastically. Turned to the man on my right –
'she could still win the election', and her charisma, vitality and
blue-flashing eyes, still could. John M was competent, better
than adequate. I was filled with gloom at my manifest inability
to answer questions on any topic. Came back here and
wrestled with my Election Address text. Completed it about
7.30, very much 'in my own write', but on the phone Jane
liked it. I stopped the car in St Leonard's Terrace, walking back
to snoop on what looked to be a street-corner meeting, but it
turned out merely to be a group of late-evening tourists with
a guide.

Ancram repeated the Cranborne line, that we must all get
together more promptly – the Friday if possible – to stop JM
resigning if defeated badly. Norma [Major], apparently, is sick of
the whole thing and urging him to do that.

---

[1] Jonathan Aitken, despite his ongoing legal action involving the *Guardian*, was
standing as the Conservative candidate at Thanet South, which he had represented
since 1983.

Tuesday, 15 April

Almost completely soft-spoken and AF because Carol Midgley, of *The Times*, said 'Max Clifford keeps telling us of something really big – but he won't tell us what it is.'[1] Luckily, for my crumbling morale, we scored seven bull's-eyes as we went along the street. She and the photographer 'had to admit it'. A little later as I said, 'I hope you will agree that I am not encountering a very high level of personal hostility,' Carol had to admit, said something about 'everybody likes you'. And we had a boost from a TV wife who said Parliament should contain people like me and Tony Benn. In the *Standard* tonight MORI showed 20 points deficit. Intractable. Could be interesting.

Garden House   *Saturday, 19 April*

My hair has perceptibly whitened and I have lost ½ stone since 11 April adoption meeting. I don't know what is going to happen. Whether we will be routed (197 seats) or Parliament hung. Soames last night bellowing that 'we will win, Alan. We-are-going-to-win!' Apparently canvass returns are not bad.

MFS GH   *Sunday, 20 April*

Last night we did sleep well. The worst point, about 8 p.m. when comment from the Sundays would be sought. And I could feel that wonderful sensation of anxiety lifting – as in a benign diagnosis. One more period of jeopardy tonight – for Mondays.

---

[1] AC had been told that James Harkess, husband of Valerie Harkess, was flying from South Africa to campaign for Robert Atkinson, on the grounds that AC was 'not deserving of becoming an MP'. The Max Clifford 'threat' haunted him for the rest of the campaign.

Then, during the week we will be at Albany. I would have to address them from the steps, like General Gordon and the Mahdi. The very last Sunday would be too tricky for them to leave it so late.

Albany, EMT   *Tuesday, 29 April*

The news is dreadful. 'The Tory Party gives up' – headline in *Independent* (Anthony Bevins, naturally, he's not a reporter at all, but a Labour Party activist). The gap is intractable, widening indeed. Can this really be the case? Yesterday we decided to watch Major's last, and only, 'soapbox' performance on (ironically) College Green. A 'papered house' and only got to hear of it because CCO rang Barbara and asked for 20 activists to be bussed round and applaud. As we walked to and from the site, the streets of Whitehall seemed curiously empty. A sense – though not to the same degree – of the atmosphere in the Palace of Westminster just before the Lady fell. Not so far distant T34s were again at the fortifications on the Oder. I was calm. 'I have arrangements for my family to travel to the Argentine.' Even though as I composed this I was conscious of lapsing into 'parody' as Peter Bradshaw (whose last entry, after a miss the previous week, was very funny).[1]

Poor Major looked exhausted, his voice flat – and Jane said Norma looked absolutely shattered. I must speak to Robert Cranborne, perhaps today, to discuss a *petit comité*[2] at Saltwood on Saturday evening to talk through next steps.

---

[1] Peter Bradshaw, author of 'Not the Alan Clark Diary' in the *Evening Standard*, over which AC would later sue for 'passing off'.

[2] On 13 February 1992 AC had noted the following as possible members, complete with partial annotation: 'Heathcoat-Amory√, Derek Conway?, G Johnson Smith√, Andrew Mitchell√, David Caneva, William Hague, Peter Brooke, Jonathan Aitken, Soames, ?Cranborne, David D, Piers Merchant.'

EMT   *Thursday, 1 May*

I walked in very fragile sunlight to the paper seller in Piccadilly Circus underground and bought the whole lot. Robert Cranborne with whom I had a very interesting talk in his delightful comfy house at Swan Walk last evening, Robert was grave, but admirable in his sense of scholarship. First we must brush Redwood out of the way. Then keep Major in long enough for Heseltine's faults (of which we are all aware) to become apparent. Much depends on timing, and how to manoeuvre. In particular, the 'structure' of the 22 committee and its executive and chair.

(On the way back a plain young lady, alone in the street, said to me, 'I hope you lose – philanderer', which quite set me back after Buck House lights where I grumbled to Jane about a young yuppie lolling back in the taxi next to us, and then he wound down the window, 'I'm voting for you Alan' – and shook my hand!)

It was apparent as the first results came in that, as the polls predicted, Labour had a landslide victory. Labour 417 seats; Conservative 165 seats; Liberals 46 seats; others 28 seats. At Kensington and Chelsea, AC had 19,887 votes; Robert Atkinson (Labour) 10,368; Robert Woodthorpe Browne (Liberal Democrat) 5,668; others just over 1,000. AC's majority 9,519.

Saltwood, p.m.   *Friday, 2 May*

Down here after two hours' sleep and looking like death. Saltwood is beautiful; a completely still day and the greens yellowy-springlike. Doves, jackdaws and swallows go about their business in the Bailey. I am so exhausted I cannot bear to look at a press cutting or a newspaper or even talk to David D, or whoever. Already Jane is quite rightly making me 'take calls'.

People in London appear to be more shell-shocked than 'in the constituencies'. Archie Hamilton was far the most compos. Asked me straight out if I wanted the 22; some stuff about Butterfill[1] had beaten him for vice and Townend[2] was going to go for it, but yes he did want it for himself. Geoffrey Johnson Smith is the Whips' candidate.[3] Alastair Goodlad was so taciturn as almost (no, delete) to be unfriendly. Perhaps because of my 'anti-European' stance. Actually he was rather unpleasant.

Monday, 5 May

Most of yesterday seems to have been spent on the phone. The candidates are a mouldy lot. Portillo, probably the strongest, out.[4] Ken [Clarke], supposedly the most genial and experienced – won't get past the hard right. Little Hague – my aphorism about 'the guy's a golf ball' has already got currency, I'm glad to say. Redwood is fluent in today's *Times* – but I don't like him. Lilley is cerebral – should be the leader, but hasn't got the oomph – white rabbit in the teapot at the Mad Hatter's tea party.[5] Michael [Howard] presents me with a problem. I ought to support him, but I'm hesitating.

---

[1] John Butterfill, MP for Bournemouth West since 1983. He served as vice-chairman of the 1922 Committee until 2001.
[2] John Townend, MP for E Yorks. since 1997 (Bridlington 1979–97).
[3] Sir Geoffrey Johnson Smith, MP for Wealden since 1983 (E Grinstead, February 1965–1983; Holborn and St Pancras South, 1959–64).
[4] Michael Portillo had lost Enfield Southgate seat, which he had represented since December 1984.
[5] Peter Lilley, newly elected as MP for Hitchin and Harpenden (St Albans 1983–97), Trade and then Social Security Secretary in John Major's Cabinet.

EMT   *Thursday, 8 May*

Yesterday I was up in the Commons. The whole thing should have been too delicious for words – but I was haunted by apprehension, and also a curious sense of hostility from colleagues, even Tebbit, whereas staff, and Labour MPs – Skinner (walking back from Church House, 'I thought the idea was to take power, not to give it away'), Mark Fisher,[1] Tony Benn – brilliant speech at the swearing-in.

Saltwood Garden   *Friday, 16 May*

Woke at 4 a.m. this morning in a panic that I wouldn't get anyone to sponsor me for the 22 chair. Got up, wrote composite letter to Peter Brooke[2] who was cool and abrupt to me in the 'Aye' lobby last night – leading to the fantasy nightmare that Peter Lloyd[3] had said, 'I gather you've put up Alan for the 22?' 'What?' etc etc. Also doubled up in seeking sponsorship from Francis Maude, David Heathcoat-Amory. *The Times* arrived, and I saw I was at 2% – same as Dorrell and only one point behind Lilley (!) – but drawing support equally from Labour and Con – so wrote also to Gill Shephard.

After EMT and one biscuit drove to House, just in time for prayers. Sent a note to Peter Brooke (*to which he did not reply* though perfectly affable). Listened to start of Devolution Debate, then urgent message from Soames. I knew what it would be about. 'You can't do this. You're mad. You'll be slaughtered' etc.

This came at exactly the wrong moment. No reply from P. Brooke; nothing on board from the others; feeling of *guarded*

---

[1] Dennis Skinner, MP for Bolsover since 1970; Mark Fisher, MP for Stoke-on-Trent Central since 1983.
[2] Peter Brooke, newly elected MP for Cities of London and Westminster (City of London and Westminster South, February 1977–97).
[3] Sir Peter Lloyd, MP for Fareham since 1979.

suspicion right across Party. I went out and drafted statement to Press Association. Told Jane on the answering machine, rather sadly went over to Trishy. Ann Perkins appeared almost at once, told me that John Macgregor wasn't now standing (!). Thought Geoffrey Johnson Smith was. Blast! Who dares wins.

Then when finally dead tired and stressed I got down here. Andrew Dalton very reproachful and disappointed ('wimpish'). As, although she was too sweet to show it, was Jane.

My line, I'm sticking to, 'don't want to split the vote' ('for the things I think need to be done'). We'll see how it is taken. My star was heavily in the ascendant. A lovely piece by Don McIntyre today in *The Independent* and yesterday in the tunnel Peter Oborne[1] was ruefully laudatory – said 'a great recalculation might have to be made'. Something though tells me I wouldn't have got it. Might next year *if* (and even that is not certain) I get on the Executive. Memories soon heal over in the House – provided I perform. But I must get my speech for Tuesday spruced up.

Tearoom frontage   Saturday, 17 May

An absolutely perfect morning of mid-May. Still wood pigeons cooing, whole place heavy with the sweet cloying odour of the Queen Anne's Lace. But I am not relaxed. Mrs Frowd this morning and we'll see what she says. Partly I am tormented by having bogged the 22 election. Lost my nerve under Soames's blustery. If only I had got Jane and not the answering machine, she would have said, 'Balls, go for it, lead from the front.' Soames rang again – said 'you *must* be more serious. If you're always on TV you're like Beaumont-Dark'.[2] Well, yes; but as Jane said someone must speak for Conservatives. In any case I'm minded to think that the old, stuffy rank of Tory MPs are different now.

---

[1] Peter Oborne, now political columnist with the *Sunday Express*.
[2] Sir Anthony Beaumont-Dark, MP for Birmingham Selly Oak, 1979–92.

They don't think like that any longer ... What put me in a panic was that nobody would 'sponsor' me. But I still should have waited until Monday – or even the very last minute.

I must speak, and question, and sit in on debates (and send congratulatory notes). I think the Party will slowly destroy itself, actually. So the tactic is to come out at an individual position.

H o C Library   *Wednesday, 21 May*

Last night at Conrad Black's dinner. Drank a tiny bit too much, and may have shouted. Influential people said why aren't you standing as chairman of the 22 committee. On the way up in the train the stars (Jonathan Cainer) had said go for it – too late. Even the 'conventional' excuse – 'better let it go a year' etc – is a cop-out. Next time could be in the context of having tried to rush it – then 'accepted colleagues' verdict' at waiting for a year.

I was in the position of the 3rd Army, and should have remembered Patton's aphorism – 'we ... don't worry about our flanks; it's for the enemy to worry about his.'

This absurd and embarrassing 'leadership contest' rambles on. In fact, as I was saying to young, intense Bernard Jenkin[1] in the aye lobby this morning, they may have 'thrown their hats in the ring', but the election campaign can't formally open until the nomination papers are filed with the (as yet unconstituted) 22 committee. The Left has now decided to make a showing for Ken, then switch en bloc to Hague (Dorrell is an irrelevance). Soames, a baleful though pleasing *éminence énorme* was going to vote for Ken, 'one's got to make sure he gets a good initial vote' – on Monday; then switch, 'it's got to be Hague'. Garel-Jones is running the Hague campaign. Let's hope he doesn't get a peerage.

---

[1] Bernard Jenkin, newly elected MP for Essex N since the election (Colchester N, 1992–97); his father Lord [Patrick] Jenkin had been an MP and Minister in the early 1980s.

Garden House   *Tuesday, 27 May*

Went over to Lympne. Michael (H) alert, and full of life-force, although he knows he's 'up against it'. Also there, particularly thoughtful, was Norman Lamont, and Rosemary. Norman was grave, but mock-statesman. Told how at 5.45 on election day he had set out for a last leaflet drop (an admission of pressure, and bad auguries, if ever there was one). Some slob of a councillor had refused to get up, but said 'would they drop in his leaflets as well …?' Then at 9 a.m. a champagne breakfast for 40 people, paid for personally by NL. Hung-over all day, and through to the humiliation of the count. What ordeals everyone suffered![1]

Refuge is taken in the assumption that Labour will hang themselves and people will say, 'this business of Government not as easy as being claimed …' Possibly. But will they then turn to the Tories? I think not. If only because they want not to admit so soon that they were wrong/conned? What part do I play? I'm guilt-free.

Friday, 30 May

The meeting of the [K&C] Executive at 1a was intensely depressing and I drove back, after 2 hours, very slowly and sadly. Not quite down to Plymothian standards, but they bickered and autogrumbled away. All the Kensington creepos were there, including that ghastly tall man who marched in front of us on walkabout bellowing at people in Kensington High Street, 'Would you like to meet the prospective parliamentary candidate?' One of them harangued the meeting about not having 'right-wing policies' in an American accent ('a Jewish accent,' Barbara said); another that we should wait for 'the

---

[1] Norman Lamont had lost his Harrogate seat to the Lib-Dems, majority 6,236.

Governor of Hong Kong'.[1] When they voted it was: KC 35; Hague 28; Lilley 14; Dorrell 2; Redwood 1. Poor Michael got zero! But an overwhelming vote for the Left. How lucky I am, to get selected there! Or at least what additional proof this offers of divine intervention.

As for myself, already I could feel my popularity slipping. And I have a suspicion that the book, and the TV series will annoy.

I spoke to Michael (he rang me at 9 a.m.) this morning. Explained I couldn't now 'come out' in the Sundays. He took it very well.

I don't actually know which candidate, *for me*, will be best. I had driven in the C-type and put £200 on Ken Clarke (now only evens).

GH   *Saturday, 31 May*

I am excruciatingly, unhealthily fatigued. Missed lunch entirely, but had a cream-scone tea – a private opening. Then trailed round with James's new little compressor and blew up tyres on the Hen (which we pushed out and it started at once, though pouring water) and the black Chev. At one point dear sweet Jane told me that she had been intermittently bleeding poor darling, and ought to see Ursell. Poor little pet. If she actually fell ill, my life would be effectively over. I would be a total recluse and try all the time to talk to her. I would close down Saltwood, I think – 'care and maintenance' – and live here half the time. But for long periods 'Ansoning' at Shore.

Perhaps it was this that has made me so utterly de-energised. I can't do Gossie – still less the Downs. Perhaps I ought to try this tomorrow.

---

[1] Chris Patten, former Tory MP (Bath 1979–92), Minister, and chairman of Conservative Party, was in his final weeks as last Governor of Hong Kong before its return to China. Aged 53, his future was much speculated upon.

Friday, 6 June

My confidence had earlier been raised by a meeting of the '92'.
The good ones – Duncan Smith, Shephard etc – interrogatingly
having an audition of candidates. Clarke, cleaned up in appearance, but not especially friendly; Hague, shifty little bureaucrat
(voice jarring, like Wilson); Howard white as a sheet, but still
impressive. Dorrell has now dropped out, but is dutch in the
tearoom (*also* white as a sheet, and looking ghastly). At one point
in the 'discussion' I bellowing dominated the room. Half-serious
Iain Duncan Smith[1] said come round here, give us a talk, take
some questions, 'throw your hat in the ring'.

Oh! But what bliss this all is. The sheer ecstasy of having
walked out of a dream, and found it to be real …

EMT   *Monday, 9 June*

Today Bill Cash[2] having a *petit comité* for a hard right grouping
after the ballot. And I will give my spiel. By sheer force of
personality I am in fact the epicentre of the 'Right'. And with
two delicious corollaries (i) I am completely independent (of
constituency pressure), (ii) whatever the solution – except possibly
a Michael Howard victory – it will be explainable.

Barbican seat   *Sunday, 15 June*

The 'leadership' contest continues. Both Lilley and Howard
welched on Redwood most odiously. I shall be voting for

---

[1] Iain Duncan Smith, MP for Chingford and Woodford Green since 1997
(Chingford 1992–97).
[2] William Cash, MP for Stone since the election (Stafford 1984–97), founder and
chairman of the European Foundation.

Redwood in the 2nd ballot in order to maximise the recognisable numbers of the Right; then for Clarke in the final on the basis that he is the weaker; least likely to last the term, easiest to attack.

1 Parliament Street   *Thursday, 19 June*

The last vote in the leadership 'contest' today. Last night I broached, at the S. Stanley garden party, my notion of a spoilt ballot paper. Didn't go all that well. Andrew Dalton sneakily opposed. I 'hid my face' while the vote was counted 14–8. Typical constituency. The hard core of party spastics who don't like a 'loose cannon'. I was originally going to write BUTTOCKS on the voting slip. A bit tricky to 'live with', although not as dangerous as at first it seems as it would be what is 'expected' of me.

The dignity of abstention must, though, be reinforced by a mellifluous and persuasive think piece written this weekend. What I can't quite make out is do I say anything at this stage – probably not.[1] I still judge, tactically, it is better for me if Ken wins, then fluffs it. It's the old '72 Heathites, against the young 'Thatcher's children' plus a shower of failed Ministers cut off in mid-career, but without an idea in their head.

The phone rang, and it was Kirsty Wark wanting an interview on *Newsnight*.[2] But I'm not sure if the timing is ripe. It's 'don't rush it' versus 'grab the opportunity' on Tuesday night, after the second ballot.

Sat in the smoking room drinking (iced ginger beer in my case; scotch and g. ale in his) with David D. Shaun Woodward[3]

---

[1] AC was still considering putting himself forward as party leader, conceivably in November 1997 ('by popular demand if our poll figures have really plummeted'), but more likely 'a long haul to 1998'.

[2] Kirsty Wark, presenter on BBC2 *Newsnight* since 1992.

[3] Shaun Woodward, MP for Witney since 1997.

hovered. Pure bliss. Was I really lounging in the smoking room, talking of politics from the inside track less than a year after I had been, in desperation, seriously considering doing a Churchill at N. Dorset?

Earlier in the afternoon, while walking along the pavement outside New Palace Yard, a voice behind me said, 'That's a very smart car of yours which slid past me this morning.'

'I love it,' I said.

'But every police force in the country must have the number?'

Thinking he was 'trying to be nice' I said, 'I never thought I'd find myself saying this: but I wish you were in the running ...'

MH [Michael Heseltine] replied by going into a long thing about 'I never could understand, you were taking the wrong briefs, we could have worked together' etc etc. I reminded him of the message I sent through Peter Levene from MoD.[1] He tried to push it aside.

When I told David D he made an interesting reply, 'you're opium now, he had to have some. He's aching with withdrawal. No, worse, you were a still smoking stub on the pavement which he picked up for a last drag.'

The delicious irony of it all. Now I'm going over to hear the count.[2]

EMT (Albany)   *Thursday, 10 July*

A year ago if you had said to me, etc etc. Last night I was elected (by a very good vote, as Patrick McLoughlin[3] said) to the 22 Executive. Most notable that there is real attendance at 22

---

[1] Lord Levene had a long association with Michael Heseltine, being his personal adviser at Defence, Environment and the Board of Trade, 1992. He had also been Chief of Defence Procurement, MoD, during AC's time as a Minister there.

[2] In the final ballot of Tory MPs, William Hague had a 22 majority over Kenneth Clarke.

[3] Patrick McLoughlin, MP for West Derbyshire since May 1986; a Whip.

elections; not like those somewhat spare grouplets that contest the Party committees.

Felt immediately an elevation of status. David D, who always keeps a lot of himself to himself, but was loyal in my wilderness years, had a chat in the smoking room afterwards. 'Get a group of the new "good" ones down to Saltwood,' he advised me, an end-of-term picnic.

Strange, his 'sponsorship'. What is going on at the back of his mind? Could it be the same sort of thing that lies in mine? (Although today I read Peter Riddell – one of the small-print merchants – complaining of 'GDP' deflation. How can a Prime Minister, unless he be exceptionally boring like Wilson, be expected to 'brief' himself on these arcane matters?)

Saltwood   *Sunday, 13 July*

My father's birthday. He would be 94, just – I think – older than Bernard Berenson was when he died.[1] Now the Great Reaper moves without disguise among my own generation. There is poor Jimmy [Goldsmith], in agony for the last 30 days at (Burgundy) where his new 'Indian' doctor is curing him (yeah) by 'withdrawing' painkilling drugs. French doctors are good at keeping you going right up until the end, Pompidou, Mitterrand, by ruthless use of steroids and others. Then, finally, the body collapses. After all it was only 1 May that Jimmy was chanting in triumph at the odious Mellor (who now, or so we are told, is to go 'straight to the Lords'[2]).

I am seated on the front step, with the door wide open, on the Coronation chair. My grandfather's diary for 1909 shows

---

[1] Kenneth Clark studied under Berenson in the 1920s.
[2] Although David Mellor had lost his Putney seat at the general election after 20 years as MP, AC was unnecessarily pessimistic: he was not elevated to the Lords.

that they were at Poolewe (with, I assume, that almost brand-new 'Katoomba'[1] riding in Loch Ewe) and that week he caught a 16 lb salmon. Just one very brief time I was there, aged 3-4, I suppose. But I can recall the smell of peat water, and the newly caught fish; and that stayed with me all my life until fulfilment with the return to Eriboll.[2]

My weight is 12 stone 4. I've put on a stone since emerging from the General Election. I am under huge pressure with Big Book. I am also looking forward to the first meeting of the 22 Executive, and 'take the temperature' of that. The cars, and practically everything else, being hopelessly neglected.

Great Hall   *Friday, 18 July*

I have this equivocal position in the Party. Many expect great things of me. I was 'lionised' at the Conservative Way Forward group meeting on Wednesday. Lots of young people. And, as I ran for a Division, a very young boy with crew cut and large single ear-ring, shouted across the street, 'That's Alan Clark, man.' I waved, and he made a finger & thumb sign – 'Top boy ...' Who else could get that, aged 69? But I am not quite clear how to capitalise.

I have to consider how to handle the Party Conference. If the TV series has already started – my line has to be 'yes, there is history' and one can learn from history; but our real task is how we re-form, and how in future we relate to the electorate.

---

[1] Katoomba was the name given by AC's grandfather to his yachts. The word came from Australia's Blue Mountains.
[2] The Clarks purchased Eriboll following the death of Lord Clark in 1983.

Wednesday, 23 July

Absolutely ideal conditions. I sit at the table in the window of the no-talking annexe. River sounds. I have turned off the air conditioning and opened the window and a gentle summer breeze comes in. Already I have been here since 8 a.m. when I arrived (every single light from Albany to Parliament Square was (just) green) in the Little Silver, put in a prayer card and had a gossipy breakfast with the boys.

EMT   *Friday, 25 July*

Yesterday we went to the end-of-term party at Buck House. One had been 'placed' (I suspect by a resentful Lord Chamberlain) on the duds day. Not a single member of the governing classes up at the top corner of the tea-tent, where, naturally, one gathers; just as the domestics separate themselves at a grand wedding and congregate around the great circular tree seat by the lavatories. I drank four of the delicious iced coffees. The iced coffee at Buck House is the most delicious in the world.

Saturday, 2 August

Blair created 57 new peers today. The Upper House is being turned into a sort of Senate (by appointment) and JM gave a peerage to Tristan!

EMT, Saltwood   *Saturday, 9 August*

In the night (4.30) 'wind-Thompsoned' – thought 'change in
bowel movement' (now a year old). The evening before coming
back over for supper I had 'field of vision' restriction (plus
'jagged' not intense halo) lasted about 18 minutes. I went on
working through it. In the afternoon I got relaxed voice ('easily
tired' – Dr Thomas Stuttaford, first sign of throat cancer) driving
back from Allington.[1] And during the night I had to tinkle at
4.10, 5.30 and 6.30 – copiously. The only frightening symptom
is return of the glaucoma. My eyes are taking such a beating at
present from the 'white screen'.

EMT   *Saturday, 16 August*

Yesterday afternoon for 3½ hours Clara and Nick[2] and I sat in
the hall of the Garden House and agreed the 'mods' necessary
to programme four, the Thatcher-Major section. So the TV will
'go out' on 14 September for 4 weeks. I think it is rather good
and glossy, though quintessentially superficial, because that is the
medium.

As for my state – I am unfit, saggy, scrawny, bags under my
eyes. I am using up my margin fast between being 70 and looking
70. (Yet I still can't visualise myself as 70.)

A little later
Went for a 'w' with Tom. The full, dark colours on every side.
Each year this time of the seasons makes me nostalgic. The great
house starts its autumn siesta. I walk in the keep while the
House of Commons awaits. Continuity. But what new

---

[1] Allington, like Saltwood, also originally restored by Lady Conway; now the home
of Bob Worcester and his wife.
[2] Nick Kent, producer, and Clara Glynn, director, of *Alan Clark's History of the Tories*,
as the TV series was now titled.

generation will appreciate it, and maintain, even skeletally, this old Venetian, faded grandeur. So important as a reservoir from which to draw strength.

Shore   *Friday, 29 August*

Our last 'real' day here. I am deeply apprehensive. So often in my life, school/Upper Terrace, Portmeirion etc, I have felt this mixture of gloom and foreboding before return. As always I think to myself – why can't one 'see the seasons round' or at least dig in for a meaningful session? Surely next year BB will be 'behind me'.

In the night I had some kind of muddled dream that James and Julie's child was going to be a little girl. Poor little darling, a rich, brainy, beautiful blonde, but what awaits her? James would be secretly disappointed, I know. He would be such a wonderful father for a little male-bairn.

This evening at 8 p.m. I strolled down to the loch and caught the high tide. Quite still, the water was, and so far in that I could use the Katoomba trailer as a pier. The sky was slate grey with wonderful passages of lemon and pink behind the clouds. I swam, more freely and longer than at any other time. Just wonderful, and I strolled back in philosophic mood. Of one thing there is no doubt. Two weeks at Eriboll does repair the physique.

Shore   *Sunday, 31 August*

We went to the island, although the breeze was getting up. Lovely, although my mind was on the return. Jane found a cowrie, and we looked at the site of the island house. As we were pulling the dinghy ashore Julie arrived at the boathouse in the Range Rover.

'Have you heard the news?'

'I don't want news. Just don't tell me.'

'Diana and Dodi have been killed in a car crash pursued by paparazzi'. So soon after my article! [in *The Spectator*]

We felt a great rage. Nothing will change, except that a lovely icon has been destroyed. Most fortuitously it was the Eriboll service that afternoon – in the Gaelic – and Donny[1] adapted beautifully. (Unlike, I was horrified to note that evening, the service at Craithie.[2])

EMT   *Friday, 5 September*

Went for a tiny drive in the R-Cont yesterday afternoon to collect my accumulated OAP (over £300) and thought how lovely it is – especially at low, vintage, speeds. That change from 2nd to 3rd, perfect in feel and unity of b.m.e.p. and engine revs.

We are off this morning to park the car in the Commons, camp in the office at 1 Parliament Street for the cortège tomorrow. In the evening, a service at St Mary Abbots, with the Mayor, dignitaries. Rather fun, in its way. And pleasing to note the discomfiture of 'the Royals' as they struggle to cope with this great outpouring of love for someone they were trying (and succeeded) to destroy – from jealousy and incomprehension. Also, can't get away from the here-I-am syndrome. It could scarcely be more convenient/privileged, than to park in both senses on the very corner of Parliament Square.

---

[1] The Rev. Donny McSween.

[2] The church for Balmoral, where the Queen and many of her family were on holiday.

EMT   *Sunday, 7 September*

Back yesterday for Diana's funeral. Very slowly and sadly one drove along in Big Red – twice yellow 'high' bikes trailed their coat at me, but I had no will to respond, and 'proceeded' at, mainly 58–65 mph (this using, by comparison, practically no fuel at all).

The day before we had been to the service at Kensington Church, a nice formal duty. And heard at the outset while waiting in the pews, the Queen's broadcast – clipped, formal, utterly without warmth and affection. Then we walked in Kensington High Street and along to the memorial – an exciting atmosphere of happening, of unity of purpose. A crowd entirely friendly, each recognising one another in this common purpose.

A quiet curry at the Kundan – we neither of us wanted to read – and then strolled back through the crowds mainly now with candles, and little make-shift shelters. We slept, not badly, in the office; Jane on the tried and proven camp bed used at Netherton Grove and even on the Le Mans 24 hours, in the fifties. I on the armchair and snoof. A rattling on the door at 5.20, and I called out 'we're in here' thinking it to be the waste-paper lady. But the voice which answered was (surely?) Trish's. I put on my trousers and staggered out blearily in the Cuixmala T-shirt. There was Trish, immaculate in a white trouser suit. I reeled off to the gents to sluice my face and she bossily moved in, rustled papers and without so much a by-your-leave to Jane, turned on the television! This, and Stewart's [Cill-Johnson] presence – triumphantly with his walking stick – in the most comfortable chair did somewhat cramp the atmosphere in the room. But the combination of cortège, TV, crowds, and the service itself was overpowering. My only wish is that I could, for the service, have been transposed to Hyde Park, watched there on the enormous screen, and applauded with the crowd at Charles Spencer's brave utterances.[1]

---

[1] In an interview in the *Guardian* (15 July 2002) Spencer said: 'Alan Clark wrote me … and said I agree with every word you said but just watch now. The press and the royal family are two of the most powerful institutions in the country and they will make sure your name is dragged through the dirt.'

EMT   *Wednesday, 17 September*

A bad night. Jane is stressed, predominantly over the dogs. But once awake – she sleeps for about 1¼ hours, from 11.45 to either side of 1 a.m. we can't hug and console each other because we both get hot (temperature rise). Was it only two years ago that we could lie wrapped in each other's arms for most of the night after making love and then enjoying shortbread ('complacently') with early morning tea?

Last night I tried to coax her into a breathing therapy and she wouldn't even try – said she was *holding* her breath, was 'too stressed' to let it out. I got out of bed in despair. It's all my fault, I suppose, Lëhni certainly is. And this bloody lawsuit with the *Standard*. Denton Hall insisting on coming down on Thursday morning,[1] while the whole of Saturday afternoon is occupied by Terry Lambert[2] going over evidence for the 31 October. The untidiness everywhere. If this clears up – but can it, ever? We both went to tinkle and Jane said 'we have no time'.

Saltwood Pavillon   *Saturday, 27 September*

A pleasant Saturday. Did 15 letters, demi-mechanically, while Jane was at the hairdresser. Rang Andrew Roberts, said 'come down' and he suggested bringing Dean Godson. Just what I like. We sparkled and enjoyed ourselves with a rosé and two Bourgogne Aligoté in their 'sleeves'. Jane adapted brilliantly with heavy-duty canapés.

This morning the news (leaked) that Hague was going to dispense with hereditary peerages (i.e. adopted Blair's 'reforms'). For me this is the last straw – already. Coming on top of message

---

[1] AC had decided to go ahead and sue the *Evening Standard* for its *Not the Alan Clark Diaries* column. His solicitors were now called Denton Wilde Sapte.
[2] Terry Lambert, partner at Mowll & Mowll, the solicitors acting for the Clarks in Lëhni's case.

to Gay Pride, Notting Hill carnival (aren't there any worthwhile causes he could send a message to?). It's got him marked. Give him a good bit more rope, though. We have the advantage that whatever he does he can't pick up any points this year.

Pavillon   *Sunday, 28 September*

I think the Party has had it. Our grip was ephemeral while Labour, even in the low, low times post-1983, had its hard core of TU and urban support. Now the hard core remains – 'it has nowhere else to go' – but the whole sticky-crap consumerist ad-speak culture has seduced our centre.

Saturday, 4 October

Today our 'last' bathe at Hythe beach.

Each afternoon we have been going down there; Jane always 'mock' reluctantly, but with her bathing dress under. It is quite delicious, the water now clean and the great long arc of the shingle like the Chesil Bank – or even Biarritz. The pleasure of swimming 'over-arm' with lots of space (too frightening, as well as too chilly, to 'let oneself go' at Eriboll) make them real bathes and put me in mind of 42 years ago.

Now I am somewhat debilitated, but still happy and well, and my shape not unrecognisable, and I thank God.

Garden House   *Wednesday, 15 October*

I came over here to browse, look at notes in general. I am still emerging from flu/cold – so feel placid and philosophic (most oddly, for the period of convalescence, i.e. after the Saturday, which was foul, my eye seemed much better, and yesterday would defocus better than for ages).

When I am in these rooms, particularly when – as today – Graham [Stewart] is absent, I feel quite 'a different order' of calmness. I look ahead to being 'domiciled' here, distancing myself from the Mains, though always ready to prowl in the historic environs and absorb the combination of nostalicism and uncertain continuity. And indeed to 'rest' it for periods.

Working here, academically but at a lower pace, advising the trustees accordingly. Only in the South for a proportion of the year; then North and serenely in the Highlands – 'still climbing Munros well into his seventies'. And, of course, in the late autumn, cutting south to the Alps, drinking wine as we cross France.

Idyllic – if there are mildly uncomfortable overtones they are there: one evocative of my father (he, too, made over Saltwood when he was 68 – I'm a year later). The moving sideways from the sword in the lake. It was almost within my grasp before Blackpool. Oh! That silly, show off (as always) aside.[1]

EMT   *Thursday, 16 October*

Jane slept badly (how many good nights does she get per year? Three maybe). Poor little soul, she carried all the problems of my (ir)responsibility. She never goes to the studio now, simply sits reading newsprint. This ought to be redundant now with the agency; but actually she finds quite interesting general things. On 19 September we had a fraught discussion about her going to her mother – and we must find time for that.[2]

---

[1] At the party conference AC had said (apropos the continuing N Ireland stalemate): 'The only solution is to kill 600 people in one night. Let the UN and Bill Clinton and everyone else make a scene – and it is over for 20 years.'

[2] Mrs Beuttler had lived in Spain for many years.

Summer Office   *Friday, 17 October*

The Sotheby's 'team' wander about for the 'Trust' inventory. The deed box has yielded its usual crop of missing, or obsolete, and unintelligible documents. I am feeble, and have ocular head-aches again, my weight is now 11.2 – alert level. I am in the evening of my life – although it is still daylight.

EMT   *Sunday, 26 October*

Yet another beautiful late autumn day. I thought, said to Jane, 'Will we ever?' now widened to 'will we ever relaxedly be able to say to each other – "what shall we do today?"'

· And yet … tomorrow I won't even be able to come to Mowll and Mowll[1] because I need to get up to put in a prayer card in order to get called for 'my place' to question the Chancellor and this first day back. The pleasure and the price.

Yesterday the all-day CPC conference and I hung in there fortified by a delicious mouthful of fish pie in the 1a kitchen. Jeffrey Archer underperformed; read, stumblingly, a speech text on 'the future of London'.[2] The future of *me*, I had warned the audience in advance, bitchily. He gave me a lift back to New Palace Yard in his Mercedes drophead – incredibly cheapo finish interior, most disappointing. I drove home in Big Red, discreetly, except unable to resist a last gallop on the Ashford concrete. Jane was in happy form and we set about, at 7 p.m., a magnificent repast: started with fresh orange juice instead of gin and tonic; ½ bottle Bourgogne '93; chicken liver pâté and toast, slice of red pepper tart; two helpings delicious venison from Eriboll and red cabbage, Anna Koumar carrots, mashed potatoes,

---

[1] Solicitors representing the Clarks in the forthcoming hearing over Lëhni, their Rottweiler.

[2] Archer wanted to be the first new mayor of London, as constituted by the Labour government.

horseradish. Then fresh apple puree, double cream and meringues. We staggered up to bed, didn't stir for over ten hours.

Thank you, God, quite literally, for my good luck.

Parliament Street   *Monday, 27 October*

A little sad. Disappointed at not being called to question Gordon Brown. And the context of what he was saying. The slow 'count-down', all the nuts and bolts of the infrastructure being put in place, for EMU at the next election. I had a good place guaranteed to speak in the Defence debate. But it barely matters now. I can't revisit it, because if I had been Secretary of State it would all be so different. Now our nationhood is being taken/given away. Along with the BA tailfins, the handguns, the sale of Rolls-Royce, the Queen, fresh from her insults in India, submitting as usual to any humiliation. There is practically nothing left of the Nation-State except the bravery of the football fans who stood up to the armed and armoured Italian police in Rome.

On top of all this is the strange sadistic ordeal of the case against Hannah/Lëhni. This is ravaging Jane, who has been warned that she might have to be in the dock for AN HOUR, and the whole case to last all day.

B5, EMT   *Thursday, 30 October*

I am so rattled and pressurised that I have lost concentrative powers. I don't know what's in my diary – even for today – and dare not look at it. A new and most unsettling phenomenon is the lesion, which I now look at every three minutes or so, on my forearm. A new basal, presumably.

I am really apprehensive about the case. (It's not that it's paranoia, I just know that they are out to get me.) Slept intermittently being woken by the certain knowledge that I will be cross-examined about my pressure on Birt, BBC, perverting the course of justice etc and even if we get a good verdict, *arrested on the steps of the court*. That's why they are pressing on with the case, so as to get certain admissions on record.[1]

Now I feel a tiny bit better. I have just seen the Albany blackbird.

EMT   *Monday, 10 November*

Yesterday we went to the memorial service and I laid the wreath at St Mary Abbots. We are WW1-minded at present. Jane has done her beautiful Passchendaele series, so upsetting. What a remarkable artist she is.

MFS Saltwood   *Saturday, 15 November*

A wonderful feeling of tranquillity as the volume ends surpassing, I believe, any other.

Yesterday we walked across wind-blown pavements and over the River Tay to Inverness Cathedral where we knelt in church (what a cold building) for the birth of baby Angus (George McKenzie). The consummation of that wonderful moment (on par with Andrew Dalton in the basement of Kensington TH) when 'Boy' was on the answering machine at the flat – just read out his names. James was ebullient last night as we waited in the (far from unsympathetic) lounge of the Station Hotel at

---

[1] The magistrates, at Folkstone, found for the Clarks, who were awarded costs. But it was an ordeal, nevertheless, AC recording in his day diary that Jane 'almost fainted'.

Inverness. And then I enjoyed what must almost be the recognitory apotheosis of my political career – a complimentary ticket for the Scottish TUC cealídh on Friday night.

EMT   *Monday, 17 November*

Yesterday I went for a good two hour walk – Beechborough and back up Kick Hill. Then strolled in the woodland, thinking of my glass of wine. Overdid it with 'Wiltshire Plait', then ate far too many old Belgium white chocolates – SLUMPED. Dozed fitfully. Woke feeling sinister – worried about brain tumour, Thompsoned hugely and slumped back feeling 'far from right'. Jane said, 'If only we could have a complete week here …' And now, even writing this, my glaucoma headache has returned.

1 Parliament Street   *Thursday, 27 November*

Spectator Politician of the Year lunch at the Savoy yesterday. Sat next to Ian Gilmour – as always funny (such an infectious giggle) and slyly mocking. Tristan Garel-J – I took at least half the meal to warm to him – told me that on the Friday after the '92 election he went straight to Major, told him to *instruct* Chris Patten to stand for Kensington & Chelsea. Neither would play (although I suspect CP would – 'if pressed'). The episode shows T.G-J's limitations.[1] So consumed by his addiction to whispered intrigue, and so infatuated with Patten that he was unable to see it from JM's aspect. Why on earth should Major, who had just won an election, want to ease the path of his most conspicuous rival? *Out*, Patten would be invaluable as friend and counsellor. In – it would be only a matter of time.

---

[1] AC had long been equivocal about Garel-Jones.

G-J remains unlikeable, and deceitful in the extreme. It is a weakness of mine that I succumbed to his blandishments dictated, I assume, by a feeling that I was one of Margaret's 'favourites'. He started to walk back across Savoy Gardens with me, then turning back, feeling, I assume, his attention and company would be better expended on others.

Yesterday the great (Friday) Hunting Debate. I wore my (brand new) O'Brien suit of faintly grey checked flannel, waistcoat and white silk shirt. A 'Parliamentary occasion' and the Speaker very nobly arranged for me to be called early (at No 3 on our side after Heseltine – himself stopped in his tracks and demolished by Denis MacShane[1] – and TK). I revelled in it; congratulating a preceding member, '… what an ordeal to have to do it before so crowded a chamber'; and fortuitously slapping down Paul Flynn.[2] And as I think about it my mind, as often, goes back to those exclusion dreams – particularly when I was *behind the chair* and couldn't go back in. Which, itself, I think must go back to the time Hugh Rossi[3] says what a pity I am retiring, and I suddenly realise the Chamber was locked and with the House dissolved I was no longer an MP. Nor ever would be.

Saltwood, EMT   *Monday, 8 December*

Early on Friday morning, before it was fully light, I walked from Albany to the House, carrying three pieces of luggage, but dressed in softies. I passed by Clive Steps – always a mixture of evocations, from Chips: 'The Chief Whip's car is waiting …' to the feeling of absolute exclusion at the seat tryst (April 1992) and 'best-attended memorial service since Aircraftsman Shaw' as

[1] Denis MacShane, MP (Lab) for Rotherham since May 1994.
[2] Paul Flynn, MP (Lab) for Newport W since 1987.
[3] Sir Hugh Rossi, MP (Con) for Hornsey and Wood Green 1983–92 (Hornsey 1966–83).

I said to Chris Patten when he staged his great party in the Durbar Court. And this time I really revelled, wallowed in the pleasures of my condition. Here I was, having voluntarily selected the wilderness and then (been) returned to a position of huge strength. The previous night, at Norland ward, people had again been saying how awful Hague was and why didn't I …? etc etc. Now I am going to enter the sleepy House of Commons which I love so much to collect my Little Silver and whizz down (more likely creep down as it's bad light and I'm low on fuel) to Saltwood for scrambled eggs. So, except for my eyes, and approaching old age, and guilt/withdrawal symptoms about BB, I would be extraordinarily happy. Absence of sexual activity I barely notice. I welcome it almost; and prostatic symptoms totally dormant. Have abated, indeed, virtually since Tom Bates a year ago.

But the future, the future of the sword is opaque. The Conservative Party is utterly shattered. Our total in the opinion polls is 22% and the Liberals at 17%. On Wednesday the 22 Committee met for 1½ hours to talk about 'the Party reforms' and when they came out into the corridor there was not a single journalist waiting. We have become irrelevant. And quite soon after our return from Christmas recess, I predict, the Liberals will be at 22 and we will be at 17%. Part of the problem, I have no doubt whatever, is the hopeless, exhausted and repetitious quality of our 'Shadow' front bench. Dorrell, Lilley, Mawhinney, Howard, Redwood, I can't think of the others, the Electorate has already said 'No thanks' in the biggest possible way. Why on earth, since most of them are saying the same things as they did in April 1997, should the public listen at all? They owe their place, in any case, not to merit, but to a series of deals patched up and traded off during the whole ludicrous 'Leadership' contest. At present, I do not see the way forward. Soames rang last night, talked for hours. Said we must rebuild around 'householders, farmers, small businesses'. I must read a lot of that new stuff from the residual Left. But will this actually be enough to fuel a party resurgence? Careful thought on the holidays required.

Anyway, after bellowing like this for 15 minutes, Soames then said he 'wanted out'. Asked me to ask Alastair [Campbell] to get Blair to make him ambassador in Paris – 'it's mine by descent … etc'.[1] Shades slightly of Christopher's [Soames] dinner at White's. He's running away. Driven out by Oborne, and Black Dog ('foul-mouthed Tory toff …' etc)

House Library   *Wednesday, 10 December*

Up early, and waistcoat for an interesting day.

I plan to stir the 22 Exec on our supporting the government to reject a Liberal amendment on Single Mothers. 'I was not sent here by my constituents to go through the same lobby as Blair, Prescott and Harman.'

Still apprehensive about my eyes and panicked last evening that they might seize up before or during my reading at the Sloane Street church carol service. But it passed off ok – after last-minute scramble to get a King James text. Earlier, in a very busy day, I had spoken to the (mature) students; and won their approval and spontaneous chat and answers. One (long face, long hair, still attractive and classy) said 'do you want to be Prime Minister?' 'Of course,' I answered, and she was delighted.

The night before (Monday) I went to the Privy Council dinner – Royal Gallery, and overflow in the Robing Chamber presided by Prince of Wales and including various – Cranborne, Ancram, TK and – God alive, how did he get one? – Atkins, R.[2] Copious and excellent wines.

The Queen is transformed, no longer the wicked stepmother with her frumpish and ill-natured features that have been permanently in place since Mrs T rescued the 1992 election. As

---

[1] Nicholas Soames' father Christopher (son-in-law of Winston Churchill, former MP and Minister) had been British Ambassador in France, 1968–72.
[2] Robert Atkins, MP South Ribble 1983–97 (Preston N 1979–83) and a junior Minister in Major government; made a Privy Counsellor 1995.

I said at the time, the whole Royal Family delighted at the elimination of Diana, and now has settled back comfortably into their favourite role – preservation of their own perks and privileges at the expense, whenever necessary, of other individuals and institutions. The Empire, the Church, the Law, the hereditary principle, the Lords, even a yacht, and now there are faithful servants who are being dismissed in droves as they modernise Sandringham and Balmoral.

MFS GH   *Friday, 12 December*

I seem to remember this is always a baddish time.

My eyes are really causing me concern – thirteen months since the opthalmicist in Hythe told me to go to hospital. I now have had a slight frontal headache and inability to 'defocus' for over 24 hours. And was advised yesterday to make an appointment (via Nick Page) with 'Spender'(?)[1] in Harley Street. Don't mind glaucoma so much – unless it stops me getting a driving licence – but am terrified of cancer of the optic nerve. 'Very rare,' Nick said, 'only in infancy and the elderly.' But that day I have read of poor old Walter Matthau (aet. 77) 'going blind' for this reason.

Then, 'on top of it all he was diagnosed as HIV positive'; i.e. the INLA man[2] is over here with the intention (according to sources) of levelling scores. Can only take it demi-seriously, but … *Plus* Denton Hall all next week; I worried that my witnesses will fold. *Plus* how *do* we get to Eriboll, with a 3-line whip on Monday? Physically impossible; and lovely to dwell here in our burrow, but fearfully bad luck on dear 'Boy'.

I must record, though, a tiny incident last week when I was hurrying to Kensington in the Porsche. Circumventing again I

---

[1] Actually David Spalton.
[2] A representative of the Irish National Liberation Army.

accelerated across Cadogan Gardens and quickly had to pull out
across Pont Street ahead of the oncoming traffic. I very nearly
was hit by a motorcyclist. It would have been terrible. God still
protects me. Whether or not he continues to do so, may he look
after dear sweet Janey, the boys and the lovely bairns.

MFSH   *Sunday, 14 December*

Extraordinary mood-swings. On Friday I was hyper-buoyant.
Filled with confidence (head-ache lifted as soon as I had finished
'filing' the *Classic Cars* column[1]), now contemplate 'trading up'
from Big Red to a 'T', and sent (foolishly and youthfully) the
'we-owe-it-to-each-other' Christmas card (which I must try and
retrieve).

   Yesterday was lovely; on our own and pottering and in the
evening *hammering* at the Green Room table. Even visually ok.
But T.O. woke us by Thompsoning at 4.30. I was still deeply
asleep. Afterwards we slept very lightly in contact until nearly
9 a.m., but didn't feel rested. Intermittently I thought how sweet
and dear Jane is to hold on to me like this. Is it because,
consciously or sub-consciously, she is aware of the INLA man?
I will write her a love letter. I ought to do one to each boy also,
but that is itself headache-inducing as it requires administrative
recommendations. I am now entering the last decade of my life.
If I pass through this I will have outlived my father;[2] but
(presumably) I will be shuffly and my voice lost timbre. I did
speak last night to EDG and his voice was perfectly ok. He has
the most incredible genes and his liver has not registered *at all*
to the alcohol washing through it, and both his parents died at
90-something. But he did speak of joints, and balance is in

---

[1] AC had been writing a monthly column under the heading 'Back Fire' for *Classic Cars* magazine since 1995.
[2] Kenneth Clark died in 1983 aged 79.

decline. Quite frankly I will never ski again. The last time was at the Davos (1991) conference where the feeling afterwards was almost like being reborn. But I do hope scrawnily to stride in the Highlands.

The point is, though, when? It is perfectly glorious – almost the early spring – but in fact before the iron discipline of winter asserts itself.

On the Green Room table we found this card ...

> *6 August 1996*
> What <u>are</u> you
> doing – London today
> when you have no time
> to spare or so you tell me.
> Well I've gone too
> don't know when I'll be
> back – to feed dogs, water
> things, iron things, tidy things
> cook things, find things –
> the 'things' wives do –
> we have so much and yet we
> don't have time for each other.
> Well make it, or lose it you
> selfish genius. It's been
> one moan all these past
> weeks. If it is my fault say so.[1]

I suppose at that time I was ghastly to live with. I was consumed by the search, not for the sword, but at least the path, through rocks and undergrowths, to arrive at the lake. Yesterday evening I said, 'I could step down now, I suppose, because I proved, to everyone, that I could come back and get adopted for the safest seat in Britain.' I still half believe that my moment may come. I cannot predict its shape. A possible coup last week – the Social

---

[1] AC had stapled Jane's actual message into the diary.

Security Bill vote (I was the only Tory to abstain on a 3-line) was thwarted, and now the whips are cool to me. The first three months of this ('98) year will be spent assiduously voting, and working out certain policy stand points (sic). If the local elections are bad, and the polls still against us I might try something in the early summer.

Although rather than attack one's own side it is probably better to state alternatives, avoid personalities.

House Library   *Monday, 15 December*

Very tired and low. I haven't eaten anything except two digestives and a small slice of camembert 'in the conference room at Denton Hall'. And yet I am not hungry. I am apprehensive about my eyes, which ache dully and resist 'defocusing'. Print vision poor. I barely think about the 'INLA man', though will lock the back door tonight. I listened to 'proceedings' all day in Court and was wearied by their repetitious quality and treadmill feel. The Judge – 'Lightman' – was beady, but I sensed hostile (perhaps having heard on the grapevine that I am 'anti-Semitic').[1] When Peter Prescott[2] recited, ad nauseam, extracts from the 'Diaries' I loathed it. I went back and read a nasty piece in the *Independent on Sunday* with 'a Westminster source' quoting unpleasantly and maliciously. Had Tristan fingerprints on it.

Everyone loathes me, or dismisses me: *The Times Diary* entry on Friday emphasising my age, if not senility. All people really want is to write *ill* of their subject.

I will dine here alone, and early, and probably without wine unless I can find a companion.

---

[1] AC was over-sensitive. Mr Justice Lightman, QC 1980, had been an admired High Court judge since 1994.
[2] Counsel for *Evening Standard*. QC, co-author of *The Modern Law of Copyright*.

Thursday, 18 December

Sitting in Albany kitchen – still in dressing-gown at 11.05; and the delightful, and unusual pleasure of the two clocks striking simultaneously 'across' each other. Very Edwardian, or early twenties. I am hugely calmer and more contented – although of course anxiety in new form will always flow into the vacuum created by the extinction of a real one, and I am apprehensive. The trial has not gone badly and the judge seemed sympathetic, although Prescott was odious at every stage. If I lose, of course, I will be open season. But my real consolation, fresh boost, is Spalton.[1] Stuttery, amiable and bespectacled (naturally) oculist. He tested me, I told him all my symptoms [here AC draws on the page the edge of a spot]. He was unphased. Said the optic nerve ok etc. And I really haven't had a headache of any kind since …! Defocusing, and periodic lights and 'flooders' of no consequence. This is such a relief; I clap my hands in prayer of thanks a lot of the time and when I wake up at night.

Just in time. As I need to think long and hard about the next three months. The real damage and threat to Parliament. The cogent conspiracy between Blair and Hague. We are actually going along with what Blair is doing.

B5   *Sunday evening, 21 December*

Travelled back from Stansted by the aero-train and changed at Tottenham Hale to Victoria Line tube to Green Park. Swift and painless. I am alone at the flat instead of, as I should be, 'thundering' with Janey and the dogs to the north. I rang Gleneagles at 6 – she still wasn't there. I'm sure she will be all right, but I did say a prayer of thanks and protection for the sweetest, goodest person in the entire world, the only one

---

[1] David Spalton, Harley Street eye specialist.

whom I believe to have not one vestigial streak of cruelty or deceit in her character. Yes, the 'what-if-died' scenario (I am always particular, see the extreme in any situation) crosses my mind at intervals. Of the smash, at the dogs being gleefully 'put down' by police marksmen as impeding, or 'likely to impede' the emergency services.

Tomorrow paperwork and the two 22 meetings. We are on the run, we MPs. The tacit conspiring of the 'New leaders'. This is worth an article in itself. But the great 'Must the Conservative Party Die?' piece slowly matures. I will put some more flesh on it on the Hermes [typewriter] at Shore.

Station Hotel, Inverness   *Monday, 22 December*

Flew up today, a joining seat taken at a very late stage by Caroline – never did get her surname. Plastered, she was, and odd. 'Ah a McKenzie tartan,' she said, spotting my scarf. I started off thinking no, oy, etc. She was completely shameless first in her verbal inquisition, then in her physical attentions. Suddenly, she started to admire and then handle my hands. I feigned sleep, but she kept pushing up close. She was a classic Norse red-head – 31? – plumpish with blue eyes and pale skin. Looking sideways I saw pleasing cleavage, with a lace-bordered low-cut T-shirt. Pushed her head on my shoulder and she held first my arm, then put her hand on my chest. What the attendants thought I can't imagine. She kept struggling and fidgeting, trying to get closer. Amazing. Quite salutary and encouraging. Derek Presley[1] met me in the not-at-all-nice Freelander and by the time I was on the concourse she had disappeared. I have barely the face to record all her compliments.

Christmas is in prospect, and my only anxiety is that James has still not turned up yet (it's 12.20 p.m.).

---

[1] Friend and manager of Inverness Land Rover agent, Macrae & Dick.

Shore Cottage, 8 p.m.   *Wednesday, 24 December*

An anxious Christmas Eve. Not since Andrew had bad asthma
at Zermatt in 1965 and Gentinetta wanted to put him on
steroids. I slept like a top – uninterrupted from 9.10 to 6.10.
Janey not so well, complained of a 'sore tummy', and said she felt
sick(-ish). I didn't put too much to this until, at EMT, she said
she didn't even want to finish her ½ cup (we were in the
kitchen; it must have been about 7.30). She was leaning against
the wall, just by the window, suddenly said 'God' or something
like that and her legs buckled, she went down with a terrible
crack (like my father's description of my mother having her
stroke at Albany in 1973). I rushed over to her, called out,
begged her to move a hand or an eyelid, could she hear me? etc.
I kept telling her I loved her. Her head, utterly limp, was at a
curious angle when she first fell, and I wondered if Nanny had
looked like that when Jane found her at Garden House. After an
age, she came round. She hadn't even felt my putting a pillow
under her head, or moving all the dogs into the wheelhouse etc.
Then she 'came to'. 'What happened?' I wanted to move her to
the sofa. She said she felt sick again. Would she like me to help
her to the loo? I picked her up, was holding on to her elbow
and her knees buckled totally. She collapsed with a terrible unconscious groaning. She vomited, but not properly. Some of it
must have caught in the windpipe and she made dreadful draining coughs. I really thought she was going to die. She recovered
a little. Still couldn't remember anything. I settled her, drove up
to the Lodge and Julie rang Dr Belbin who said he would come
straight over to examine her in the kitchen; then the ambulance
and the paramedics. Now she's in Raigmore [hospital] and
(naturally) the floor sister is guarded. She is 'tired' and all wired
up to a heart machine etc. X-rays. Blood tests. Would I be able
to take her away tomorrow? Unlikely.

Poor, sweet, sweet Janey who was game and pleasant even in
this tearful adversity.

I took the dogs along the shoreline; back over the top. I

thought of how catastrophic if she died. I had to see it in personal terms. I would withdraw utterly. 'In mourning.' Instantly become a recluse (and a pretty scrawny one. All I have eaten today is bread and butter!).

But even so. Things are cyclical. The hubris (partially intended) of that card. The extraordinary good fortune that has blessed us this year. There had to be a downturn. I'm off up to the Lodge for dinner.

Shore Cottage   *Sunday, 28 December* [1]

Immensely contented and at ease

We have been sleeping 9½-10½ hours per night. Jane not yet 'quite right', and Tom is ill-at-ease, now definitely in his closing months and wanders around the house making little wheezy noises. How unhappy is he? Head of the house until the end. Nineteen years old next month (Feb).

I am reading simultaneously Rhodes James's *Lord Randolph Churchill* and WSC on the same subject. Hugely enjoyable to read of:

'The announcement in *The Times* this morning immediately and sensationally terminated the Christmas calm in political circles. Holiday plans were abruptly cancelled ...' etc. [2]

and the calm in the knowledge that I can myself now go back, wreathed in fantasy yes, but *potent*, and push through the doors marked 'Members Only'. Who (save me) a year ago would have conceived of this as in any way feasible, still less likely?

Now I am going upstairs to write letters to RRJ and David

---

[1] AC has written above this entry: 'Poor handwriting for being written on knee in wheelhouse as Jane's artist's materials over table.'

[2] This is how Robert Rhodes James, in only his first book, wrote of Lord Randolph's resignation. Winston Churchill's life of his father was published in two volumes.

D. Later I will be on the hill and will go to the little church and pray thanks and a hope for protection – particularly of that tiny baby who kicked and chatted so merrily and conversationally as Julie was changing him yesterday.

Shore Cottage   *Tuesday, 30 December*

Tremendous gales today. For the first time since arriving I have taken no long walk in the daylight hours. Last night I worked on BB, some correction in green pen of bound (red) Book I. Thought how good, how melodious it is. Much – or perhaps not so much – to do. But it ought (personal anti-prejudice apart) be a prize-winner. Worked also on the Intro, and showed a page to Jane which she liked – 'reads so well'. (I had woken in the night and worked on it for an hour; so easy to potter across the landing and into the little stripped-pine, pent-roof study.)

The routine at the little croft is snug and restorative. I rise around 7 (or whatever time it may be that has given 9½-10 hours sleep). I let out T.O. who hates the wind and always heads for the grass bank along the stream where habitually, in former times, he would Thompson. But now he is so unsteady on his pins that I have to head him away. Quite shivery in my dressing-gown and slippers/mules, 'damn you, Tom', I can be heard saying. But T.O., bless him, is always regular.

Perhaps because I am impatient to get back to it. Perhaps because intermittently I think I am 'starting' a head cold, my temper degenerated (wind always makes me rattled).

Cursingly I amassed quantities of fuel for the Tyrolia, with staged back-up piles in the little store, the big store, and (Jane's idea) a 'flu stack' right next to the stove.[1]

---

[1] Elsewhere AC notes: '… set to at the Tyrolia stove, which nearly always picks up with newspaper and kindling, i.e. seldom needs even a match … I can sit with the little door open at the wood crackling merrily with an orange flame.'

Up at the Lodge I collected some old *Telegraphs* and getting back here was made uneasy by news of an INLA assassination inside the Maze prison and a tit-for-tat murder on IRA men by the UVF. I hid this so that Jane wouldn't see it. She is very sweet and uncomplaining, but her voice timbre is down, as is her life force. As I thought she has done some perfectly beautiful Dürer-like pictures of feathers and seashore *trouvées*. I hope she recovers enough while we are here to enjoy it.

I fear that when the gales abate the snow will start. I do not want to be cut off here, and already, very slightly, I have at 7 days (effectively 5) got 'wandering feet' and think of the Mains, and the piles of correspondence, and the 'white' computer. Am I like this because I feel I have little time left? Can't effectively be much more than 5 years surely – which isn't much. Like my father standing impatiently about in the hall of the châlet in 1977.[1] Or is it that my energy still comes back fast? A bit of both.

Jim Lees-Milne died at the weekend. 89. Suits me. But there were references in his diaries to 'recurrent bouts of cancer' (uh?).

---

[1] Lord Clark visited Châlet Caroline only once; it was not a success.

1998

We're not sleeping well. Last night I was convinced that I had jaw rot (for want of a better word) under Bertie's [Arbeid] great bridge. For some reason I am getting a pulse, off-and-on, in the upper palate. I can feel it (rot, not pulse) now; and wonder if it is related to my occasional shooting headache on the R. side. I had been put out by how *old* I looked (Reagan – but with his heavy polish) in the 60-minutes CBS film.[1] And Jane, of course, had been upset by some references. The whole day has been completely frittered. I had hoovered out the Discovery. The 'side' in the kitchen is cluttered. I went over to GH briefly and was alarmed at how slow I was getting the green ink corrections into the machine. Ion now wants to 'set in stone' a delivery schedule, which both depresses me and makes me feel cramped.

Also, Chris Patten (Phil Patten I call him, a 'wishee-washee', the Chinese laundryman, as *Private Eye* do) has surfaced increasingly and everyone is saying how he has huge political career ahead of him. (What about D. Owen, by the way?[2]) I don't know what I have to do to be taken seriously. Win the *E Standard* case, for a start. I am too busy now even to open Romeike.[3] Everyone is out to get me. Radio silence from Denton Hall.

Still most unfit. Much of my listlessness explained, perhaps, by the fact that the scene, the Commons etc, really is changing. Politics has become different. I am old now, also. In my last decade before a true sage. I don't want to die, but if I do, let it be on the Creaggan Road and my last sight being of little Jane's face.

---

[1] The American CBS TV channel had included AC in a 60-minute documentary, filmed after the Kensington and Chelsea selection.
[2] The fortunes of the Social Democratic Party, of which David Owen had been leader since 1988, were in steep decline.
[3] Romeike & Curtice – cuttings service to which AC subscribed.

EMT, Saltwood   *Saturday, 24 January*

Last night DD rang. We did one of those long tours d'horizon
that I once so much, yet so wistfully, used to enjoy during the
period I was out. How delicious and nourishing it is now to
conduct the conversation as an equal. We talked through and
round Hague's clumsy attempt to interfere on the 22. He takes
a more extreme view of the Exec's situation than I. 'Why didn't
you speak?' he asked. It wasn't because I funked it; more because
I don't think the time is ripe, but it is ripening. Each of us is
approaching our goal stealthily. Leadership for him; chair of 22
(probably come first) for me.

That is why a low profile – except in the House – is important
for me at this stage as my book moves into preparation.

DD rightly said that half the Party don't come in to the
Chamber any longer. The running is done by the 'new intake',
and the 'four horsemen of the apocalypse' (who they? – Forth,
me, DD and Maclean[1]).

EMT, Saltwood   *Friday, 30 January*

Yesterday the unpleasant experience of being sacked (over
lunch) by Phil Hall[2] – who seemed, as his words ended, to
change from an enthusiastic *naïf* into a ruthless and beady 'senior
executive' in steel-rimmed spectacles. Went back to B5 feeling
immensely tired. Couldn't, just had the sense not to, go to bed
and zizz, as Tip came round with some pheasants. Lovely and

---

[1] Eric Forth, MP for Bromley and Chislehurst since 1997 (Mid Worcestershire,
1983–97); David Maclean, MP for Penrith and the Border since July 1983.

[2] Phil Hall, editor *News of the World* since 1995. A week later, though, AC noted: 'Am
cheered by the fact that my 'departure from the *N of W* coincided with their dis-
closure' that a fellow Conservative MP's daughter was "a hooker". He added: 'So
cruel and irrelevant an attack on a colleague would make it impossible for me to
write for the paper anyway.'

giggly as always. Went off on his little bzzip scooter – in which
I fear he does the most horrifying dangerous things. He crisply
cornered out of Albany courtyard.

Saturday, 31 January

Just a note, I should have done one long ago, an appreciation
rather than an obituary of dear little T.O. Still, and unshakeably,
'head of the house'.

Now he's in his twentieth year, the toughest and most
indefatigable of all terriers. Keegan, at ball-play in the pool, and
incredible football performances – 'a dog against ten boys' with
the Essen school.

Very, very slowly, his faculties and performance have declined.
Today, quite a good morning, he briefly did seahorse still, but in
the last 6–8 months he has slowly withdrawn, even from
scampering down the drive to get the papers and waiting at the
Barbican gate to go off like a rocket to the 'black' postbox. He
has gradually lost his sense of smell, can't even pick up cheese
on the floor until it is literally under his nose. Sometimes he is
very blind, and is almost totally deaf. As a result he often looks
unhappy. But he is still in routine. Up 7ish, excellent Thompson,
in kitchen for EMT in his 'saucer'. Sleeps a lot during the day,
but will enjoy a car drive. I now carry him up the stairs and
'throw' the 'markie' for him on his bed.

But he can still, and did until a week ago, manage the back
steps. He is still the all-knowing puppy, and I will never let him
down. But oh for the elixir! I see my own decline – if I avoid
cancer or stroke – following this pattern.

House Library   *Thursday, 5 February*

An EMT note, really. But the (even) more congenial atmosphere of the House Library I now prefer [to 1 Parliament Street]. Yesterday was very full indeed. There is something about Wednesdays – because rather than in spite of the early start – that causes it to be filled to the brim.[1]

So, blearily and creakily staggering to get dressed (yesterday's shirt – why?) went without EMT to the Members Lobby where Tapsell[2] was already crouching in the messenger's chair at 7.28 p.m. Exceedingly rich (or so one must suppose – 'I don't deal for individuals, only for countries'; 'I'm not a stockbroker' etc etc).

There were three of those interesting morning adjournments. House totally empty on our side except for Anthony Steen[3]. Libs everywhere; many 'New' Labour members who had ousted our own people in May. I had quickly to bodge together some remarks about organic farming, Scottish communities, 'affordable' housing etc etc. It is really too depressing. There is our great Party, its historic roots dependent on rural dwellers and walkers in the countryside – and we don't even turn up, still less illuminate the Debate.

Later Soames performed massively, and statesmanlikely on the Middle East peace process. His father would have been delighted.

Then came a total shambles. Little Letwin,[4] cheekily with his detailed sequences etc etc tried to do to 'Cookie' (as Labour call him[5]) what David Maclean had two weeks ago so brilliantly

[1] AC adds, if irrelevantly to the matter in hand: '"causes it-always-to-be-full" – second half of a pentameter.'

[2] Sir Peter Tapsell (Kt 1985), MP for East Lindsey since 1983 (Nottingham West 1959–64; Horncastle, 1966–83).

[3] Anthony Steen, MP for Totnes since 1997 (South Hams 1983–97, Liverpool Wavertree 1974–83).

[4] Oliver Letwin, MP for West Dorset since 1997.

[5] Robin Cook, MP for Livingston since 1983 (Edinburgh C February 1974–83), Foreign Secretary since 1997

done to the Paymaster [Geoffrey Robinson]. Walked into a firestorm. Stuttered and stalled. Michael Howard[1] speaking from the backbenches (why?) equally useless. Fatchett[2] (reading a text clearly written by Robin C) said:

> 'The Right Honourable Gentleman, since 1 January, has tabled no written questions on the EU Presidency, the Middle East peace process; the crisis with Iraq; the Dependent Territories; or China ... He seems to regard the position of Shadow Foreign Secretary as a sabbatical between his period in the Home Office and his rumoured high-paid job in the City.'

Poor Michael! Ever since the Ann Widdecombe assault (could so easily have gone 'either way')[3] and then the nil score among the voluntary workers, he has been losing ground. What on earth can he do next? He's not even, like John Moore, boyish-looking.[4]

House Library   *Wednesday, 18 February*

I went to Enoch's [Powell] funeral. A beautiful, perfectly chosen service. Not one word out of place – which is hardly surprising as he wrote it all himself bar (sic) John Biffen's address which was even better. In the congregation outside Ronnie (I had a

---

[1] Michael Howard, MP for Folkestone (Saltwood in the constituency), Home Secretary 1993–97, had been shadow foreign secretary since the election.

[2] Derek Fatchett, MP for Leeds Central since 1983, Foreign Office Minister.

[3] Ann Widdecombe, MP for Maidstone since 1987, had, as Minister of State at the Home Office (1995–97), criticised Michael Howard, the Home Secretary ('he has something of the night about him') over his sacking of Derek Lewis, head of the prison service.

[4] John Moore, MP Croydon Central February 1974–1992, Transport and Social Services Secretary in the mid–1980s, had for a time been seen by Margaret Thatcher as her successor. Later, in his early fifties, he went into financial management.

mental block, as always, on his name until someone came up to us – 'Ronnie') Grierson[1] he said 'have you written yours yet?' or perhaps it was 'I assume you've written yours?'. 'I'm not 70,' I answered, hearing that EP had written his in 1983 when he was, in fact, just 70.

1 Parliament Street   *Friday, 27 February*

Why is it that I do not find this office particularly sympathetic? Greatly preferring the House Library, where I now have established 'my' table, recognised by staff and messengers alike being the first small one on the right by the window as you come into the *silence* room.

On Wednesday of last week we [22] had a meeting with little Hague. (Still terrified of me, I was glad to note; caught his throat and swallowed when he had to say 'Alan Clark'.) Pretty disparate. Some, but not total, brown-nosing. Hague in his usual stuff about our being 'arrogant and out-of-touch', said the polls were 'just turning now'. I said my bit, that I was 'arrogant and out-of-touch' and proud of it, and still got large audiences – cited Kent University, overflow room etc.[2]

The following day Norman (Archie)[3] was in the tearoom and talking a lot of rot about Euro-MP selection and how we would now be putting the 'good' ones at the top of the list. 'What *is* a good Euro-MP?' I asked. He scowled, blackly.

---

[1] Sir Ronald Grierson, vice-chairman, GEC, 1968–91.
[2] Three weeks earlier AC had noted, 'Hague is slowly emerging from his "right wing" carapace (as I predicted to the '92, within a week of getting back, that he would – "Hague is *of the Left*.").'
[3] Archie Norman, MP for Tunbridge Wells since 1997.

EMT (kitchen)   *Thursday, 5 March*

Came back last night having 'not eaten all week'. *Delicious*
2-egger, demi-braised venison and rhubarb and clotted with
remaining ½ bottle of Palmer '88.

Exeter Station   *Monday, 9 March*

Been down to Bratton, leaving Saltwood at 5.35 in the Porsche,
which I dropped at Carrs for its big service; borrow a Golf again
(v nice – and no problems at all).

The whole place very scruffy indeed. Only the 'studio' is
pleasing with Campling's door,[1] and the giant (and, as it now
turns out, not invaluable) Duncans for the Queen Mary.[2]

It's strange, for ages I was sad and calm and nostalgic about
Bratton. Now I see that we never really got it right, should have
planted dense shrubs etc. It was monstrous of my father to keep
us so short of money that I had to sell the fields – 'the cream of
Bratton' for £500. I did write (most of) *Barbarossa*[3] there, and I
recall walking up the 'dump' road, looking over 'Bennett's' gate
and feeling immensely content. Not much later came 'Jollyboy'
and 'more run' in the white pushchair.[4] Also pining for Tilfy and
the magic afternoon with the girl from Bray Shop. But I only
developed into real living at Seend – Anna Koumar[5] and the
banks of sweet peas in the 'secret garden', which we 'dedicate to

---

[1] Robert Campling's painted door is now on one of the Saltwood tower office
walls.
[2] Duncan Grant, Bloomsbury artist, had, on the recommendation of Kenneth Clark,
received a commission to paint huge pictures for the *Queen Mary* liner in the
1930s. They were rejected. Jane and AC bought them in the 1970s.
[3] *Barbarossa*, AC's third volume of military history, following *The Donkeys and The
Fall of Crete*.
[4] 'Jollyboy', yet another name for the Clarks' elder son James, who so enjoyed being
pushed at speed in his pushchair that he invariably asked for more.
[5] The Clarks' cook.

the church'. So it seems perfectly natural and proper that Seend survives (and the garden and workshop too) and is now 'dedicated' to the Amazings.[1]

In the second drawer down of the 'Rye' desk I found a lot of old diaries, of the early 60s. Somewhat mannered writing. Written, indeed, more 'for publication' than subsequently. There are a few lines worth saving. But in the main it is a time-warp, and of a time when we were pushed for cash, and made-do-and-mend. Even when I was 'local MP' I never really got it *up*, although a lot of '2nd house' allowance money went on it, to hold my position in my last Parliament.

'My last Parliament.' Hm. Everything seems to be collapsing. The Tory Party really doesn't *make any sense* at present. Just running behind, fetid, panting. Now I read that the Queen is cutting down as fast as possible – on ceremony, while the dear House of Commons is going to change for ever if PR is brought in. How crazy to get rid of the coach and uniforms! I remember watching the Birthday Parade in 1982 and thinking – yes, all this finery and ceremonial. But these chaps can shoot, and fight. Undoubtedly the display that 'only we can do', that is what should be impressive, and unique.

There must be few things so tediously misleading as the 'focus group', a lot of total strangers sitting round in a room trying either to show off or recycle the fashionable clichés of the moment. Yet they are dominating the 'forming of policy'.

So all in all, I am pretty low. Of course I can say fuck them, fuck-you-all. But I am sent back to have one more try at the sword. At present I am lost in the undergrowth. I say, keep calm and concentrate on BB.

---

[1] 'The Amazings' – Andrew and his wife Sarah, who had a habit of using the word 'amazing' to describe everything.

EMT   *Monday, 23 March*

My 70th birthday approaches. Hard to believe, in some ways, when I sit at the table in the tearoom. What do colleagues think? There is a man of 70? Yesterday I tried to avoid Garel-Jones, but as everyone else went up to the new compulsory arse-lick at 5.15 on Mondays – the 'Forward Look' meeting – I was stuck. He boasted a lot about money – but unconvincingly – retold a story about UBS securities relating to a cousin of his who (very) allegedly had 'a billion dollars'; then got into his soft-sell approach on EMU. Did get through three cigarettes though, I was glad to see.

But I am creaky in my joints. Erection is a total loss – except for the one curious and reassuring experience on the Inverness flight. My arms are weak now (and look it).

I have arrived in Parliament at the very point when it is being 'marginalised'. Neither leader wants to have more to do with it than is possible. Blair because it's a nuisance, interferes with news 'management' by the exploitation of 'focus groups'. Hague because it raises issues about majority support – particularly of the 22 Executive.

Patience, but not *too much* patience. Let us see how the local elections go, and what is our rating when the summer winds down.

Harrogate   *Sunday, 29 March*

On Friday evening we set off for Harrogate Central Council. V jolly as we had the eight centre-seats on the train. Jane and I had bought pleasingly at Fortnums and I went off and got a 'bottle' (of Australian Chardonnay). How lovely and friendly and uninhibited K&C are compared to any other constituency I have ever visited. We were at the conference hotel (the Moat House) and I had hoped to be lionised a bit more than I was.

That evening the atmosphere was sceptical. To a journalist (*not* quoted, I'm sorry to say): 'There's a limit to the number of times he (Hague) can say "you're a lot of obsolete anomalies who ought to be ashamed of yourselves".'

The next day, though after a somewhat jaded opening by Cecil [Parkinson] (how many more times is he going to do this?) along came Hague. Tory audiences are far more conformist than Labour; they are utterly undiscerning. Hague's performance, though illuminated by some good lines and showing stamina (he went on for over an hour), was strangely flawed and insubstantial. He had clearly watched my pro- grammes, the way he went into *history*, and talked about 'one nation' (which shows (a) why he is so scared of me, and (b) how/why he never talked to me about it or anything else).

Poor old Archie H[amilton][1] was there totally on his own, both at breakfast and walking about the street. He came on and did his speech of support and penitence – deliberately forced on to show there was no 'breach', a stooping figure broken, all conformist after the KGB interrogations, at a show trial. He's finished. But will I be able to take his place?

In the train coming back Michael Spicer said, 'Thought they can get rid of us (the 22 Exec) at the next elections, of course.' Could be all or bust, though David D ought to be a great help here.

Theresa May[2] is the upcoming bête noir as I spotted some months ago. Yet she is the No 1 conventional plug at the moment. Even John Bercow[3] in whose Buckingham constituency I spoke on Thursday, was fulsome (though not as fulsome as he was about me in his vote of thanks). A strange and long drive that was, in his F reg Ford Sierra leap-frogging along the M-way. When we arrived an unmistakable smell of burning brake-pad which I had thought, hoped, might be coming from HGVs

---

[1] Sir Archibald (Archie) Hamilton, chairman of the 1922 Executive since 1997.
[2] Theresa May, MP for Maidenhead since 1997.
[3] John Bercow, MP for Buckingham since 1997.

adjoining us in traffic jams. And on the way back John's view of
high-beam was bizarre. So much so that some big lorries were
reduced to putting on their reversing lights.

EMT   *Friday, 17 April*

Two things have depressed me lately; dear little T.O. steadily in
decline. Periods of 'remission' are now so short. He was, miracu-
lously, 'seahorse' just for a few feet the other day after his
morning Thompson. But he now doesn't run expectantly to the
Barbican gate and wait while it is unlatched, never will again.
He is terribly muddled and almost blind so bumps into things
quite hard. Night before last he had a 'turn'; not one of his worst,
but wouldn't come out of it properly. So last night we gave him
a one-third child's aspirin and he slept better.

   The photos of me with the babies (Albert and Archibald)
show an old, maddish man, scrawny and streaked, aet. 73 – first
time I have ever looked *more* than my age. I wake at 6 a.m. with
ringing in my ears. I dread getting a stroke, like my mama.

Garden House   *Sunday, 26 April*

I was on *Frost* today. Unhappily scabious he looked, and *distrait*.
His hand shook when he passed me the butter at breakfast; and
at 8.50 a.m. he took out and offered me one of 3 huge Havana
cigars. Jack Straw, Home Secretary, controlled and capable, 'a man
of power'. Ten years or a little more ago I remember 'slapping
him down' when I was junior employment minister and he was
a backbench socialist 'trying to find his way'.

   I am 70, and feel much weaker. I am really sad that I can't
make love to Jane any more. It's different from last time when
for years I didn't really notice her. Now I look at her and think
how sweet and attractive she is.

Garden House   *Saturday, 2 May*

On the way back from the post I saw an amiable, though rumpled
figure hammering in 'Garden Open Today' signs. It turned out to
be Harland, whom I have not ever consciously met. 'Last year
nobody came,' he said. I took Jane up there at teatime. Absolutely
lovely. The age of the rhododendrons and azaleas – some going
back to 1820. A lovely boggy valley of a garden with endless
glades and dells and sudden *aperçus* and vistas. That's why it is
called 'The Garden House' (hitherto I always thought because
of his fruit farm).

The house itself, long and low, must have been sensational in its
heyday (could have been 1911, or 1922). Now needed a lick of
paint all round – but sympathetic. The little summerhouse where
we had an excellent scone tea (though served in paper cups) was
cottage *ornée* 1860 or earlier and presumably attached to an earlier
building which was pulled, or burned, down. The green tennis
court was spongy and ill-maintained, indeed the whole place bore
signs of one-man maintenance, with the marks of tractor tyres on
the fairway. But the more magical for that very reason. There
appeared to be four generations around. Old Harland (aet. 95, or
so he looked) had parchment skin and needed to be helped.
Liquidity is clearly a problem, as with so many valuable (as this so
clearly is) properties. I felt nostalgic there, and at tea thought of
the tennis parties, and their personal desires and tensions.

Why is it that good manners and the domination of the
world's oceans by the Royal Navy did coincide? Now both have
vanished. I'm sure there is a linkage.

MFS GH   *Saturday, 9 May*

On Thursday evening I collapsed from a very late tea at B5 and
we went to dine at Brooks's. Collapsed in bed. But around
midnight I knew I had to go to the count at KTH. Expensive

taxis as I was *cum* a ½ decanter of claret. A little tension at the Earls Court and Pembridge tables, but the Rolls-Royce machine had performed. Barry [Phelps] strutted and paced, like an archduke in his dinner jacket. His Labour opponent came up and said how he had wanted to meet me, and how when he was canvassing people would say how much they admired me.

House Library   *Wednesday, 13 May*

I did two TV clips, spoke in the Drugs debate – deliberately, so as to take revenge on George Howarth;[1] admired Blair at PMQs; sparkled at the Defence Committee. It is bland, 'perfect' summer weather 68°–73° I would guess and the breeze flows in from the river. Yesterday I was so exhausted. My limbs are stiff, and weak in all the joints so that I can barely walk properly (a symptom since walking back from Sandling one night a couple of months ago). I am utterly desexualated. I drink, I suppose, just a tiny bit more than I ought, with wine every day. And yesterday I was melancholy all day long, because of something concerning which I had long fantasised – the Ecosse Rallye actually coming to Eriboll, and stopping at Ardneakie; it was taking place and I was not there. Where's the C-type? What's happening to it?

I must write about something which I have long avoided. Dear, game, lion-hearted little T.O. is now in his last stage. He can't even 'seahorse' again; even when he tries he stumbles suddenly and falls on his chin, so now only walks about bandy-legged and his spine a little twisted. He sleeps a great deal, sometimes he bleeds from his scrotum. Often he is very 'bad' and bumps into things. But still he will eat, and he is not incontinent and only two or three days ago caught his 'markie' at night-night with that same old satisfactory clunk of the jaws. He is

<hr>

[1] George Howarth, MP Knowsley North and Sefton East since 1997 (Knowsley North 1986–97), had been Parliamentary Under-Secretary, Home Office, since the general election.

19½ years old. It's fifteen years since we had him on our election address in Plymouth, and an item in the *Western Morning News*. Watching his decline is depressing; not just for its depiction of a game little soul slowly being dragged down, but also for its implications for me, at 70. And my suspicion that recovery will be more difficult, as decline steepens over the next five years. And then old age will supervene.

Saltwood, EMT   *Saturday, 23 May*

The day in 1940 (is it the actual day? I know it is the date, but am finding it often difficult in my writings to clarify the day of the week, but this is so important for atmospherics) of the Cabinet meeting when Halifax argued for a 'settlement'. We could not do it then. We had to fight to a point when we had proved our mettle, which we did on 15 September, and a few weeks later in the desert.

Are we better or worse off now?

House Library   *Thursday, 9 June*

A fortnight since the last entry, but seems a month at least. I 'mislaid' the brown, 'Scilla Hotel' gift briefcase containing the journal and so missed recounting a lot of incidents – most pleasing of which probably being Jeffrey Archer's 'fine wine dinner', and the cast and conversation. Last night Rocco Forte, good(-ish), but house too *Italianate* in its decoration, stuffs and drapes and curtains – though lovely Burne-Jones drawings in the hall; sketches, or so Rocco told me, for the figures in the Berlin museum.

As it is, I am depressed. I am *so* oppressed by work. This evening I have five, simultaneous [constituency] invitations, plus there are two votes at 6.45 and pre-10 p.m. I wanted to do Transport Qs, but had to go up to Sue's[1] where there was a stack – I mean a stack, 10″ high or so, of signing.

In the morning I went out to Aubrey Finsberg. Even worse than I suspected. A shed, open, corrugated iron flapping. A youth bashing panel deafeningly the moment one got involved in conversation. The poor C-type stripped of its body panel at back, looking like a write off, dirt and discarded wires and pieces everywhere. The mystery of the 'crankshaft pulley' – how? and when? I just felt terribly tired and sad. Something told me she had gone. A lot of braggadocio about 'doing our best, Alan'. Sort of balls, but not the slightest chance of getting it ready for 26 June or 26 July or August, September or even 26 October. I was really furious. I have a hate thing with mechanics and just like builders (workmen). Only P. & A. Wood are orderly and compos (worth every penny).

Saltwood, tearoom terrace   *Friday, 12 June*

First entry this year from a favoured spot. Brian has started to scythe the sycamore slope and we are near to the longest day (by which, I hope and trust, BB will be delivered and I will be quietly awaiting my first tranche of £50). I am calm. Fax from Knight Frank saying that Bratton sold for 186. I had hoped to get 200. This will just restore our liquidity ration, and allow me to use the royalty payments and BB to produce (at last!) 'solvency'. Very nearly dislocated everything today by buying the ever-so-nice 'lightweight' VDP 3-litre tourer at Goodwood (Brooks's). Authorised John Leyland to go to 41. Fortunately it made 49. Would have been huge fun to clean and activate, but came back, looked at the Hen and was reasonably content. My cross remains 91MX, but we had a lovely outing. Jane brilliant at the

---

[1] Sue Line, AC's secretary.

autojumble stalls. And v splendidly dismissed the Barn VDP by saying that it looked 'teeny bit Wolseley'.

I spoke last night at the dinner; just about ok, I suppose, but goodness knows what I looked like under the lights. Sat next to the v attractive Mrs Jane Major. Paid £2000 so can't complain.

Parliament Street office   *Thursday, 18 June*

In that slightly rattled, dry-mouthed condition one gets into following a 'gaffe'.[1] I don't in the least regret speaking out on behalf of the 'fans'. Part, as Charles Moore said, of my *weltanschauung*. But usual correspondence of cor-there-he-goes-again type. And Conservative Central Office – predictably – got in the act 'condemning' me.

Great Hall   *Saturday, 20 June*

This is midsummer weekend. And, as usual, I make an entry from the prayer seat on the long table in the Great Library where, at 7 p.m., the sun is still high.

The ramblers were down all day. I was somewhat (sic) dreading them, when we met them at 10.07 at Sandling. I walked with them as far as Acrise. When I first 'offered the booking' I said to Jane 'this will be the hottest day of the year'. And sure enough, after weeks of thunderstorms and winds this is what it has turned out to be. I turned at Postling Road and walked back to Sandling; waiting by the station my pulse was erratic, at 130+. But as soon as I had swum it was back to 78

---

[1] On BBC's *Today* AC had praised the 'martial spirit' of English football fans in Marseilles involved in fighting French riot police. 'Football matches are now the modern equivalents of medieval tournaments.'

(some doctors might have said 'don't go in the cold water might risk a stroke'). They came back for tea and the atmosphere improved, with the groups fantasising.

Poor Aspers is dying. What will happen to the animals? Do they know their protector is in travail?

I got the better of everybody over the football-supporters 'gaffe'. Central office are briefing against me, as always. 'Tough on dinosaurs; and tough on the causes of dinosaurs.' Hague is ill, with flu.

Saltwood, EMT   *Monday, 22 June*

Big Book is finished. At 8.50 p.m. last night I put the very last sentence onto the computer.

Thursday, 25 June

I dropped a tart note to Sebastian Coe[1] off at 32 Smith Square with copies of all my fan letters.

On the way over I had been striding along, saw cross-faced Roy Jenkins[2] in his little purple car turning into the Lords car park. Returning I looked up at the Palace and inhaled great lungful of air, I took pleasure in its appearance like some lovely ridge in the Highlands, and knowing that I have climbed it.

---

[1] Sebastian Coe, former athlete, MP for Falmouth and Camborne, 1992–1997; Private Secretary to William Hague as Tory Leader since 1997.

[2] Lord [Roy] Jenkins, former Labour Minister, one of the 'gang of four' that broke away from the Labour Party to found the SDP, which he later led.

House Library, 11.40 p.m.   *Thursday, 2 July*

I felt rather dreadful before 'turning in', at intervals in the night,
and even on waking (though recovering now, on Indian tea and
grapefruit juice). Dinner at Wilton's with Soames and
Woodward. S crocodile, so occasionally shrewd; but unfocused,
too easily distracted in conversation. W is good, but of the left
of course; and makes mistakes of judgement – like plugging 'the
Governor'. All agreed that Hague must go. But not, naturally,
this minute. He's now been 'staying out' for over ten days. Quite
ridiculous with medical science in its advanced state – look at
Mitterrand (or Yeltsin) not to mention Mrs T, Winston, Anthony
etc. The Party can just about carry him. But it simply means he
can never be ill again, like Michael Heseltine being allowed only
one heart attack. The boys want, of course, to replace him with
Clarke. Almost as difficult, I would think, to get the Party to
swallow K as to swallow A!

I hope this weekend to do some thinking – for the first time
almost since Scotland. But at the Carlton Club finance meeting
yesterday evening all the men in the room were glowering.
What a dreadful, seedy mediocre bunch the party apparatchiks
are! There were some Nellies in the doorway and I 'gave' one a
kiss for the photographer – which caused a huge coach-tour
whoop to echo round the crowded room, to everyone's
disapproval, except for dear Michael Ancram, who was speaking.

EMT   *Monday, 13 July*

Last night we went to bed at eight – slept shallowly until it
became dark, then deeply. This morning at 6-ish I said
something to Jane and she answered 'ye-es' in a very sleepy
drawl that reminded me of when (twice) I have visited her in
hospital and she has still been under anaesthetic. In a curious
way her very sweet nature comes through. And very briefly I

had a sad projection forward – which of us will die first? Me, I hope. But then would dear sweet Janey be nicely looked after once I was gone? Who would spend 'quality time' (new *in* phrase) with her; what about her pets? She is so patient and kind.

Sunday, 19 July

A lovely hot day, almost the first of this summer. I am sitting out by the tearoom (not in use this year). I drank the delicious new Riesling and could be at a café table beside a *place* in Normandy, 'putting the world to rights'. If I was also sexual I would be completely happy. With this one exception, my good fortune is so TOTAL that it makes me apprehensive – both as to possible reverse, and also regarding my debt to 'put something back in'.

After all, the three little grandsons; BB delivered; the safest and most pleasing of all seats – to which I am perfectly suited; the nicest part of the summer ahead. It is gone 8 p.m. and very still, with exceptional golden light in the left-hand sycamore. Swallows, jolly now, still swoop and chatter excitedly although they, and all the birds, are about to retire.

Bratton   *Thursday, 23 July*

Yesterday I was absolutely depressed. The sad, final news that Tom – missing since 8 p.m. yesterday – had been found dead or drowned at the Towers end of the moat; its many sad reminders of – in slow motion – my own steady decline. Then an inconclusive (as nearly always) meeting of the 22 Executive followed by 'the Leader's address'. Hague really awful. Trite, insecure, verbal disconnection. Worse, I think, even than Ted. Certainly Major was incomparably better. What is to happen to the Tory Party?

Last week DD, who is proprietorial for me, suggested I give a lecture on the constitution in our history, preferably at Conference with Robert Blake somewhere around. Just right, if it weren't for the fact that if BB 'flunks', which clearly is going to, my reputation (always partially spurious) as a 'historian' goes with it.

Now this afternoon, after getting up at 5 a.m. we are at Bratton for the last time.[1] It is smiling, and I sit in the front garden after a lovely tea. I have practically no pangs (though disappointed at the price of £180,000). It took us 5½ hours to drive here from Saltwood. The West Country is inaccessible in the summer months, and much here has changed, with the death of Mrs Lintern and David's sulkiness, and the unpleasant publican. It is peaceful, on a sunny July afternoon, because there is no background noise, no 'M-way roar'. But the house looks dreadful from outside now, paint peeling off all the windows, and a generally neglected air.

I bought it in a rush, driving down to Okehampton on the Bank Holiday in the Olds 88 after we saw it when cruising through to look at a National Trust property in the north, where we might have been tenants. In fact we did not live here very long. Under pressure from Nanny [Greenwood] we went back, after the birth of Andrew in 1962, to Rye, first to No 30 (an awkward, vertical house at the corner of Watchbell Street and Church Square); then with some Trust money to the Wades (No 12), bought, heart-stoppingly – for £9800. We still used Bratton as a summer place. I remember particularly the lovely Whitsun of 1963 with the Grahams staying, using the [Citroën] ID Safari to go to Bude. In winter we were at Zermatt (though interrupted that year by the typhoid scare, being only saved by Taugwalder's [lawyer] greed from closing the sale of the châlet at 120,000 francs. This we continued until 1964-ish and bought Seend Manor, living first in the Manor, then at the Park, and as

---

[1] In a note three days later AC recalls how he and Jane were 'absolutely knackered' after the double drive – Saltwood/Bratton/Bratton (Broomhayes)/Saltwood.

I often write in many ways the most physically fulfilling period of my life and long walks with EDG on the plain with the Beagles and the 2CV.

Then, captivated by Enoch, and courted by Alan Warner and his crew at Langstone (Havant) I approached politics.

My father moved out of Saltwood in 1971 and 'new readers join here'.[1] Bratton remained intermittently while I was Plymouth MP kept going by periodic grants from our 'second-house allowance'. But now we haven't visited (much less lived) here for seven years. 'More Run' has surfaced – my *Rosebud*. The furnishings will be dispersed around the family.

House Library   *Tuesday, 28 July*

Last night I was so exhausted. I could barely drag myself to 'Pembridge' [ward] party – the last of the social round. Did *not* sparkle. Had come straight from Hague talking about 'the State and the Community' at Carlton House Terrace (being *not* recognised by the tittle on the desk when I arrived). 'What a lot of waffle,' said the elderly man on my right.

I went to Pratt's, drank a glass of white wine, felt too tired to remain and returned to B5. Ate an Eccles cake bought at the tearoom counter, tried to ring Saltwood – engaged. Dialled Eriboll – engaged. Talking to each other (again). Read a long passage about German strategic policy in winter 1940.

Outside Long Garage, Saltwood   *Saturday, 1 August*

Yesterday was our wedding anniversary. Forty years. Janey still looks incredible; I have deteriorated since last summer when the famous Christmas card photo was 'snapped' by Caroline Stroyan.

---

[1] See *Diaries: Into Politics* which begins in 1972.

In the early mornings I am so stiff and weak that I almost fall over (as, presumably, like my father – and grandfather – I will at some point in the next decade). I am hypochondriac about my jaw – is it rotting slowly under Bertie's great carapace? What does one do when the teeth go? Like the king elephant in *Babar*, it is the end. No more photocalls either.

BB is going to cause me damage. I will not be the Party's historian and (as I had intended) its sage; still less its Maxime Weygand.[1]

Wednesday, 12 August

Although we have been sitting by the pool (the last 4–5 days have been incredibly hot) saying that we wished we need not move, now suddenly the pull of Scotland is felt. As at the House (catalpa trees in flower) so at Saltwood where the hollyhocks have more than half lost their petals then the season has changed gear. We must assert ourselves and when we return the air, and the colours, will be different. So tomorrow, up the A1 with the customary 5.50 a.m. 'through the gates'. For the first time ever, though, without T.O. on his 'jump seat' – although his hairs are, as Jane would say, copious on the seats and carpets.

I am fractionally better, and would have improved more if in fact had been to bed earlier, as one had intended. Down on energy and zest, though. No press-ups by the pool this year, or weights, or Gossie in the evenings.[2] I had a nasty frisson walking in the old family garden this evening. How many more times will I see it, in its August fullness? Two or three (with luck) in my present condition; then perhaps another four or five as a buffer, or demi-buffer.

---

[1] Maxime Weygand, who was recalled in June 1940 to take on the crumbling French Army.

[2] By October he is noting, 'I have only done about three sets of two press-ups this whole year.'

Shore, Wheelhouse   *Tuesday, 18 August*

Last night I slept – without interruption of any kind, barely even 'surfacing' – from 10 p.m. until 7.10 a.m. Opened my eyes, said a few words, then slept again until 8.20. After lunch I slept in the deckchair in the wheelhouse until woken by Hannah for the 'w'. Each time we are in Eriboll I sleep like this ('too much') for the first week. I remember Peter Morrison[1] when I asked him what he 'did' at Islay just answered – 'sleep'. That is what Scotland is for.

At tea in the wheelhouse I looked across and thought – 'if two years ago I had been told that I would be sitting here, and beside me a beautiful little baby boy in a high chair being fed by Julie with chunks of fruit salad, I would have thought, "there is nothing more I can ask for …"' Two roots of the generation tree now started in the soil. But continuity is now as much in God's hands as in mine.

What an incredible two years it has been! Was it only that long ago that Sarah Baxter interviewed me at Bournemouth – 'reinventing himself'. But of course in that time I have become much older. My limbs are feeble and achy in the joints. So much so that at this rate I will be bufferish at 73; while I want to be a mixture of Bill Deedes and (as it were) Paul Johnson.

What of poor old Aspers, I wonder? He must now be at death's door. Or rather, Death be at his. I watch the obituary columns quite eagerly; each contemporary down is a private score. This is the counterpoint of getting much-sweat and bladder compression in the night thinking of how much I have yet to do to assert order.

---

[1] Peter Morrison, former MP for Chester, junior Minister and Mrs Thatcher's campaign manager when she lost the Party leadership.

Shore Cottage   *Saturday, 29 August*

The holiday is over. Two lovely last days; yesterday we went out in Katoomba (I felt queasy, but 'held on') and dined up at the Lodge. Today a great walk all around the forestry plantation taking 'Bok' as well as the girls. I bathed twice, and Jane very gamely joined me for the last one this p.m.

The recall of Parliament.[1] Yes, it is a chore, cuts into other 'options' for departure day. But just think of it! What would I in 1992, 3, 4, 5, or 6 have given to be recalled from Eriboll to an emergency sitting of the House of Commons! And at the same time to be leaving behind James and Julie and the tiny baby Angus! How can I even for half of one minute start to whinge or question my unbelievable good fortune?

EMT, Saltwood   *Saturday, 5 September*

Demi-serene. I performed in the emergency session. I stumbled – why? Slightly alarming in retrospect – calling Madame *Deputy*-Speaker, then my honourable *members*, but got professionally into my stride. 'I am fortified ... ('all too true', chuckled that bearded nameless who bothers me from the other side; v unfair as I hadn't drunk anything all day, but no one would believe it) ... by fact that deputy leader of the Liberal party has just withdrawn his name from a motion signed by his own chief whip' (this thanks to injunction from Mackay[2] and Michael Howard).

It was a most classic example of the House of Commons coming alight while the two front benches sat mute, looking at

---

[1] Parliament was reconvened to pass emergency anti-terrorist legislation in the wake of the Omagh bombing by the 'Real' IRA.

[2] Andrew Mackay, MP for Bracknell since 1997 (Berkshire East, 1983–97); deputy chief whip 1996–97. Opposition spokesman on Northern Ireland since 1997.

the floor. A quite brilliant speech by Richard Shepherd, almost on the verge of a breakdown, inspired people to argue.[1]

Ashford train   *Wednesday, 9 September*

The time seems to be galloping past now we are back. This year the September second half of holiday is blighted by the launch of BB. I feel lethargic and passed over; and just lately I am reading a lot about Chris Patten (his book is just out) and his impending 'return' to politics.[2] I can get sad if I think of being finally 'out'. But am I to die in harness? When I am over at the Garden House I think of my retirement there. And when I walk through the rooms at Saltwood now I can half feel my own death. Almost an Orphée-like revisitation.

And yet the 'practicalities' oppress. Three days ago we thought that we might clear one piece, delivered from Bratton, from the Hall, and decided to move a small chest of drawers up to Andrew's room … Like everything at Saltwood tampering with the mud and wattle dam released first a dribble, then a jet, then a cascade. The chest seemed better in the bathroom. And that in my bathroom beside Jane's (summer) bed. Thus 'releasing' the ludicrous wooden washstand, which has been her bedside table for the last 25 years into the passage. This involved a total re-organising and cleaning of the original (Rye) chest in my bathroom, polishing the Herman box, the glass desk-top, rearranging the photos etc.

One minor point of interest in the back lid flap of the inlaid writing case we found a letter beautifully written in copperplate complaining about his 'posting' to Ireland, the 'brigands', the delays to the stage [coach] and so on. 'While writing this I have

---

[1] Richard Shepherd had been the *Spectator* Backbencher of the Year in 1987 and *Spectator* Parliamentarian of the Year in 1995.

[2] Titled *East and West* it proved a bestseller. But would Patten return as a saviour of the Conservative Party? Patten, shrewdly, did not rise to the bait.

a sword at my side and a pistol, cocked and loaded, on the table before me.' For 150 years or more this has been the 'norm'. How then, about the Peace Process?

Thursday, 17 September

I wrote an article defending Bill Clinton and – unbelievably – on being asked for a quote Hague's office said, 'Mr Clark periodically makes a spectacle of himself, but most people know his views are not those of the Conservative Party.'

Sunday evening, 20 September

All depends, really, on the Book and how it is received. Robert Blake reviewing it for the *Sunday Times* – this could be critical.[1]

A lovely still late autumn, with the barometer rising. How delicious to live on here, just daily tasks. The Mains, the Garden House, the Woodland (both sides), the cars.

But I've tried this; withdrawal symptom too strong (because, of course, I know that the next big 'event' is death).

So what is to become of me?

Rebecca Salt[2] has fitted up the whole week, like an official. Doesn't leave a single gap in the diary, not even to tinkle, still less eat.

---

[1] Lord Blake, who had himself written an earlier history of the Conservative Party, was good-tempered.
[2] Rebecca Salt, publicity director, Weidenfeld & Nicolson.

House Library   *Wednesday, 23 September*

An absolutely beautiful still September day, the barometer rising all week. A special agony at leaving Saltwood (at least I did bathe, briefly to stimulate the system out of its abject and listless depression) because of a feeling that there really are so few left – ones when I can still stride, if not prance.

'Don't go, *don't* go. Why are you leaving? How can you leave us? Always you do this, and always it makes you unhappy; and always you have the same excuse – "must" do this or that (utterly transient; ephemeral and draining task) and, at the back of your mind, "next time, next year I really won't." But that's not true. You think we will always be here, and that because you love us we will always love you and protect you. But in the end, we will be gone. *Please* give us a little time ...'

Thus I felt the call from the trees and the corn-stubble and the songbirds.

Zermatt   *Tuesday, 29 September*

This is the time to come here. And now that the silver birch and the larch are so grand their leaves filter and dapple the sunlight. The house is set back from the street, blocked on the southern side by the Kariad, and its screen of trees in leaf protect it most pleasingly.

We started off as on a meander but, as nearly always in the Alps, it turned into a quite stiff (for the first day) expedition. A nice young man, beautifully dressed in a navy overcoat with his lady (in a black fur) smiled and took my photograph in the old inn; they were on their honeymoon as we were just exactly forty years ago.

Last night I had difficulty getting to sleep. I tinkled five, finally six times quite copiously. In the morning Jane found blood on my pidgy bottoms. How? Why? Unsettling. I am absolutely desexualated. A nullity. Up until only two years ago I would always wake with a sleepy erection at 5.30. Seven years ago we started again out here. Absolutely delicious, never been sexually happier with Jane.

Saltwood   *Thursday, 15 October*

Conference – AC1800 parked 'modestly' bang outside the very Blackpool-like (we were of course in Bournemouth) 'Trouville' Hotel. Then Eastbourne for the 'bonding'. I turned up in a 3-piece (sic) suit with a pink shirt – tight collar, accidently chose a size 15 instead of 15½ – and OE tie. Surrounded by reporters as I got out of the cab. 'It's a statement,' I told them.[1]

Later
'Do you want to be Mayor?' Jane asked.[2]

I just don't know. Or rather I do know and the answer is, by a narrow margin, 'yes'. But what I do not want is a campaign for the mayorality. Yes, the ideal scenario remains, as Moira Stewart[3] put it, 'become Mayor, then after two years strike for the Leadership of the Tory Party.' And certainly the odds on this are no higher than, two years ago, they must have been for a 67-year-old animal rights activist with a lurid private life and a record for colossal indiscretion, plus falling foul of the Police, HM Customs, and the Scott Inquiry to get selected for the safest Tory seat in the country.

Or the Speaker, conceivably?

A nice lead piece in Cross-Bencher [*Sunday Express*] to which – interestingly – NO ONE referred the following day at

---

[1] A Central Office spokesman had said: 'we don't want people turning up in suits.'
[2] The Labour government had decided London should have an elected Mayor. Candidates were beginning to jostle along party lines.
[3] Moira Stewart, BBC newscaster, in conversation with AC at a literary lunch in Kensington Town Hall.

Eastbourne, except DD slyly in his cups at supper. I did say to Jane – here we are discussing these marvellous possibilities and here I am with three lovely little grandsons and a safe seat – surely some catastrophe is due to strike? I try and avoid hubris, but do, of course 'show off' (*épater*). Not quite the same thing, but invites Nemesis none the less.

House Library   *Tuesday, 20 October*

Last night the first meeting of the Sybil club. The unlikely duet of Bill Cash and Shaun Woodward have invited twelve 'interesting' colleagues (ten MPs, two peers) to meet on a monthly basis and talk things through.[1] No factional lines. Ruffley (clockwise), Simon Burns (an unexpected figure – but pleasant), Bercow, Cash, Tapsell, Q. Davies, Gowrie, Woodward, self etc.[2] Robert Blake talked, or rather read in very poor light at a slow pace a quite nicely composed text – the plot of the novel, its lessons etc.

All of the contributions were worth listening to. An enormous amount of drink was consumed. Quite suddenly at the end of the meal after port and Sauternes a selection of new, and delicious, clarets were proffered. I smoked, most rarely, a Havana cigar. We 'broke up' at 12.55 and completely stupefied I left the Porsche in the street asking Shaun's butler to feed the meter from 8.30 a.m.

In spite of walking back at a fine pace and reading at some length from my own published *Diaries* I woke up quite quickly

---

[1] Political dining club named after Disraeli's landmark novel, *Sybil: or the Two Nations*. AC sometimes misspells it 'Sibyl' (after the hostess Sibyl Colefax?). The Woodward-Cash 'Sibyl' met at Woodward's Queen Anne's Gate home. Like Bill Cash, Woodward was wealthy, but politically they were on opposite sides of the Conservative Party. One black-ball excluded.

[2] David Ruffley (Bury St Edmunds since 1997), Simon Burns (Chemsford W since 1997; Chelmsford, 1987–97), Quentin Davies (Grantham and Stamford since 1997; Stamford and Spalding, 1987–97); Lord Gowrie (chairman of the Arts Council since 1994).

– bitter vomit in the upper throat. Should have got rid of it at once, but this would have meant losing a lot of quite good food as well. Dropped back off, woke again – cold. Tinkled and immediately and strongly came over Norwegian Embassy. Only just got back to bed; a bit worried about cerebral haemorrhage. This symptom is now definitely linked to (far) too much drink.

Shaun showed me two little pencil sketches done by a woman of Winston on his very last day [in the Commons]. The last one, of him making his way out of the Chamber with his stick, achingly moving.[1]

House Library   *Wednesday, 21 October*

I walked this morning across Star Court, wet and exhausted, and was reminded of that strong, upsetting, and never wholly eradicable relationship – my last, indeed my entire, two years at MoD. A long time now; next year it will be ten years. I get a kind of satisfaction now, looking back at passages when I felt bitterly unhappy, but now think – 'well, I got through that …' Many, many times I think of 'x' and would love a 'chat'. But I don't make contact not wanting to let down Jane.

Parliament Street   *Wednesday, 28 October*

This, to all intents and purposes, is the final entry.[1] I should have started it at Shore, where we were last weekend for the christening of the bairn. So lovely Shore, 'the little house', as Jane calls it, with the light changing and the husbandry and the panelled 'work-station' and, of course, the wheelhouse.

---

[1] The artist, Juliet Pannett, worked for the *Illustrated London News*, which is why she had a ticket for the Commons' press gallery.

As so often (and I expect that I will return to this) I turned my mind to shifting the centre of gravity: Saltwood on care-and-maintenance with only the Red Study and a semi-stripped Music Room intact. The most symbolic of all transfers the hens to the sleeper-shed taken place. Would I then get on 'Boy's' nerves. Quite probably, certainly on Julie's. An ironic mirror image of my father at Garden House in the closing years. We could be at Saltwood for periods only; probably mid-June to end July. Zermatt in October; conceivably, and again in end March early April. Christmas would alternate.

At the moment, though, it is not feasible. The House consumes me still, I love it. I want to come home early on Thursday, but must wait and speak in the Quarantine Debate because I always promised myself that whatever else happened to me if I should ever 'get back' I would speak for the animals.

I still haven't described the Christening – so pleasing in the little candle-lit church (Mary's iron candelabra) and the Catholic ceremony – Fr John Maguire – much more significant. Afterwards we did pile into the jeep for the Christmas-card photo. The last occasion for some while, I fear, when we will all be under one roof.

Saltwood, in bed, Summer Bedroom   *Monday, 2 November*

Third day of a cold. Saturday night was dreadful, 100.5° at 3.30, I lay diagonally restive – 'simply on the floor at Mother Teresa's, nothing to be done' etc. Hannah occupied most of the space. Jane carrying forward the analogy saw her as a cow, also ushered in to lie among the sick and dying. To complete the image, there was no water.

Yesterday I was mainly in bed, though did totter down to 'run up' the C-type. I'm reluctant to part with the C-type; but have gone right off cars. That bloody 91 MX – a bill for £20. And

what, incidentally, of Bratton? It's just a write-off. A nil amount.[1]
Had a 'Lem-sip' last night so slept round from 11 to 7 a.m.

EMT   *Tuesday, 10 November*

A very long 'cold', now in its twelfth day and still bright green,
chestily and my voice tenuous in the extreme which worries me.

After the Remembrance Service on Sunday I spoke to little
Dr Jonathan Munday our new Mayor of the Royal Borough,
said I'd been feeling shaky for eight days and had lost my voice.

'Feeling ghastly for ten days, eh?' Vomiting, diarrhoea? No.
Shortness of breath, chest pains? No aches in the joints? No.
Waterworks, digestion? OK.

Hm. I trailed the idea of getting throat cancer from 'straining'
the voice. He spluttered. Spoke reassuringly about the vocal
chords.

We drove back in Big Red. But I am far from right.

Saltwood   *Saturday, 14 November*

I refuse to close this volume until I am 'feeling better'.

Saltwood   *Tuesday, 17 November*

'November is always a bad month for you, isn't it?' said Jane at
EMT.

'Yes,' I answered. 'I know that I will die at ten minutes to three
on a date in November – probably between the 4th and the 10th.'

---

[1] Although the buyer had, as AC notes elsewhere, 'welched' on the deal, we 'very
clever to have pouched deposit'.

1 Parliament Street   *Thursday, 19 November*

My first entry[1] and I am low, uncertain, and 'not myself'.

Now (tomorrow) coming up to three weeks with my 'cold' and, pace Mrs Frowd, 'spot' on the trachea. No longer green, but voice tremulous and with a low endurance. *Only very slowly* recovering energy. Is this Eric Forth's (many colleagues have had the germ), 'you think you're getting better and then it comes back at you'? Or more sinister?

I am gloomy that it is a step-change. Will never quite recover off the back. Last night, eating solo and lightly in Wilton's, a *very* old buffer next door asked me how old I was. '70'. 'I'm 70' he said ('you look and sound — he was v quavery — 80'). 'You'll have a stroke this year' he said. Hm. On inquiry turned out to be a rather dim 'explorer'.

B5   *Monday, 20 November*

Going to give myself a fresh treat and looking at a C-type which Gregor Fiskin is offering at £475,000 (!)

House Library   *Thursday, 24 November*

I drove up this afternoon in typical November afternoon weather. Poor light, moisture, mist, heavy rain that could almost be snow. I felt listless, and exhausted. Already I had cleared out the hen houses, and put in fresh straw, then over to Garden House to clean up my *New Statesmen* 'Diary' which last night most perversely went *off-margin* in the biggest possible way. Once more I am condemned to stay all day Friday and then

---

[1] In what would prove the final manuscript volume of AC's journal.

a mock speaking engagement – but it is in John Hayes's[1] constituency and he is a good guy.

Am I pre-cancerous, or even cancerous? Certainly I get sudden fluctuations in body temperature. Last night Jane woke me. When she is hardly awake she speaks in absolutely normal, conventional tones, which I don't like in the middle of the night. Worrying about Bratton, which *is* a bore of course. I don't mind (much) 'taking a bath', but don't want there to be no bids at all.

Surgery for two hours, switching on the lights for 'ML Welss',[2] followed by a book signing. I drain myself. And tomorrow early for the Savoy and a Hague breakfast.

Tower Office, Saltwood   *Saturday, 28 November*

This week I put 100,000 Coats into the Eriboll Trust. All too easily they might have been (in the mid eighties/early nineties, when I was jobbing in them at 200-ish) the balancing element against the *Times* dollar portfolio. It is less than fifteen years since I identified the asset objective as 'a million Swiss francs, a million dollars, and a million Coats'. Now they are 25½p! So on a negative basis I suppose that is 'phew!'. 'Shows what can happen' etc and just as well, as Bratton clearly isn't going to sell and we will be down £180,000.

I am a lot calmer. I feel myself to have recovered, and today pulling some 'fruiting bodies'[3] and pottered pleasingly in 'classic-car' weather standard for November with moist road surfaces and condensatory precipitation.

I just took a few moments off to go through and be told that it was pheasant this evening. So opened a bottle of Lynch '62

---

[1] John Hayes, MP for South Holland and The Deepings since 1997.
[2] Chelsea and Kensington food shop.
[3] AC's name for brambles.

(the best claret of all time, *I* think) from the case which Jane found among a full case of Yquem '67 and Margaux '61 in Peggy's pantry, under the Great Library, of all places. I think a lot about the Party and my mission – conceived last January. I will, I hope, draw a dividend on my many speaking engagements, my appearances at the top of the fund-raisers league table.

Later (Monday)

I was inspired to write draft notes for a speech to the AGM telling of how I felt I needed to 'break out'. Went up to the bath, there noticed the ulcer on my shin which has been there on and off for quite a time (originally thought to have been hit while walking through metal parts in, as it were, the workshop).

How long has it been there? Certainly not changing as now, but often a little red scab. At once deep gloom, a full onset of hypochondria so soon after finally emerging from the viral 3½ weeks.

Now it is a lovely, fine gusty morning, but I am low and feel my leg. As soon as one realises oneself to be afflicted it's 'what's the point?'.

Tuesday, 1 December

Have done a couple of medias today; the (potentially hateful) Leasehold Reform Lobby; then 3.15 Pinochet[1] on 'Westminster Live'. Last night I heckled – demi – Hague on the 'Forward Look' Committee on the Lords and PR which has got me on to *Today* on Wednesday. Most people in the room (even, e.g., Ainsworth[2]) agreed with me.

As I walked back this morning from Millbank I passed under

---

[1] Britain was refusing extradition demands from Spain over General Augusto Pinochet, former Chilean dictator, who was living under house arrest in a house in Surrey.
[2] Peter Ainsworth, MP for Surrey E since 1992, opposition deputy chief whip, 1997–98.

the windows of the office of my old friend EDG from which sometimes he used to hail me. It was fun in those days popping in there every Tuesday before lunch for white wine. But I was far more frustrated then than I am now. My constituency was in a mess, intense dislike and unease. My political prospects nil. My private life uncertain, as my finances.

Now I am happy and fortunate. Last night sat at my desk, rang Jane, didn't know what to do. Aimless Beefsteak or House dining room? Chose House, ran into Ancram, dined with him and joined by Goodlad who was a little uneasy about being nominated Commissioner. A bad press and Patten has announced that *he* would like it. 'You'll get it,' I told him.[1] Later he said that 'once your radar shuts down even a bit (we were talking about Tom King being deaf) you're finished. You're out.'

Goodlad told me that my radar was always at 360° fucking even when I was out of Parliament.

Leaving the dining room I was taken in by little Duncan.[2] Beautiful, but a weenily bit tiddly, and we sat in the Savoy Room to be joined by Ainsworth and then – TED.[3] Mellow and pleasing and a white dinner jacket. His eyes are still alive, very.

Quite like old times.

Ashford train   *Friday, 4 December*

A couple of days ago I was depressed and flaccid. I came across some 'poor' reviews of my book – which has unquestionably proved a 'disappointment' (and, in its reception, to me). I seemed

---

[1] AC was wrong: Patten became a member of the European Commission in 1999.
[2] Alan Duncan, MP for Rutland and Melton since 1992; PPS to Health Minister 1993–94.
[3] Sir Edward Heath, aged 82, Father of the House, having first been elected for Bexley in 1950.

to be pointless in the House. Perhaps even the 22 Exec[1] would be taken away ...

Then, at the Wednesday PMQs, Hague walked into an ambush which (as it turned out) he had set up for himself. He started asking Blair about 'a deal' to include hereditaries in the reformed House of Lords. No one – either side – had the slightest idea what he/they were talking about. Soon it became apparent from Blair's responses that Hague himself didn't either. Robert Cranborne[2] had done a private deal to save the Cecils' skin and give the hereditaries a toehold in the 'new' House (because of course there never will be a 'stage 2'; there never is). At first sight it was monstrous. The corridors were buzzing and little Liam Fox[3] caught up with David D and me in the Library corridor as soon as we left the tearoom and said it was 'the greatest act of betrayal in the history of the Tory Party'. There was uncertainty, bewilderment and resentment abroad. Most colleagues were low. Another filthy setback (although there was little blaming of Hague's handling).

At the Executive there was much complaint. Everyone agreed it was a miserable affair and the *balance of resentment* seemed to be against Robert. Suddenly there was an agitated tapping at the door. Lidington[4] burst in, white as a sheet and wild-eyed. 'William has just sacked Cranborne and wants to come and address the full Committee in 20 minutes' time.'

Hague himself was 'grimfaced'. Quite clear, but how his voice does *grate*! He's quite like Harold Wilson minus only the bogus and infuriating penchant to suck on a pipe. Wilson, though, would never have got into this jam. The next morning I was woken (one had 13 votes the previous night after 10 p.m.) by *Today* programme and croakily and (when I saw the transcript)

---

[1] AC had been elected to the executive of the Conservative backbench 1922 Committee earlier in 1998.

[2] Lord Cranborne had been Leader of the Opposition in the Lords since 1997.

[3] Dr Liam Fox, MP for Woodspring since 1992, Opposition spokesman on constitutional affairs.

[4] David Lidington, MP for Aylesbury since 1992, Hague's PPS since 1992.

incoherently said we were in a 'double-sided mess'. All day, clips
and bites. I judged it right to be 'loyal'. But the fact of Hague
afterwards accepting the 100 exceptions does seem to show that
in fact he's all over the place. And in Sunday's (today) morning
papers he had briefed that he intends to reform the Upper
House 'root and branch'.

As Jane remarked, 'one's instinct is to support Robert; but
from the Party point-of-view I suppose that one must stay with
Hague – for the time being at least.'

Gratifyingly, Alastair C[ampbell] came on the phone for 35
minutes on Friday night (twice offered me a peerage, incidentally).
In the end we were cut off. I assume that the Downing Street
switchboard were changing the tape. So when it immediately re-
rang I said, 'Are you at No 10?' It was Soames! He gulped and
moaned. A little later I phoned Cranborne. Hannah answered,
coolish. 'Robert will ring you back, maybe tomorrow.' R came to
the phone at once. Spoke for another half hour. Two sides to this
tale. Funny about the 'epicene young men' who forced their way
into the Peers meeting *with* Hague (quite discourteous and
improper). Told of how when he said, 'I can resign now; or later, or
you can sack me', Peter Carrington[1] stepped forward, venerably, 'As
someone who, so to speak, has experience of resignation, hah-
hah, could I suggest …'

'*NO.*' Hague pushed him aside. 'Yah sacked.' It is an indescrib-
able mess. I wrote roughly the same piece for the *Mail* (rejected);
then for the *Mail on Sunday* (rejected), each time being paid for.
There is the usual talk of the succession. Ken [Clarke] crazily in
the wings; Maude hovering. Neither is realistic.

But 'the front *is* collapsing' – as I predicted.

At least it is a lovely winter's day, and crisp underfoot. We are log-
splitting and stacking. I have my Mains, and my old-timers. I am
content. (My 'ulcerly leg' is healing itself.) The little boys, Albert,
Archie, were here yesterday en route for Broomhayes and divine.

---

[1] Lord Carrington, Margaret Thatcher's first Foreign Secretary, had resigned in 1982
at the time of Argentina's invasion of the Falklands.

But there is just this void. I can only barely see the lake. Over Christmas I must think very carefully.

House Library   *Tuesday, 8 December*

Oh-so-low driving up (in mist and rain). Last night Lëhni suddenly got *full-blown* ear flapping (as in 'full blown' AIDS). On and on she paw jabbed it, yelping and whimpering all the while. We rose, blundered about; Jane found Miss Bett's Powder – stored in a Colman's Mustard tin.[1] Later she paw-licked oh-so-jarringly. 'An *early night* always involves an interruption.' Old and true saying. Perhaps it was depression induced by recalling how we would start leaving Tom down there after he had one of his fits and sometimes he used to bark, and we pulled the blankets over our heads. In the morning we would go down half almost hoping that he would have 'died in his sleep'. I am still nostalgic for Tom and miss him when I come round the corner for tea at the end of the day and the log fire is burning merrily.

I am lowered more than I care to admit by Max Hastings' unpleasant introduction to Bradshaw's *Not*.[2] 'Many Conservatives loathe him', etc. Realised, of course, that the 'Chairman of the 22' who was quoted as saying that 'Don't people understand that Alan's not *pretending* to be a shit? He really *is* one,' would, can only, have been Hamilton. Read over the weekend account in *Grauniad* of man of 73 getting, and dying from, cancer (written by his daughter). If I am rejected … General gloom.

Fear God, and stay calm …

But why, incidentally, won't Jane pray? Too frightened of it working, I suspect.

---

[1] 'Thornit', a patent medicine from Miss P Bett, Thornham, Norfolk.
[2] Selected columns from Peter Bradshaw's pastiche Diary as they appeared in the *Evening Standard*, now published as a paperback.

EMT   *Monday, 14 December*

Heading now into pre-Christmas week with the election to the 22 Executive and the 'Clarkson' show behind me.[1]

Elections ok, so much so that I would like the results, the numbers that is beside the names, published. As I said to John Bercow these are the only (beside Parliamentary committee scrutinies) posts in the Party that have true democratic legitimacy. The whips have woken up to this and now try and get their men in, as a matter of routine, to guard against 'truth' in the coming year (this year particularly). So we have to put up with Jacqui Lait[2] whose matronly good living-ness got her through.

Wednesday, 16 December

Left Big Red slightly 'skew-whiff' (spelling?) in Piccadilly as the [Albany] courtyard was full up with loathsome, idle-rich up for Christmas shopping, discreet 'office parties' etc. So this morning my own internal alarm clock woke me at 4.50 and I dressed in softies over the pidgys and went down; as I started it I was aware of a strange, youthful, walker-of-the-night leaning on the pedestrian railing and attempting to catch, or rather pinion my eye. Plainly he thought I was stealing it and wished to 'bond' rapidly before going off to a squat.

Now it is an hour later and I am enjoyably on my third cup of Irish Breakfast tea (the best since the great Pakistani package of 1987).

These last days have been somewhat muddled, with much 'exposure'. I have been uneasy (lightly so) about health matters.

---

[1] AC had appeared on a 'sofa' show hosted by Jeremy Clarkson, the motoring writer.
[2] Jacqui Lait, MP for Beckenham since November 1997 (Hastings and Rye, 1992–97).

Intermittently throaten to the extent of being gravely plus upper-respiratory early symptoms. Almost a head cold being 'dealt with' by immunisation established after the great three-weeker. For a good deal of the time this makes me depressed, or worse, and I think of my shrinking life expectancy. The approach of the end of my 'leave period' and back to the Scarpe when I go through Purgatory before d.o.w. in base hospital and being reborn – as what? Please not as an orphan, or 'pet' animal. (Talking of which, I took time off to go and cheer up a tiny group last night who were standing by Barry Horne placards astride New Palace Yard entrance.[1] I'm afraid they were un-attractive, not to say dysfunctional. And yet the animals are so important. I am prepared to take risks for them.) More cheer-fully, did a book programme last night with Pat Hollis – still pretensions of attractiveness – and Philip Gould.[2] I was prepared to be objectionable to PG but he won my heart in the Green Room by saying 'why don't you take charge? You should take over …' of the Tory shambles.

Earlier the 22 had assembled to hear Hague. Still pretty dread-ful. Baroness Elles,[3] who was opposite me, looked at him the entire time with a strange expression of distaste and contempt that reminded me of Mama. At the end there was *spastic* desk-banging.

At the start that old trouble-maker Keith Simpson[4] tried to criticise my 'naughty' teasing on Clarkson. 'It's not a current affairs programme', I said, 'but a Sunday evening chat show.' He

---

[1] Barry Horne, animal rights campaigner, who had just ended 84 days' hunger strike while serving an 18-year sentence for arson.

[2] Baroness [Patricia] Hollis of Heigham, the government's social security spokesman in the Lords since 1997, author of a biography of Jennie Lee, one of the creators of the Open University and wife of Aneurin Bevan; Philip Gould, strategic and polling adviser to Labour Party. His book, *The Unfinished Revolution: How the Modernisers Saved the Labour Party* had been published in October.

[3] Baroness Elles (life peer 1972), former Conservative foreign affairs spokesman in the Lords, MEP Thames Valley, 1979–89.

[4] Keith Simpson, MP for Mid-Norfolk since 1997, Special Adviser to the Secretary of State for Defence 1988–90, and a former lecturer in war studies at Sandhurst.

changed the subject. How many other Tory MPs would be asked on? And would they not be wet blankets, or embarrassing? Ann Widdecombe is now taking bookings for March 2000. This made me feel terribly tired when we talked about it. She and I (Hague excepting, for particular reasons) are the only two Tories who can fill rooms. So over Christmas I must *think*, and plan how to advance. At least two walks to Beechborough?

First thing must be a proper Question schedule. Phased speaking engagements. Briefing journalists. Am I doing this a year late? I suppose so; like (and because) delivery of BB was a year late so for the first six months of this year I was frantic, immersed in the Library. 'I have my friends' (Neville). Cheered by the 22 Exec I must be graver also. Papers and lectures. A Pamphlet? I've a feeling that 'western man is superficially content, but oppressed by forces of which he is aware, but cannot easily identify'.

It's wonderful, as I write this I feel full of energy, intellectual vigour. It's 6.37 and I have been up for an hour and a half. Just thought of a sly device. I will wear a dinner jacket to Dr Munday's [reception]; this making it look as if we 'have to go on' which I did on Monday when I took Jane to Archer party. He really rather sweet and plucking as he showed his most recent acquisition – a Tenniel drawing of Dizzy slumped on the bench. He does have taste, Jeffrey. And it is elusive. Alas his status sinks. The room was 'B' list as Jane immediately noted. We went up in the lift with Basil Feldman,[1] ran into Geoffrey Howe as were leaving. 'Going on to somewhere smarter,' he observed.

EMT kitchen   *Friday, 18 December*

Rose early, pleased at the approaching hols. But could do no more, once tea made, than sit glazedly. A mile of tasks. Yesterday, exhausted after being 'on the go' continuously. Should have

---

[1] Lord [Basil] Feldman, holder of many senior posts in Conservative Party.

asked PM 'so one bombs Iraq for three days ... then what happens?' But didn't quite have the *go*. [Douglas] Hogg,[1] on my right, called; then Soames pompous, but incoherent.

Scooped up a mass of folders and signing ullage and took the 8 p.m. train signing most of the way.

Saturday, 19 December

Bratton sold at auction yesterday. Jane was crossing the bridge, just by the Bratton 'box' implant when a message – quite calm and jolly – reached her. So that chapter is now closed. I was apprehensive that the room (the Red Lion at Okehampton) would be empty. But it was sold to a man from North Lew who hadn't even been inside (saw it that morning) for £167,000. Almost forty years ago that I went there in the blue Olds '88' on a bank holiday Monday in order to exchange contracts – yes, in Okehampton. Estate of Leroy Fielding for £2,500.

The whole Bratton sequence is so filled with *ifs*. If we hadn't been so hard-up that we had to sell the field ('Cream of Bratton') to Hortop, I was ready to buy the connecting vicarage strip, possibly later bits of Eversfield. Fortunately we did always have the châlet and wintered there. *If* Jane hadn't miscarried/had to work so hard when still drained by having Lilian. I remember coming back in the blue 220 after being in Germany (when I first met 'D'[2]) and thinking I must have cancer of the gum (in fact an abscess). And, particularly, first 'calling' the little boys in their blue cot.

Now I have just enough liquidity to 'carry' me (DV) until the Giorgione millennium exhibition – if it ever takes place. In all probability I will set up a 'small' sale to try and pull another 100 or so.

---

[1] Douglas Hogg, MP for Sleaford and North Hykeham since 1997 (Grantham 1979–97).
[2] David Cornwell (aka John le Carré).

My plan would be to:

£90 – Coutts MM (60)

£30 – Barclays Classic (30)

£30 – adding to the family holding of Coats – at present going down again. And, incredibly unhealthy chart.

My leg 'ulcer' has very slowly healed to a tiny pink spot, half the size of the original 'lesion'. I remain 'throaten' – now seven weeks intermittently. Especially in a.m. and when voice is 'tired' in the evening. I must say, though, that practically everyone in the House of Commons is mildly, or totally, throaten at the moment. We are, though, getting into 'see your doctor' territory.

Now I must stop to restore some order in the dining room as Christmas is approaching and the whole house is full of lovely greenery and decorations.

Saltwood Tower Office   *Boxing Day*

The Amazings left this morning, squeezing most deftly all their belongings plus two 'show' baby box trees, plus all manner of presents and groceries into their 4-door Golf sedan – with the two little boys confidently strapped into their 'space-tracker' safety seats.

When first they arrived my heart did sink a little – 'how the hell are we going to get through this?' – three nights etc, and I am getting worried about little Albert, the princeling, who seemed peaky and chesty and easy to tears. In fact it was fine, and Albert 'recovered' amazingly (sic) and ran about and climbed things while Archibald was benignly *Winston* at all times. Now a delicious sense of relaxation – a couple of non-dies (tomorrow and Bank Holiday) then a week 'off'. Then a firm, but engaging week of 'duties', but no movement outside the walls. I won't at present, think of scheduling, or look at my orange PFD[1] diary.

---

[1] Peters, Fraser and Dunlop, AC's literary agents, who had for more years than he could recall provided him with his annual office engagement diary.

But I would like this mini-cloud to lift so that I can think of the *grand perspectif*, how to be 'un homme serieux'. Last night a nice (though somewhat croaky) late night talk in the red study after Jane had gone up to bed — she has a dreadful throat and dry cough at present. The Amazings were alert about politics and the state of the Party. But at no time did they say, as an adjunct to 'who is there?' — 'why don't you do it?' or 'Do you think you have got a chance?'

If I can clear up my health (and I'm afraid this means going to Nick Page for a blood count) then I can establish my schedule of tabling, asking, working up my thesis: 'western man is everywhere threatened by forces of which he is aware, but cannot identify'. This is most easily done with a couple of glasses of Lynch 62 in the hand. Slowly start to incorporate into speeches.

Boxing Monday, 28 December

Soames rang last night. We talked and I felt better because together we have time-warped. Could have been Oliver Lyttelton[1] and Julian [Amery]. Lovely to do this from inside. But the Tory party has in fact changed out of recognition. We're not 'new Tories', we are the remains of a beaten, scattered rabble which has in large part discarded its weapons. What we need is a revived guerrilla army that will start a long march and live on the captured equipment of its enemies.

---

[1] Oliver Lyttelton, later Viscount Chandos, served in Churchill's War Cabinet.

Saltwood Green Room   *New Year's Eve*

Full-blown head cold. Most unusual so soon after (four-fifths) recovery from upper-respiratory throaten that went on for eight weeks. I sit here gasping and blowing my nose. It damages eyes, and diminishes concentration and energy. Naturally I would feel that I have still got time to recover before return before, even, the TV crew come down on Thursday. So, just a little uneasy at this calendine turning point. Now I have to go and print/compose (on the grey machine which I loathe) letters to Brodie's (for James) and Sotheby's (for Jane).

1999

The first time I have written 99. Low water; heavily upper-respiratory and uro-genitary – often quite insistent and then back pain. This has affected work output of course. Slowly, oh-so-slowly, I am eroding the cliff of paper on the Green Room table – but after trying the device of recategorising into 'file' and 'urgent attention'. Many boxes are extraordinarily and bizarrely mixed and muddled, and occasional nuggets surface. A clear and orderly breakthrough by Monday evening – but is this feasible? We promised ourselves not to 'work' on Sunday. All too clearly I see the approach of that familiar situation – 'Anything for one more day …'

Particularly important this week is to work up my pamphlet, but this means going to the Garden House, ideally with a glass of good claret.

And then there are these basic headings where I must make progress – Trust structure (I have an insurance demand for £16,000 for Jane, but haven't really any idea how it all works); insurance, household and cars; and the car folder itself.

For the first time this morning I have the pages of the orange PFD book to look forward. Hold it. And we both agreed that we are not yet strong enough to put up and fill in the new '99 chart.

Monday, 4 January

We had a two week 'holiday' in prospect, a lovely open unencumbered stretch holed up in the Mains. Now, just past the half-way point we should be full of enthusiasm and returning vigour. Of course this was the Monday when the holiday actually ended, it was simply that we had intended to stay at Saltwood, 'receive engagements' here instead of travelling. Now, though, it's arrived, and we are, arguably, in worse shape than when we settled back – that delicious moment when the Amazings had packed up and left and we sat by the Green Room fire on Boxing Day, joined by the dogs who had been excluded for three days. For a start, we have both of us remained chesty throughout. I ran through full-blown head cold, now in its tertiary, phlegmy-cough phase. I would sleep nine hours plus (quite often unbroken), but we're exhausted still. During the day I can get sweats and also 'go' genito-urethrine. Final blow – sweet Janey put her back 'out' last night, this morning could hardly move at all. She's so sweet-natured, never really grumbles – but has been looking decidedly pale and drawn of late. 'Still,' I said, 'we could either or both of us be coming back in an ambulance from an accident on the M25.'

DV.

EMT   *Tuesday, 5 January*

Still wet and close. I am chesty and unhealthily on-the-step. This morning to Jane's astonishment I dressed before EMT. Semi-conditioned to 'Dave-at-eight' although we have in fact got the whole of this week.

Last night my usual one-hour conversation with DD, burgundy balloon in the hand. The Labour Party are being buffeted. Whelan has gone – but under odd circumstances. To Alastair [Campbell] earlier I had said, 'praise him, don't fire him.' That's three quite important ships sunk in a week[1] – all while Blair himself is on holiday still.

What can one make of all this? We can't claim credit for it;

---

[1] Peter Mandelson, MP for Hartlepool since 1992, and New Labour's 'master of spin', had been forced to resign as Trade and Industry Secretary, following revelations of a loan (to purchase a house) made to him by Geoffrey Robinson, who had also had to resign his position as Paymaster General. Charlie Whelan, press secretary to Gordon Brown, the Chancellor of the Exchequer, was blamed for leaking documents relating to the loan.

there's no credit around, anyway. We mustn't gloat, and I prefer the line that it diminishes the whole of Public Life and is to be deplored. It is/should be cowardly Labour while we (should) seem to be political and crisp. Some hope! The Party can only think in terms of wankers like Willetts[1] coming forward with ideas for clipping the benefit and education policies 'at the margin'. I am not applying, enough, though to what I should be myself doing.

I turned off the lights on the tree for the last time yesterday; what a beautiful tall specimen, short of the height of the lower hall by 2-3 metres only, and like Wolf [the Führer] was filled with sadness and foreboding also.

EMT   *Thursday, 7 January*

A *nuit cassé*. Awake from 11.45 till past 3 on and off. After I came back from tinkling second time (2.30-ish) Jane said, 'are you ok?' 'Not really,' I said. I felt illish and sub-prostatic. I sweat hugely at night. During the day I am feeling incredibly tired. Yesterday we went out to the Garden House and while Jane and Eddie were wrestling (from time-to-time literally) with a tap in the kitchen I sat at the desk feeling utterly exhausted. I read parts of Graham's book on Churchill – very good, almost excellent.[2] Made me feel sad for my own. Jane, when I said I felt illish, said again, and rightly, you're trying to do too much. One coined:

1997 – 'A ticket back to heaven.'

1998 – 'You may be too late.'

1999 – 'All he does is whine.'

---

[1] David Willetts, MP for Havant since 1992, opposition front bench spokesman on education and employment since 1998.
[2] Graham Stewart's *Burying Caesar: Churchill, Chamberlain and the Battle for the Tory Party*. Stewart, AC's researcher on *The Tories*, had been given the use of the Garden House at weekends.

Sandling train   *Monday, 10 January*

Was in excited form; hair wash, looking 'beautiful', clean shirt,
pressed suit, etc. 'First day back at school.' Then Big Red totally flat
battery, plus strange grey TV-tuner lying 'prominently' on the boot
floor close to the little Lucas charger. Caught by Penny Newell
(wife of former Lord Mayor and daughter of Paddy Ridsdale[1]) for
unanswered – I've never heard of it – invitation for 10 February.
Black tie. Greatly crowded by all these invitations/functions.

I do hope this isn't the year of setbacks, when (at last) I still
not get to feel, but to show my age.

Later

London seemed almost deserted; traffic light, an icy wind
scouring the streets. In deep gloom I walked to Parliament
Street. I felt tired and old and barely yesterday it seemed I had
been in high spirits (though exhausted) at the prospect of the
Christmas hols. The frightful constricting feeling that comes
from a blocked-out chart (with more waiting 'to fill in the
corners') plus an uneasy feeing that when actually I do get
a release ticket I won't quite be myself any more, to put it
lightly.

My prostatic-urethric symptoms are now more or less
constant, which is quite an acceleration from, say, December
when they were intermittent. A fairly constant strain always in
the groin after peeing, plus a hard to define feeling that is not
quite right. I fear I must ring Nick Page and have a blood and
significantly PSA test. Then it comes out. 'Oh dear' – what do I
do? I certainly don't want to be cut up and mucked about. I
dread the leaked (as it is bound to be) publicity signifying the
end of the old Al – the Clarkson Show prancer. Can't do it.
Can't do it quietly because (a) an MP, and (b) the constituency.
Have I got time to be still compos while I consolidate the wills,

---

[1] Lady Ridsdale, DBE 1991, chairman, Conservative Wives Association, 1978–91,
married to Sir Julian Ridsdale, MP for Harwich February 1954–1992.

and get everything in order (ugh!). (Just rang Nick Page – on holiday, pity, but am booked in for 10 a.m. on Thursday).

Yesterday I went to the Forward Look committee at 5.15 – a bore this function, at a slightly awkward time. Mainly fantasy strangely coloured by 'we're-still-in-government-really' aura. People trying to score good-boy points, but the whole thing decidedly tactical – if that is not putting it too high. It's Hague, who now uneasily sits in, hears every suggestion, or invitation to pronounce policy, or even attitude, who just swallows and looks away – e.g. Angela Browning[1] made a very important point about Iraq, the unfinished business etc. Presumably Hague is entrapped by some Privy Council deal so that in return for snippets of info he doesn't make Party criticisms? Old trick. I raised the question of the EU Parliament. Surely we should at least address the question of whether we want to 'call for' (six) individual Commissioners to be accountable/sackable? Do we want the EU Parliament to be more effective, or not? Possibly 'not'. But we must be clear.

Later the Sybil. Simon Heffer.[2] People shouting. Shaun W said Hague should not have been away while the Labour Party was getting into all those messes. Shaun is the most resolute critic of Hague in the room, always. David Howell,[3] as often, was impressive. David Davis had a ghastly cold and I found myself sitting next to him. Damn, Damn!

House Library   *Wednesday a.m., 13 January*

A lovely crisp day, I cursed and muttered as I dressed – could have taken another two hours in bed (slept without waking

---

[1] Angela Browning, MP for Tiverton and Honiton since 1992.
[2] Simon Heffer, now political columnist on the *Daily Mail*; his official biography of Enoch Powell had been well received.
[3] Lord [David] Howell, life peer 1997, MP for Guildford 1966–97. Energy and Transport Secretary in Margaret Thatcher's first government.

from 11.5 to 7, but none the better for it). An extraordinary free run in the Porsche, got from Albany to Norman Shaw lights [at Parliament Square] in under three minutes (!). Yesterday I felt dreadful. Doom-panicked in the morning and rang Nick Page – back from holiday, so when I see him tomorrow he will be (his first appointment) bronzed and youthful ...

A condemned man, I trailed out to Fulham Broadway to 'attend', or re-attend the Chelsea village inquiry. In the council chamber I sweated at intervals, took my pulse, felt flushes. My rate would not go below 78 – sometimes hovered above. I am still harbouring germs.

But when I got back here how lovely and enclosing the Palace is! I took a piece of cake, cheese and a pot of tea and settled behind the screen (Janet Fookes' position) in the tea room and started to reread Routledge for the extra work the *Observer* want.[1] Last night I saw Mandelson in the corridor. He was white and shiny and distrait. Had lost weight. Ah, politics!

Saltwood   *Saturday, 16 January*

In limbo. But after Nick Page's consultation I slept eight hours for the first time since Scotland.

Bratton money in and earnings building, no o/d (except Barclays), calm about cars, still getting media attention, looking forward to *Observer* tomorrow. If PSA okay must really devote myself to a strategic plan, then talking to Anji Hunter[2] and Alastair. DV. Before the consultation I whispered to God that if it can be done this will be the *year of dedication*. If it fails then spectator, or buffer.

---

[1] In the light of Peter Mandelson's resignation, AC had been asked to revise his review of *Mandy: the Unauthorised Biography* by Paul Routledge. He called it, 'that most tedious of all literary phenomena, the virtual biography'.

[2] Anji Hunter, the Prime Minister's personal assistant.

I do like life, and am eternally grateful even if it stops tomorrow — or today.

House Library   *Monday, 18 January*

A draining morning with the Aon man (Moffat). Jane out to Tom Bates and was told she needed a mammogram. Poor darling! This made her low, but very sweet and quiet.

I drove up oh-so-unassertively in the Porsche. Went straight (in softies) to Parliament Street and cleared/signed complete folder. 'Withdrawn' but — therapeutically — in bare feet. The task done, and preparing to go across to the House, I suddenly realised that I felt terribly homesick. I miss Janey at these times, and am sad that effectively we only get one holiday a year — a long period when we can plan things and go on the wing. And only two days, if we are lucky, out of each week. Which means that each year out of 365 we only have 130-ish to each other. So how many days have we got left — a thousand? Perhaps far fewer. I hardly dare write the PSA, for myself:

> Under 3 — irrepressible
> Under 4 — confident
> 4.2 – 6 — worst of all – DECISIONS
> Over 6 — so what? Just plot what happens; but played, of
> course, into gloom and apprehension.

And yet must always remember these last two fabulous years — it's now exactly two years.

House Library   *Tuesday, 19 January*

(Still) no letters so had to ring Nick P using the little door-phone in the Library corridor and, briefly, thinking that I might faint if the news was really bad. In fact it was ludicrous: nought-point-five. My health *in the clear*; the sheer, total delight of daffodils and birdsong and lengthening days; the relaxed enjoyment of planning jaunts and trips and going 'on the wing'.

But there is the obverse. I have now got a clear two years to make my mark. Perhaps practically too late starting, although BB was useful to have 'behind' me. A heavier handicap is all this ludicrous boxed paper that eats into one at Saltwood when I should be philosophising on my screen. Just at present I am totally exultant, and dreamy. Must somehow get away to pray at the weekend, and Beechborough, too.

Saltwood   *Saturday, 23 January*

I have been upper-respiring for nearly three months on and (v occasionally) off. So although I should be *relancé* by the astounding clearance from Nick Page – actually set the dial back further than when first measured – I am very creaky, and enervated. I glaze over and shirk and flinch from obvious tasks. This morning incredibly frustrated trying to make cars respond. Batteries, carburettor needle sticking and petrol flood, damp terminals, etc etc. Quietly I went into the family garden and attacked fruiting bodies. A slightly petty piece in *The Times* by Matthew Parris attacking me for my 'love' of animals. This is the third time he has been unpleasant about me since I came back. Triggered, I suppose, by my – much acclaimed – Mandelson review. Essentially, all Parris is interested in is homosexual politics; the emancipation of homosexuals. Hey, just a minute, I thought they were emancipated? No, no, I mean really emancipated; so that unpleasant, overt heteros like Alan Clark are seen in a minority, and a slightly disgusting one to be racially discriminated against. Anyhow, I doubt it will have done me any harm. But this year I must attack. Opening say, 'This can't go on.' I attribute no blame, I do not seek to personalise the problem, but the Party is in mortal danger. If we went into a general election now could lose another eighteen seats. And that, actually, would be the end of the Conservative Party.

House Library   *Wednesday, 27 January*

I am wretched – why – it's so unfair.

Still going upper-respiratory (*again*) on Thursday as I got home. Held it off during the weekend, but deteriorated on Monday with *Willie's eye* – so postponed 'Blakeway'.[1] Slept poorly that night – though not as poorly as last night – and weeping so profusely on Tuesday morning that walked, 9-ish, to Spalton. Diverted, at some distance in time to F[oculist] in Wimpole Street. He amiable, if anything preferable to Sp., almost too laid back. Gave me chlorphormical drops which I got from a nearby Pakistani chemist who gravely showed a picture of himself with Omar Sharif (now somewhat portly and cum a triple bypass).[2] I seem to have deteriorated during that day. Voice went at the Courtfield and Earls Court AGM. People are *definitely* less friendly now. 'Where's the bright, ebullient Alan Clark?' asked John Major at dinner. I announced my 'flu' and was pleased to note that both he and Tom King moved away to more distantly laid places.

Slept intermittently, woke feeling cold (but not shivery) almost replay of that last afflicton. Made a little 'Ceylon' tea, inhaled from Vick and boiling water in the eggtimer saucepan. This morning temp 99.8°, pulse 89+, gobbets of green. No voice at all (it had gone speaking to Jane the previous evening). Left eye now also inevitably Willie so popped chlorphormical into that one, also.

---

[1] 'Willie's eye', named after the rheumy eyes of William Whitelaw, former MP, Minister and Margaret Thatcher's deputy; Blakeway, an independent TV production company.
[2] Omar Sharif, Egyptian-born actor, whose films include *Lawrence of Arabia* and *Funny Girl*.

Tower Office   *Saturday a.m., 30 January*

And still this strange virus shifts its territory. Last night, fourth
in a row, 'chesty' and phlegm-bound. At 3.30 found difficulty
tinkling, thought that the 'germs' had shifted location to the
waterworks (as in May '75) v depressed and muck sweat. Then
remembered that Nick's letter had said urine test (last week)
'... had shown no indication of possibility.' Tinkled splashingly,
more or less at once.

Expectations disappointed. ... Matthew Parris brilliant,
but highly unsettling piece the previous day.[1] I've let a whole
year go past.[2] BB, which should have given me status, hasn't
really.

In the meantime the Party is in total dumps. People are
simply losing interest – period. The climate, and the scenery, is
shifting. For some reason I don't have the energy really to
tackle this. Most colleagues (like most constituents) 'don't
want to know'.

It is 11.30 a.m. on a grey January day. On the morning walk
I looked up at the Mains (we walk around the moat now, in
order to avoid contact between the dogs and the public), said to
Jane, 'For four years all I wanted to do was get back through the
bulkhead door that has no handle; now what I would like best
is to settle at Saltwood, order my affairs, restore the Great
Library and study, travel and drink good wine.'

---

[1] *The Times*, 28 January, headed 'It's time to panic: I don't know what the Tories are
about. And neither, it seems, do they.'
[2] A few days before, AC had asked, 'And when am I going to get started?' Mike
White [*Guardian* political editor] said, 'Look at Ann Widdecombe. She just kicked
the door in ...' As a further alternative AC confided to his diary (10 January 1999),
'My game plan, if I don't break out in some way in the next 18 months, is to get
Alastair to fix my being Speaker in the next House.'

House Library   *Tuesday p.m., 2 February*

Last night we went to the Christie's dinner for the Monet Exhibition. All the paintings beautiful, dazzling you could say and all cleaned (save the beautiful fog-bound view of the Palace of Westminster and the seagulls) to the same sanitation standard. The two of the Contarini Palazzo in Venice, some of the water-lilies, particularly those with the willow branches reflecting, were incredible.

On the way up I had started to develop a sore throat. How could I be getting a sore throat now, at three weeks plus intermittent 'upper respiratory condition'. And to think that when it started I just thought it was the ordinary flu-cold, had my day 'on the floor of Mother Teresa's waiting room' and expected the recovery pattern to set in thereafter.

However, this morning I read the accounts of SAD [seasonal affective disorder], and cheered up a bit. Sparkled in the tearoom. And today a wonderful Parliamentary occasion, the House of Lords debate[1] with speeches from Ted, John Major, Robert Marshall-Andrews[2] and Rick Shepherd. Ted spoke, personified gravitas. Good voice still, carried well, miles ahead of Enoch who started in his seventies to go 'piping'. Yes, I should have spoken too, but had no time to collect my theme, nor energy to sustain it.

Tuesday, 9 February

I am always quiet and melancholic-reflective after Shaun's dinners. Bed at midnight and half woke several times with v slight feeling that something was 'physically wrong' (like being

---

[1] To debate the government Bill to reform the Lords, bringing to an end the hereditary peerage's right to sit in the House.
[2] Robert Marshall-Andrews, a QC, Labour MP for Medway since 1997.

precursor of flu). Oh-so-gloomy on waking. What is the point? The Conservative Party is a husk, its place has been taken. I am old now, and my enthusiasm wanes easily.

Dinner was the usual shouting match. Willie Rees-Mogg just the limit, bit deaf now with intellectual hair cut.

Before going in Tapsell had shouted: 'I want Alan Clark to lead the Conservative Party' and on the way out Willie said: 'You could be a kind of Reagan, really,' and I reminded him of his favourable article after I was selected.

Drove back (risk-takingly[1]) in the Little Silver. I had Positano steps coming down the B staircase [Albany], just controlled it, then halted and spat at the 4 St James's Street Island and realised I had to go to Brooks's and essay a vomit.

I am not myself the morning after Shaun's dinners.

Saltwood   *Friday, 12 February*

Memorial service today for Alan Hardy.[2] Saltwood Church absolutely overflowing. Robin Leigh-Pemberton through to Ann and Bob [Felce] – although no sign of Eddy Rothschild.[3] Reg [Humphriss] uttered a pleasing biography of Alan, who was a big man with an *enormous* stomach, one of the largest I have ever seen. He was exceptionally rich, owning much land (a small part of which he recently sold) and having inherited from his old father, 'Skinflint' Hardy, his beautiful and exclusive gardens. He married Carolyn, a beautiful and lively student of Wye Agricultural College who rode a 250cc BSA 'Bantam' motorbike.

Afterwards, walking in the woodland, Jane asked what I wanted 'in' my own memorial service. The first time the subject has come up. Originally I said (post *Diaries*) I just want to

---

[1] At some later date AC has added an alternative in green ink: 'oh-so-ill-advisedly'.
[2] Alan Hardy, local landowner with exceptional collection of rhododendrons and azaleas.
[3] Edmund Rothschild, a senior member of the banking family and a keen gardener.

disappear, like *Zapata*.[1]

I suppose if I am in Parliament still I will have to have one at St Margaret's, W[estminster]. Must have a choir, I said, to sing the hymns and 'God be in my head ... and at my departing' (probably at end). Also the hymn 'Guide me, O thou great Redeemer' and 'He leadeth me' (psalm 23 sung as a hymn). All prayers and lessons in the Old Form. Lesson: *Genesis* – 'In the Beginning ...' New Testament:'the star on the edge of Galilee'. Reading: the Housman lament from Enoch's, with an introduction by me to be read by James. Who shall do the address? Then it all disperses.

EMT, B5   *Tuesday, 16 February*

Returning to the House I was desperately hungry.[2] Cranborne was in the Gallery and I tried to persuade him to come out to dinner at once. He couldn't. Soames, always ready for a nosh, agreed to get a taxi for 7.10 and we went to Wilton's where he paid for the food and I the wine (bott Montrachet, not v good at £65; a Volnay for £55). Usual discourse; grumbling. Party absolutely no idea what it's doing or where it is going. At the end Nicholas was Churchillian. As David Davis said, when a short time ago I told him 'I'm on the verge of making a declaration ...', 'Who's going over the top with you?'

This morning I felt odd when I rose. It is a lovely crisp day. But I don't throw back the bedclothes any more and spring up as I used to for twenty years in here. I'm 70 of course, and this morning I had mild alcoholic poisoning. Yes, I'm *ok*. Low testosterone is a tiny price to pay (when occurring naturally) for a PSA reading of 0.5.

---

[1] Zapata, the early 20th-century Mexican revolutionary, was shot dead, but his ghost was said to return. AC at one point in the early 1970s affected a Zapata-like moustache (see photograph *Diaries: Into Politics*).
[2] AC had been in a TV studio.

This is an easy week except for the absurd and ludicrous 'Listening to Britain' session on Wednesday evening (contrived of course to clash with the 1922 committee). Papers in order, none. A nice long weekend at Saltwood. I must go for a week rebuilding the fabric a little. But really I need three weeks for that – Zermatt or the Highlands. And that is impossible. This year I will know whether or not I 'miss the bus' and just concentrate on the heritage. Trusts, maintenance and inventories. A dear old patriarch.

I read Chips a little. Exactly 61 years ago Anthony Eden resigned and Chips, to his huge delight, was made PPS to Rab. He was 41 and for him it was, I suppose, the equivalent of being Minister for Trade.[1] Whitehall in those days being smaller, and the Magic Circle far, far tighter. This was the moment when Chamberlain made his bad decision – to go for the 'friendship' of Italy. He should have seen things globally, but (comparably to John Major) he simply did not have the confidence to set up a great carve-up conference plus backing it with selective re-armament.

Tower Office, Saltwood   *Saturday, 27 February*

Yesterday I was nearly killed – nearly killed myself, rather – accelerating hard on a greasy road in Big Red in (as it were) Bilsington. The great vehicle slewed and skidded. I found myself going head-on at a truck sixty feet away, lifted off, thank God did not panic or brake, skidded past. The whole incident over in 3-4 seconds. It would have been a pure accident. Dead. But a 'mystery'. Dead straight road, head on crash, etc. Spared. Like being spared to go back to H of C. But am I anyway now doing

---

[1] Chips on 2 March 1938: 'Of course I cannot believe it, I, Chips at the Foreign Office.' Rab Butler had been made Under-Secretary of State for Foreign Affairs, with Lord Halifax as the new Foreign Secretary. AC was appointed Minister for Trade in 1986.

enough? Jane cautioned me against 'creep-back' on Thursday. Plus, for the first time in our lives we found ourselves talking seriously about accounts. Jane rather sadly said what does she do, how does she see Saltwood after I've died and my earning power has gone?

EMT, B5   *Tuesday, 2 March*

For some time I have been shirking a full considerative entry – one that faces the fact that I am not *doing* enough, or my profile is sinking. Last night Tony Bevins[1] cautioned me against 'shooting' until the Euro-elections are out of the way ('otherwise you will do yourself damage – perhaps irreparable'). A bore, and only four weeks of summer left then. *But ...*

Then, at dinner, Michael Spicer[2] came in with the news that automatic reselection is now in the rules for everyone. Full meeting, all members eligible, secret ballot etc. What a draining prospect! Another giant tour de force in KTH. Also a cramping of my style (for the remaining two years) as a rebel standard-bearer. Back in Easton territory[3] after all (as of course is the CCO 'intention').

House Library   *Wednesday, 3 March*

Yesterday I had my AGM in Chelsea Old Town Hall.

A straight victory. Virtually no opposition. I am dominant, ran

---

[1] Anthony Bevins, the son of Reg Bevins, working-class Postmaster General in Harold Macmillan's government, had been twice political editor of *The Independent* (1986–93 and 1996–98); he then moved to the *Express*.

[2] Michael Spicer had been on the 22 Executive since 1997.

[3] AC is remembering his clashes with the party organisation at Plymouth Sutton, where a leading light was Mrs R. M. (Betty) Easton.

a joke combining wind-power and Jeffrey Archer through an oh-what-a-good-boy-was-I recital to a fine peroration.

At the 'President's Party' afterwards people congratulated me. One man said he 'nearly' (sic) said 'why don't you take the helm?'(as it were). I drank a glass of delicious iced white wine in the kitchen and was effusive. Janey drove me back to the House to vote, then to Albany. A hint of 'that's that, then'.

I have really no excuse now not to achieve this year. Health, wealth, seemingly. But was exhausted, listless.

At lunch today in the Members Dining Room John M[ajor] said how uncharacteristic of Blair to chuck PM's Questions twice a week. How they used to hog our time. Every Saturday was blighted by Tuesday. The middle of the week blasted out. Thursday practically the only 'free time'.

EMT   *Friday, 5 March*

Last night on *Question Time,*[1] which I have been trying to avoid for months, in Maidstone. Probably went as well as could be expected. Asked about sex on TV I said 'They're only actors. It's simulated sex, isn't it ... Myself I prefer the real thing.' A charming, civilised black man said how sex should be pinnacle and when I responded and deplored the yob culture, said how footballers and pop stars were 'role models'. Dimbleby got agitated and said 'Role models etc ... Do you consider yourself a political role model?' 'That's for others to judge,' I said – and the entire audience clapped delightedly!

I was buoyed up by my 'triumph'. I haven't seen the tape yet, and may have been *too oggly*.

Last night, after lights, I hopped out of bed again and prayed – just pure thanks, for the fact that now I am an MP again, and

---

[1] *Question Time,* BBC 1 equivalent of Radio 4's *Any Questions?*; David Dimbleby (b. 1938) had been presenting it since 1994.

for the safest seat in the country. While last time I was on to him I was wilful and pluckingly defiant.

I had a long talk with Dimbleby at dinner. Usual beef about BBC management. He would like to have been Director-General, now says he is too old (!). But a pleasant man really.

Saturday, 6 March

A lovely Saltwood day. The wind is unpleasant, cold rain that is almost liquid snowflake. Yesterday I spent polishing a hostile review of George Walden's 'memoir'[1] (and my instinct instantly proved right, because just at the end I caught a most typical, and (designed to be) unpleasant passage about myself). Yes, I do very vaguely recall doing a *Today* programme with him. Apparently I didn't 'speak' while we were waiting. Sounds typical, listening, as I have always thought him an ill-mannered waste.

We spent most of the day in Papa's study in the Library block, Jane painting the wall, I 'sorting' books and Liberoning the leather surface of the great desk. That's a marvellous room, such lovely things. I have hung the 'Babars' behind the big Bratton sideboard which has now displaced the big, old, ill portrait of my father taken in 1978.

As (per) usual, all I want to do is stay down here. Just a few lightning forays. The weekend gone by so fast and at present I am very tired in the mornings and sleep on after Jane has got out of bed.

---

[1] George Walden, former diplomat, MP for Buckingham 1983–97. He called his memoir, *Lucky George*. AC in his review in *The Times* wrote: 'part memoir, part autobiography, part half-baked docu-fiction novelette.'

EMT   *Monday, 8 March*

Lovely fine morning, and fall in atmospheric temperature so
that you can see your breath, which hangs in the air. I thought
of little T.O. and gloomily half worried that I am getting more
like him. Sometimes just standing, unable to remember what I
am going to do. One of the dogs' towels is white with black
blobs on it, and when it lies on the floor by the Aga it could,
out of the corner of the eye, be Tom.

Tower Office   *Thursday, 11 March*

Today I screeched with pain and frustration at being unable to
find the insurance certificate for Big Red, so can't tax it. Everywhere I rummaged I found *needy paperwork*. Had meant to come
down last night but was – as usual between 5 and 7 p.m.
Connex'd[1] at Charing Cross; unhappy travellers ('customers') on
the concourse; inaudible, but bellowing high speech-rate
announcements; unhappy and unrecognisable trains appearing
one-at-a-time at unfamiliar platforms.

  Why do I do all these speaking engagements (still)? Plus endless sundry appearances and journalism. Partly for the money,
yes; the odd monkey and grand accumulate at almost the rate
they were doing in '92–3. Partly also to 'keep my name forward'.
In the tearoom queue yesterday afternoon I said to Gerald
Kaufman,[2] 'Thank you for your article bolstering my leadership
bid, which will be irresistible once the Conservative Party is
down to a dozen seats (there being only seven which we hold
by a majority of more than 50%).' He turned and looked at me

---

[1] Connex South East won the franchise to run train services out of Charing Cross
   including the Dover line. It quickly gained a reputation for unreliability, perhaps
   no worse than its British Rail Network South-East predecessor.
[2] Gerald Kaufman, MP (Labour) for Manchester Gorton since 1983 (Manchester
   Ardwick 1970–83).

very seriously, 'Alan, I honestly believe that a successful leadership by you would be the only way left for the Conservative party to survive.'

I am pleased by this. And by MacShane, who said, 'Why don't you become Shadow FCO Sec?' Also by Barbara [Lord], when I raised the question of re-selection, shall I write a letter, etc etc, said, 'Oh no, I don't think there is any feeling like that. There may have been when you were selected, but not now.'

But in the train today I read Heffer, who said, 'Bring back John Major.' Heffer of all people. With the exception of Alan Clark I think he has by now plugged every single senior member of the Tory Party.

Saltwood   *Sunday, 14 March*

A really happy day. Fine. First day of spring, and we released the tortoises. This morning I was on GMTV 'sofa' with Alastair Stewart,[1] and tried (not unsuccessfully) to be *statesman*. Ancram also there. And I (Chips) 'made a conquest of James Landale'.[2] Then back down in time for 'boilies' and collected some lilac from the railway line after Jane brilliantly forced the pace in getting the Mehari to belch merrily into summer life.

Finished cutting the Bailey and drank (unusually) some of the Marquie's red Puligny Montrachet. Before that went for a drive in the blue Chev (block almost dry, as it turned out!). Then Julie and baby Angus turned up. I feel intensely at ease and optimistic.

---

[1] Alastair Stewart, news presenter, originally with ITN.
[2] James Landale, political journalist on *The Times*.

Tower Office, Saltwood   *Sunday, 4 April*

It is Easter Sunday. I have changed my 'work station', first from Garden House, then to the dining room here, now to the original Summer Office.

My eyes are giving me a bit of trouble – blurry, intermittent inability to defocus leading to periodic headache. I have an antipathy to the crabbed scrawl in the blue Banner notebook. And mindful of the pre-booked (I already have one of the contracts, but not signed it) £450,000 for 'The Early Years',[1] think that with posterity in mind I can now type a bit. The 'Mouse' makes it so much easier to tune and correct as you go along, apart from anything else. Harold Nicolson typed (most evenings); so, I think, did Dick Crossman. Tony Benn dictated into a machine. Chips wrote in longhand. (Or did he? Robert [Rhodes James] in his introduction does not confirm this. I will telephone to Robert this evening; have been looking for an excuse for some time. He will like to be asked his opinion on Kosovo, but I must also ask him *how he is*, as there is news in the tearoom that he has had a 'successful' (yeah) operation on his colon.)[2]

Of course a pre-printed is less secretive. If only because it can be read by any nosy parker who finds it. And if it is in a hiding place it will be read – even 'pirated' – still more avidly. It might be possible to get a ring binder with a lock on it; even to have one made, I will ask at Smythsons.

It is a fine day, and our priority must be the yard and the badge room before the swallows come back (according to *The Times* they have already arrived in Dorset). Last year we never did the yard, or the workshop at all.

On Thursday morning I felt absolutely happy, relaxed and

---

[1] AC had agreed to make a selection of his early diaries, as a 'prequel' and had pre-sold the serial rights to *The Times*.

[2] Since his retirement as an MP in 1992 Rhodes James had returned to writing and was currently at work on a sequel to his study of the later Churchill (to be called *A Study in Triumph*), but became ill with what was later diagnosed as cancer in 1998.

independent. A Bank Holiday weekend, and the week following ahead. That was a working day, with 'Bill', the Atco delivered. Chris the PSA carpenter, Alan-from-the-garage, and others making their claims. But after that we would be claim free. Yesterday most of the morning went on cleaning – really cleaning – out the hen houses. I was muck-sweat and 'adversarial' in the Chinese dungarees. V exhausting, but after tea I felt traditional enough to walk the Seeds and the valley. Then shunted all the cars round so that the line-up is not jarring (l to r) Cont 'S'; R-Cont; Buick RM; New Bing; Summer Car; Ghost. All on the button except the Buick whose battery is on slow charge up at the village. An American is being brought over on Monday week by Robert Coucher[1] who has a very 'hot' R-Cont. Could be fun, provided that Saltwood does not scowl and drizzle.

But one of the reasons I am typing is that a full-scale *résumé* of position-and-prospects is overdue and can be properly set out.

I am hugely depressed about Kosovo. Those loathsome, verminous gypsies; and the poor brave Serbs. The whole crisis is media-driven. Editors have no idea of, or respect for, the truth. They are concerned simply with *scooping* their rivals, and/or pre-empting counter-scoops. But an orthodoxy of public indignation is built up, stoked up, you could say, and the politicians have to respond. Each editorial conference is concerned with how still further to raise the 'temperature'; each political session with how best to be seen as 'seizing the initiative'. I have spoken in the Commons debate, written in the *Observer*, been several times on television – but no one is interested. I doubt that I shall get another invitation.

And this also throws into uncomfortable relief my own *lange pause* since returning to the Ho. I have got good relations with the constituents – as good as can be expected anyway – still. I

---

[1] Robert Coucher, editor of *Classic Cars*, for whom AC wrote his monthly column, 'Back Fire'.

can command media attention — Frost, Alastair Stewart — and
often I refuse bids. I have an enormous backlog of speaking
engagements, and turn down many, often, culpably, from
universities and young people. 'One of the few people who
brings a bit of colour to the Conservative Party' etc.

But (with the exception of Oborne) I am never tipped to
be 'brought forward'. 'Friends' like Bruce Anderson will never
do so. Never have, indeed. Even during Mrs T's reign it was
always regarded as a mixture of joke and accident — except
during the immediate aftermath of the Def Review paper to
Andy Marr. I suppose my high peak in this Parlt has been
when Jonathan Holborow rang from the Lab Party Conf in
1997 to say that I was the tip for 'stalking horse' that autumn
(this was before the Party electoral system changed) and just a
few weeks later I blew it (and a lot else besides) with my
reckless and intemperate comment on the 'solution' for
dealing with the IRA.

Now a huge change of mood infects society and politics. I
must contact April whatever-she-was-called whom I met at that
PR party in Kensington. What have I done with her scrawled
address? It has extended out of touchy-feely, Diana-caring into
a *correctness* that has become an orthodoxy. So that 'human
rights' can override all considerations of national sovereignty,
even of UN Articles and the authority which depends on them.
The 'democratic right of protest' now extends its immunities
from prosecution or even restraint to demonstrations here in
London, and other cities whose governments are not in any
degree to blame for the 'plight' of the demonstrators.

I suppose the first intimations of this were those ludicrous
Moluccans who used periodically to make life intolerable for
everyone, whether tourist or inhabitant, in the Netherlands. Once
a group exceeds critical mass in a situation of disorder, be they
gypsies, 'new age' travellers, asylum seekers, squatters, they acquire
both immunity and access to the media; who will aggrandise
their cause of complaint and seek to find, or to concoct, various
'human interest' angles from which to illuminate it. I heard a

ghastly story from Keith Simpson about an (Italian) TIR driver
who noticed that his truck appeared to be full of 'refugees'.
Virtually incapable of speaking English, he telephoned on the
lorry phone to his employer in Milan. 'Go straight to the police,'
he was told. The unfortunate driver saw a sign off the main road
to an RAF station, with sub-headings one of which was 'RAF
Police'. At the perimeter gates the puzzled redcap phoned for
instructions, was told to contact the local station. Needless to say
the local police (it was in Norfolk) wanted nothing to do with
the situation, said it was for Immigration. 'Immigration' said the
same, as the 'subjects' had already passed through the cordon.
Finally, after a pretty crisp harangue from the station commandant
a couple of police trainees and a squad car did turn up and took
the miscreants off to a 'hostel'.

Saltwood   *Wednesday, 7 April*

Skip day. We have been out of doors most of the time loading
junk, total detritus accumulated over God knows how long into
a skip.

My health not yet right. I felt terribly sleepy, almost Shore-
like at 7 a.m. Jane gets up and goes down. I follow about 25
minutes later. An exact reversal of the 'quiet hour' routine
which prevailed for so long. About half an hour into loading
the skip I began to feel really tired again and useless. It wore
off, then Ann Felce arrived to talk me into lowering her rent.
Subtly fault-finding as usual. She said that I should high-
pressure hose down all the garden seats. Fucking cheek. None
of her business.

She muttered something about her horse, Northern Starlight,
running at Ascot this afternoon. I thought I'd put something on
it, partly so as she wouldn't be able to gloat if it went well, and
popped down to the bookies, gave them a couple of new red

boys, plus two purps on Skip'n Time which Lynn had ably spotted on the card later in the afternoon.[1]

Have I been *herniac* these last few days? What a bore. It felt unhappy when I was humping on to the Mehari great sacks of wet grass from mowing the Bailey. But I think it is Christopher's Revenge – having been 'triggered' by desperate twisted straining to get a box of Lynch '61 on to its side in Peggy's pantry in order to read the label. Solicited by Christie's I am contemplating the sale of a very few cases of (really) 'fine wine'. Apparently Palmer '61 is worth more than Yquem '67, being £6000 per case.

EMT, Saltwood   *Thursday, 8 April*

A manuscript entry (much disturbed by 'TC' who either pulls at my pen or, from my shoulder excruciatingly, at individual hairs on my scalp). I woke in the night with the knowledge that something unpleasant had happened. First time, really, since heard of the Sevenoaks rejection from 'Ann Barrow'. James has lost his seat on the council in Durness.

Saltwood   *Friday, 9 April*

I woke this morning after a good night, but realised that I was a little sad, almost unhappy, tho' that is too strong a word, and ungrateful to God and the Fates. I just don't feel any sense of either freedom or excitement, or anticipation aka Rho J and Lord Randolph Churchill – '… all clubland was agog' etc etc.

---

[1] Northern Starlight came in 2nd, but Skip 'n Time romped home first at 6 to 4.

Saltwood   *Saturday, 10 April*

Just watched myself on GMTV – *too* pouchy, 106 years old, so
puffy and eye-bagged. I must not let crews come down here
with their own lighting. I look too awful – though still all right
in the studio. Jane and I had a lovely evening in the Gt Library.
Such potential, but slightly shaming in that we have neglected it
for 30 years.

Saltwood   *Sunday, 11 April*

Now the holiday is over. Never been near the Green Room
table, or done more than lightly scratch the KGV workshop, the
yard, or the badge room. Or, more seriously, written more than
one page of 'The Early Years'. But we have worked ourselves to
exhaustion practically every day. Jane has been brilliant,
everything from the swimming-pool loo revived, the skip
loaded, the yew pruned down by the Long Garage.

Little oh-so-meek George Ramsden was here, yet again, on
Saturday. We finally 'dealt' and I exchanged some more of the
Wharton books for a selection of my father's 'personal' library
(sold by Celly for £20,000 en bloc in 1986 to Zwemmer, or was
it Maggs?) and a cheque for £2000. I would have settled for less;
he might have paid more. In the end I found him quite
sympathetic. He said that suiting books, bindings and 'runs' to
shelves was 'like arranging flowers'.

Jane agreed to the terms, and thoroughly joined in as we
explored the Gt Library and laid our plans. An incredible room,
but many of the books are not in a good state, greatly to our
discredit as we have barely touched them, or the furnishings, for
25 years. My father's study on the other hand, has been
thoroughly done over and is quite perfect.

How is my health? I am at least half sure that my l/h hernia
has re-torn, although Mrs Frowd (only last Friday) said not. Last

night I was woken by 'pointing' pain inside the left hip. At one point I had such a sweating attack it was almost like a hot tap running over one. And I am still v down on energy, though not as much as during the 'viruses'. It is probably something to do with SAD as one does feel better when the sun comes out. But I have done no yoga, nor even walked to Beechborough Down.

Later
I talked briefly to poor Robert. The cancer had spread out of his colon, and he had been on chemo. But was calm. The Cambridge oncologist was 'satisfied'.

Brave he was, and calm-sounding though just a little weak of voice.

Later we watched the Jimmy [Goldsmith] film. And a huge pang at the shots of Cuixmala. Not enough of Jimmy, but what there was conveyed his incredible magnetism.

Very typically the script closed with a sneer ('right to the end he was a bad loser …'). Of course the media have never forgiven Jimmy for hating them, and never quite worked out how to get even – not unlike their relationship to Jonathan Aitken.

B5, EMT   *Wednesday, 14 April*

I am 71, and listening to the Albany blackbird doing his repertoire. Outside it is cloudless, but cold.

Saltwood   *Sunday, 18 April*

I am low. Last night a tittles from the *Mail* had left a message asking me to comment on 'Cardinal Hume's cancer'. Uh? I did not return her call. But on the nine o'clock news we were told that he was 'carrying on' though with 'inoperable cancer' – at the age of 76. I don't understand this. You don't have cancer at that age surely without any warning? 'Cancer is the last barrier before Old Age' etc. And at 76 you have arrived at old age.

I am down on energy and depression is in the bones. Literally, almost, as when I go and tinkle at 3.30 a.m. all my joints are so stiff. Last night Lëhni had not come up so I left the bathroom door open. I wondered if possibly I might meet myself, now dead and wandering about, not wholly at rest, to monitor things. I am not particularly frightened of death, but I do not want to die as I am enjoying life. I don't want to be reduced to ash – obviously; nor do I like the idea of being buried – not, at least in a coffin or a stone-lidded vault. Best, perhaps to *swim* and meet God, falling like a giant leaf into the undersea garden.

I never get at the cars; I'm more concerned, in truth, to conserve the fabric and inventorise the contents. I can get back into wistful mode, enjoying the garden and *an easy routine*. This is the eternal tension, between the sword in the lake or standing down.

I think if my health picked up back I would still go for the sword. But I do love Saltwood, and am so lucky to be here.

House Library   *Wednesday, 21 April*

Yesterday I networked. The Southend expedition was a success. Teddy Taylor[1] drove fast, but not well, in his blue Ford (I later found out that it was a Cosworth, and had done 173,000 miles). I gave the lunch all four barrels. Went well, and questions also, although the return journey, in light drizzle, took longer than coming in from Saltwood. We slowed down past 'City Airport', through a pointlessly long tunnel, then crossed Tower Bridge, but didn't turn right until far too late. I was glad to be the passenger.

---

[1] Sir Teddy Taylor, MP for Southend East since March 1980 (Glasgow Cathcart 1964–79).

A hint of HE's reception getting ready for the great Margaret Thatcher anniversary dinner at the Hilton. 'Why have you come here?' asked a reporter. 'To hear Ted heckle,' I answered.

But at my table I was demi-lionised by David Young, Basil Feldman and particularly and interestingly, Phil Harris.[1] Lita Young gave me some good lines – she is firm and bouncy, like a *diva*. Then who should come over, but Michael Ashcroft! Talked about setting up the lunch. 'Alan, these are all women you are suggesting,' he said.[2] Earlier Victoria Borwick had embraced me, also raising her leg tango style. Several men, youngish, had sought me out and expressed admiration. A move-on from the sort of function I used to go to as a nervous aspiring candidate in Monday Club days – or even later as an obscure MP. But main personnel hardly changed.

Saltwood   *Saturday, 24 April*

Jane left for Spain today. I drove her to Gatwick, and now I am *en garçon*, with fish cakes in the fridge which I never really seem to be very good at cooking, they break up in the pan.

It is wet, and I am extraordinarily tired, keep wanting to drop off, like when prowling about the House of Commons after a ten o'clock division. This is because we drove back down last night after the Association dinner, not getting to bed until gone 1 a.m. Soames spoke. He was big, and *mixed*. Good, very good, and moving on Churchill as an artist, his sense of colour; and a pleasant, funny style with his *racontes*. But Soames was abrupt with questioners, told one 'trouble-maker' that he should 'change his Party'. They don't go for that much in K & C.

On the Thursday I had been most terribly depressed by a

---

[1] Lord [Philip] Harris, carpet entrepreneur and contributor of considerable funds to the Conservative Party.

[2] Michael Ashcroft, controversial Conservative Party treasurer; AC had earlier sent a list, noting that Ashcroft, 'wants lunch, which is good of him considering how rude I was in my reply to one of his demi-reproachful money-raising letters.'

quite brilliant op-ed piece in *The Times* by John Laughland, whom I had never before heard of, but I rang Andrew Roberts who said he was very good and emboldened I took his number and entered into a brief conversation on the telephone. Laughland illustrated by ruthless logic the inner meaning of NATO's persecution of the Serbs.[1]

Garden House   *Sunday, 25 April*

Little Hague continues to make a complete hash of things. Why is it that journalists cannot work out a bum steer and one with intelligence? There is talk of a reshuffle and whose face is prominent? Why Theresa May, of course.[2] This is because there is nothing they like more than an internal row which translates into 'left' (good) versus 'right' (bad).

Whoof! The Sandling Train!   *Monday, 26 April*

I have had a dreadful two days. A paltry supper of four tiny fishcakes, and lights at 10.50. Woken by *paws on board* – TWICE. Walked alone (dogs bolshie and puzzled), and very nice and fulfilling it was. I noticed a thread of dead grass on the 'family' camellia, went to pull it away and to my great delight saw a beautiful new nest! No eggs yet, so hope that 'everything turns out all right'. Made some scrambled eggs (quite incredibly, my only culinary attainment over the entire period, as it turned out)

---

[1] 'The war is being fought to destroy the very principles which constitute the West. This is not moral, it is megalomaniac' – *The Times* heading to Laughland's piece.

[2] The MP for Maidenhead was 'spectacularly promoted', said the *Daily Telegraph*, to education and employment spokesman, 'a phenomenal promotion that has surprised many, for while she is clearly competent she has done little that obviously merits so swift an ascent.'

and Douwe Egbert instant coffee. Sunday papers all garbage. My hernia seemed to be pointing uncomfortably, but I decided to clean off and black the hinge iron on the Great Library door, wanting something to show Janey when she returns. First I tidied and reorganised the Red Study.

The hinge blacking v arduous and time-consuming with its many stages of wire-brushing, rubbing, painting and brush polishing. Dogs came on the walk this time, but were bored, would not attend on the getting of 'layer pellets'. An egregious tea (not 'high') at 5 p.m. with a little camembert, then to the 'work station' to continue on the Stephen Glover piece.[1] I sipped some chilled wine James came on the line; pleased and calm, but fussing about the (old) safe-deposit book key. Took 35 minutes. On and on went round the clock hands. No point in preparing dinner. I tiptoed through about 10 p.m., opened TC's cage door, took an old slice of Jane's sultana cake (all that was left) and up to bed, where dear, dear 'H' had already pitched her tent. This morning up v previous. Neither dog interested so went down to the site with a camera.[2] Predictably, it 22-window-clicked, had only one exposure. Went back: fed hens with stray bits of old bread found in a green Fortnum bag. Then made some instant coffee (no EMT) and two slices of brown toast. Then to print letter to Colin Paine of Shepway [council] and *Mail on Sunday*. Then back down to finish Glover piece. 'Colin Paine' rang and wanted an instant site meeting. Next down there and heard his 'compromise' suggestion. The unpleasant, hard-faced engineer was in evidence. Just back to Saltwood in time to put on a suit, gallop down, muck sweat, to get into Bill's (he wearing a sleeveless vest) red Vauxhall. Slept exhaustedly and intermittently in the carriage. On arrival a solitary, badly served lunch in the Commons. Then to Sue, masses of supportive letters, and across to Statement. Not called.

---

[1] Published under the title 'Why I Hold Journalists in Low Regard', in *Secrets of the Press: Journalists on Journalism* edited by Stephen Glover (1999).
[2] Shepway Council were at work on anti-flood measures.

Walked back to Charing X with incredibly heavy briefcase that I was not at all looking forward to carrying from Sandling. This is not a comfortable period.

House Library   *Tuesday, 27 April*

Keith Simpson, yesterday in the tearoom said to me '... and Alan what do you make of all this?' ... (the ludicrous Hague, Lilley row).[1]

'I find it profoundly depressing.'

'But you don't really, do you, Alan? This kind of confusion and reverse should be giving you pleasure. As, I suspect, it is to not a few of our colleagues.'

I sometimes get irritated with Keith. He is mischievous, in general and often towards me personally (*passim* his spastic 'mock' letter of invitation to the Garden Party). But I enjoy his company. And he was after all the first to spot the personal analogy between me and Maxime Weygand. Recalled at the age of seventy-something to take command of the shattered French Armies – but with the private remit of keeping them intact so as to maintain 'order'; to defeat, that is to say the battalions of 'workers', who had taken advantage of the political situation in both 1848 and 1870. DD encourages this and sometimes refers to it. Anything is possible, that I do know.

Delightedly, I fell back into this fantasy. 'Yes. I think of the atmosphere in the C-in-C's dining room (not 'mess') in Damascus. On, say, the 27 May 1940.'

Because this was not a simple colonial outpost. Surrounding them are the names – Saone, Krak des Chevaliers, Chastel Rouge, of the great crusader fortresses, so redolent of French

---

[1] Peter Lilley, in his role as Conservative Deputy Leader, had been accused by William Hague of speaking out of turn in ruling out big private-funding solutions for health and education.

chivalry and military prowess. And also, occasionally or so they had
been conditioned to believe, of English perfidy and cowardice. In
the presence of great art — in the case of the crusader castles the
absolute apotheosis of medieval architecture both ecclesiastical
and military — one is entitled to feel contempt for the *little worms*,
their mediocrity and plodding quest for everything that is banal.

1 Parliament Street   *Wednesday, 28 April*

Last night a dinner at Shaun W. Michael Portillo came and,
somewhat to my surprise, *was* impressive. Towards the end he
said that if we were going to talk about the leadership he would
have to leave the room (pompous and guardedly shifty).

This morning bad headlines — 'Tory Party in mutiny' etc.
Breakfast in tearoom subdued by presence of Jacqui Lait, big
frumpish ex-whip who disapproves of me and everyone like me.
But afterwards a pleasing little conclave with Eric [Forth] and DD
in the 'Aye' Lobby as Hague apparently insists on coming to the 22
this evening. Bloody cheek, I say, it's not us who needs the pep talk.
Are we or are we not, do we rate above, or below, a focus group?

So I really do look forward to this evening's Executive; and I
am enjoying being an MP. Even Peter Luff,[1] waiting for a taxi,
said he ought to fit *you* in …

1 Parliament Street   *Thursday, 29 April*

A day of considerable turmoil. Dreadful (for Hague) headlines;
MORI figures still further collapsed.[2] At about 11-ish were told

---

[1] Peter Luff, MP for Mid Worcestershire since 1997 (Worcester 1992–97).
[2] 'Hague fights to save his political life'; MORI showed 56% for Labour, 25% for
Tories; Hague's personal rating dropped from −26 to −31, meaning that twice as
many disapproved of his leadership than approved.

that there would be a meeting of the Executive on Tuesday (as soon as we return from Whit recess) and Hague would address us. The Lobby was in considerable turmoil, and I spoke to several – though not all – journalists. By 6 p.m., though, he had 'bottled out' and the meeting was cancelled. Order, counter-order, disorder. I left and drove to Gatwick where, at 10.15 p.m., I picked up Janey, sweet and refreshed from a week at Benalmadena.

MFS   *Saturday, 1 May*

Yesterday was stressful. Too much going on and 'things' against one, like the Discovery battery giving trouble. I had to drive over to Dover, but even the New Bing seemed to have a 'flat spot' and some fault with slow running. I'm really off cars by now. The place is full of catalogues – Brooks's, Christie's, Coys etc. I 'couldn't care …' Quite fancy Nick's [Beuttler] 2CV, of which he sent me photos; alternative – so what?

Today, though, has been lovely. We sat on the 'summer seat' at the end of the moat for salami salad and 'Max' attended on us, while other birds flitted about busily. I am more tranquil, I don't (it seems) have glaucoma after all. Spalton wrote today. My hernia less obtrusive; my weight back to 11.4 (+) and reasonable ½ erection in the morning.

But how do I get *noticed*? Do I make a speech, or give a lecture, or arrange a TV news conference, say? The great test, the 'New Paternalism' and the glowing reviews. I would talk to DD, natch; also Michael Gove.[1] I had a call through to Alastair, but he was still away. What is lovely is the sunlight, which does just slightly raise the vitality quotient.

I do thank God, though, everything is so lovely.

---

[1] Michael Gove, opinion page editor on *The Times*.

Sunday, 2 May

Really hot sun, and the comfortable knowledge that tomorrow it is not 'Dave-at-eight', but a free day.

But, a potential setback this morning. I had cleared out the hen house, then dashed off a letter to Stewart Steven[1] and rushed up to the post. Around lunchtime I was busy at Bill Holding's[2] shed when I started to feel *odd*. Almost like dropping off (before 'lights') when different reasons and evocations move across the consciousness. I had been contemplating a glass of Puligny Montrachet, but thought first to go down to the Long Garage. But by the time I got there I was feeling peculiar. Headache by side of skull, v livid. Half 'Hungarian embassy', almost sickish. Sat on the seat by the VW axle and started a sub-panic sweat. I worried about a possible stroke. Just about pulled out of it. But had no appetite for a salad of prosciutto-melone, which Jane concocted. Felt, and continue to feel, incredibly sleepy, almost as if v late last night (which we weren't) and/or jet-lag. May be linked with o/d-ing of sunlight which is affecting my blood count. I daren't (although Jane urges me to) put up my feet and drop off for fear of how I may find myself when I awake. Boring, and rather frightening also.

Summer Office, Saltwood   *Tuesday, 4 May*

I seem to have virtually no appetite, and I no longer like alcohol, not that it makes much/any difference. Am I heading for cancer? And if so, where?

A nice bath and hairwash from Jane before getting dressed,

---

[1] Stewart Steven, now a columnist with *Mail on Sunday*, had remarked on the quality of *The Tories*.
[2] Bill Holding's, the Saltwood garden shed, not only for tools and powers, but also, sometimes, the Mehari and other cars.

but doing my nails I saw in her mirror that the bags under my eyes are very pouchy.

Later in the day I felt stree-ange; almost light, as with a high fever – indicating some body out-of-balance factor. I am being eaten by stress.

I drove up v slowly in the little 911, then had three cups of tea, an Eccles cake and a slice of Stilton; calmed down at the prospect of a calm week.

Thursday, 6 May

I sit now in the Library, and I am ill-at-ease and *light*. It is a strange condition, a Lenin-Stadium variant, but in that case I could take refuge in a secret sexuality. But I am not myself; and particularly *put out* by the non-performance of alcohol. Last night a pint of beer in Pratt's[1] – made no impact whatsoever. I seem to remember Cindy [Frowd] saying that this is an incredibly bad sign. At one point (middle of January) I said, 'something-something-cancer-of-the-spleen'. Nick did, I think, hear it. But made no attempt to 'pick it up'.

How do I get out of this? Saltwood is no fun without sex or wine. Calm discipline and thought. But my self-confidence (due to its link to testosterone, perhaps) is down. Do I see my way?

That evening, Great Library (study)
A very sad blow. TC died (was killed) at Lëhni's hand. He/she had popped out on my return, had a drink and a good meal from his dish. I had a pleasing double poached egg (having come down on the 3 p.m. – excellent – train). We decided to stroll down and look at the workings, and putting my shoes on at the asthma rail I suddenly heard Jane shouting – knew at once what it was. Lëhni had clamped him *on the nest*.

---

[1] Pratt's – club owned by Duke of Devonshire, at Park Place, SW1.

We are absolutely shattered. We stood together looking at him on his tablecloth on the kitchen table. So warm and plump, he seemed. I hate the sudden invasion of death – 'in the midst of life we are in death', and was unhappily reminded of the vulnerability of the sweet young. Happily, as soon as we got back from our short and melancholy stroll, the phone rang and I said that may be the young; and it was Boy – very compos and lovable.

When Jane met me at Sandling I was 'Depressed Prince Enters Clinic' and she said how 'good' I was looking. Fun to be home – 'for three days of prayer and contemplation' I said (little knowing of the setback ahead and unhappily aware of inner lippen which seem to die down but quickly revive after 'eating'; or being 'caught'. From the day diary I see it is only 5–6 days old.

It is very great loss to lose a jackdaw, because they are magic birds, and carry reincarnationary powers. Last night (was it a portent?) I am almost in tears as I remembered the little dog – mentioned here earlier – whom I used to wave at and occasionally bring milk for at the top kennel by Eriboll byre; and how I had let her down; and is she, I assume, now dead? Not dying, I trust, too unexpectedly but I hope to meet her – greet her – in Heaven.

Sadly I thought about it all as we walked back up the path from the workings. Just to die, or induce death – not so likely to be treated. Like, almost, being sick. It may make you feel better, but actually *doing* it is horrible.

Jane produced some photos including one tiny almost unrecognisable shot of 'x'.[1] I have that of her a couple of times. Could she have been reincarnated? All mysteries.

Little Alan Duncan, sitting on the Front Bench while I was waiting to speak in the London health service debate. Said (after

---

[1] A few months before AC remarked about meeting 'x' – 'that extraordinary, obsessional and almost ruinous affair (out of which, indeed, my marriage to Jane emerged so much stronger, "miracle" and all).'

I had praised him on his article in the *H.S.N.*), 'Lining yourself up for the impending vacancy.'

'We don't want a vacancy.'

Self: 'You do if you've got a good chance of filling it.'

He was delighted: 'Only if you are my campaign manager.'

'Ditto,' I said.

Saltwood, EMT   *Friday, 7 May*

We buried TC today at noon, in the *Pavillon*.

He was laid in the little portable hamper, with a host of personal 'belongings' selected from his diverse and conscientious 'nest' assembled over so long and with such Herculean effort. That special silk scarf (which he used to keep purloining even after it was 'reclaimed') also his/her tiny, miraculous eggs; her 'tin'; a biro, a clothes-peg, a silver spoon and the little horse-brass of Jane's which she had carried (although heavy) all the way along the passage from the back stairs windowsill. 'Money-for-the-journey', an 1868 Victorian sovereign which had for several years been lost on the floor of the Winter Office and which I knew his magic would lead me to immediately, and I put my hand straight on it, beneath the desk. Brilliantly, Jane made me snip off with the kitchen scissors a ¾ length of the grey marker ribbon from the orange PDF day diary, which he would always try and remove at EMT, and this was about his person.

It was a sad, a very sad, little ceremony. Last night in bed a sad couplet from the childhood nursery rhyme kept going through my head:

'All the birds of the air fell a sighing and a sobbing …

– as they learned of the death of poor cock Robin.'

We are very very low, at losing someone who had so much magic. Did I betray his trust? Accidentally – yes. But perhaps it is this which makes me so dejected (and Jane, also, I suspect). I did say, aloud, a short prayer for him/her. 'I don't want to say it aloud,' I said. (Jane and Lynn were both in the Pavillon.) 'It'll make me cry.' 'Cry, then,' Jane said. And quite right too.

For the rest of the day I was completely dejected. I had no energy at all. And a recurrence of toothache in the right lower wisdom (which is, of course, 'false', i.e. made by Bertie Arbeid, or whatever that root specialist was called). This must be sinister. I was also made lower by inner lippen which seemed to be expanding.

I feel now as if I may be about to die, possibly quite soon, 'nearing the end of my life.' A huge sadness, as if I am/may be looking at so many things for the last time. Somehow I am going to be cheated of my chance to get hold of the Tory Party, and this realisation, coming on top of the accumulated stress, will do me in.

After lunch dozed off in the Pavillon, deeply. Then wrestled with fruiting bodies on the GH bank. In its own way even this was depressing because of the sense of neglect, and the way they have been killing the azaleas. Tea, and we decided to go for a walk, along the front. Almost empty, mild, and tried to take in lungfuls. Some nostalgia for the great days. We returned along the shingle, and could almost have plunged in the sea, which felt inviting. A clinical regime, as in 'Depressed Prince Enters Clinic'. Then a nice bath, and into pidgys. Trying to calm down and de-stress. Now going in to dinner, but afflicted by a particularly unwelcome symptom – the absolute non-effect of alcohol. Normally this is a time when wine inspires the mind. Not at the moment. There has been (on our TV screen) little Hague, in his 'Bruce Willis' haircut (whatever that is) and his dreadful flat northern voice. I find it just awful, skin-curdling, that the Party – our great Party – formerly led by Disraeli, Balfour, Churchill, Macmillan, Thatcher (even) could be in the hands of this dreadful little man who has absolutely no sense whatever of history, or pageantry or *noblesse oblige*. The whole enterprise to be conducted on the basis of a Management Consultancy exam tick-box, and the 'findings' of a 'focus group' 'Is not the 1922 Committee a valid "focus group"?' as Eric Forth, justifiably, complained.

Saltwood   *Saturday, 8 May*

The date (although not, of course, the *day*) of the Norway Debate in 1940.

I woke this morning so depressed. The pile of *germane* – or is it mundane? – tasks. Terry [Lambert] wants a copy of the Trust Deed. Where are the Wills? I am fairly certain that I will be dead, or at least *hors-de-combat* in 6-8 months. Weight now 11.4lbs (+).

The message light on and it was Keith Simpson wanting 'a word' about little Duncan. This, + two cups of Indian made me feel better. Today we are going over to Lynx (by Land Rover) to collect (one of) the XKs. Why bother? My taste for the cars is gone. The white XK is an icon, but the rest … The minimum stable (so often attempted in the Dealing Book): Discovery, S16, 'little black (?)', SG, XK120, prob 4¼. I am quite minded to go out in 9AKC, now the Chev Summer Car. And there is also the Chapron.

Later, My Father's Study
It's 5.30 p.m. and back to an almost habitual, or usual condition of feeling slightly better after a full (Indian) tea (in this case backed by fish cakes and Heinz ketchup) except for anxiety about rear r/h wisdom toothache. But 'hernia' has virtually disappeared. We went to get the 'noisy car'.[1] Also an enormous bill for the grey 140. Quite nostalgic, almost upsetting, going through Rye – oh the pining to 'start again'. But I did 'start again' it must not be forgotten, in Parliament. I do worry and get 'depressed' very easily, that I have so much to do before I can die at peace – for sweet little Jane for whom I am feeling very loving at present – and for my descendants. Trusts and inventories.

Sometimes, as now, I feel pretty ok, but I am not looking very young.

---
[1] 'noisy car' – the XK20.

Saltwood   *Sunday, 9 May*

Just in from the walk, a lovely mild spring/May morning. Felt so tired and listless on waking, I barely wanted to get out of bed (at 7.20 a.m.) and go down to EMT. In many ways this 'Depression' is extending out into a 'Nervous Breakdown'. But I am not frightened of dying; just scared of packing up. Dirk Bogarde has gone, at 78 (same age, almost, as my father and still seemingly a long way off).

How do I ensure that I stay in command of the Mains, but with everything clear and composed for Janey? I really love her. And I love James when I hear his voice on the phone, so clear and compos.

I am almost near-to-tears. Not at all as programmed. Where is *FE*?[1]

Later, p.m.
In the afternoon, quite hot, I went for a walk to Beechborough. I have for long been fascinated by this property, often remembering in its first heyday the girl (owner's wife, presumably – much, much later after my Jaguar article in the *Telegraph* – she wrote to me) quite nice-looking with long hair who drove a faded metallic blue 120, nearly always with the hood up, and I used to see her on the A20. They were a young couple, I assume, trying to make a go of it with bed and breakfast.

Of course in those days I was living mainly at Saltwood, 1955-ish I should think. I often think that I should have bought the whole place, lock-stock-and, which I could probably have managed then; painted it all white, and filled it with pre-Raphaelite paintings, Alma-Tadema, Leighton etc. But as Jane points out had I done so she and I would never have met. Because then I was getting restless, and quickly bought Watchbell St, and first started to see her and Pat at 'The Lookout'.[2]

---

[1] The 2nd Lord Birkenhead's two-volume biography of his father, F. E. Smith.
[2] At the end of Watchbell Street; one can see across to Camber.

This afternoon I made a point of climbing over the battered
iron railing fence to the 'lake' (in reality a freshwater reservoir).
A strange and romantic mystery pervades this location, with the
overgrown reeds and water lilies, the occasional wild moorhen.
Something, perhaps, of Leslie Hartley, *The Go-Between*.[1] But, less
happily, I found out only a couple of months or so ago that the
main house had been a convalescent hospital for the Canadian
Division in the Great War. Eighty-four years ago, give a week
or so, fell the anniversary of the very first use of poison gas in
the attack (on the Canadians) in the Ypres salient on 28 April
1915 when those poor brave soldiers stood on the parapet to
raise their heads above the cloud and continue firing. Their
only mask was a handkerchief soaked in bicarbonate of soda.
How many of them must have been hospitalised afterward to
Beechborough, with their lungs terribly damaged.

I was rattled because time passed and I had agreed to return
in time to take Jane to the Rhodi and Azalea walk up in the
American garden, plus I ought really to write a piece (at their
solicitation) for the *Mail*, on Kosovo. Got back too late, so we
had tea in the Pavillon. Then went for a run in the White Car,
first time out for years, to try and capture some Jaguar music,
but too much stuff (as usual) in the way.

Saltwood   *Monday, 10 May*

I am really 'poorly'. I wake utterly demoralised and so low that
I want only to drop back asleep. I don't want to do anything in
particular, no zest. Not even a delicious anticipation at going up
to the House to see what 'unfolds'.

On the walk with the dogs I no longer brighten at the
thought of coffee and a fried egg and bacon.

---

[1] 'A *Go-Between* trysting place in a hot hot July,' as AC described it in November
1995.

Later, House Library

Driving up this morning in Big Red I felt incredibly sleepy and de-energised and zest-free. Had hardly got the other side of Ashford, and was doing 75-ish, unassertively and being over-taken – almost as if in a big old American. I thought to myself, I actually *am* having a nervous breakdown.

I think what was wrenching at my heart was a little con-versation I had last night on the telephone with James at Eriboll. I suppose at one point I may have said '... got to go now; I'm in a rush.'

Very very sweetly, not at all cross, he said, 'Almost from my earliest childhood, when I wanted to talk to you, I can remember you saying, "I haven't got time just now." But now you are still saying it to me. You still very, very often say it. But I am your son and heir. There is so much I need to talk about. It is to the others that you should say this ...'

I really love 'Boy'. He has got a lot of greatness in him. I told him that we had now decided to come up over Whitsun, he and I would have a really good 'w', and look at the plantings together. But he wanted to talk *then*.

How awful it will be if I were to die (or still worse he) without our ever really having *taken time together*.

My hernia has cleared. And my 'inner lippen' is not notice-able. But I do seem to have jawline aches. It may be just because I clench, or grind, my teeth, including the giant 'bridge', in frustration when, notionally, sleeping.

What am I meant to be doing now – 'with myself'?

Not only have I lost my palate for cars, and to some little degree for the heritage; but also for politics, at present; even for political gossip. It is a Sibyl tonight, but holds out no promise. Douglas Hurd is g. of h. Even more boring and self-regardingly pompous than TK, who still bogusly pom-posticates from the backbenches when called (which happens far too often).

I did get into the Kosovo statement, and forced Robin Cook to exculpate the RAF from the destruction of the Chinese

Embassy in Belgrade. Then up to the 'Forward Look' Committee in room 21, right up on the top floor. Hague jarringly ghastly, as always. I could feel no tremors of inside track, even. Into a black tie for the Sybil, signed a few oddments. I have got rid of a couple of unpromising speaking engagements. One at the Oxford & Cambridge Club, where Commodore something-or-other had the cheek to 'suggest' that it might be more 'tactful' if I did not mention Kosovo; also one for Nick Winterton[1] that had all the makings of an ordeal: return fare £155 – monstrous that I should have to pay this; and totally impossible to return from Macclesfield without changing trains at Stafford, and anyway they only go to Euston. Saltwood weekend ruined.

Anyway, on the Thursday I want to use the occasion of a quite promising Liberal Opposition Day with an amendment to cut Hague's salary because he is so useless, making my own cerebral speech about what the Conservative Party is/should be. Plus masses of overdue sorting of paper.

This actually *raises* stress, although it ought to abate it. There is little Derek Fatchett,[2] a clear victim of the Ministerial destruction-test – the classic 'HE's Reception syndrome having to be revived' (they failed) – 'while fighting for his life on the floor of the pub'. Heart attack; dead. I could almost, almost, retire to the croft; leaving Saltwood care-and-maintenance. But what about the constituency? What's he up to? Etc. ('Doctor's orders.') But that really would be the end – of me; in every sense.

The only way I can recover real freedom is by getting Wills and Trusts into concrete. Then, 'Come-and-get-me, Larsen'.[3]

---

[1] Nicholas Winterton, MP for Macclesfield since 1971.
[2] Derek Fatchett, Foreign Office Minister, died suddenly aged 53.
[3] A phrase from a 1950s American television series.

House Library   *Tuesday, 11 May*

Sybil no fun really. I was between Bill (Cash) and Oliver Letwin, to whom I am now warming a little more. Hurd, predictably, was largely Position-Paper balls. When dear Bill C finally weighed in about Europe/generally I rose and left. Drove (!) back having discarded my black tie and boyishly donned the grey cashmere pullover. As I said to my fellow diners, 'I am utterly demoralised.' Shaun told me that Gordon Reece[1] was in hospital in Houston *waiting to have his tongue taken out* (would it be called a *labiectomy*? Oh dear). Cancer. 'Started with a cough.' No it didn't, I thought. Can't have. He had a bad cough, I would think, went to the doctor who said 'let's just take a look, open wide', etc etc, and then … 'Hey, what's this?' How awful for Gordon. The great John Diamond saga excruciatingly continues.[2] How fortunate one is. I can't let my mind roam over that dilemma.

One part of my depression, as I sense my palate dulling for so many things is that it may in the end *go* for my real reservoir of strength and inspiration – Nature and greenery or, worse, 'At peace in the Highlands'. Then, actually, I see how those in Deep Depression can at that point suffer acute despair – John Webb from Devizes church tower.[3] One pleasing development to record. Stirrings this morning. And in the tearoom I suddenly realised that I was enjoying *looking at* that waitress, what's her name? (who I have long in the abstract – in her striped blouse she is *exactly* like the cutie in a 'Careless Talk Costs Lives' poster of the 1940s – fancied) and I still get testicular writhings, tho' mild. Perhaps another next week before Whitsun in the Highlands.

---

[1] Sir Gordon Reece, influential public relations adviser to Margaret Thatcher.

[2] John Diamond, a journalist and married to Nigella Lawson (daughter of Nigel, sister of Dominic) was writing regularly about his experience of throat cancer.

[3] John Webb (d. 1991), a clerk at the House of Lords and a friend of AC and Euan Graham, who committed suicide by jumping from the rampart at the top of Devizes Church.

Later

It's 6 p.m. and Sue has made a mess of my going on TV at Millbank. They've 'got someone else'. Adds to the general 'what's-the-point?' syndrome.

I am so demotivated. I ought to write a great speech for Thursday. Don't at present know if I am going to succeed in getting out of Nick W at Macclesfield.

But this afternoon I started to feel ill. Just very slow and sleepy and uninterested. My mind went back to little T.O. Sometimes Tom just *stood*, wherever he was, and often he would get (deliberately, as I believed, and unthinkingly allowed it to irritate me) 'caught up' with bits of furniture, fireguards, the cross-bar of a kitchen chair, or whatever. I rang Andrew about my will. Did he want anything in particular?[1] Poor little Albert has dreadful chickenpox. He came to the phone and spoke so beautifully; clear, and with perfect diction.

I am so down on energy. This has always been my most precious asset. How is the whole thing going to end? I am apprehensive – undoubtedly an anxiety derivative. Classic Lenin-Stadium. So that I can't even look forward to the Scottish May-week jaunt; or the summer hols – *enfin le clef* – the Palace, and Public Life, closed off. Before then, though, certain vicious *hurdles*. Most daunting, the Saltwood Garden Party. Invitations, lists, coach reservation, crockery, cheap (huh!) champagne.

Followed disagreeably soon by the XKs. It's strange, now about the XKs.

I'm not even in the mood to clean up my own two, plus the 'C'. Also the *retraite* of P & A Wood. 91MX is there, but nothing happening (not even a bill) and no response. In theory we are doing the BDC Europe Rally next year, and the Rolls Jordan ('Crusader Castles') rally in September.

Not interested, old boy.

I would gladly *write my own chit* and stand down, as a crusty

---

[1] Andrew replied with a 'hope to get' list – 'a hard choice as one looks to the future, and with it goes the terrible sadness that accompanies it'.

heritage-man. But just a minute! We've had this before. The tortured withdrawal symptoms, the pining – part 'x', part FE etc, all inflamed by the material for BB as it accumulated; and the intermittent flow of letters from people saying why don't you go back, take the helm ... and all the delusory temptations of articles and TV shows.

But if I did, again, 'step down' I'd break the White Office vow, and would deserve anything. Perhaps I should pray again, this weekend. Talk to God. He is understanding, and helpful.

Wednesday, 12 May

I am seated in the doorkeeper's chair by the chamber entrance, having come in early in order to write a place-card. There is an account in *Chips* of Winston Churchill sitting in one or other of these chairs (when actually Leader of the Opposition) before a late-night Division and making jokes with, and waving at, passers-by, while puffing at his cigar.[1] All sounds a bit gaga to me.

I still feel awful. Too many times have I made this comment, in the last seven months. I suppose it all (the destruction of my immune system) goes back to October, while suffering from the onset of that strange upper-respiratory virus that shattered, and reshattered us both over many weeks and did, I believe, inflict great damage. Long for relief – and the melancholia of having passed away pre the sword, on the reeds at the water's edge, would be almost welcome.

---

[1] 'Winston smilingly made his way towards one of the Porter's chairs and asked for snuff, which the attendant handed him in a silver box. Then, surprisingly, Winston looked at the chair (which he must have known for 40 years) as if he had never seen it before in his life, got into it, and sat there for fully five minutes, bowing and beaming at other Members who looked at him through the little window. A boyish prank. How endearing he is, sometimes. A few minutes later, however, he was making what was to be one of his very greatest speeches ... to a crowded and anxious house ...' *Chips*, 28 September 1949.

Later, House Library

Pull-yourself-together, Clark! If I were told, 'yes, you can go back *IN*. The price is a colossal and draining change on your paper load, and your "Diary". But the condition of this is that you "disperse the load, and get stuck in to a regularisation of your own fiscal structures".' Of course I would have assented. Now these latter two conditions – draining though they are – have got to be 'addressed'.

There is one rather disturbing psychic phenomenon to which I am minded to refer. Often in my bedroom I will, have for many years, suddenly get out of bed and pray for a little boy who is being terribly and mercilessly bullied and/or abused. Now this has slipped into the kind of WWI image – the Scarpe, Arras, all that – which is sort of out of *real* into *virtual* time. And the 'little boy' is of course Albert, or Angus. And I may be watching in agony as a disembodied spirit, and unable to act.

The wills are a total mess I must get them redone properly – everything to each other, and no legal gobbledegook. I must also, though, write to darling Janey – a real text of love, and commiseration at all the frightful things, paper-mess, 'How-do-I?', 'Where-is?' etc that I bequeath to her. Investing and private values. Car values and historian. All something of 'a note to my literary executors'.

Soon I am going up to the 22 Exec – full meeting.

House Library   *Thursday, 13 May*

I've (almost) had it. Don't really see my way to make the 'Great Speech'[1] this afternoon. My energy quotient is almost nil.

---

[1] In a draft note, dated Wed 12 May, AC had written, of the debate, '*make an impact*'. And later, 'Impact is certainly what it would have made. I could have got it in, but semi-peaked because that awful little git Hague had already *sold the pass* at the start with his "support" or, as I now realize I should have described them – "plaudits". A perfect high-profile background to the speech I want to make in the debate tomorrow.'

Intermittent jaw-like aches, seem to have lost weight again. I feel, and am almost certain, that soon I am going to die ('Tom' just standing). Before my heart actually stops, I must get the Trust docs out so as to be absolutely clear where we are. This is itself a major undertaking because of boundaries (sic) of 'Private Apartments'.

For the first time in my life I see no recovery scenario; nothing to kick-start (*passim* Nick Page) and 'put a spring in my step'.

Saltwood   *Saturday, 15 May*

Last night I had a useful mental catharsis, and slowly began to feel a little 'improved'. I couldn't raise Eriboll, though left a couple of messages on their answering machine. Andrew I did speak to, and apparently he is considering changing his job to become a City 'trader' (!) a 'flipper' they're called, apparently; I must ask Keith Pinker what that is. We chatted a bit. I explained how 'low' I felt. I asked him to promise me always to look after sweet Albert, the 'Prince' who might be in jeopardy of some kind one day. Also that if I died before Jane he would always ring her every Sunday. Also ahead of Christmas, just to talk through 'arrangements'. It is so lovely for old people to have very young children scampering around at Christmas. They must never be allowed to feel left out. He said he would.

If I get my affairs – Trusts, inventories, bequests – in order then I *can* take the risk of dying, or inducing death (on, say, the Creaggan or the Schonbulweg) in order to evade misery. I don't really know how ill I am. If I look back over recent scares – 'urethric' (but PSA 0.5, it turned out); 'herniac' (lifted immediately); failing vision (passed glaucoma test) – I should derive some reassurance. In the late 70s I used to worry dreadfully at the prospect of financial obliteration – at the hands of the tax 'authorities' and C. Hoare & Co who held the deeds of this place. I had this analogy of the last days of the Reich – how should one play it, how good will the V-weapons be? Sometimes this was useful in getting to sleep. Now I am falling back on my ramparts, the siege of Acre, is the Keep secure? If I am convinced that it is I will be more at peace.

Now I am stopping to type out a new (real) Will.

THIS IS THE LAST WILL AND TESTAMENT of me
ALAN KENNETH MACKENZIE CLARK of
Saltwood Castle Kent CT21 4QU

1. I hereby revoke all former wills and testamentary dispositions made by me.

2. I APPOINT my wife Caroline Jane Clark, and my two sons James Alasdair and Andrew McKenzie to be the Executors and Trustees of this my Will.

3. My Trustees shall be empowered to make and retain investments in the name of any nominee or nominees reasonably deemed by them to be reputable, and to seek advice concerning matters of Administration from Mr Graham Camps of Bird & Bird, Solicitors, of 90 Fetter Lane or, failing him, from Mr Terry Lambert of Mowll and Mowll, solicitors of Castle Street Dover, and to pay any reasonable charges for such services.

4. I HEREBY BEQUEATH unto such of my two sons JAMES and ANDREW as shall be living at my death and if more than one in equal shares absolutely a cash sum of an amount equal to the upper limit of the nil percentage rate band (at the time of my death) in the table in Schedule 1 of the Inheritance Tax Act 1984 (or any statutory modification or re-enactment thereof).

5. I GIVE all my possessions and property, both real and personal (to include cash and equities and chattels within the meaning of section 55 (i) (x) of the Administration of Estates Act 1925) to my wife CAROLINE JANE absolutely. And this I do in the knowledge and expectation that she will make

such later distribution by way either of gift or bequest as I would myself have done, were I alive, and in consultation with JAMES and ANDREW, and carrying always in the forefront of her mind the interests of our grandsons Albert, Angus and Archibald

6. (mss additions) I have hereunto set my hand etc etc plus witnesses Lynn Webb and Edwin Wilson, Housekeeper and groundsman, and their addresses.

Saltwood, Tower Office   *Sunday, 16 May*

We went over to dinner at Allington yesterday. Just before leaving, in the Pavillon, I started to feel decidedly odd. Full Lenin-Stadium. This did not abate in the car, was aggravated, indeed, by being unable to find the place on the road map, where-do-you-leave-the-motorway etc. Jane, though, brilliantly sleepwalked on to both the exit and the route. On arrival I remained uneasy, though. Felt that I might have to absent myself at some point to go and sit in the car. Was some kind of cerebral occlusion building up? Something had told me to get page 1 of my new will signed and witnessed, or perhaps even bring it so that, gaspingly, I could have signed at the scene – drama! The fact that I hadn't added to my anxiety.

The Worcesters have done a good job on Allington. It is cleaner and tidier than when Jane and I first 'viewed' it. But I certainly wouldn't want to live there instead of Saltwood (or Shore, or Broomhayes, come to that). Jane rightly loved Margaret's long, modern kitchen; an example of what we ought to do here with the Green Room and Embersons. But that wing is very well built, and would entail major demolition reconstruction, RSJs, dust and disturbance.

When I came down this morning the little grey cockatiel was dead on the floor of his cage. He has been a bit withdrawn and huddled lately, and we were concerned, although he has been like this before and recovered. I was very sad and depressed by this, the second intrusion of Death in two successive weeks. Bad-things-come-in-threes, all that. I don't like to think about it. In fact I was not so traumatically moved by his death as I had been at the loss of TC. My great regret is that I never managed to get him out, and have him walking around on the kitchen table. But I really did love the way he would greet me when he heard the back door, or even the telephone door. And how to get attention he would do the whole Benny Hill repertoire (this would amaze strangers, particularly workmen). He and his female consort once escaped and flew over the Knights Hall to the woodland. How well I remember walking across the moat and up along the woodland desperately whistling their tunes. It was the grey one who returned and Jane, with amazing speed and skill, nipped and pouched him (that same morning) off the Laurestinus by the garden entrance. We agreed that that is where he should be buried (discreetly in a linen napkin as a winding sheet) and he will be able to hear the telephone, and listen to conversations.

Stress builds up in me. Quite a lot of the time I can feel sickish, and at night I have these strange dream sequences, not exactly bad or even narrative (as in the 'Saltwood Dream'), in which some non-specific but apparently insoluble problem occurs; recurs, indeed, every time I go back (not always easy) to sleep.

This condition is not going to lift until I have created the kind of relative order that would allow me to 'step down' not just from politics but from Life itself.

Curious; I always used to be certain that a time would come when I withdrew from Public Life and simply concentrated on finance, and establishing durable structures. We tried that once, in 1992; but then came the lure of the will o' the wisp, and the great triumph of 23 January 1997. After that anything seemed possible, but now my political career seems to have hit the buffers (sic); being loathed by the Leader, and undermined by his courtiers. From the Constituency itself unease is reported back at my 'disloyalty' (aka the Eastons and Latimer in Plymouth in 1974[1]).

So if I can just get my will completed and valid, and the Trust structures settled and properly filed with boundaries etc. Also the contents inventory and private history and putative values ('the map of the oilfields') then serenity might be in sight.

Later

Just got in from the interment of the little grey cockatiel. It is too depressing, almost an RFC mess in 1917. Jane found a perfect spot just under the Laurestinus and we carried over from the Knights Hall a huge XIXc terracotta chimney liner which just serves to protect the grave mound and into which we scattered a lot of wild bird seeds from his dish. It will be humid in there and they may grow, exotically.

I am unsettled by a story which Margaret had recounted to Jane. One evening, with Bob away, she had encountered a couple of intruders carrying beer cans (worst possible sign). On inquiry they, objectionably, shouted that they were 'ramblers'. Later she found that they had cut their way through the chain-link fence with long-handled metal shears.

If I get to have a 'w' with Boy in Scotland, or Andrew also, how do I explain to them our plight? We are menaced, almost, as the law is structured; at the mercy of the rabble, and their yob nominees. Vandalism, road rage, casual larceny. There is a huge tide of scum rising, motivated by vulgar preference, *schadenfreude*, envy and class loathing. There is nothing we can do as they and their modish sympathisers have monopoly control over the whole legal process. But we are the counter-revolutionaries. Like XVIc recusants we must lie low, drawing strength from our own certainties. And we must be patient, and prepared for when our day may come, and by the action we then take we will stand to earn the gratitude of all our people.

This afternoon we drove over to Harland's in the Discovery,

---

[1] See Alan Clark *Diaries: Into Politics.*

and wandered around. Part of the idea was to get tea, which
arrangement I had ballsed up last week by being out too long. In
fact it was a swizz – 'tea and biscuits'; and in polystyrene cups.
Jane was so sweet and loved the shrubs and blooms and made
plans in her head. My love for her, and a premonition of parting
soon, made me terribly sad and I thought that I ought to write
her a proper letter. I thought that I ought to 'go into' the question
of how and where I am buried. It has got to be by the fig tree.
Better in a winding sheet, against the earth, than a cold vault. But
I would so like to have her beside me, when the moment comes;
the stretching out of the hand, or the foot. I am sure it is right for
us to dig our grave there. Afterwards we can always 'go to
Scotland' when the usual time comes round, and our spirits will
frequent the many haunts there, from the place where once,
nude-bathing, we saw a seal very close in. And, of course, the
Birkett Foster rocks and also, for Tom's sake, the burrows.

On our return we took the dogs into the woodland and
wandered back from the Old Family Garden along the stream. A
delightful stretch; all Jane's vision and doing, and I well remember
at the time she was envisaging it and giving instructions to
Holliday's men I was lukewarm, and limp. On the telephone I
spoke briefly to Tip, who asked me what was the matter? The more
I talked about it the more 'anxious' I found myself becoming. I
have a very steady jawline ache which frightens me, plus nervous
about going to bed and trying to sleep. I am having a bad time at
the moment. Tip, very splendidly, could hardly understand.
Looking back I don't think I would ever have envisaged it being
'like' this. Or indeed 'it' taking place at all. What a waste …

House Library   *Tuesday, 18 May*

Today I hope to speak in the Kosovo debate; and I have a slight,
'half-pointing' headache on the right side of the skull. Had this
before, something linked to the eyes and the need to 'defocus'.

Sandling Train – Ashford   *Wednesday, 19 May*

I am so utterly down – on the verge of tears, because everything is so lovely – the morning sunshine, the birdsong, the scents and sounds. And sweet Janey so adorable, such lovely *company* as well as being so attractive-looking. I hated saying goodbye, even though 'formally' until the weekend.

I really dread, dread (almost as a child must) dread being parted from her. I write these dreadful entries, partly as a kind of exorcism, partly for the fun (can tell myself) of turning back to them when I am 'better'. One of the things that most depresses me is the loss of *joie de vivre* so that (as I have repetitiously noted) I no longer spring from the bed in May and autumn full of eager anticipation at what the day may bring. Nor do I feel lance after the morning Thompson.

One thing to look forward to, it's not *too* bad a week. Will give Terry's dinner the Press[1] piece and on Thursday back lovely and early (I have just, this minute, satisly filled out the warrant for a return ticket). On Friday, Cindy Frowd who might, ought, to *therapise* me. If I can get 'better', next week is the Flower Show, and the drive north. Providing no more setbacks. I must talk to God.

Later, House Library
Illish-feeling and utterly disillusioned. Self completely unreported in today's press (as Jane rightly cautioned me, 'Matthew Parris will never mention you …'). Out of the Members Entrance Porch and across New Palace Yard and thought – I'm absolutely sick of all this. Nothing left to go for – it's all draining and/or aggro. I want out.'

A measure of my decline into this strange condition. Walking back from Charing Cross I would, in earlier years, have been jaunty, confident, pleased at – almost *inviting* – visual recognition in the street. An MP striding towards the House of Commons!

---

[1] AC's piece for Stephen Glover's collection, *Secrets of the Press*.

A condition, a *mise-en-scène* I have been pining for ever since I first used to hang around the TV crews on College Green while OUT (in '93-ish, I'd guess) and said to Nick Budgen 'who's that buffer over there in a hat?' and he reproachfully told me that, '... if I may say so that is just the kind of mistake you can make when you are no longer one of the Parliamentary Party'. (It was, in fact, Iain Duncan Smith.) Now, this afternoon, I am back into a state of raging anxiety. As soon as I got to the office I could feel it getting aggravated as I redid the Engagement Diary with Sue. The dreaded great green book first introduced by Trish. The secretary's battering-ram. Speaking engagements and social (the Norland 'Summer Party' etc etc) I could feel myself getting 'unhappy'.

Once back here I got to thinking – 'how do I get out of this?' Perhaps the really haunting spectre is that I would have to turn my back on the lake, and the prospect of the sword. This would mean (a) announcing that I would not contest the next Election or (b) arrive at the same position by openly applying to be readopted (the Muzio gambit, or the *Coup Royale*). Once done, either result would make me secure. Would lift the have-you, could-you pressures, the correspondence, and the sense of obligation and possible lurking ambush.

At the same time, and in parallel I must confirm the Trusts in existence, the validity of the wills, and such insurance cover as there may be. (Some little runt of a 'Loss-assessor' turned up at 10 a.m. to 'look at the wiring, and the security' and wasted my time. Any insurer will turn to the most convenient (for them) excuse to keep taking the premiums but dodge the claim.)

How feasible is this scheme (or 'game-plan'?). Well, of course *c'est possible parce que tous est possible*. But we've sort of been here before, have we not (like, say, in 1991-92)? I will pray, perhaps with Janey, at St Leonard's (maybe on Thursday) and then we will talk it over *viciously*.

I love Janey so much now. It is terrible how I miss her. I long for contact – it is almost like a child, waking in the dark in fear and calling out. I need the mummy to come in. It is a physical reassurance, and she is so reassuring and willing in the things she says and her lovely giggle. It was partly grounded, of course, this melancholy, in reminder of how horridly I treated her; it is ironic indeed that now I *really* can't do without her, even for a little while, and salutary also that I should be punished for my callousness in former times. Additionally, and 'at the margins' I suppose that I have been made uneasy by the antics of that nasty dark-haired 'student' who is *rights-ly* turning on J.D. Salinger,[1] and selling his letters. I can't bear to think of something happening and hurting Janey again. One is never safe, I suppose. But she should really be able, her position is so strong, just to laugh it off. I suppose that's why I keep repeating to myself how uniquely special she is and has always been.

Pavillon   *Friday, 21 May*

Talked this morning to 'Dr Thomas Stuttaford' (no, actually, I did) whom Jane brilliantly spotted as writing on depression. He v splendid, quick and almost reassuring. Said I could be dosed (there is a school of doctors who think in these terms) remedially with Serotonin. 'Replenishes' (sic) the brain. I don't hugely like the sound of this.

Max[2] is around, flies down benignly; a very different kind of presence. I give him didgys from the EMT tin.

---

[1] J. D. Salinger, author of *Catcher in the Rye*, became a recluse and used any means that the US courts could provide to avoid biographical material from becoming public.
[2] Max, one of Saltwood's jackdaws.

Pavillon   *Saturday, 22 May*

I am relaxed here – quite therapeutic – and let the mind run over the sad death of my old friend and in today's obituaries.[1] Too many deaths at the moment. Are we going to be able to atone for TC after Jane briskly and competently scooped up a (*very*) baby jackdaw and has been nurturing him on the Aga?

Felt awful this morning. A *nuit-demi-cassé*, Guderian on the Meuse in 1940 (exactly this time in May). Woke with an awful headache. Artery muscles in the skull just above the collar-line. Then suddenly *caught unawares* while dressing and retch-vomited tea and biscuits into the wooden loo. Still only 11.3 (+) on the weighing machine. Went down to Cindy Frowd, who was far from reassuring. Said I still had a retentive virus (possibly on chest). But that my *liver* is right up the creek, which may explain loss of appetite and indifference to wine. A bore and sinister. Fats banned (like Janey). I could barely eat my delayed breakfast. Scrambled egg decidedly what was not wanted. I've noticed that I've been off egg yolk, in its various forms for some time recently. Sinister. Liver cancer always starts with jaundice, doesn't it? Looked up the symptoms: 'extreme lethargy, weight loss, loss of appetite'.

This pretty well finished me. Jane very splendidly saw this, and said 'Go to Bed' (in the Summer Bedroom). But I was afraid of doing that; too much of an admission; so came over here and put my feet up wrapped in the 2-tone brown cashmere rug. Mrs F had told me that we must go abroad for two and a half (!) months. No. Not Scotland. *Abroad.* Would that we could. Well, it would be lovely, and probably therapeutic, to go to the châlet. I wouldn't mind going via Colombey, either. But if we do go to Shore sitting in the wheelhouse, or walking the Creaggan should be pleasing. Although the Highland melancholy is never far away. We'll see.

But I am not 'right'. No, not by any means. I feel so tired and

---

[1] Robert Rhodes James had died on Thursday, 20 May.

listless. Duty/projects tower over me. Not just the Trust Deeds, returns, and inventories, but do-we? how-can-we? is-there? jarrings connected with the Garden Party. Ultimately the apotheosis of falling-in-a-dream beckons – '*told by his doctors to rest for two and a half months*'. Would de facto signal my not standing, or being selected to stand at the next election, but what about the White Office vow? Awareness of this certainly heightens my stress level, as also receiving encouraging notes like that yesterday from Dr (sic) Morgan of Trinity Coll, Dublin, '… it is not impossible that you may find yourself at the head of the Conservative Party'.

As I became drowsy I found (as one can) a formula. Michael Heseltine! Doctors' orders, etc; of course – Al and Heseltine! In no time I dropped off into a perfectly acceptable zizz.

Later, that evening
We then went over to Garden House to collect a plant. It is really nice over there, always. And, as often happens I felt a sort of wistfulness for the early days working on BB, which had so much promise – and was very good, but late getting completely finished and always bound to be panned. I wanted to find something on the shelves on the Battle of France 1940 (the Meuse crossings etc) but couldn't, though left with Leo Amery's diary,[1] always one of the very best reads.

We then did the 'w', woodland as always. It can make me sad, will I be doing this next year? etc.

Back at my desk I decided to phone Mrs Frowd: 'If I had liver cancer would you have picked it up?'

'I didn't pick up cancer anywhere … You are still carrying a virus around.' (Hey, just a minute, I thought I was suffering from deep depression?) She wants to see me as soon as we are back, clearly expecting an 'improvement'. But I am not looking forward to the trip as much as I would be normally. No point

---

[1] Another diary much read and re-read by AC: *The Empire at Bay: the Leo Amery Diaries 1929–1945*, edited by John Barnes and David Nicholson (1988).

in going to Gleneagles, and the treat of eating in the conservatory, and their excellent *carte de vins* – if you can't *consume*. Must try not to be too much of a wet blanket for Janey.

Pavillon   *Sunday, 23 May*

I sit here (ironic how often I seem to find myself getting like my father, with cashmere rug, writing pad/text on the knee) and am feeling awful and apprehensive, having woken with a headache, then uncontrollably retch-vomit on the 'w', just at Lynn's Bank. Now wonder that I may be getting jaundice (was it vaguely like this at Eton, when it started, in 1942?). Utterly without appetite, have indeed an aversion to food (couldn't even eat a didgy with EMT). Just thinking about releasing PA statement – 'Alan Clark to "rest". The MP, 71, suffering from strain, has been advised by his doctors to "take a complete rest" and has cancelled all public engagements.' This will obviously affect my position in the constituency, and also in the House, itself.

Summer Bedroom, 12.30 p.m.
It is early afternoon, in May, and I am frightened. Jane, perfectly sensibly made me come up here – the full sickroom, pad on, teddy [hotwater bottle] warmly dutiful.

I feel very weak, I doze intermittently, and can't 'keep anything down', not even half a tumbler of water. I'm just convinced I'm getting jaundice and have (or am just about to contract) liver cancer. I feel as if I am dying, as indeed I have for several months. There doesn't seem to be any escape from it – except to 'pass away'.

I don't want to leave Janey, and Saltwood which [I] love and the birdsong. There is evidence of one of TC's little messes on the duvet. Sadly I remember how he used to come up and find me here in the early spring when it was a 'sickroom' and once fell out of the window and into the rose.

I am fussed about the impending (tomorrow) flower show. Billy Wallace's famous intelligence of sitting next to the QM and feeling sick ... Am I going to have to dash from the tent – that special, unmistakable and stooping dash into a giant handkerchief?

I will, I suppose, tell the boys. I would like to have them with me when I die, as I have always said, like the squire in *Tom Jones*. Just to hold all their hands and tell them – what?

I have not felt so ill, or been so low – a mixture of fear and gloom – for a very long time.

I see, incidentally, that it is exactly three weeks to the day that I had my little turn in Bill Holding's shed and walked down to the Long Garage wondering if 'anything' was going to happen.

Later

A symptoms note. I feel viral. Very much 'the floor of Mother Teresa's waiting room'. No sense of improvement of any kind, however slight. How do I get out of this? It is, literally, incurable. Jane, with some truth, said, 'I couldn't drive north in this condition.' And of course it is so true that driving on the A1 adds to the strain. Don't want to miss the trip. Train or plane? I need the hills, but I am very, very weak now, like Tom? My little simple 'tea' hasn't come up yet; but already I am feeling sinister.

Summer Bedroom   *Monday, 24 May*

I spoke to Angela Rhodes James. Made me worse because Robert, it seems (after coming back from Australia and another 'go' of chemo), walked into his house and simply went upstairs to bed (he was feeling terribly weary, 'because I think his liver was packing up') and just lay down – and died. 'It can happen, you know, sometimes', i.e., exactly what I half want to do, half think quite soon is going to overtake me. It is strange up here, and creepy, as the wind blows the rose branches against the

window. The blackbirds, though, sing 'goodnight' enthusiastically.
I am more depressed, I think, than I have ever been.

Summer Bedroom   *Tuesday, 25 May*

I am still in the Summer Bedroom. It is a fine Tuesday in May.
I am behaving exceedingly like (because, I fear, I am) someone
'with' cancer in the '20s or '30s. Yesterday started better; we
drove to Barton Court for the Chelsea Flower Show. I took a
taxi to Nick Page. Then I walked round to Dr Muncie, who is
attractive. She ran the ultra-sonic scanner over my abdomen.
Images linked to a screen nearby. At the conclusion she claimed
to have noticed that 'everything was all right'. This cheered me
massively and I made a triumphant entry to Simon Hornby's
lunch tent.[1] Shook little Nick Brown[2] by the hand, then flirted
with the red-haired married lady on my right. Disconcertingly,
though, a glass of Sancerre had only an adverse effect.

It is very, very busy as the Royals have to be greeted at 4.50
and said goodbye to at 7.15. I was typing at my desk on Monday
morning just longing for an excuse (for Jane, possibly), an
instruction to abandon it. If anyone at that time had said 'you
are going to have to sit next to the Queen at tea' I would have
protested quite literally that it would have 'made me ill'.

The whole thing amazing (sic) confirmation of the status of
Chelsea as an utterly incredible constituency. At the gate fell into
conversation with the Bernsteins (David and Anne) when a figure
half attached himself – it was Heseltine (!) – 'in the papers' this
morning, Henley are thinking (sic) of de-selecting him. He looked
a bit wildish.

---

[1] Simon Hornby, President of both Royal Horticultural Society and Chelsea Society
since 1994. A former chairman of W. H. Smith, he had also twice been a Conservative
parliamentary candidate.
[2] Nick Brown, MP, Minister of Agriculture since 1998; (Labour) for Newcastle-
upon-Tyne East and Wallsend since 1997 (Newcastle E, 1983–97).

Jane – darling sweet Jane, she does so much – drove all the way home. Ate a small amount of curry and naan.

Later

Janey was sitting on the bed. 'Are you going to blub?' She nodded. 'Come over here.' The poor sweetheart, her lovely grey eyes were full of tears. This is my real sadness. I just can't bear to be away from her – for so long.

Summer Bedroom   *Wednesday, 26 May*

I forgot Jane's birthday – how could I? Only remembered when Sarah rang this morning. Last night quite soon in I was woken by her pretty face against mine, she was distinctly wet with tears. I am so sleepy I suppose I just dropped back off; but was soon rewoken by her touching my cheek, and hair and face. Jackie Kennedy and Jack in the Dallas infirmary. Poor little love. 'I don't want to lose you,' she kept saying. I am so exhausted I couldn't respond properly. What made her wake up to do this? For us both this is a deeply unhappy time.

Before supper I had made a start on a Saltwood note for the boys. However, at the end James and Julie rang and were compos and cheered us up – have now definitely decided to provisionally (sic) drive north.

Later I prayed. 'God; I am frightened. You have given me so much, everything really; and particularly my little love, whom I betrayed. How I wish I hadn't done so! The thing I fear most is leaving her. She is so good, so important. Please, please will you care for her also …'

We went up (1.27 train) to the 'mayor-making.' First looked in on Graham Camps.[1] He is reasonably reassuring, and Jane agreed. Then to House, taking tea except I risked a slice of apple

---

[1] Graham Camps, partner of Bird & Bird, solicitors, Fetter Lane, London.

strudel. I went up to the 22 Exec, felt illish when I repicked Jane up at the Family Room, but just got to KTH, where cheery black attendant thanked us for our Christmas cards. Improvised my way through both the ceremony and the reception (I see Barry Phelps looking at me fishily these days). [Andrew] Dalton hanging about, but not effusive at all. We cut the dinner, then drove back in Big Red. I had most recklessly eaten a canapé. It had the miraculous effect of making me hungry! So on getting back I had a tiny Jane-2-egger cooked in oil. Slept pretty well.

At one point yesterday Nick Page rang about the results – he was talking about a coloscopy. 'Cancer of the colon is the 2nd biggest killer of men after lung and (I would assume) prostate.' And I thought of Robert Rho J.

I must not go on whingeing. It is fearful-making just being in the Summer Bedroom at the end of May and so feeble. Don't quite know how we're going to get to Scotland, or what I will do when I get there.

As for the medium term. I agreed talking to Jane that what I really want is to *cancel engagements*.

Now with some trepidation am going to speak to Nick Page and hope he doesn't say anything unsettling.

'There is no evidence of any liver, kidney, pancreas or heart disease; and the second blood tests are all normal.

'This tends to confirm the clinical impression that there is no disease here and I suspect it may be the psychological factor that lies behind all this …'

This *has* calmed me, and made me feel hungry. I'd like a yoghurt and cereal.

Pavillon   *Thursday, 27 May*

So hot this May morning. Adding to my misery, in a curious way, because I love the month of May. I went over to the Great Library. I thank God for everything. He has given me so much since I wrote the Plymouth selection speeches at the head of this long table in June of 1972. And then of course, supremely, helping me at K&C. I asked him to help stabilise me and me to stabilise myself. I could not forgo the long march (to the reeds by the lake's edge). But I am so down on energy that everything seems to accumulate and get me down!

Today Lynn made a brilliantly perceptive suggestion. Jane was shopping, but 'Bill the gardener' had sort of made a balls-up of the Atco. The clutch had started to slip again and he had taken off some of the shields. Wanted to take off clutch, but 'could only be done by bending it.' Certainly not, I said. I cannot bear employees who abuse machinery – as they all love to do, and it irritates me every time I hear the Mehari going.

'Nothing for it,' Lynn said. 'You'll have to retire and take a job as a gardener.'

What bliss! But how totally illustrative of the sort of dilemma which, probably more than anything, is 'stressing me out'.

Summer Bedroom   *Friday, 28 May*

I am suffering from *apprehension*, triggered by an initial attack of panic (brought on by what?). Last night, e.g., couldn't raise Eriboll though left several messages and got this awful child-in-the-dark panic – of which I had had an attack earlier on at Garden House when Jane suddenly disappeared and wouldn't respond to my coo-ees.

Now I am really low. Everything seems so ephemeral.

By the evening AC had deteriorated – feeling awful, headaches and wanting to be sick. Jane recalled sitting up in bed in the middle of the night saying 'I think you've got a brain tumour. I'm going to call a doctor.' That morning he was examined by Chandrakumar (the Clarks' local GP) who said he wanted him to have a brain scan. Despite AC's protests Jane drove him to the William Harvey Hospital at Ashford. By

*the time they arrived he was so dehydrated he could no longer stand and
had to be admitted in a wheelchair. The scan revealed a massive tumour
and despite it being the Whit weekend it was arranged for him to be taken
to King's College Hospital, London, by ambulance – Jane recalls someone
apologising that it was not 'as comfortable as one of your Bentley's'.*

*Jane drove up to see him on Sunday. No longer dehydrated he was
in typical AC form, ordering everyone about. The surgeon, Nick
Thomas, had arranged for AC to undergo surgery the following day. AC
takes up the story:*

King's College, SE5   *Whit Monday, 31 May (pre Op)*

Just woken and (a bad sign) thought I was in France. Actually in
King's College, SE5 – quite nice private room.

Jollier last night; boosted by talking to both boys, doctors and
Jane. Watching TV. Fell asleep instantly 11pm. But head filling
with putative engagements for today ...

Woken, panicking, by drip alarm. V sleepy. In came nurse and
changed reservoir.

Slept totally till 6-ish. Then started looking at clock. Could
easily have depressed you (no!). Is this a function of the tumour
itself? Heaven knows what it will be like when coming 'round'
(sic) from the anaesthetic.

Yet last night the Registrar was charming, said I was the only
person who could rival Blair's combination of charisma and
authority.

Saltwood Summer Bedroom   *Friday, 4 June*

Green ink! Originally reserved for holidays (Z or E).

I am back from (in a sense) the dead. I nearly – sic, etc – died
last week. Tried to get through to Father Michael [Seed] etc.

That second operation … 'to stop the bleeding' … on Monday (!).
My physique (Nick Thomas, surgeon, very splendidly said to
Jane, 'biologically, he's young') has taken a real battering. Last
night Janey, quite brilliantly drove me back in the Discovery in
the dark to get here at 2-ish. (For five hours she had devotedly
sat in my room at King's College while we both watched the
three blood-transfusion sacs drain down.)

Yow! Did I creep − first real slip-change down into old
age/infirmity with the walking stick − through the Garden
Entrance, up the front stairs, line of route in reverse etc. And the
previous two days in hospital I could hardly straighten the legs
out without setting the heartbeat knocking, the blood coursing.

But today, physically, I am doing more and more. It's the mental
work, any kind of analysis which is what I am really trying to
avoid. It particularly does/did affect the brain. But quickly leads
me into unwelcome little naps with observationalist dreams
involving my father, which make me a little frightened.

This morning I woke, thought myself to be a little short of
psyche. In spite of reassurance from Nick and Chandrakumar I
know it could quite well be George VI valet.[1] Certainly the best
(least 'controversial') way to go. Pin just been on the answer-
phone. 'I shall be so cross if you go ahead of him,' Jane said.

But to some extent the whole episode has 'cleared the air'. At
least outline parameters will have been set, and I have been able
to talk seriously to the boys. Also (sadly) I have withdrawn,
effectively, from public life. This at least should reduce the
number of neuro-toxins circulating in the skull (if I stick to it,
and try not to strain the mechanism).

But the only way for real peace of mind is to wind the whole
thing down.

As a start I should ask − if I had died in a collision last
weekend and then reappeared, what would Jane have wanted to
ask me?

---

[1] George VI was found dead by his valet in the morning at Sandringham; he had
died peacefully in the night.

Sunday, a.m.

Less batteredly pensive. But feeling so empty. I must be terrifyingly anaemic, ½ panicky about the haemoglobin and awful green, vile-smelling colonic cancer Thompson.

I seem to be wasting.

But yesterday went out, really needed the stick, to Tom[1] and back. Turned at the garden entrance and went to the well. Then on to the sun-dial in the rose garden.

In the evening a personal handwritten letter from Blair. 'Come back and give me a hard time.' Utterly delighted and moved.

Baddish night. Awoke and apprehensive from about 1.30 round past 3.15.

Jane, though, snuggled up and was quite incredibly lovey and reassuring.

Summer Bedroom   *Sunday, 6 June*

Helped Jane start C-type (which she did brilliantly). She also coaxed the white duck and her brood out of the conker-tree door.

But I am really worried about constipation (I think this is partly responsible for a recurrence – sic – of headache). Appetite ok-ish. Not sick. But it is all impacting.

I am catastrophically depressed. How is this all going to end?

Much fiction being generated about 'recovery'. 'You'll be back' etc etc. But my objective simply to 'get comfortable'. Tie up ends that need it, and then calm down for George VI valet.

I'm very, very weak. But at least I'm getting (bounding, almost) out of bed a good deal.

I don't, though, want to read anything about myself.

Also, am fully dreading 'next stage'. How do they get the stitches out?

I never want to go into a hospital again.

---

[1] The grave in the Bailey of Tom, the Clarks' Jack Russell.

Monday, 7 June

7 *a.m.*

Another fine day. I would have been prepared to go up to
King's College, but am dreading it. Now Nick T will himself
come down this p.m. I still wake feeling ghastly at 2.50–3.10
(incredibly bad luck on Jane). Rewoke 5-ish and my plight came
crashing in. Almost couldn't quite believe it. But mini-step. At
8-ish heard duck and ducklings under pressure. Leaped from bed
and out into Bailey in pidgys and bare feet.

Sad that, what a way to go; if I have to. Thanks be to God and
Janey in particular.

Tuesday, 8 June

8 *a.m.*

Nick came down yesterday p.m. and took out the clips. Forty in
number. First 'reasonable' night. (Unexpected, strangely, after
being told, indirectly, that you've 'got' cancer.) 2.50 a.m.–3.10
a.m. not so bad. This morning quite hungry and ready for
action. Even went down, and 'did' the padlock. This is the first
morning that I haven't felt absolutely ghastly. At present, watching brief. Must not get involved in office paperwork (neuro
toxins etc). James may be here tomorrow, which I'm looking
forward to. I am over-active. General frustration compounded
by 'big' Bill who (after ego-ly asking for a 'manual' for the
compressor) oafishly using the Countax and then blocking out
the Bailey for most of the day, I would think.

My special worry, is, of course, colon blockage, if not cancer.
But I would think the anaesthetic is now 'out', almost, of the
system. I leap from my bed the whole time and am quite ready
to 'take over' the Countax, e.g. from 'big' Bill. I am still quite
composed about George VI valet (but today I am not – so far –
glazing over into, and then resisting, mini-coma).

But when it happens the transition must be smooth. There is a
hell of a lot of heavy-duty paperwork still to be put in place (the

worst sort of situation). I have now wound up a notch in imagery. It's reconstructing Vichy after the fall of Paris. But I am doing too much admin – the sort of thing I ought to be avoiding.

A nice round. Did Roman Tower, then Welsh, then round the half moon and Jane drove me back from Towers in Discovery. Dear Hannah still pawing me. I can progress forward, ready to force the pace. Chandrakumar coming (jarringly) at 7.30. But will not ever (DV) go into a hospital again. That's why I am so worried about a blockage. Then went to have first bath in the Cork [bathroom]. I have lost weight, a stone, and look like a thin old man. I recalled a lovely high spot of physicality and natural delight when Jane and I bathed naked at the slipway round Eriboll shore towards the sheep fence and a seal came up and said hello and we waved at him.

Wednesday, 9 June

Really frightened at about 1.30 a.m. I must not sleep until I have seen 'Boy'. Sweet Janey blipped (the first time) at EMT.

1. I am really ill.
2. Never going into 'hospital' again. I am now the chieftain at the Mains.
3. So it may be George VI valet.
4. Or I may go, doing something. Nothing anyone can do about it.
5. So diminishing I have got to force the pace a bit.
6. Potter about. Make free with the place. Reacquaint yourself with the Long Garage, the Great Library.

Long talk with James, before I got deafer and deafer and my arms weaker and weaker. Walked in the Bailey a little, smoked salmon 'snack'. Sleep one hour after lunch. I am weak. Arms tired. Frightened of being sick.

Thursday, 10 June

First 'good' night. Plopson at 4 a.m. and again at 10.30 a.m. after breakfast. Arm fatigue diminished. Lovely talking to James about Eriboll, Burrs,[1] lots of things. Jane still incredibly pretty and fresh-faced.

I'm still a tiny bit worried about visual co-ordination and have had a brief left foot-toe panic. But more energy, less fearful (spelt also with a 't') though still hate falling asleep ('naps') in bed. More energy. I must try not to look too far forward. I'm alive. I feel better. If I do a Simon Fraser[2] the situation is more clear for my successors.

Whether or not I will be spared gradually to consolidate my position as a Renaissance Count is still to be seen. But even if not, better King George VI valet now than cardiac in the ambulance on Monday p.m. when I wanted to fetch Father Michael.

At 8 p.m. drove and turned XK140!

Friday, 11 June

'Not quite right' (?mark, eyes, throat, toes etc etc) – frightened of falling asleep – strange dream patterns. But found that achieving is the most therapeutic. Did the gate and just came back now from winding and setting the stairs clocks.

Lilian due at 10.15. Will bugger (sic) my plan for a supplementary Thompson. But long to see him too. Then it's just me and Janey after today (which is looming with cars, mowers, etc.). Her wonderful remark – 'now' (i.e. post-King's) 'it's all bonus'.

---

[1] Burrs, shop and property at Tongue.
[2] Simon Fraser, Master of Lovat, had died suddenly in 1994, in his mid-fifties a year before his father, the 17th Baron.

Later on Friday, 11 June
I just list what God has given me today (lunchtime):

1. A long talk with Andrew.
2. A general feeling of being energetic 'on the case'.
3. The will and impulse to go down and phone DD.
4. A strange feeling of fulfilment (much reduced glazed 'napping').

Later
Been ruthlessly stirring myself. Bast'd *Express*. Rang *Classic Cars* etc.

Almost 'normal' over in Bill Holding's with James. Putting compressor on Countax; trying to start Mehari, etc. Appetite normal.

Two black spots. Thompson still y. Funking suppository in case it doesn't work. Eyes a bit out of focus. Dread 'consultation' looming next week on 'Radio Therapy'. Nasty decisions.

Also livid with 'Bill' who has broken every machine. Want to break him. But 2 days now with Janey at peace.

Saturday, 12 June

A nasty night – usual panic time.

Arm weak, sight awkward, difficulty in defocusing. Suppository/Thompson while Jane in Hythe. Morale rose. Had a nice lunch (smoked salmon and macaroni cheese). Series of cat-naps and deliberated. Seem much *livelier* today.

Went to join Jane in the woodland, I drove Countax back (!) – What a way to go, etc etc. I am much tireder today, and looking awful.

Sunday, 13 June

V good night. Arms less feeble. (Suppository Thompson at 11 p.m.)

Get stressed talking to Jane about 'Big' Bill. I'm more worried about stressing her – she's so brilliant. Even Countaxed the woodland yesterday.

But I feel that God has given me additional strength. I am hungry and have written a checklist.

Later

Best day physically. Worst day morale – blood in (utterly inadequate) stool 11.10 a.m.

Arm weak on and off all day. But blissful afternoon. Starting Chev, Big Red, Barnato (to reverse) and Jane gets Mehari going. I thank God for such happy times.

Monday, 14 June

V good night.

Unbelievably manic this morning. Plopsons. Had started 3 letters and dictated EMAP to Sue.[1] Jane has brilliantly put Bill on notice. Irritatingly the garden is full of schoolchildren. Soon the Amazings, including Albert, arrive. If it wasn't for eye trouble (defocusing v difficult) I'd be *in the lead* at still not quite two weeks. God is being marvellous to me.

Tuesday, 15 June

A bad night. Indeterminable. Jane didn't sleep well either.

But semi-redeemed by double plopson at 5 a.m. and 7.30.

---

[1] AC's monthly column, 'Back Fire', for *Classic Cars* magazine.

Weight exactly 11 stone. Eyes (left now too long-sighted) only remaining worry – radiotherapy 'consultancy' (will talk to Nick first).

Calmly concentrating on getting Estate in order, so the transition (sic) can be smooth ('seamless').

I really love being out-of-doors. But decided to 'overdo' things. Yesterday was apotheosis with the blonde babies crawling about on the grass while Saltwood 'shop' was run by Lynn, Andrew and Jane.

Later that evening I walked the upper woodland.

11 a.m. I continue to be amazed at my recuperative powers, grateful to God. Spoke C. Hoare & Co on Jane's behalf. Cut verges a little and spoke to Bill in the Bailey. Spoke about arrangements generally. Then Sue.

Now I must lie still for a bit. Outside a girls' school is on a visit. But all temptation is lifted. Particularly, and most liberatingly the whole congested diary; 'speaking engagements' etc.

I can plan with a calm mind. As Jane said, 'it's all bonus'.

Wednesday, 16 June

a.m. I can scarcely believe that I am where I am. 2 plopsons this morning (without aid). Coping with Coutts, Eriboll Trust, Bill's letter of dismissal (although this 'fussed' me at breakfast). Feeling full of energy. Eye-focusing only remaining symptom.

God has been incredible to me. It's 2 weeks and 1 day.

I shook hands with Eddie in the kitchen. Is this 'my best day'? There must be a reaction … (or, DV, not).

Friday, 18 June

Just back from 'w' to machines! Tired – but v good plopson at 7
a.m. (they are so much better in the old wooden[1]).

Talked things through with Jane at EMT. Whole affair is in
many ways perfectly timed.

I look at my engagement diary. Sunday, Church Service in
Chelsea. Rest of week, and the next, impossibly demanding,
each weekend eaten into.

For what? 'Image projection.' For what? '… if you shall find
yourself …'

But actually whole strategic position had altered with Tory
'triumph' in Euro elections.[2] 'Hague walks tall' etc etc. Stuffing
Shadow Cabinet with 'young Turks'. My position would have
been greatly weakened, but the 'engagements' would remain.

As it is I can devote myself, with a clear conscience, to
Saltwood and the family. Every day is a day gained, and being
put to good, satisly, or constructive use.

Will I succeed in being the Renaissance Count, but still
holding myself ready to do God's command?

Monday, 21 June

Yesterday was my best day. Felt energetic, grappled paperwork,
moved cars around (SI Cont turned round to face out; XK140
moved to Bill Holding's etc) and striped – most of – Bailey.
Cindy Frowd came and also did good. A lovely cheese and
cauliflower dinner. I slept excellently – best yet.

But this morning we were up early, and ready at 9 a.m. with
John Williams with pump and hoses for pool. Initially I was
amazing.

---

[1] A Saltwood lavatory with wooden seat.
[2] With only a 24 per cent turnout, Labour's poor showing was soon discounted.

But later Chandrakumar arrived to take some blood. Checked on haemoglobin (what's the point?) accompanied by a *nurse*.

He let fall the dreaded word oncologist about Coulthard (or whatever he's called)[1] and his radiotherapy. Actually this depressed me dreadfully and today I feel weak in the arms, tired, and at intervals cold. I 'overdid' it striping on the tractor and I seem no longer to have the almost manic level of energy for proper work. Almost a hint of back to square one. It's strange, because I am feeling better and my weight has now crept up again to over 11 stone. I now realise that the great benefice of Nick's operation (excision) was the return of enthusiasm, almost of *joie de vivre*, so that last evening, e.g., I classified all the Coutts, C. Hoare statements.

Now I am listless and my morale low. I feel somehow as if I am already undergoing radio therapy. The VCC visit and even the XKs[2] on 18 July hang over me, because I so love the blank time with Janey.

I must go to Eriboll and see Angus and the Birkett Foster rocks before a decline sets in. That week, just for a few days on the sleeper seems the best bet for a little 'pic'. I somehow can't realistically envisage myself, certainly not at yesterday's peak form, being there for long in August. I am sad today, the first, almost, since the operation three weeks ago.

Tuesday, 22 June

Woke depressed. Weight still 11. Talked to Jane at EMT, mainly about after my death; how my spirits will always find her at 'Tom and Eva'.

---

[1] AC thought he was related to the racing driver, David Coulthard. In fact the oncologist spelt his name Stewart Coltart.

[2] The Veteran Car Club and the XK Jaguar-owners' club, who had arranged days out for members at Saltwood.

She made a remark that really chilled me. I will be so vulnerable on my own, 'just an old lady with a couple of dogs'. The moment my death is announced all the crooks will converge on the place.

This morning I am low and frightened. God please deliver me a little (last night Nick T very good on the phone, said 'no contra-indication' for glass of red wine!).

Far my worst day from the point of view of morale and apprehension. When I rang Canterbury the woman on the extension said 'oncology'.

My physical symptoms are ok. I do things, like being outside, I'm 'getting better' if it were not for this awful overhang – Chandrakumar blood test and the 'oncology'. Only God can get me out of this.

Wednesday, 23 June

Another stage to make, I fear, a reversal of both fortune and direction. I have been getting steadily better each day, since the operation and since (especially) my sortie to Saltwood. Last night I was incredible, and even this morning 'normal'. But from today I will be in a morale-based decline. The oncologist appeared at 12.30 and I did *not* take to him. Quite clear (as I have all along both suspected and know) that radiotherapy is both disagreeable and useless. 'No cure, so don't expect one' etc. The word cancer was freely mentioned a lot.

Almost at once I decided to go on a sortie to Eriboll. We sat in gloomy silence at lunch. Then I went for a walk in the woodland. Now I am very sleepy and going to risk a nap. It's so sad, as I was really 'making medical history'.

Friday, 25 June

A good night. I always sleep well after Cindy Frowd has been.

Yesterday evening I mowed the *wanderweg*.[1] Had spoken to Nick who said 'ok' to go to Scotland and he would write the prescription for boost steroids which John the chemist has very gamely agreed to provide. Am I up to the journey? Tinkling and Thompson, Macrae & Dick[2] on arrival etc. Jane is very pre-occupied at the moment. How very ironic that our plateaux of serenity should be disturbed by these two car events, VCC and XK.

Saturday, 26 June

I am writing this in my father's study in the Great Hall. I am low, more depressed than I have been for a very long time.

A bad night. Headache, eye-tension derivative. My head felt so hot. Poor Janey, so long-suffering. I was near to panic; all these horrid little malignant tendrils starting up again. There is absolutely nothing that anyone can do – except possibly the very last stages of cortisone/steroid dosage.

I am made apprehensive immediately by this bloody VCC coming tomorrow. But more so by the imminence of the Scottish trip. I want to go to Eriboll asap; there are certain sites – Birkett Foster, the Creaggan and summit, Tom's game bank, some of the beaches and coves where we used to nude-bathe – into which I have got to lock my spirit before the body gives up. Why am I so feeble? I seem to be worse than for a couple of days. I dislike the bright, hot June sun. I hate the bluebottles which buzz round me whenever I settle. Just back from Cindy Frowd. Jane drove me down and I felt slightly carsick. She

---

[1] The mown grass path from outside the towers.
[2] Land Rover dealers at Inverness. The Clarks always bought their Land Rovers there.

didn't seem to do much for the eyes – unlike on Thursday. I wonder about my blood test. Chandrakumar is keeping himself to himself. Perhaps my haemoglobin is still down – but so what?

Later back in MFS GH
I seem to have done an awful lot today, but feel knackered. I swam (!) – in the ¼ full pool. Delicious. Should have done two circuits, and funked it. Then on the walk in the woodland at 6 p.m. I felt so exhausted I thought I might have to lie down. Read my grandfather's diary for 1912 this time. At Poolewe, fishing, what a lifestyle! Why drink yourself to death?

I napped after lunch under the fig tree, and sweet Hannah came over to see if I was all right as I didn't come on the 'w'. I love that dog, she is so quiet and devoted. I felt awful again. So weak, and this is new. Arranging, etc, a lot of chairs, tables etc for tomorrow.

I don't want to die until I have seen Eriboll and there I may be able to contrive it.

What I particularly don't want is to lose some faculties, vision especially. This is a bad time. What I don't understand or like is why I am not so strong as I was 3-4 days ago.

MFS GH   *Sunday, 27 June*

I must record a wonderful day (against all expectations).

I rose early, moved things, fussed. When the visitors and their rather boring brass-age cars, were assembled I mingled, spoke to them (shades of Robin Tavistock in *Country House*), felt pretty amazing. Jane was pleased with the way everything went. Saltwood 'putting on a show'. Then I slept, went on the 'w'. But I still feel as if I am 'getting better'. Quite remarkable. If I didn't have radiotherapy and Chandrakumar's silent blood tests hanging over me I would be over-confident. Came over here

after tea and said a prayer of thanks. It's lovely this kind of demo
that God can do anything.

Brian Moore came in his red Ghost with 'Alpine' tourer. I
remember how fast the car was the first straight out of Vienna
and told him so.

Later I reminded Jane how lovely and romantic was our
meeting at the Monaco landing stage in Venice, then going on
to Trieste, making love in the hotel room before dinner; and
then the rest of the magical [Alpine] rally.

I have this divine serenity at present. I do hope it lasts.

Eriboll Wheelhouse   *Thursday, 1 July*

It's incredible. At 8 p.m. I sit in the wheelhouse. Troubled only
by a full colon (blocked, presumably, by a(nother) tumour). But
what an achievement to be here! Came up on the day train
yesterday from King's Cross. A lovely journey with attentive
staff, although I became adversarial with the passengers including a man of my age who sat on the other side of the aisle and
seemed to be observing us and listening to our conversation. He
did not, irritatingly, appear to have prostate trouble. (Nor did I
come to that.)

Derek Presley[1] met us with the latest Discovery – very
pleasing indeed. Jane drove and stopped at 9.15 p.m. at the new
curry restaurant in Bonar Bridge. Amiably they produced a
beautifully packed and labelled take-away and as we drove along
to Lairg we ate one of the most delicious meals I have ever
consumed. It was dusk and drizzling when we arrived, but still
I walked in my raincoat alone and with the big stalking stick to
the boathouse. On the shoreline I thanked God for getting us
here 30 days after Room 17. Then a cup of Ovaltine and slept
like a log, as did Jane.

---

[1] Derek Presley, managing director of Macrae & Dick.

Today I have done a lot. Incredibly walked around the walled garden, going to Birkett-Foster, sawing some logs. Almost like old Eriboll crofting days.

But one little additional bonus. Yesterday morning we arrived in good time at New Palace Yard and while a cab was being summoned and loaded I went up to the tearoom – alas almost empty except for Cheryl Gillan.[1] She was nice. Did not as I should have done tip-toed round and stand briefly at the Bar of the House. It would have been my very last time; just as, too late, it would have been in April 1992 when the badge messenger said, 'You can't go in, sir, you're not an MP any longer.' The Speaker had just announced the Dissolution.

I was lionised by many, especially by the policeman; and the taxi driver who took us to King's Cross. But it made me not in the slightest bit nostalgic. Because, with Hague consolidating there is absolutely nothing I could do.

Wheelhouse, Eriboll   *Saturday, 3 July*

This morning, for practically the very first time since the 'illness' struck I felt a certain anticipatory elation when getting dressed after a good plopson and prior to walking with Jane to the boathouse.

The Eriboll magic. Yesterday I went to the Creaggan, lifts [by car] for some of the distance, but walked the last bit to the summit of the col and then across to the little knoll (which featured in *Love Tory*[2]) and round it. This made me very tired. I couldn't dine or linger at the Lodge, but I ate five of Angela's oysters and slept virtually without interruption for ten hours!

Today we went to Arnabol in the new Discovery. I felt very

---

[1] Cheryl Gillan, MP (Con) for Chesham and Amersham since 1992.
[2] *Love Tory* – Michael Cockerell's 1993 BBC film, made at the time of the publication of *Diaries*.

tired on and off, but the pluses are unavoidable – especially no more weakness in the arms or muddled obsessionalist dreams.

How I wish that I could stay up here and just cure myself by God helping me to regenerate (as he has done so brilliantly up until now). But tomorrow we return, for me to be slowly and systematically destroyed. But how wonderful to have come up here, and tasted its strengths and touched all the beacons.

Monday, 5 July

We got back last night after Jane had driven heroically from Eriboll-Inverness (Scotch mist started on the Moine) and London, H of C car park, to Saltwood.

Didn't have a very good night. Worried about the little pea-chick which had drowned accidentally.

But this morning after an excellent plopson I am serene, having been to all those lovely places where God could at any time take my spirit if he chose. I am now back at the Mains and must look to him for strength.

Later

Soon I got lower and lower. All those bloody chits from Dept of Oncological Radiology etc. I am homesick for Eriboll. The sweet oystercatchers all came in a flock, full strength, to say goodbye to us yesterday morning at 6 a.m., when we were loading the Discovery. I see always the beautiful view of the shoreline from boat house beach and hear the slap of the wavelets. That is heaven for me. But today I seem to be an awful long way from it; and it's very inaccessible. There I would gladly lie down and die. But the gulls and the hoodies [crows] would take out my eyes, which would be upsetting for Jane.

Later still

I bathed today, one length. The first this year. Thank you, God

MFS GH   *Tuesday, 6 July*

I'm very tired. But today I went to Canterbury for 'planning' –
i.e. fitting the mask.[1] All quite encouraging

Then I did a lot of mowing, also swam two lengths – just like
the old times with Lëhni waiting aggressively on the steps.

I don't have much of an appetite, and after my 'nap' was
muzzily headachy. But it cleared with the tea. And here I am in
these lovely rooms, still acquiring strength and confidence. My
blood test, haemoglobin etc totally ok (as Chandrakumar was
forced to admit).

Looking back at the PFD diary, and the period 4–6 June, my
progress is really incredible. I dare not even write down what
God could do if he chose so to do. I am happier now than I was
in those days. Partly I suppose my recuperative powers. Partly,
also the impact of the wonderful Eriboll memories, especially
the Creaggan knoll, the boat house and the oystercatchers.

Pavillon   *Wednesday, 7 July*

I have been coping with Stuart J. Dawes and the repaired Atco
and Countax. I am feeling really tired and feeble. Back a notch;
and this makes me depressed and apprehensive. I woke, and felt
utterly exhausted and shattered, like in the early days here (6
June etc). I am not eating enough. My appetite is on a hairline,
and am losing weight visibly. But God can get me out of this as
he has every gloomy situation …

---

[1] A clear plastic face mask used when undergoing radiotherapy of the head.

Later, Garden House

I am in my father's study. I have eye-headache coupled with some dizziness. No great appetite.

I virtually finished the Bailey with the repaired Atco. A delicious machine, but fills its green box in 1½ stripes. Felt very tired, but swam one length. I remain depressed and apprehensive. Just like May, I fear.

I think about when I may 'take my leave'. Once I get to Eriboll to the boat house, I am so close to heaven. But to get there is so difficult.

Whereas here, with all those lovely things around me, it could always be '*Suddenly at Saltwood*'. My eyes are not good today. They ache. But I am not as bad as I was in the first week in June, when I was almost frightened of falling asleep.

The Catholics are coming. 'Guild of the Divine Sacrament' on Saturday. I hope I'm up to it.

Pavillon   *Thursday, 8 July*

This, so far, is my very lowest day. I am so de-energised, almost like May, and have an unpleasant, eye-related frontal headache.

Napped after lunch, but couldn't even (literally) take the plunge. Resorted to splashing my face, which did no good.

Before lunch I was standing in the Great Library with Jane and Lynn. A month ago I used to go over there on my own just for the fun of arranging books. This time I had to sit down, couldn't do anything.

I dread the inference that there must be another tumour lurking in there. X-rayed today in Canterbury. But then what? I feel that I am cut off especially from Eriboll. All I want to do at present is 'rest'. My eyes complain if I do any kind of paperwork, like, e.g., even writing this note.

Progress has come to a halt.

Later

After tea (always the best time) I got a good adrenalin fix. Rang Anji Hunter to inquire if Blair would like to come to the Mass on Saturday. Long chat. Felt 'tons better' at once. The combination of female admiration and political inner loop.

Friday, 9 July

A(nother) very hot day. I am de-energised, utterly, almost like I was in May; and I have horrible eye/headache. Cindy Frowd said that I was much better than when she first started which cheered me up. But after my 'nap' I am filled with gloom. Prayed in the Summer Bedroom before going to join Jane in the woodland.

It all seems unending. But how does it end with cancer of the brain? Mark Boxer and Jock Bruce-Gardyne.[1] Do you lose your faculties, vision, speech, balance? I wish I could conceive of an escape route. It is just so difficult to get to Eriboll. And anyway I must, I suppose, give the treatment a chance. I fear, though, that now I am degenerating into an invalid ...

MFS, Great Hall   *Saturday, 10 July*

The Guild of the Blessed Sacrament have just left. A wonderful hot afternoon and by 4 p.m. the Inner Bailey had the appearance of a garden party. After my 'nap' I felt ill. No energy, no appetite, and those filthy headaches.

Last night Jane gave me a little reflexology on my thumb to

---

[1] Mark Boxer, cartoonist ('Marc'), journalist, editor of *The Tatler*, died 1988; Jock Bruce-Gardyne, journalist and politician (C, South Angus 1964–Oct 74; Knutsford, March 1979–83), died 1990.

ease the head pain; and amazingly it worked – I dropped off almost at once. But today is *so* fine and lovely it's terrible to be captive on a hot July afternoon in the Summer Bedroom. One should have serenity, be laughing, and with a feeling that there is still a lot in reserve.

Father Michael came up trumps. He produced the Marchmain case out of *Brideshead*, gave me sacrament for the sick, oil, holy bread etc.[1] For a few minutes I felt cured. But it soon reverted. No appetite, or energy, headache. At periods I am back to May – which is particularly lowering.

Summer Bedroom   *Sunday morning, 11 July*

I am ill today. Headaches, no appetite, weight implacably stuck at 11 stone. It is really hot and fine, but I am exhausted and sleepy. This is strange and rather unnerving. Even in the early stages of my recovery I was full of bounce.

Howard Flight[2] has just made some rather splendid remark (about leaving the EU) from the Treasury (Opposition) front bench. And been 'reprimanded'.

Later

Feeling really ill, still. I collected all Jane's share certificates and brought them up here to see how they should be consolidated. 'Quite a nice little list ...' But feel eye-related sea-sick. I know I am exhausted, but surely food is as important as sleep?

---

[1] AC often quotes from Evelyn Waugh's *Brideshead Revisited*. If he saw life imitating art one wonders if he knew that in Waugh's novel art was imitating life? As Waugh explains in his diary (13 October 1943) he drew inspiration from the death of his friend Hubert Duggan, and the priest saying: 'Look all I shall do is just to put oil on his forehead and say a prayer. Look the oil is in this little box. It is nothing to be frightened of.'

[2] Howard Flight, MP for Arundel and South Downs since 1997.

Monday, 12 July

Continued to deteriorate during the day. Sweet Janey cried, heart-rendingly, after 'lights'. 'I don't want to lose you …' The laughing, the chatting, the strength. I went down and rang Nick Thomas who (as always) returned the call immediately. He was unwelcomingly grave. Authorised 2mg of D/M[1] per day. But spoke of 'new' cyst. Could be removed surgically. I am so depressed. The stagehands are now fiddling about with the curtain(s). I took a D/M, and slept pretty well; though immediately on waking unease and pain starts to come through the eyes. I remain very, very exhausted and sleepy. I don't see how this can end now, except with my dying. I do not look forward to the gravediggers clumping about. God, please help to keep Janey's morale up.

Later
After breakfast (of which I did not partake) Jane went down to a 'site meeting' at the Workings (stream). After a bit I came into the Green Room and just started to get things 'in order' when I had a 'little turn'. Quite frightening. I could have fainted, or just sat down and passed out; or perhaps be sick? I felt ill, and see how Robert Rhodes James (and others come to that) can just give up the ghost. I panicked and appealed to God. Reading the past, marvellous, entries, He has given me so much strength, and favour. At the moment my sights are set on 'clearing' the XK visit.

After lunch
I don't think I have ever felt so terminally ill, headache on both sides. Weight won't even now read at 11 stone.

---

[1] AC's shorthand for Dexamethadone, one of the drugs he was prescribed.

Summer Bedroom — *Tuesday, 13 July*

I sat on the bed here, feeling feeble (just had a bath because I, and the pidgys, have become poofy).

It turned into rather a sad little morning.

Jane and I had an argument about the size of the D/M dose (not easy to calculate owing to the confusion of the milligrams and micrograms). Lynn was in the kitchen and Jane ran out crying. I swallowed all eight, told Lynn to find her in the greenhouse and tell her I had done so. I read a piece in *The Times* about a new cure, but with a poor prognosis.

I then retreated to dictate the review of Graham's book[1] to Sue on 6212. This took quite a while. No sign of Jane. So I left a note and went out to walk in the – her – woodland; lower path and twice I missed my footing and fell. I was quite frightened. Only God can give me strength now. I don't really want to die now, or here. Back to the old conundrum. How do I get to Eriboll and the oystercatchers? I suspect that Jane will thwart this. She does not want me to die in the north, probably for administrative reasons.

So I am low. The D/M has banished the headache, but the eyes can still induce nausea and dizziness. What is my *raison d'être*? If there is ever going to be an *être*?

Bonjour Tristesse; comment tu vas – ou vas tu?

Green Room — *Wednesday, 14 July*

Very, very low and depressed. I feel sick (again, it is the breakfast). Couldn't even manage EMT (a new low). We talked about my present arrangements. Poor Janey is going to be under *so* much pressure.

---

[1] *Burying Caesar*, Graham Stewart's first book. AC was by no means alone in praising it.

Later (back to bed)

The most depressing of all conditions, when you can measure your regress. I now have no energy to do anything. And all the escape routes to Eriboll seem to have been closed off mainly by logistic difficulties – distance, Lynn's hols, the dogs. The fact must be faced. I'm weaker than I was on 30 June – with the triumphant return to the tearoom, and the Station Hotel in Inverness later that day.

Back in Summer Bedroom   *Thursday, 15 July*

a.m. Eyes really ache. So no appetite at all. How do I emerge from this? Dreading the XKs.

Wrote Jane a letter for our wedding anniversary [31 July] and gave it to Lynn.

We went to Canterbury. Not much encouragement. After the skimpiest lunch I had ever consumed, tried a nap, but disagreeable, blighted by a non-obsessional dream sequence. On waking up – where am I? What's going on? What's next?

7 p.m. Now – 'sick headaches', accentuated by where is the hat?[1] Jane has finished mowing the Inner Bailey. Started to sort – not a good idea – some of our Eriboll photos. Made me so homesick. Surely there can be no location better suited to taking leave of one's earthly body. How to bring this about?

Saturday, 17 July

Feeling simply dreadful. Is this how Death approaches? This morning I could eat no breakfast to speak of. The smell of bread

---

[1] The Clarks' name for a cardboard receptacle in case AC needed to vomit.

frying made me nauseous, as I was going out of the kitchen, Jane snapped 'why?' at me. I tried to explain, but was, I recognise, soft-spoken in the extreme.

'Your problem is', Jane said, 'that you want to die; but are frightened of dying.' Too true. It is the journey that scares me. Partly, I suppose, due to those unpleasant dreams that recur. It is only a few weeks ago that I was buoyed, in the Great Hall, etc. etc.

The Amazings are coming in this afternoon to help with the XK rally. Poor Jane is so exhausted. Can one wonder? She does so much. (Jane has just brought me a glass of cool sorrel tea.)

Garden Entrance, Terrace   *Sunday, 18 July*

The XKs parked all over the place. Andrew extremely competent in coping. The blue, the white and the grey cars all 'won' awards. (So there!) I said to James on the phone. Fitting, somehow, that my impending departure should be attended by this huge retinue of XKs. 'You must think positively,' was all he could say. Useless advice, although well meant.

Monday, 19 July

This morning I am in absolute despair, though can still be talked out of it by Janey.

I remain low, and frightened. What is my objective? Just to get through this, I suppose, and return to good health – or at least to feeling like I did a month or so ago. My brain seems to operate on two halves. The second one is muddled and potentially obsessional. I have been quite wary of it for some weeks. It seems to subsist on creating bogus problems and then attaching spurious solutions to them.

I am very unsettled, and more than a little frightened.

Tuesday, 20 July

Yesterday in mid-afternoon I felt so ill I wrote Jane a note.

Darling
I think I'm going …
    The divide between giving up life and *being sick* is a narrow one.
    You must not forget how much I love you, and regret having caused all this 'aggro'. Talk to Fr Michael. He knows.
    Also get a message to the oystercatchers. And to Tom, also. I will always be *for you*.

A x x x x

When I was writing the note Jane was crossing the bridge, and heard me calling … we are very psychic, and she particularly.

Saltwood, Summer Bedroom   *Thursday, 22 July*

Woke this morning after a 'good' night and suddenly realised that my mood had altered. I thought that I was 'feeling better'. Alas, soon back into whirlpool. Tried to contact Macrae & Dick, via Julie; this infuriated Jane (for whom I must be a hopelessly trying companion).[1]

Only redeeming feature on the horizon (sic) is the arrival in September of that same *Discovery* from Macrae & Dick. If it coincides – as I think it will – with the end of my treatment, then it does open up the possibility of getting to Shore Cottage for nice contemplative period. At the moment the day does not seem quite to have acquired a finite shape. And I am not quite happy that I am using the time properly.

---

[1] Jane had given the number to AC, who must have misdialled it; hence his call to Eriboll.

Earlier this p.m.

I have been doing a certain amount of contract note work to clear the decks for Janey, and all. I was thinking well at least I'm still living. But the actual end is very nasty to contemplate. Just going downstairs and Nick Thomas on the line. Looked at the scans: 'There is really nothing more that surgery can do ...'

I really don't know what I should do next. I am scared at losing my faculties and dying without dignity. How I wish that I could hand on K&C to Tip. He would be so good there.

I still don't feel very well, but what is really horrible is the knowledge that you can't 'get better'. God could help, but why should he? Still, I might, I suppose, have died already like JFK.

Saturday, 24 July

A good night – 9 hours. However, at EMT, when I turned to Janey and said, 'you know what worries me about the difficulty of getting to Eriboll?' 'Hello, here we go again', she answered in good humour.

I had just re-read my note to her of Monday ('I think I'm going'). Feeling so dreadful telling the XK Rally etc and asking her how she could get a message to the oystercatchers, which would have to be 'his body is somewhere else. But in spirit will always linger here and seek your consolation ...'

Yesterday, I'm glad to say, we did quite a bit of work in consolidating her investment list.

Later p.m.

Over in my father's study for cool and shade from 'the glare'. Dreadful eye-ache, of the kind one used to be able to relieve by D/Ms. Once again (as last Monday) I am absolutely miserable. Feeling trapped almost to the point of panic. How to get independence back? That wonderful feeling when we stopped the little demonstration Discovery beside the stream on the evening of 30 June after that incredible curry en route from Inverness. I was unsteady on my feet. But the oystercatchers guided me. Slept perfectly, because I knew I was safe. 'Don't thank me,' God said, 'thank BLJ. She brought it about.'

Saltwood Summer Bedroom   *Monday, 26 July*

A lot of hustling and bustling with different doctors. My treatment starts tomorrow and in some apprehension I look at the tube of Biafine Emulsion[1] which is meant to protect the skin from burns and (can it?) disfigurement. Last night felt ghastly. At one point it could have been 'Suddenly at Saltwood'.

Green Room   *Tuesday, 27 July*

Jane drove me back today from the first day of treatment at Kent and Canterbury Hospital. My vision has gone and I am most worried about it; now see double images, particularly vehicles coming towards me, which quite underlines Nick Thomas's early caveat.[2]

I am very very in despair. Where do I turn? Something told me, again and again, 'don't come back from Eriboll.'

A little later I rang Broomhayes and spoke to Lilian. As I said later to Jane I do love the way they have all settled in, after a fashion, on to the Seend scene. One of Seend's premier families. After all, the little boys can't be much less aged than when we were there in the sixties and we were making waves at (say Ned Whiting's) and forging memories. A lovely, friendly, beautiful

---

[1] Nick Beuttler, AC's brother-in-law, sent the cream, available over the counter in France.
[2] AC had been told not to drive for three months after his operation.

place in Wiltshire. I will always remember the first time I saw Broomhayes, when we were looking over 'Miss Usher's', as it came to be called, and thought – 'gosh, there is a plum'. So neat and pi – 'building society advertisement'.

Blast, as I wrote this I am finding it more and more difficult to focus, and to alter focus.

Now it is Wednesday, 28 July

The very favourite date in a Parliamentarian's diary. All over. The great long recess is finally under way. For me the delicious feeling of relief is irrecoverable. And the prospect of the Pait weekend.

This realisation ought to be coupled with a feeling almost of triumph. Aha! I've given them the slip etc when it first seeped through the anaesthetic in June. Now I'm trying to escape something nasty. No sooner back from Canterbury than a headache, usual mussy kind linked to the optic nerves began to creep back. The Bailey in July at 1 p.m. was full traditional Saltwood. Beautiful, sunny, warm, hollyhocks burgeoning. I suppose that I should just have stripped and plunged in. The shock of the cold water … what a way to go! A nice irony after all my earlier physical exultations there.

I look at a 'piece' in the *Sunday Times* – 'stars (sic) all home in on Scotland'.[1] A map and illustrations. This made me very sad, the knowledge that I am not physically in shape to enjoy it, because of bad vision, headache, and extinction of appetite. Also, let's be fair, loss of *status*; tied in with impending loss of life itself.

---

1 The Clarks and Eriboll were included.

Green Room, Saltwood   *Wednesday, 28 July*

Oh dear, I am down! Actually I do not think that I have ever
been worse. Came back this morning from Canterbury ('radio').
A man with an unattractively shaved head in the waiting room.
Now I see, piecing together what is on the label of the cream,
'*ne pas appliquer sur des brûlures infectées.*' Oh dear! Those awful
close-ups in articles about cancer of huge scabeous sores,
blackish and overtly malignant.

At present there is a huge vacuum around my life. What am
I actually waiting for (that is of course itself exceedingly
carcinogenic)? No more comradeship drinking, shared and
competing ambitions, gossip, taste.

These are all the things I love in (and about) life. Perhaps that
is why at present I am getting so many nostalgic evocations –
the N7,[1] the café at Kalpetran,[2] even, Jane remembered, the
great expedition down to Zinal when she and (I think) both
boys met me in the Porsche.

Well, weather it as best I can.

At some point, as the news gets worse, I find myself resolving
to take a bolt. Head for the highlands and put my body at God's
mercy.

Saltwood Summer Bedroom   *Thursday, 29 July*

Talked with Boy on topic of Zermatt. Did I imagine it or when
he rang off I thought the word Treuhand was mentioned?
Suddenly realised this might be the answer to everything. Stuff
(sell) a lot of the Sotheby's inventory, which I have got 'forward'
into the AG!! Slept more calmly after a nice vol-au-vent supper.
Must talk to Janey today, or asap.

---

[1] The old route to the south of France.
[2] A halt on the way up to Zermatt.

Just back from Canterbury – yes, it makes one so tired it's unbelievable. I'm up here now and ill, but don't even want to sleep, daren't would be truer. I'm in a dead end at the moment; both physically and morale-ly.

I've got this nasty headache – literally a 'sick' headache – and am really scared of losing my vision, possibly totally. Jane didn't deny this possibility, but did say 'think of the sounds …' (at the water's edge). Then I couldn't induce a coronary; I'd just have to drown myself and be buried off the 'machine' or thereabouts, but how do I get there? It is all so miserable.

AC's wedding anniversary letter, to be opened on 31 July, but written on Thursday, 15 July

Just back from a visit to Kent & Canterbury, not a very good day …

Hello, my sweet Janey!

I am reminded that only 41 years ago I was somewhat apprehensively sharing digs with Celly and Caryl in Victoria Road Westminster – a short distance from Grey-Coat Gardens.

At that time I was already bonded, and would soon formally be *pledged*, to the sweetest, kindest, most percipiently intelligent human-being I would ever encounter. What a union that would prove to be!

Those lovely 'fair-heads', of every generation! And all the sympathy and knowledge for *plants* and *animals* that has radiated out from you and transformed the whole ambience of the family seat. (Am I getting a bit illegible? If so, damn, and apologies.)

For every minute of the day you have worked for me, us and the family. Worked *too hard* (Henry). A hundred times I ask myself how I could have been so cruel to you. Fool Clark, fool. *Nasty* fool, also! What's the use of my saying you are, will always remain, the only true love of my life? If you should ever need me, I will, I hope, be possibly at certain known localities in the grounds (of each property, even Zermatt).

Love, love, love from

A xxx

Saltwood   *Sunday, 1 August*

Fact is, I've got brain cancer. And it is fairly disagreeable.

My body realises that there is no hope. I mean what is the next stage? The next (local) demon with which to wrestle?

My wrist shakes – why? Shades of little T.O. I could not eat, even put into my mouth, any of the delicacies prepared at lunch time today. Or even the 'accompanying medication' which hourly makes Jane very depressed.

I am afflicted by a kind of despair, also.

The Amazings coming in tomorrow. What can I say to them?

The house is like an oven now, excepting the rooms on the north side.

JANE

Although AC did not know it as he wrote, his entry on 1 August would be a true 'last', as he would say, the final entry in a journal that he first began writing almost forty-five years before. His eyes troubled him; he stopped reading and writing and often found the glare even from a clouded sky too much to bear and asked for the curtains to be kept closed. He may have lost his own will to record his decline, but Jane now took up her pen. In a spiral-bound A4, green, soft-covered notebook she started recording the events of each day. What follows are extracts:

Day 5 of radiotherapy[1]   Monday, 2 August

Al got dressed and so wobbly – came downstairs on his bottom, me placing his feet on each step. He is really bad.

Day 8 of radiotherapy   Thursday, 5 August

Took ¾ of an hour for the pill saga and 1 minute piece of toast to be completed. I long for a meal that I don't have to get up every few minutes for some whim. I long for Al to take the pills without having to yet again explain what each one is for (more than twice, it's 4 or 5 times).

He is now off dried fruit – the sight, the smell etc. Lunch soup (spud garlic parsley) and tomatoes, slice ¾ of apple. But he radiated such depression I felt completely drained by its silence.

10.25 came to bed – Al had eaten *no* food nor had he even taken his pills.

---

[1] AC had started a course of radiotherapy at the Kent and Canterbury Hospital, with Jane driving him there and back daily from Saltwood.

Day 9 of radiotherapy   *Friday, 6 August*

It's 7.20 a.m. Have bathed and made breakfast. EMT in bed writing this with Al sitting on the edge of the bed trying to be sick and soft-spoken. I feel ill with the struggle ahead – long for a dark, warm place that is silent, snug and I can sleep.

Car luckily in Bailey which was easier. Do not think he could have done back steps and slope. Late leaving which I hate as it's so rushed, but in spite of 3 traffic lights made Canterbury by 9.10, time to offload Al into a chair and for me to put car in car-park and to run back. Collected pills for sickness on return. Into Pavillon – lunched there and Al rested – I made him go under the willow for this as Pavillon too hot. Had got from Rabies Room wheelchair of Bonny mama. Tyres pumped up well and Lynn gave it a good wash. It is jolly good.

In and upstairs via chair – had to walk from Huega tiles as chair would not go through gap. Upstairs on hands and knees.

Bed 10-ish – tired, but no early start tomorrow.[1]

Rest day   *Saturday, 7 August*

Rained in the night hard, but cleared up and now fine. Woke at normal times, but Al slept well – and only tinkled once at 5.30-ish. Lovely lie-in. Didn't move until 8, swam and made EMT, gave Al his sick pill – he didn't have a biscuit – but did drink a cup of tea.

In bed all day dozing on and off. Peed again at lunch. He ate *so* little – 3 teaspoons of spud, a scrape of cheese – then a curtain rest, tea v poor – I had walked dogs etc and went up with tea to find him on the floor in the passage by the banisters. Got him up and back to bed – he has bruised quite badly and small abrasions on his elbow/arm R.

---

[1] The radiotherapy department at K&C Hospital did not operate over weekends.

It seems to have had the effect of completely unhinging his mind. He mumble rambled – did not really notice anything. Seemed far away – on about a PhD and being on water. Quite frightening and he was so good in a.m.

Supper 1 banana whisked in milk (½ cup), he had 2 spoonfuls v reluctantly and then pushed it away saying it was going all round his head. Told him he was a b fool and of course it wasn't. Couldn't, so he drank some more, almost ¾ of it, which was good.

Rest day 2   *Sunday, 8 August*

Bad night. He woke for a tinkle at 1-ish, but could not get back to sleep, so nor did I – at 4-ish or bit before he decided he had a headache so I had to fetch dry biscuit so he had something in his stomach before pills.

Raining – swam, made tea and porridge for Al, which he did eat (small yellow bowl used). Al in bed all day – peed not in pot so changed pyjamas. Have got wheelchair upstairs to take him to loo.

Just been upstairs. He just lies there making bizarre zany muddled sentences or mostly just saying nothing, but lying looking miserable. I find myself so demoralised now being in the room, so deeply depressed by it all.

Decided to run a bath and give him a wash and hair wash, too. Back in chair and left him in it by window (curtains closed as bright sunlight), made tea, and only into bed after tea – just left him. He has been sick. Damn, damn. Not a lot, says it is the vitamin pill so *they're* out.

Cut his toenails and filed rough skin. He looks so much better. Wish he would read a little or take an interest in things.

Day 10 of radiotherapy – only 10 to go   *Monday, 9 August*

So rushed didn't even do hens today – oh dear, oh dear.

Mrs Frowd came 4 – was pleased with Al's progress.

Over to GH to collect other chair – back with Eddie pushing it – he stayed for tea,

I mowed Tom's grass – and potted up aloe vera in greenhouse. Lots of tomatoes now.

Came in from the Pavillon about 8 as Al wanted to go to the loo. I had a breakdown as first couldn't negotiate the small rise by yard door, then hit a lot of things in outer lobby, and ended by kicking everything to right and left hurling boxes of papers, chairs etc. Shouting at poor dog (Lëhni) whose paws were slightly in the way. Broke down in tears in Cork bathroom with Al on loo.

It's 9.40, I still haven't had a proper meal and am desperately tired. Al would not eat *anything* tonight just lying there hiccuping, retching.

This whole thing is a ghastly nightmare. I do not know how it will end.

Day 11 of radiotherapy   *Tuesday, 10 August*

At 20 to 12 woken by movement, but Al still lying down – then the noise of a pee. I can't believe it. He is peeing in the bed, just peeing. I confess I freak out somewhat – it's through the sheet, underblanket and saved from mattress by electric blanket and New Zealand wool underblanket – pyjamas naturally sopping. I take them off him and hurl them out of the window; all the while he tells me he hasn't peed. Change entire bedding, put sheet into machine, feel sick. Poor darling Al. Both take long time to fall asleep. Up 6.45 – swam, did hens, breakfast, porridge, tea, coffee for A which he didn't drink today and ate not all porridge. Into car in good time, but oh dear I had left it switched on. Battery *totally* flat. All change into dear S16[1] and into K&C. Saw Stewart Coltart afterwards and he gave me the shattering news that it was pointless to go on with R – unkind to Al and the family. He shouldn't be like he is after 11 doses, bladder going, no balance, lack of appetite etc. Very bad sign. I was in tears – Al had gone out of the room for a blood test. In my heart I *knew* it wasn't right although trying to look positive. We went to find Al, me with tears pouring down my face past all those people waiting – Al didn't really seem to have taken it in – has he? I don't know – although I was in tears he made no sign of compassion which isn't him at all. A gloomy drive home in suitably torrential rain, which stopped at M20.

Into Pavillon as usual and in to Lynn for a good cry. Lunching, he ate a very small amount of spinach and spud the size of acorn which produced retching – and half a pear. I am to cut down on Dexamethadone – only 2 a.m., 2 lunch, not the tea or supper ones any more.

It's strange I feel numbed by this news – waves of tears when I sat in Pavillon for tea – he didn't notice at all. Earlier I had come back from hens and walk to find he had an accident with water bottle so had to change every stitch of clothing. Dressing him quite difficult as he is limp, but if you say move this way or that he can't seem to work out how to.

I love God, but this is such a cruel way to demolish such a brilliant brain – I dread to think what lies in store.

Talked to Andrew, Sarah, James and Julie. They are equally shattered. Amazings will be here Thursday and James as well. How long we have got only God knows – but miracles sometimes happen. It is the eclipse tomorrow. For us it was going to be a turning point – but now the beginning of the end.

---

[1] An old Volkswagen Golf, used as a runabout.

Eclipse today, 11.20 for us   *Wednesday, 11 August*

Sister Angela Rourke (Irish?) district nurse came 11.30 to 'assess' Al and offer me advice and what have you. Got v cold during eclipse and quite dark – v cloudy, could just see a crescent of sun. Light amazing as it came out so beautiful and bright – '… and let there be light.'

Walked dogs – saw Eddie who was terribly upset at the news. Back – Al tried to pee, but failed – he won't drink or eat. Noticed spots on his chest and back. Tried to make him drink water – he was terribly sick after 3 sips – oh God, why? He looks so desperately unhappy and knows only too well what is happening.

9.15 Rang Mummy – she poor darling is v ill too. I should be *there* as well as here.

Crisper and fine day   *Thursday, 12 August*

Spots are worse now.

I didn't bathe, thought I saw worm in pool. Threw in remaining chlorine tablets. Have a headache and feel sickish. No breakfast for Al. Helen Blake from hospice team came, stayed for *hours*, Sister Rourke also came. They discussed anti-sickness pills etc, etc and saw Al. Thought the spots needed something. Dr Mohr coming later to see them. Andrew, Sarah and boys turned up, Cindy Frowd turned up. It was awful – *so* many people – meaning well I know, but I'm not so sure they don't make you worse – *counsellors* – not for me. I need them for making Al's life unpainful, painfree and for access to commodes, sheets, waterproof etc.

Tup brilliantly mowed Bailey and dealt with battery problem – it was totally flat, wouldn't take a jumpstart at all. He also shaved Al and helped move him from Cork to bed, while I ate lunch. Came with me to find depot to collect mattress etc etc. Would *never* have found it if he hadn't come with me.

Went and sat with Al in bed. He did eat a tiny sandwich and sipped tea. Then a bath – will it be the last? He is so vulnerable and frail. I dread him falling. The Zimmer is brilliant, very light, but strong and good for confidence.

Overcast, but dry and windy   *Friday, 13 August*

No night disturbances, but I slept badly waiting to leap out of bed. The dogs were intolerable, scratching and panting on and off all night. Must deflea. Up at 6.15 as Al wanted to pee – got in commode, which he thought ok and used. Thompson and tinkle so v good. I think Al *better*. Just a little bit – the pills against sickness seem to be working so he kept down breakfast. Made damson purée. He had two 2 tea-spoons.

Very fine and windy after wet night   *Saturday, 14 August*

Al has not spent a penny now since 3 p.m. yesterday. I do hope James will come before it is too late. I am tearful. Al has just drunk a ¾ cup of tea! More muddled today. Have asked him if he wants to say anything – he likes the idea, but fears it would be too melancholy – his journals through my pen.

Asked Al what he thinks when he looks out of the window.

AC: a path through a jungle really and I suppose the … I am being consulted about it.

JC: Carry on, turn back?

AC: you can sort of divert.

James arrived as I was putting him back to bed just in time as he is now difficult to move. My back is going – I get on the bed and pull him on and up if alone.

Feel I rather abandoned dear Al as he was in and out with James, but James had some nice talks and shaved him, which was good for Al's morale. He was also quite tough about drinking and breathing.

If this is a game of snakes and ladders we have met the biggest snake — a veritable pit of them.

Still, crisp and sunny   *Sunday, 15 August*

8.30 I must get up. We are lying side by side. Al completely silent and looking so vulnerable and *young*. Not an old person at all. Tup saw him, said how much he had lost weight from Thursday's visit. It's lovely having everyone about, but I feel I am more with them and *cooking* than with Al. We had a Sunday lunch of roast venison, Yorkshire pudding, spinach, beans and spuds. V good for me as I ate well! I took my tea up and lay in the bed with him for 2 hours talking and weeping. It is so hard, he does not really respond as if a river was between us, and he can't/won't hear and can't/won't respond. But I know he hears as when I queried God's role in this he stopped me and said I mustn't blame God. I don't, but why does God think *I* need proof of his powers — what is he trying to say to me, to us both?

Monday, 16 August

Al turned as I put the [EMT] tray down and said, 'Is that all the ships?' I affirmed it was.

Al seems to be slipping away from us. No breakfast (or EMT) – only sips of water.

Dr Chandrakumar and Gail (District Nurse) came 12.20. Dr C briefly saw Al and the rash, and agreed it was caused by drugs – why don't they say *medication*? He then took me and Gail into the Red Study – I called in James and Andrew and he told us it would not be very long now. It is inevitable and so like a dream gone badly wrong – a nightmare of depression. I still keep hoping for someone to say it's all ok.

It is 3.35. I foolishly asked Al to say something I could remember – something nice about his BLJ. He stared silently away – and when I walked out called me back saying he thought the question 'was about level playing fields on the battlements'. But still no words of endearment – I long for some sign, but he is not really here so I must be content with a squeezed hand and not grumble.

He was so dear as I struggled to get him on to the bed and comfy saying I was angelic. I told him I couldn't let anyone else sit in the room and nurse him and he was so pleased and reassured. Being really ill, if you are a proud and private person, is so cruel it is only your loved ones you want round you at this moment.

Cool heavy rain, but sky blue, too   *Wednesday, 18 August*

Dr Chandrakumar came 12.30-ish – I like him. He does not go for the make-him-eat-drink-and-force-his-bowels-open stuff. Is really quite spiritual in that way – agrees the most important thing is to make sure there is no pain, which, thank goodness, is the situation now. Was v kindly worried about how I was coping and agreed to be my doctor and will put me on the NHS. Talked about what to do when he dies – I did not know and had asked him. I have to notify him if possible – no objection to him staying here and undertakers were always on 24-hours call. It's all essential information and I am calmer for knowing everything.

Earlier Stewart Coltart had come – he is nice too and did not rush us, but gave his time. He took a look at the rash and said it was Epanutin – his wife was a dermatologist and he telephoned her and she confirmed this – so at last we do have a culprit – ok to stop it tonight as still in blood for a bit so perhaps by the weekend it will start clearing. He does not complain of it, but it looks v uncomfortable, and is really everywhere, but face, hands and feet.

Crisp, windy, but fine   *Thursday, 19 August*

Gail, the quiet District Nurse came – do hope we can continue with her – and was very pleased with Al. Said to Lynn how different from Monday he was. She will collect the new anti-fit pill and drop it in at Lynn's. Al tinkled well and is so much better and more smiling – I'm aghast at the fact I was shovelling in that little green and white Epanutin pill every night and it was causing so much aggro to his blood/skin, poor darling. Late lunch as he dropped off – but he did have some soup and almost half an apple. Drinking quite a bit more. Have put on Gail's recommendation 1 Redoxon into one of his drinkers.

New anti-fit pill is a lovely violet colour!

Rang Mummy whose legs are still v bad – she goes tomorrow to have stitches out.

Crisp and fine today   *Friday, 20 August*

Poor dogs not walked as James did not want to be left to get Al on to commode. He is quite different from Andrew who is a genuine carer. J just like Al would be.

Watched while we had tea the boys and little boys and others playing on the lawn. It was fine and sunny and I cried tears for a future that Al was not to share. It is like a terrible dream and you wake and it's real and oh how I long for it to be not so. Al is not aware of my crying whereas tears would have upset him before – that too is hard – we are already apart yet still both alive and close. Strange.

Crisp and v fine, heavy dew   *Saturday, 21 August*

A quite good night after tinkling at 10 and then asking again at
11, but it was a blank. We cuddled instead, but he was not really
here – a strange faraway look on his face. He had left me and I
must realise this will happen more and more. He has always been
my other half, but the branch is nearly off and the scar will take
time to heal over. It is strange to see and feel him and yet know
he is fading away from me.

I am writing this on Sunday and only did the above and my
mind is a complete and utter blank as to what happened on
Saturday. I'm going mad, not Al. Talked to Nick [Jane's brother]
or was *that* yesterday. Shit, shit, shit. I am going completely gaga.

I know I wanted to go to the church, but a wedding was in
progress so that was out – and somehow it was hard to leave the
place.

Overcast day   *Sunday, 22 August*

Awake on and off but all seems well. Finally fall asleep as usual
after 6 and woken by Al throwing the duvet back and wanting
to 'dump'. Half asleep I shot round and helped him on to the
commode, but too late and I got it all down left leg of my
pyjamas and I later realised it was a little on floor so he trod that
in and all over front of commode legs tinkly etc and his pyjamas
too. A disaster for first thing and *most* tiring.

James came and popped him into the bed as I was going to
wash him – but before that he suddenly announced he wanted
to dump again so off we got and more produced. Tup came and
we got him back into bed and comfy.

Breakfast reduced one to tears of frustration – he had wanted
porridge, but when it came he refused to taste it. Toast and
honey minute little mouthfuls – 1st one spat out – and gagging
ensued. Coffee ½ a cup ok. Went and made Weetabix + warm

Complan milk. ¼ only but after 3 egg spoons Al was gagging and trying to retch, so hardly anything.

Started on 'the pills'. 2 D/M + anti-sickness, 1 anti-fit: difficult now as he will not swallow it in one go so it stays in his mouth dissolving. After the 2 D/M and anti-sickness, he said 'I must dump' so out of bed and on commode – just saw in time. He had got his tinkle out and pushed it back in – as more foul-smelling diarrhoea and large pee came. Back to bed (alone so back twingey). Put pyjama top on as it is colder although sun now out. Made hotty. I only managed a bit of toast and cold cup of coffee – am quite exhausted.

11.45 now and I am lying on the bed while Al sleeps 'Venice train'. He was dear though and said he was sorry about all this. I said I found it so hard that he no longer seemed to notice if I wept and I wished he would weep with me – are we in this together or not, I said – if you can't cry with me who can you cry with? He said he didn't want to give in and only to God could he cry, and we would look back on this and he would remind me of our conversation. Yesterday – I might have thought it possible – this morning I feel there isn't any hope. Everyone says it will be up and down, but oh it's so terribly cruel – when you are up you think all will be well, this nightmare will end, we have a future to share.

It is a horrible, horrible, horrible thing to watch someone you love and who has such an incredible brain slipping into Kafka rambling and yet suddenly lucidly ticking one off for not reading something properly.

12.10 I must go downstairs now, have been sitting writing this up or reading *Sunday Times*. Al is asleep still – his face is getting much thinner.

It is the silences I find so depressing. He just stares ahead. Does he hear? I think so but he can't answer. We talked about how I would miss politics. What fun this last year or so had been since getting back into H of C, fun for me for once as I could share some of it.

I asked if there was anyone he wanted to see – any messages to or for anyone – he just looks ahead or talks so quietly it is impossible to hear and he never repeats it as it is obviously an effort to answer at all.

Supper was lovely fried squid – done by Julie in a jolly good batter. Al asleep – but did not stir when I kissed him. His dear face as I look at him sideways is falling in – oh dear God what a foul and miserable thing you have sent us all on such a beloved husband and father – everything has a reason, but I do not know what this is.

Crisp and fine again   *Monday, 23 August*

8.30 Al still asleep. Made coffee and grapenuts for myself and a piece of toast. Al said, 'You have been crying – so have I.' He seems quite different again, more on the ball and not so muddled. Another cruel quirk of this awful cancer – another 'up' to give us hope before a steeper decline again to despair? He had coffee and noticed today I had put sugar in it! Liked the idea of grapenuts and had 3 spoonfuls (teaspoons) and then two small pieces of brown toast and marmalade – and more coffee (nearly 1 cup of coffee). Drank nearly ½ Redoxon. I stayed with him – carpet swept the room and polished about, talked – he said he felt a weakening of his grip, but I tested it and it is as strong as ever – found him the wrist-strengthener which he used while talking. Quite good form, some wires crossed.

Grey and overcast and light rain fell today   *Tuesday, 24 August*

He seemed good this morning – fell asleep late a.m. and slept over lunch, which is now the norm. I took up soup and yoghurt, but not wanted. Sat for a bit, but left a note and went downstairs to do some bills – red reminder from the telephone as had not done them. Heard a noise and went up to find Al half out of bed having had an accident – changed pyjamas, sheets etc and got him back into bed. James came to help. He is now so heavy and dead-limbed it is awkward to move him – his face is now so thin you can see the 'plate' where the operation was, and his ribs, backbone and hip bones plus legs are too depressing. He is bones with skin and v little flesh. We talked, but he is quite muddled now – will try the lavender anti-fit, but not the anti-sickness one.

Late now after 11.30 and Al thirsty – suspicious even of water so offer to get him a piece of melon – downstairs to find J.J. still up. Back upstairs and Al takes one look/smell of melon and starts to choke retch – frantic trying to get upright. I rushed for James who held him upright. He sat on the edge of the bed lucid compared to earlier and not keeling over. Drank some water and took Epilium – while we talked to him. Julie came through and he lay down and we sat with him and talked.

Wednesday, 25 August

Michael Howard telephoned. I rang him and told him all not well. He was shattered by news.

Thursday, 26 August

Quite a good night for both of us. No sign of Bromley so *hope* he/she will appear again. 2Boy fine and jolly.[1] Al asleep as I write – sleep now and v calm. Just woke him calling Bromley – but it was 2Boy on the window. Al said good morning to me on

---

[1] Two jackdaws.

coming round, but otherwise just stares out of the window or ahead – looking so dreadfully sad.

He has now lost so much weight he looks like a PoW. Slept on and off, is low today – Helen (hospice nurse) came. He was monstrous and grimaced crazily when I tried to lift him and then flatly refused to speak to her at all.

Had tea with him and we chatted. I asked if he'd like Reg or Michael †,[1] but he did not answer and when he did much later on being re-asked said no.

Up with Complan for supper. *Very* little – he became quite fussed and asked about it. Was it poisoned, as they were trying to poison him? Andrew with me and we tried to reassure him, but this accounts for the fact he will not eat or drink.

Fine, cloudy, cooler (windy now)   *Friday, 27 August*

Dr C and Gail came and we have organised everything for a drip should he need one – Gail returned with an enormous tin and bags of medicines, which I have locked away. Al woke and peed, but I was not there and although we were in the kitchen it is obvious that isn't any good. I or someone should be *in the room* from now on as he is not aware of anything today and does not know he has peed or remember to call out. It is a dreadful down day. He does not even speak much, but when I kiss him and tell him I am here he half smiles, which is lovely.

Made tea and upstairs Al asleep. Woken and I went round and he asked for a kiss so he could remember my taste. We talked about it all. If it was for a reason what was it? He said he knew what I was doing for him and thanked me. Stayed until 7-ish – half asleep holding each other's hands.

---

[1] Reg Humphriss and Michael Seed.

Heavy dew, but v fine and dry, few clouds   *Saturday, 28 August*

Bromley appeared at the window for food. 'You tried to spike him,' Al said. 'No', I said, 'I've just given him a biscuit.'

Up to church with Julie – had a good cry. Felt better for it. James came back with a paddling pool and choc ices. Al actually ate a bit.

Did Al's nails and massaged his feet, creamed his arms and hands. He spat out the fish and peas. Is in a non-speaking mood, which is irritating to say the least.

Out now to do poor dogs who have had no walk or supper and it's 7.35 – I only walk around the top woodland and upper terrace. Back, gave them supper and met James who had taken up lovely picture of swimming pool to Al. J said he was very lucid and loving so I should go up and be with him. Told him I had been there all afternoon and he was just pretty non-speakers to one and I was bloody fed up with him.

He was not loving and friendly so I left him and came down after changing for lovely dinner of squid. Bed 5 to 10. Al asleep, covered him up and kissed him goodnight – (no response).

Heavy dew, v fine early autumn   *Sunday, 29 August*

5 to 5 I leapt out of bed and ½ asleep got bottle ready etc, but he had in fact peed lightly – so changed pyjamas and pad. He did not say a word, just glared. I am going to find this phase *very* difficult and depressing.

It's now 12.30. He doesn't seem good at all – not a good colour and stays mainly asleep. He was dear, though, and kissed me and said I was his BLJ and thanked me when I sorted him out after Thompson.

The children and young have been sitting outside in the sun with paddling pool in use and general jolly chatter/tears etc. It's another world out there, inside here my world is crumbling and yes, I am frightened.

James sat with him for 45 mins, came down and was quite rude when we said supper – he said he was going out for a fag. I then said don't worry I'm going up to bed and went out to get dogs. Dear J came out too and totally broke down in tears: 'I'm nearly 40 and I'm crying. I love him so much.' We both agreed it was absolutely vile to watch someone you love so much being destroyed by such an awful thing. He had his fag and we went in, both calmer.

Dry, overcast, warm　　　　　　*Bank Holiday Monday, 30 August*

Lost count of 'tinkling' 'dump' dramas. Sat in his room all afternoon as he dozed, but he is in a non-speak (to me) mood so it is really depressing. I might just as well have a nurse sitting in here and just go off outside. I sometimes wonder if he recognises me at all. – (yes, he does).

Staring into space, not talking – feel terribly low today. A lovely walk which restored me round the moat with the dogs and then with J J and A to see the combining. Bob kind and stopped the machine for Angus, but it is really so huge he was overcome. Bed late, too late.

Written at EMT, 7.40　　　　　　　　*Tuesday, 31 August*

A fairly ghastly night. I am so overtired by everything and things rather came to a head by a call for peeing at 12.40 and then nothing done at all. I fell back into my side of the bed at 1.05 and then another call 10 mins later (or rather not a call, but a throwing off of the bedclothes). Held the pee bottle until gone 2, but had a row with God and tried to tell Al how tired I was by all this and that I would have to get nurse in if this carried on. You always think you can cope, but you can't.

Tiny pee done, but he was a dear and whispered he knew how much I was doing and he was sorry. We talked and I lay with my head on his dear bony chest while he tried to stroke my hair. Oh dear, darling Al. Oh God how I will miss you. I dread the future without my soulmate. I dread being really alone without his wisdom, strength, fun and companionship. For 41 years we have been together, through ups and downs. Can I live without him? For the children's sake I must remain strong – the 'Dowager Empress' he said I would be. I must not let him down.

Woke this morning dragged to the surface by light (6.45), turned to Al and found he had thrown back his side of the duvet and peed. Down, laundry on and out for my bathe, up again with EMT. Al asleep – breathing v shallow today. Like dear Tom, you look closely to see if it is so.

Helen came, said to reduce his Dexa by 1 so only on 2 pills a day. She came up and saw him as Andrew said he was awake having peed again. I stayed and changed him. Tup saw Helen out and J J and Tup had a chat to her. She is worried about *me*. So is Dr C who said I should have 24-hour nursing for him now. I simply wouldn't, not while he still is aware of what's happening and although sometimes he looks through me and glares he will suddenly smile and say 'I know what you're doing and you are incredible' – or tonight he said he loved the gentle look I gave him. How could I just let a stranger take over? It is my job and I will go on.

Seems cooler, but still dry, high cloud, heavy dew again   Wednesday, 1 September

It's now September, the whole summer has gone by in a surreal way. I look out at the changing season from afar lost in this high-intensity 'drama', which is taking place in the Summer

Bedroom. Cannot get him out of bed any more, now too risky.

All the family off this a.m. to Dymchurch, girls by car, boys in the little train. Went on the beach on the way home. They are back now, said beach was lovely. Angus bathed so is now wrapped in James's T-shirt.

Dry, fine day, no wind, heavy dew   *Thursday, 2 September*

Woke before 6 to strange noises, put out my hand, but no response at all. I panicked. He was 'drowning' in his phlegm. Tried to put another pillow under his shoulders – not wildly successful. By 6.15 I thought it was the end. Terrible noises and looking v v bad. I rushed down with dogs to see if Tup and Boy there – no sign. Back up, caught Tup going down so asked him to fetch James, who rushed out of room to 'go for a pee' the minute he came in. Poor James, he is only making it harder for himself.

Al still open-mouthed, open-eyed, twitched lower jaw – a very minor fit possibly as it later (1 hour) turned into a shaking of shoulders, arms and hands, so I unpicked my hand from his very firm grip and took a little pill out to pop under his tongue, quite difficult and it was still under his tongue when much later Tup and I moved him to my bed to change and wash him and put a fresh sheet on the bed.

No sign of Reg on telephone, so Tup drove up, but he is obviously away. Tup brilliantly thought of Norman so I went and rang. Patsy, his wife, answered and said he was doing a service, but could come up at 10. She would go and find him. She rang back and dear Norman was coming straight up. He is *so* nice, a truly good, holy man. Both boys came in and we said prayers and he was anointed with oil. Felt so much better for it, and in a way I was glad fate had decreed it was Norman. Although I like Reg, we have known Norman longer and he has been a good man to know. Feel *so* much better that someone

came in time; I would have felt guilty before God if I had failed
to have him blessed. Waves of calmness are there now.

11.45 Realised he had had *no* medication and so Andrew rang
Helen (hospice). Gail will come to put in syringe driver. When??

In fact the syringe driver was put in after 7. Dr C came 6.30-
ish and saw Al – confirmed he was in a coma and unconscious
and we discussed S-D. James said a fit would be very distressing
and so when we realised the S-D would not do anything, but
peacefully end him we all agreed.

Dr C came back and Heather the twilight nurse, whose own
mother had died of cancer, came to put it in. I could not stay
for this as it somehow seemed to be wrong to violate the body.
Andrew stayed. Everyone being really kind. Al had been in a
coma, but could squeeze your hand until about lunchtime – his
breathing so rasping through the mouth, eyes open, but not
aware. Oh dear God what a waste, what a waste! It is this I mind
so much, not just the fact I shall be losing my soul mate of 41
years, my lover, my friend, my companion, my dearest husband
– oh *how* I shall miss him! What an empty horizon stretches
ahead, so frightening I cannot think of it, so am blocking it out.

It is now 20 to 10. I am lying on the bed beside him, his
breathing fast and noisy, his chest tight and violent in the
breathing. I hold his hand, but no response, his eyes now closed.
How long can his body hold on to life? I talk to him of what I
will do, the office, the woodland walk, the brambles on the cistus
bank as well as the woodland. Keeping the paperwork in order,
the bank statements in order, my life in order, a Lady Dunn
minus Beaverbrook. We were always such a good team and now
I shall be leaderless. Still the faith he always had in me will be
my inspiration. I must not let him down. The Dowager Empress
shall reign.

Now v hot and sunny   *Friday, 3 September*

Sat on bed or lay on it beside Al most of the afternoon. Flies
bothersome. I am paranoid about them settling on Al. Do they
sense he will shortly be dead? Finally went for a walk round the
garden while Andrew sat with him. Several scares, but tonight
(10.20) he sleeps ok, head slightly on one side. Eyes sometimes
open and still clutching the crystal.

Sarah and Julie both come in and boys a lot. James (and Tup)
really worried about *men* bothering me – how *dear* of them. I
simply do not see it at all.

Rang Col tonight – Celly out and Fr Michael out too.

Hot and sunny   *Saturday, 4 September*

Not an impossible night, difficult for me to sleep, but Al seemed
to be sleeping quite peacefully – one or two hiccups, but then
restarted. Talked at 4 to him, was sure he knows. Then at 10 to
6 Hannah got on the bed, plus Lëhni. I put Al's hand out so they
could smell him and he opens his eyes and I *know* he senses they
are there – a lovely moment.

Later back from a bathe and making EMT I tell him I'm back
and have bathed and I love him etc and he squeezes my hand (I
had cleaned him up, he had 'dumped' a little and peed – so now
he is lying comfortably). Oh such magic moments, but cruel too
as you suddenly think perhaps it's stopped and all will be well.

Washed hair. Celly rang, was very sweet and sympathetic. Nick
rang worried about me. We both agreed Ma seemed perkier.

Back upstairs with bowl of cereal I had dashed down for –
now in bedroom with papers and mail. Cutting from Romeike
and Curtice from the *Express* saying Al thinking of standing
down and I was going to support his decision. Furious, *hate* the
papers. What untruths they can publish. I shall have nothing to
do with them after it all comes out.

Stayed in the room all day on and off. Lunch came up, lovely cauliflower cheese. Father Michael telephoned, is coming down this afternoon. I went and rested with Al – fell asleep so Fr M had to wait – it was ok. Everyone gave him tea and talked. Then he, Fr M, came upstairs. Tup came too. We said prayers and Fr M anointed him with oil (been here before I thought). Downstairs and Fr M and I to Red Study where he talked and he told me Al *was* a Catholic. He had made him one on 10 July when he was with him. He had written down notes of that day. Sarah brought us tea. I was gasping for a cup, then I went back upstairs, Tup had very kindly stayed with Al. I must say I could have shaken Al. I felt quite hurt he had not told me he was made Catholic on 10 July – he only said he had blessing for sick and communion secretly. Why when we can't talk about it do I only know – for a short minute I actually hate him for holding something as major as this back. I had thought we shared all these things. How could he exclude me of all people? In a way it's quite good as I can now distance myself much more.

Tip came in surprised to see me sitting on *my* side of the bed, not 'in the crack' by Daddy. Showed him the letter Fr Michael had written for me. I was cheered up by the fact he didn't think Fr Michael *had* given Daddy last rites. I thought it poor compared to Norman Woods's which was v moving. This was very much a Catholic priest saying something for someone *not* a Catholic. Swing back. I do *not* think he was fully received.[1]

We talked about burying Daddy. I said he'd always wanted a shroud, not a coffin. James has not managed to hire a Kubota [mechanical digger].

---

[1] Jane's journal, Wednesday 8 September: 'A fax from Fr Michael. Long and rambling, sticking to his tale of Al's conversion, but tonight while cleaning my teeth I spotted Al's Day Diary which reminded me I had his journal in my drawer – how silly of me, I could look and see what happened. As we suspected – only the sacrament of the sick. Do you not feel Al would have written up at length such a major thing as being received into the RC church? Of course he would. He didn't, because he wasn't.'

Al died at 11.45   *Sunday, 5 September*

Slept fitfully and woke with a jolt at 3.20 (Al's time) as Al was breathing differently now, shorter, tighter rasping breaths – with sighs every so often. Lay awake beside him. He is incredibly hot, 'muck sweat', but his arms are very cold and body temp ok. V hot hands and face.

Jolted, no jarred by 2Boy and dogs at 6.45 so let them out and came back to bed. Tup up getting EMT for himself. Down a bit later for EMT and a bowl of cereal. No change from Al upstairs since then although shot down to have a word with Sue. Washing machine flooding the floor downstairs – wish to goodness J had left it alone. It's much worse than just being temperamental with spinning.

Upstairs all morning. Janice [nurse] came 11-ish to change the syringe driver. Al's breathing still bad – and I noticed when I changed his pads that blotches were appearing under his skin on his legs and knees, reddish purple, and on the soles of his feet. Janice says this is the body's way of shutting down. Lynn came up – looking very well after her break in Britanny – and saw Al.

While we were there, she was just leaving, Al's breathing changed and I said we must get the boys in. Luckily, really luckily they were both outside in the courtyard and came running up. Within 5 or 6 minutes Al had died. Silence, then gasp and a little breathing. More gasps and pulse now weaker. He just looked so peaceful and you really felt his soul and spirit had left on their journey, a wonderful calm feeling entered the room. We all stroked him and talked and kissed him. It was such a lovely ending. Then we all hugged each other. The end of an era. Rang SEDOC and a doctor came up. Rang everyone, Ma, Nick, Celly, Col etc etc.

Reg coming up at 3.30 – was very nice and calming. Quite happy to bury Daddy and will ask Norman to help. Rang the gravedigger who can do it and will come tomorrow, at one o'clock. Dr C came and checked Daddy, and was very kind and concerned about me.

Walked dogs. Was sure I felt Al above going towards Roman tower. Talked at length to Celly. Michael Howard telephoned. Was terribly upset by news. V kind.

A big stumbling block. We have to have Shepway's [local council] permission to bury Daddy in the grounds. I am quite shattered. Fear they will say no. It has all gone so well. I do pray that we can bury Al as a family without pressure and where we wanted to, *when* we want. Delay will inevitably mean he will have to leave to go somewhere cooler. To bed after a bit of a sibling outburst over the fact Norman and Reg cannot go ahead without Shepway's ok. Julie very kindly came in and had a chat.

Monday, 6 September

So-so night, only jarred by worrying about possible problems with Shepway. No worries about Al beside me. In fact it was lovely as I could talk to him still. Much nicer than an empty space, which will come tonight, perhaps?

Up 6.20 writing this and the first of many LISTS! Downstairs breakfast. Did I have any? No, don't think so, too tense. Reg telephoned at 9-ish with Shepway's number, a Sandra Francis. I dialled it. A really nice woman answered and it was Sandra. She was so sympathetic and I cried, but wonderfully it is all under control and she doesn't see any problems at all. Oh *what* a weight lifted off my shoulders. I feel so calm. Had got myself in a terrible state if the answer had been 'no, not possible'.

Immediately wheels set in motion. James doing base for shroud (wood base). Andrew organised to collect death certificate and have it registered. Sarah has gone back to Broomhayes with little 'fair-heads'. Gail came and took syringe away. Julie and I bought flowers at farm shop in Sellindge. Back and then Reg and Michael Marsh and his son arrived to dig grave. MM and son *really* nice couple. Reg very calming and we discussed placing of chairs and bier. Grave was dug in record time and looks very pleasing. Walked dogs and fed hens on return. Saw Graham who is coming, and Eddie, who is still terribly distressed. Picked bay and wild clematis and a few white sweet peas. Did some flowers for the Red Library – organised curtains for table after tea.

Andrew dressed Daddy, who, I must say, had made our room a tiny bit high and window had to be shut because of flies. We have prepared him in his Cuixmala t-shirt, white silk shirt, his favourite battered cords and his suede shoes, his blue neckerchief. He looked very nice. Tup had re-shaved him as well and sprayed him with Roger & Gallet. Downstairs with Tup – he seems to have got heavier somehow. Have all helped to wrap him in his shroud, beautifully done by Julie and Sarah, and he has taken with him a lot of softies: pricklepins, heart stone, Creaggan early heather, seaweed, markies for dogs, digestives, fruit cake, H of C miniature, Zermatt rock, 2 Swiss francs, his armband, his racing vintage goggles, his H of C pass and a travel warrant, 1 handkey.

Supper omelette in kitchen. James insisted on lasagne.

Bed very late 11.30, but feel so much better.

Tuesday, 7 September

Today is Al's funeral – the first overcast morning which was lovely. It rained the day he died and now a dull day. Up quite early and bathed and made EMT, took it and a bowl of cereal back upstairs to bed. Got up at 8 and downstairs, made some cake as nothing to offer people, then organised everyone and saw Al out of the house on to the Mehari and round on to the table in the Knight's Hall. A white damask tablecloth of Great Granpa's with Albany gold curtain over and then the shroud on its wooden base. Did the flowers, 2 large bowls. The white urns inside the blue pots – full of chrysanths, lilies, bay, rosemary, old man's beard and Russian vine and hops. We put our individual posies on Al – peace lilies from Hannah and Lëhni, mixed little bunches from all of us. Very pretty it looked.

Dashed up to wash hair and change at 5 to 11. Felt very shaky, but hope I looked ok for Al, black plain linen dress, black stockings, black shoes, hair clean and loose. Only jewellery my diamond cross Al had given me, and my sapphire rings.

Celly and Col had arrived, and Sue[1] joined me when I was doing the flowers – dear Sue she was so shattered. Lynn, Peggy, Eddie and Graham, and Canon Norman Woods and Reg Humphriss, resplendent in flowing robes. Julie looked lovely, and so did Sarah and both boys very dashing. I was so proud of them. It was the nicest funeral I have been to, intimate and personal and I do hope Al would have been pleased with me. Sue dear and kept saying how proud he would have been of you. The first part of the service over we went across the lawn to the grave. Reg blessed the grave and consecrated it and after a short prayer we lowered Al into it and I threw or rather shovelled 2 spades of earth on to him, the first one rather splendidly landing on his tinkey. All then to the Red Library for sandwiches, gossip and coffee/tea. Both Reg and Norman were so complimentary about it and said it was one of the nicest funerals they had done.

When everyone had gone Sue and all of us retired to the kitchen to thrash out the press releases. Kept to what Al had wanted – 'Suddenly at Saltwood on 5 September. He wanted it to be known he had gone to join Tom and the other dogs.' Good and zany. Informed the Queen first as he was a PC, then Press Association. Phones frantic after that and camera crews at the gate.

Just talked and watched TV and listened to radio. The coverage is absolutely fantastic. On and on it went.

At 9 bizarrely the new Discovery turned up and so James and

---

[1] Sue Line, AC's former secretary.

I went up to the layby by the M-way and swapped our old one for the smartest vehicle ever owned by me.[1] Back and into bed very tired, but so pleased it all went so well.

---

[1] Bizarre is no exaggeration. Ordered earlier in the summer from Macrae & Dick, it had been brought south from Scotland on a car transporter, but the driver's tachograph reading forced him to stop near the Dartford tunnel. The only solution was to go and collect it. But with press cameras still massed outside the castle gates, Jane realised that to drive out past them in her old Discovery on the day of her husband's funeral only to return an hour later in a spanking brand-new machine was to invite trouble. Headlines of 'the merry widow' variety might be the least of it. So Jane and James waited until early evening, when, with deadlines passing, the press began to drift away. By the time they returned with the new Discovery the castle gates were deserted. Phew!

ACKNOWLEDGEMENTS

This third volume of Alan Clark's diaries would not have been possible without Jane Clark's support. Having decided to give the go-ahead her help was unstinting, although I know how daunting, difficult and stressful she found the process at times. As well as giving me free range through Alan's journals, day diaries, indeed anything that might prove useful, she also painstakingly read my transcripts against Alan's originals, even to the extent of peering through a magnifying glass at enlargements of particularly intractable entries. We shared moments of triumph – and exasperation – at some of the reading tests AC left behind. But knowing as she did the background to so many of the entries proved an enormous help. Any errors are, though, mine, and I would be glad to hear from readers who wish to offer comments that should be taken into account for any future editions.

Jane was also the most generous of hosts. I am very grateful to her.

Let me also thank here James and Andrew Clark, who separately provided invaluable expert knowledge on Eriboll, cars and their father's official visit to Oman in 1992.

After seven years as Alan's publisher, my editorial involvement in these diaries had its origins in a conversation with Michael Sissons, who represented Alan as his literary agent for more than forty years. I appreciate his faith in my abilities as well as his wide general knowledge.

As with the work of editing the earlier volume of diaries I wish to acknowledge here the many supporters who responded to my calls for help, not least in compiling footnotes:

Antony Beevor, Nigel Nicolson (and not only for his masterly edition of Harold Nicolson's diaries), Graham Stewart, Andrew Roberts, Simon Heffer, Katie Campbell, Susie Dowdall, Nigel Reynolds, Matthew D'Ancona, Michael White, Katy Heslop, Michael Cockerell, Hugo Vickers, George Weidenfeld, Gerald Isaaman, Simon Jenkins, Bruce Anderson, Dean Godson, Alan Williams, Brian MacArthur, Tim Heald, Carol MacArthur, Robert Coucher, Ilsa Yardley, Douglas Matthews, Jane Birkett, Christopher Silvester, 'Google' and the staff of the London Library. For the paperback edition Shaun Woodward, Juliet Pannett, David Ruffley among others.

A number of books were invaluable aides: let me single out for a general and often precise understanding of the events of the governments of John Major that cover much of the period of these diaries, *Major* by Anthony Seldon (Weidenfeld & Nicolson), undoubtably the most comprehensive source. Not for the first time I doff my hat in acknowledgement to Anthony's talents as a contemporary historian. As readers of this volume will note the diaries of Chips Channon are frequently mentioned. Robert Rhodes James's edition (Phoenix Press) has been well-thumbed. I am grateful, also, to *Knee Deep in Dishonour: the Scott Report and Its Aftermath* by Richard Norton-Taylor, Mark Lloyd and Stephen Cook (Victor Gollancz). The lines from Keith Douglas's 'On a Return from Egypt' are quoted by permission of Faber & Faber.

My colleagues at Orion and Weidenfeld & Nicolson put up with my absences. I would like in particular to thank Anthony Cheetham, Peter Roche, Adrian Bourne, Bing Taylor, Katie White, my assistant Victoria Webb, and the ace Orion group production team headed by Richard Hussey, aided in particular by Erin Hussey, Helen Ewing and Iram Allam.

Finally, but not in the least, my gratitude to my wife Sue for her patience and understanding of the time I spent with the diaries in a year when we also twice moved house and home.

Ion Trewin

INDEX